Latin American Women

Contributions in Women's Studies

The Chains of Protection: The Judicial Response to Women's Labor
Legislation
Judith A. Baer

Women's Studies: An Interdisciplinary Collection
Kathleen O'Connor Blumhagen and Walter D. Johnson, editors

Latin American Women

HISTORICAL PERSPECTIVES

edited by Asunción Lavrin

Contributions in Women's Studies, Number 3

 Greenwood Press
Westport, Connecticut • London, England

Library of Congress Cataloging in Publication Data
Main entry under title:

Latin American women.

    (Contributions in women's studies; no. 3)
    Includes index.
    1. Women—Latin America—History—Addresses,
essays, lectures. 2. Women—Latin America—
Social conditions—Addresses, essays, lectures.
I. Lavrin, Asunción. II. Series.
HQ1460.5.L37   301.41'2'098   77-94758
ISBN 0-313-20309-1

Library of Congress Catalog Card Number: 77-94758
ISBN: 0-313-20309-1
ISSN: 0147-104X

First published in 1978

Greenwood Press, Inc.
51 Riverside Avenue, Westport, Connecticut 06880

Printed in the United States of America

10 9 8 7 6 5 4 3 2 1

Contents

Tables

Figures

Illustrations

Foreword

This book is the result of the search for a social group that has up to now eluded historical examination: the women of Latin America. The absence of women in most of the historical sources that we used in the classroom or read as graduate students challenged the contributors to this book to undertake the task of reconstructing a part of the past universe in which women of Latin America lived. We all have a strong personal interest in the subject matter and a shared faith in the validity of this study. From the outset, most of us felt that in-depth studies of specific subjects would be the most fruitful approach to generate a broader interest in this topic among our colleagues and future historians. This is, then, a book of perspectives captured in the form of essays. The word *perspective* is used here to encompass our standpoint as historians, the broad view that time allows us, and the personal interpretation of each writer.

During the planning and assembling of this volume, the editor and the contributors had a group of potential readers in mind: students and instructors in Latin American Studies and Women's Studies. We hope that historians, political scientists, sociologists, and anthropologists will find in these essays the kind of historical data that will give meaning and support to their comparative studies or that may help to explain contemporary situations. Most of the material dealt with here is pretwentieth century, and all of it is based on original research carried out by the contributors. The emphasis on the pretwentieth-century female experience stems partly from the fact that all of us are historians. However, it is also the result of a conscious choice made by the authors to produce studies that would help fill the lacunae of information on that period and would help balance the recent output on Latin women by social scientists. We also wished to prove that the situation of Latin women in society and in the family during the period under consideration was far from being homogeneous or so well known or understood that it could not be dismissed in a few paragraphs of "background" information.

The essays in this volume attempt to offer some representative material on women from the sixteenth through the early twentieth century in the main areas of Latin America. This in no way implies that a complete or balanced coverage of the subject has been achieved. We are still far from such an ideal. In order to come closer to that goal much research needs to be done in all areas of Latin America and on all members of its class and human mosaic through those four centuries. This is only the beginning of a long and hopefully stimulating line of research. The last chapter of this volume identifies some trends and patterns in the studies available and the needs for future investigations.

Now that our task has been accomplished, I wish to thank all of the writers for their continuous enthusiasm and steadfast dedication to the completion of this volume. I also owe special thanks to Professors Peter Smith, Franklin Knight, and Susan Socolow, who read this manuscript *in toto* or in part and who helped to strengthen it with their judicious comments. The staff of the Latin American, Portuguese, and Spanish Division of the Library of Congress, especially Evert Larson, offered continuous aid in the process of research. Berta Casanova, endowed with great precision and patience, typed the manuscript beautifully. My husband David has read and criticized all my writings throughout the years in an anonymous labor of love. It is high time that he received acknowledgement in print for his moral support. Cecilia and Andrew, my children, did not make any intellectual contribution to this book, but they were very understanding of their mother's busyness.

Latin American Women

Introduction

The need for a separate field of history devoted to the personal experiences of women and their similarity to or difference from those of men has been increasingly recognized by historians in the last few years. This had led to the legitimation of this area of research and the subsequent deepening and refinement of its subject matter. Historians of Latin America have yet to undertake the study of women either as a group or as individuals in a meaningful, thorough, and innovative manner. Very few attempts have been made at incorporating women or subjects related to them in scholarly works. In 1954, William L. Schurz departed from the usual pattern of historical writing by including a chapter on women in his popular book *This New World*.[1] Subsequent authors of survey histories of Latin America have not followed Schurz's example. Whatever little information on women as a group has found its way into textbooks or monographs written in English has generally been woven into the narrative in such manner that it has appeared to be of secondary or passing interest. Marriages have been treated as men's clever accomplishments for family consolidation or social mobility. Indian and black women continue to be seen as the means of sexual satisfaction for the conquistador or the male white elite and, as such, the blameless cooperators or victims of men's oppression. The white upper-class woman is assumed to have been relegated to the confines of the home and the family and to lack a history of her own.

Some individual women have escaped historical anonymity for some highly personal attributes or deeds that contradicted accepted stereotypes in their own society or ours. There were those who gained note for their heroic acts during the conquest or the independent period, such as Inés Suárez, Beatriz Alvarado, or Policarpa Salavarrieta. La Quintrala, a female landowner in Chile, is remembered for her sadistic practices and suspected crimes. La Monja Alférez gained notoriety as a transvestite. The mistresses of well-known men have never failed to attract the historical curiosity of scholars and popularizers as well. Such women as Manuelita Sáenz, Eliza Lynch, or the Marchioness of Santos have earned their niche in history. Sor Juana Inés de la Cruz and Eva Perón are also perennials in colonial and contemporary historical writing. Other names could be mentioned, but the point needs no belaboring. The emphasis has always been put on extraordinary women or on their uncommon achievements, whether personal or political.

We have long abandoned the heroic theme in history, but the canons of Carlyle are still being applied to the history of women in Latin America. As a result, we have developed a "great woman syndrome," whereby only prominent females are the subjects of what pretends to be the history of Latin American women. This concentration on exceptional individuals is the result of compensatory history, which tries to redeem the anonymity of the many through the brilliance of the few. Such an approach does a disservice to our knowledge of the past. Although not denying the influence of outstanding figures on the course of events, history extends beyond personalities. In the case of the history of women it is necessary to stretch the boundaries of our inquiry and to concern ourselves with their attitudes, motivations, and actions, both as individuals and as members of the family and other social institutions. The objective of an inquiry into the roles, status, thoughts, and actions of women should no longer be that of finding superhuman beings, but rather of considering normal individuals who were engaged in everyday activities and were representative of their times and societies. This will not be an easy task, since for certain periods of Latin American history—such as the sixteenth through the early nineteenth centuries—it is frequently necessary to ferret information from diverse and sometimes unpredictable sources. The late nineteenth and early twentieth centuries are more generous in their offerings. However, scholars will have to face some problems regardless of the period that they choose. Perhaps the most important will be the collection of scattered data, its organization, the definition of topics of concern, the clarification of methodologies, and the acquisition of a special sensitivity that this new subject deserves. New perspectives will demand new sources and new methods.

In the past decade, due to the growing importance of social history, there has been an increasing awareness that investigation of the participation in the social and economic processes by largely anonymous groups of people—such as women—holds the key to a better understanding of some historical situations. At present a more open-minded attitude and a better climate exist for carrying on legitimate historical research on the role of Latin American women in the history of that region. Since the mid-1960s a number of historians have been underlining the relevance and significance of research topics involving women, the family, or feminine institutions.[2] However, the accomplishments of such research have been, so far, limited in size and scope. Only a few books completely devoted to women in Latin American history have been published in English, and the body of periodical literature is modest.[3] This situation is understandable in view of the short span of time passed since the first attempts were made to break ground in this field. Nonetheless, the time is ripe for superseding this state of affairs.

The essays offered to the English-speaking reader in this volume are the results of the most recent investigations by a group of historians who have taken a deep and serious interest in the study of the female past in Latin America. Their main concern was to contribute to building a body of historical literature that would provide some answers to the innumerable questions now posed and to spurring the interest of other historians in searching for answers not provided here. These essays are perforce diverse in character, style, and methods of investigation. All initial efforts are bound to underscore the multiplicity of choices and directions rather than the ultimate unity of the goal pursued. Furthermore, the different and sometimes disparate ethnic, geographical, and class circumstances of women in Latin America, not discounting the research preferences of the historians themselves, conspire against any thematic unity other than that provided by our common subject of study: women, their role and participation in the historical development of Latin America. At this early stage in the process of investigation, with such a limited number of well-researched historical studies available or in progress, it would have been futile and even detrimental to try to saddle themes to the essays other than those of very general character. Questions of theoretical relevance that are possible in other, more developed areas of women's history—such as that of American women, with many more years of research and publications behind it—are as yet difficult in a field that has only a patchy record of works published in Spanish, Portuguese, and English. Thus, diversity of objectives and multiplicity of foci are inevitable at this point and, to a large extent, preferable to highly speculative generalizations built on questionable grounds.

All these essays, nevertheless, have tried to revise the stereotype of the Latin women as a passive element in society by emphasizing the role of women as doers or agents. Women of all classes had their own areas of influence and made significant contributions to society, whether or not this is fully appreciated or perceived today. This is not to deny that the status of women—that is, their position, *vis-à-vis* men in society— was lower and still remains lower than that of men. However, to assume the oppressed minority group interpretation would not only be unimaginative—since it has been the only one so far used—but could lead to an intellectual *cul-de-sac* once all the forms of oppression are exposed. The approach that we adopted assumed that all women were more than objects, having in them a significant dynamism that was not only channeled into the preservation of values and institutions, but also proved to be fundamental in the formation and development of Latin America societies.

The initial bewilderment produced by entering a relatively unexplored field of research was caused mainly by the necessity of readjusting our vision to new forms of seeing reality in order to open new paths of investigation. Searching for specific information on women demanded from each of the writers in this volume a concerted and sustained effort to "look under" some traditional topics and sources of information in order to find material on women that had been previously neglected or overlooked. It is almost an understatement to say that, in general, we did not look into the records of the ministries of war or finance or any other referring to political or governmental decision-making activities, since women have been banned from such areas until fairly recently. The search took place in civil and religious archives, municipal records, notarial books, newspaper writings, genealogical and family history sources, records of charitable and educational institutions, minutes of women's conferences, and writings of women themselves. No questions about exceptional women were asked. Women were treated as members of their specific social class, ethnic group, or station in life. What ideas affected these women's behavior in society? What were their reactions to certain specific historical moments? What factors limited their participation in social processes? Did these women break with traditional prejudices and attitudes, or did they conform to them? The essays in this book answer questions such as these and try to present women not isolated from their social complex, but constituting an essential part of it.

The existence of many misconceptions about the status and role of women in colonial society called for a general discussion of this topic in both the Spanish and Portuguese possessions. The essays by Asunción Lavrin (chapter 1) and A. J. R. Russell-Wood (chapter 2) undertake this task by studying Mexico and Brazil, respectively. These two essays outline some general issues without attempting to provide a detailed picture of both societies. The emphasis is largely on white women, because most of the readily available historical sources of the seventeenth and eighteenth centuries provide more material on them than on women of any other group. A focus on the women of Spanish or Portuguese descent is a requirement for more detailed studies on Latin women and provides an index to the values of the ruling elite.

Both studies underscore the importance of institutions such as the family, the vehicle through which social and economic status was preserved. The white woman in both societies had the specific role of maintaining the family's status and its racial purity. As a consequence, she was subjected to a great deal of protection and was the object of a considerable degree of sublimation. Both protection and sublimation could imply restriction rather than freedom for women. Although this is true, reality was nonetheless not confined to restriction alone. Both authors leave no doubt that women could and did pursue activities of their own as independent agents, a fact that adds a significant new dimension to the interpretation of the historical role of women in the colonial period and that most histories neglect or ignore.

These two general essays stress the need to examine the behaviorial prescriptions made for women in colonial society and the most common masculine attitudes toward women as a necessary step to achieve a fuller understanding of women's options and actions. They also stress the importance of the roles performed by single, married, and widowed women and the social demands made of them in each of these three states. Russell-Wood's tentative, but interesting, observations on the demographic structure of the family and Lavrin's discussion of the incidence of behavioral defiance of moral codes illustrate some of the many aspects of colonial women's lives that have escaped historical attention.

Although there are many similarities in the attitudes and patterns of behavior of women in Brazil and Mexico, it is apparent that women in the former were more passive, more restrained, and less enterprising than in the latter. One may hypothesize that the pervasive influence of slavery in a less urbanized milieu, which made many fewer intellectual and material demands upon women, contributed to this situation. In the future other studies should focus on smaller geographical areas and shorter periods of time in order to confirm the general trends outlined by Lavrin and Russell-Wood and to emphasize local and chronological nuances. Further research should also provide more detail on the structure of the family, the influence of women as heiresses of their male relatives, the social and economic meaning of marriage arrangements, and the deeper meaning of female deviations from normative rules of behavior. All these topics should make our perception of interpersonal relations in the colonial period more acute.[4] Obviously, nonelite and rural women should receive more attention.

Little is known or understood as yet about the impact of the conquest on the female indigenous population, the way in which this event changed their lives, and their contribution to the organization of sixteenth-century society. Although the role of the Indian woman as mistress of the conquistador has been underscored,[5] other aspects of her life as a member of society have not been fully explored. The Indian woman was a very important element of society as part of the labor force, providing diverse services to the growing urban centers, while undergoing herself a transformation as a result of the contact with the Spanish culture. Elinor Burkett (chapter 3) explores the impact of the conquest on women and their subsequent adjustments to the demands of a new social *milieu*. Burkett suggests the existence of a special relationship among urban working Indian women and describes a significant labor and social split along sex lines due to the different activities performed by Indian men and women and to the different attention and treatment that they received from the Spaniards.

This essay offers a challenging reinterpretation of the activities of Indian women in colonial society, inviting future comparative studies with Mexico and other areas where Spanish and Indian population and cultures faced each other in an urban situation. It is clear that studying Indian, *casta*, or black women merely as objects of exploitation can be fruitfully superseded by considering the complexity of their relations with the racial and social elites or their participation and positive contributions to the building of a new society.

Home was the sanctuary where women were regarded safe from the temptations of the world and where they would fulfill their natural destiny as mothers and wives. Yet, because the family in Latin America has traditionally been patriarchal in character, it is difficult to envision that even in this sphere, regarded as their own, could women be other than secondary figures whose main occupation was to look after children and husbands. Although there is a great deal of truth in this situation, it would be erroneous to assume that such represented the total truth. Among the socioeconomic elites, husbands and fathers recognized the unwritten privileges of women as mistresses of their homes (*amas de su casa*), controlling the management of domestic affairs.[6] This degree of authority could be stretched to meet extradomestic situations. When the men were missing, women could assume their role. This social phenomenon was not confined to the wealthy, since among the poor, for whom consensual unions were quite common, a significant number of women were the heads of households.[7]

The character and strength that women developed within their homes two hundred years ago can be gauged in Edith Couturier's study (chapter 4) of the female members of the influential family of the Counts of Regla in New Spain. This work examines the personalities and actions of the Regla women as an illustration of the roles of females in the upper-class family. The portrait of the lives of several generations of women provides an opportunity to learn about the intimate nuances of their lives, their power and influence, and the limitations on both. While most historical studies of Latin families follow the lives of men, few have attempted a sustained narrative on the women. This essay proves that such a project is possible. Investigations similar to this could yield revealing pictures of women in other areas of Latin America. Carefully researched studies of women within the family are essential to reconstruct one of the areas in which their functions received the most recognition and also to measure the degree of this recognition. It is also necessary to establish whether the values determining intrafamilial relations have been preserved or adapted to changing socioeconomic circumstances. A better knowledge of the colonial family and its evolution through several generations is indispensable to evaluate what internal structures have remained constant—and thus have become traditional—and what transformations this institution has suffered under the impact of industrialization, access of women to education and their incorporation into a broader labor market, rural-urban migration, and so on.

The choices of life-style for upper-class women in Latin America have changed greatly in the last 150 years. The limited alternatives of marriage and profession of the colonial period were substantially altered in the nineteenth century with the growing secularization, urbanization, and industrialization of the region as a whole. However, during the colonial period religion was a very important element in women's lives, providing moral guidance and education. For the rich and the poor alike, religion and religious institutions offered a channel for spiritual fulfillment and charitable endeavors. With the foundation of the first nunneries in Spanish America in the 1550s, profession became a choice of life for colonial women, but this choice was reserved for a small number of women of the white elite. The argument of the unpreparedness of the indigenous woman for profession, which concealed an unmistakable feeling of racial prejudice, deprived Indian women from sharing in the highest form of religious experience until the eighteenth century, when the first convent for Indian nuns was founded in Mexico City.

The Franciscan *monasterio* of Corpus Christi, founded in 1724, is the object of the work by Sister Ann Miriam Gallagher (chapter 5), who has studied rather than the institution itself, the nuns who professed in it. Given the dearth of information on Indian women in the colonial period and in the nineteenth century—the contemporary scene is better covered by anthropologists—this work has the value of unearthing some of the motivations guiding Indian women into profession and providing us with an insight into the socioeconomic standing and values of the indigenous groups in colonial Mexico. This is also one of the few group profiles of Indian women available for colonial Mexico. By studying the social extraction of all the nuns who professed during one hundred years in Corpus Christi, the author reveals the strong sense of social hierarchy among the members of the Indian community, a sentiment resembling that of the white community. The vast majority of the nunneries founded in Brazil and Spanish America remained the enclave of the social elite. As an Indian convent, Corpus Christi of Mexico City was an atypical institution, but one which in historical perspective is an extremely interesting and valuable example, precisely for its uniqueness.

More typical of colonial attitudes were the religious foundations for white women. In her study of the four convents founded in Bahia, the capital city of colonial Brazil in the seventeenth and part of the eighteenth centuries, Susan Soeiro (chapter 6) found a racial, economic, and social exclusivity similar to those present in Spanish America. Daughters of planters, merchants, and bureaucrats crowded the ranks of the professants. Class and race were key historical determinants in these institutions. This essay underlines the relation between demographic and economic factors and the foundation of nunneries in colonial Brazil. It proposes that economic and demographic cycles determined changes in the Portuguese Crown's policies, which either allowed or restricted the creation of such institutions. Soeiro endorses a suggestive interpretation of the convent in Bahia as the institution that took out of circulation those women who could not contribute to the preservation of the power of the socioeconomic elite or were misfits in their society. Although the approaches of Sister Gallagher's and Susan Soeiro's studies of nunneries are quite different, both of them serve to illustrate the fact that the significance of religious communities in colonial Latin America lies beyond their mere religious purposes and that they can give us clues to the economic and social standing of women, their families, the prevailing social attitudes, the royal policies, and even the economic structure of a given area.

Major intellectual changes affecting the manner of viewing society and the roles of its various members took place in the second half of the eighteenth century. These changes, embodied in a philosophical outlook that has been labeled as the Enlightenment, naturally affected the social role of women. The most important social changes related to women were proposed by French thinkers, who advocated their education and their incorporation into society as being equals to men and enjoying the same rights. The Spanish Enlightenment adopted some of the ideas of the French Enlightenment, but the emphasis was on social regeneration and economic efficiency. French and Spanish ideas were disseminated in Spanish America through periodicals published in several of its major cities. These journals devoted a significant number of articles to the discussion of the role of women in Latin America society, indicating a new awareness of the presence of women in society.

Johanna Mendelson's work (chapter 7) surveys the contents of these articles with the purpose of determining the models and values of femininity upheld in the late colonial period. Mendelson stresses the fact that the ideas expressed in these journals, whether sympathetic or not, were those of men, not of women themselves. As such, they still do not represent women's universe. An important concern of this group of "enlightened" men was the education of women as a means of upgrading their performance as wives and mothers. While not questioning the biological and psychological nurturing functions of women, the male writers of the journals endorsed what was going to become one of the driving themes of the nineteenth century: the education of women.

As mirrors of personal opinions and social attitudes, the journals also give evidence of the strong tendency among their publishers to define women's role in terms of class, separating the image of the lady from that of the women in lesser stations in life. This concept of social class is one of the most important historical factors in the definition of the Latin American woman's social and individual roles. The significance of the opinions expressed in the journals is that they were formulated at a historical time when the educated male members of society were reassessing the past and planning for new and "reformed" societies. Since the roles proposed for women did not mark any departure from the past, it is not surprising to find few changes in men's attitudes toward women or in the women's life-style in the first half of the nineteenth century.

For the Spanish and Portugese colonies, the period from 1810 through 1825 was filled with the traumatic experience of achieving independence from their mother countries. In the ensuing years important political and economic changes took place in most Latin American nations, although in different depths and at different rates. How women were affected by those changes is an issue that remains largely unknown. We know almost as little about women in the nineteenth and early twentieth centuries as about women in the colonial period. Thus, the essays by Evelyn Cherpak, Cynthia Little, June Hahner, and Anna Macías are welcome additions to the meager literature on that period.

The participation of women in social and political change in Latin America has been one of the favorite subjects of study of contemporary scholars in several disciplines.[8] Social and political change in the twentieth century, however, has not taken place in a vacuum, and the participation of women in these processes should not be detached from its historical roots. Women participated in political uprisings, conspiracies, and popular riots in the colonial period, but it was during the wars of independence that all over Spanish America they had the opportunity to be part of political change on a large scale.[9] Historical literature in Spanish is not lacking in books praising the "heroic" qualities of women at the time of the wars of independence. Works in English have taken little notice of women's efforts during that period. Evelyn Cherpak's study (chapter 8) examines the manifold contributions made by women supporters of independence in northern South America. The female participation in political change in these wars took the expected forms of combat by the boldest and of spying, camp following, or supplying economic aid by others. In this historial instance, as well as in others in which women have participated in wars, there have been two main types of women: the female soldier and the camp follower. The former achieved respect and rank among her male fighting companions by assuming masculine roles and projecting an image of active leadership that modified her femininity. The camp follower, on the contrary, performed the tasks expected of a woman in traditional anonymity. Only the female soldier is remembered. This situation confirms the assumptions that under certain circumstances the imitation of male behavior gains recognition for women because the male is always considered superior.[10]

For the most part, women's participation in the wars derived them few rewards, even for the heroines, who hardly ever received pensions or the material gains that men enjoyed. Women collaborated in the movement without further political ambitions because they were not trained to think politically or did not regard themselves as political beings in the same way that men did. Many saw their participation in the wars under the light of noble sacrifice, which had for long been one of the main normative guides of their behavior. After the wars most women retreated to their traditional role. With few exceptions, men were equally unprepared, emotionally and intellectually, to see women acting differently. Such attitudes, strengthened by restrictive civil codes based on the

Code Napoleon, limited significantly the civil rights of women during the first century of national life, leaving them with few options of behavior.

Among those options, three became the most important avenues of expression open to women after 1830: charity, education, and feminist activities, the latter in the last quarter of the century. Cynthia Little (chapter 9), in a case study of Argentina from 1860 through 1926, analyzes those three options. Throughout the colonial period the Church had served as a bridge between women and charity. In the nineteenth century, with the Church losing ground in its social and educational functions, women channeled their activities through lay societies such as the Sociedad de Beneficencia in Buenos Aires. Charitable work was held appropriate for women, fitting well the image of nobility and dedication assigned to the feminine sex. While having few, if any, political implications, this work utilized women's energies in a manner beneficial to the State. Charity work was imbued with a strong sense of class consciousness, and, as Little points out, it remained a static, conservative form of social activity that did not contribute much to changing social structures. Nonetheless, charity gave lay women the opportunity to exercise themselves in the process of institutional decision taking, a prerogative that only nuns had been able to enjoy prior to the nineteenth century.

Education, one of the most important personal gains for women in the nineteenth century, showed a geographically and socially uneven gain for Latin American women. Nevertheless, it gave those who benefited from it a sense of social and personal achievement rarely enjoyed before. Education also allowed the recognition of women's intellectual capacity, though this fact was slow to be assimilated even by women themselves. They did not register in university courses in significant numbers until the 1930s. Since the late eighteenth century, education was supposed to prepare women to be better mothers and wives. Education as a personal achievement was seen as an ornament to womanhood, an acquisition that should not clash with traditional concepts of woman's higher destiny as mother and wife. This continued to be the case during the nineteenth century and the early decades of the twentieth. As a social function, education was utilized by the national states as an extension of maternity for the service of the motherland. Few men raised any serious objection to the incorporation of women into the labor force in that role.[11]

Perhaps the most significant offshoot of education was the development of a self-consciousness among some women that led them into feminist militancy.[12] Little underscores this important connection, which was reflected in the ideological content of Argentinian feminist groups. Feminism appeared in almost all Latin American countries, mostly among the urban educated women. In Argentina, as in other nations, feminism helped to win broader civil rights for women, but not necessarily the right to vote. The vote was regarded as an extension of legal and social equality, but not as the main target of feminist demands, which focused on social reforms such as the control of prostitution and alcoholism, the adoption of protective legislation for working women and children, and the liberalization of the civil codes' restrictions on women's status.[13]

Argentinian women enjoyed one of the highest levels of education in Latin America in the late nineteenth century. Feminists there could expect a greater receptivity to their ideas and a larger number of interested listeners. In countries with lower educational levels and stronger attitudes about women's essential ties to the family, feminism or merely the idea of women's right to an education and a higher status within the family and in society found a slower acceptance. Such was the case of Brazil, where a small group of women who were educated enough to realize their unequal situation made tenacious efforts to make men and other women aware of the necessity of change. In her essay (chapter 10), June Hahner describes how these women used a new tool accessible to them, the printing press; and starting in the second half of the nineteenth century, they published a substantial body of feminist journals. Largely unknown until now, these journals can be regarded as the vehicle of expression of women emerging from a patriarchal society into the twentieth century and are doubly interesting as the first Brazilian publications for women, by women. The editors and the reading public were obviously middle-class. However, their concerns were not only for their own social and economic group, but for women in general, although in a manner more idealistic than practical.

There are two main themes common to all the publications cited by Hahner: first, the demand for the recognition of women's intellectual equality to men coupled with their right to a complete education and, second, the advocacy of women's rights as individuals, whether at home or in the larger arena of society. While the male editors of the earlier Spanish American journals studied by Mendelson never advocated women's participation in any sphere of social life other than the home, the Brazilian women editors eventually ventured beyond the boundaries set by centuries of tradition. Time had not passed in vain. This essay points to the potentially rich source of women's history offered by journals written or managed by women. The study of newspapers by women or for women should yield meaningful insights into the untapped area of women's awakening self-consciousness, their reactions to rapidly changing social conditions, and some of the conventional prescriptions ruling their lives.

A variant form of feminist activities and supporters appears in the Mexican peninsula of Yucatan in the early decades of the twentieth century. Women who supported feminist ideas were not alone in their position. Male intellectuals and politicians raised their voices to advocate the same ideas.[14] Anna Macías's study (chapter 11) of the activities of Felipe Carrillo Puerto on behalf of women's liberation illustrates the actions of a man who supported a radical form of feminism as an important part of his political platform. It is ironic that when some reforms were introduced—birth control and legal divorce, for example—they were not palatable to most of the women of Yucatan. The case of Mexico, where success was ultimately attained by the moderate reformers concerned with protection for women rather than with abrupt departures from accepted social mores, indicates the complexity of women's own attitudes and the importance of other factors, such as the economic and educational level of the female population and the political manipulation of the issue of feminism.

A comparison among the contents of the Brazilian feminist journals, the records of the First Feminist Congress in Buenos Aires, the activities of the Yucatecan feminist leagues, and the minutes of the 1923 Congress of Women in Mexico City should help to illustrate the similarities and differences among the various Latin American feminist groups, born out of different social and political conditions at various times. Generally, Latin American feminists were not radicals, but reformists. Was this conservative trait a result of deeply seated social attitudes? Did it delay, rather than help, women's full incorporation into political and economic activities? Such questions point to our incomplete knowledge of the circumstances that contributed to the acceptance or rejection of different forms of feminism among various social groups in Latin American nations and propose an agenda for future research.

I have expressed some reservations on the advisability of making generalizations applicable to all Latin American women based on regional or period studies. There are, however, a number of themes suggested by the works in this volume that bear examination. Perhaps the clearest of all is the relevance of social class and ethnicity in the determination of attitudes and behavior. Although most of the essays deal with white middle- or upper-class women, the writers are fully aware that the options and experiences of women of different socioeconomic levels and ethnic origins were not alike. For example, only a partial view of the Indian female world has been historically explored—and mostly in its urban context, facing Spanish cultural values. Yet, the urban Indian female experience points to the development of a new set of values and behavior catering to the Spanish society and borrowing from it at the same time, but still maintaining its own identity. An Indian nunnery meant the complete adoption of the conqueror's religion—a successful acculturation—but the community's racial pride and emphasis on the social origin of the professants denote strong ties with their own traditions and world. Although the historical experience of the black woman remains largely unknown, the little evidence gathered so far also shows that her world was quite distinct from the Indian and the Spanish. The strength of ethnicity in the determination of attitudes and behavior in the woman's world, nevertheless, remains to be explored in full and should not be overstated. Urban nonwhite women readily adopted many traits of the Spanish culture as they became affluent. Social climbing and acculturation obliterated racial differences in life-styles and patterns of behavior.[15]

Class distinctions in female behavior have been obscured by previous blanket acceptance of stereotypes originating mostly in upper-class customs.

The essays in this volume point to nuances in the adoption of values, forms of behavior, social demands, and expectations that are directly correlated to class. The feminist movement of the late nineteenth and early twentieth centuries is a case in point. It reflected the aspirations of the educated, urban, middle-class woman, and it used the vehicles of expression and social pressure available to this class: newspapers, novels, poems and similar literary tools, and even sympathetic influence of male politicians.[16] The programs suggested by some of their leaders, consciously or not, set goals more akin to their expectations than to those of women of the working classes. With few exceptions, female labor leaders seldom joined feminist associations.[17]

The family, as the center of socialization, kinship, and control and transmission of property, is one of the most powerful themes running through the essays. That many of these roles retain their validity even today seems to indicate that the Latin family is traditional in character, although this point needs further refinement.

Some other characteristics of the family bear further examination. The patriarchal character of the Spanish and Portuguese families has been supposed to have been the typical *modus vivendi* of all families in Latin America from the sixteenth through the twentieth century. This notion assumed the existence of a dominant father figure exerting all the legal powers inherent in *patria potestad*. To start with, only the white and perhaps the *mestizo* family have been used as models. The evolution of the indigenous and black families throughout this period is much less well known. Although legally and de facto the white and *mestizo* families were patriarchal, there existed social circumstances that accounted for variables breaking the inflexible mold into which family relations have been cast up to now. The high incidence of informal unions in Latin America since colonial times allowed the existence of households in which women were the head of the family. This phenomenon has been better described for the contemporary scene than for other historical periods, but current research in historical demography is building considerable evidence to support the theory that matrifocal families coexisted for centuries with the more common patriarchal type.[18] The fact that many of these matrifocal families were of low-class and mixed-blood origin further complicates the picture. Class, slavery, and urban poverty were all important ingredients in the formation of this variant of the classic family stereotype. Other circumstances such as widowhood gave women a familial and social role that was not previously taken into consideration. Some legal devices provided women in the Spanish colonies with rights that compensated for restrictions rendering her subordinate to her father or husband. These contradictory circumstances will eventually help to explain some conflicts within the family that have been observed by historians and contemporary social scientists. Nonetheless, marriage, as a factor contributing to the stability and strength of the propertied classes, and women's role within the mechanism of transmission of property and preservation of the socioeconomic system remain important aspects of the family as an institution, particularly prior to the twentieth century.

The concept of the centrality of the family in the social network from the sixteenth through the nineteenth century will also remain unchanged. United by the bonds of kinship, families influenced politics at the local and even the national levels. They are also detectable in the economic underpinnings of spiritual institutions, such as the Church, that relied heavily on intrafamilial ties for membership and patronage.[19] The extent to which these factors have retained or have lost their validity in this century indicates the degree of continuity or break with the past. The measurement of such factors is perhaps the task of the social scientist, but the historian must provide the parameters for measurement. Another area of mutual cooperation is that which relates to hierarchical relationships between male and female at home, at work, or in politics. The historian can usually find roots for the contemporary situations described by anthropologists or sociologists in early Spanish or even indigenous prescriptive literature.[20] Both the thread of continuity in family relations and the interrelations of the sexes deserve further study in order to determine the precise meaning of traditionality and modernization in these areas.

Sharp definitions of femininity and masculinity and a consequent polarization in education, socialization, and division of labor between men and women are themes inherent to the Iberian and indigenous worlds. The definitions of what was properly masculine and feminine and the specific forms of behavior that they generated seem to have had a lasting influence on Latin American culture. Both European and Indian sources establish very clear models of proper behavior from childhood through adulthood. Separation of the sexes after a certain age, preservation of female honor by the individual herself or through the family, fidelity of the wife to the husband, and dedication of the woman to the task of motherhood mark the boundaries of acceptable femininity in these societies. Femininity was closely identified with good, chaste, loving, and demure behavior, physical and emotional weakness, and the need of man's strength and attention. Those values were inculcated through education and preserved by a set of normative restrictions—personal and social—that women were expected to observe. Protective devices such as physical guardianship or legal and institutional safeguards prevented the loss of those desirable traits of femininity and buttressed the normative restrictions.

The canons of the Spanish male world are better known than those of the Indian, black, or *casta* men, and it might be premature to attempt any definitions for these latter groups, especially for the colonial period. However, one may say that personal assertiveness, economic and personal responsibility for the family and its women, and careful distinctions about the degree of respect owed to the proper or "improper" female were values held in common by most men of all classes. The concepts of *machismo* and *marianismo*, so much under discussion today, need not be repeated here, but it is appropriate to point out that they could not have evolved without the supporting foundation of several centuries of attitude formation.[21]

Beyond the discussion of class, race, family roles, and sex polarization as themes of great importance in defining the Latin female historical experience, another question posed by these essays is whether there exists a commonality in that experience. Historians have been more sensitive to the significance of class and race than that of sex in Latin America. They have not considered to what degree women share attitudes and problems owing to their nature. It is obvious that inequalities arising from class gave women of the social elite advantages over those of lower status. The wealthy used the labor of the poor to lead more comfortable lives. High-status women could command men of lower status with few or no questions raised. There were *patronas* as well as *patrones*. However, under some circumstances all women shared the burdens of imposed inequalities. Sexual ascriptions leading to subordination have been felt quite heavily by women in some periods, such as the nineteenth century, when legislation placed them in a position of complete dependence on men under the guise of protection. In the larger social arena, legislation and male attitudes made the majority of women ineligible for participation in the government and divested them of any opportunity to exert political leadership. Until the nineteenth century the majority of women were undereducated as a result of their gender, regardless of their abilities. With few exceptions, they were also barred from participating in large-scale business. Their early socialization, by stressing the functions of their sex, conditioned women to accept such limitations. These are common experiences that affected all women and that convey a feeling of repression, if not outright oppression in some instances.

However, there is an inherent problem in any interpretation that sees sex as a factor leading exclusively to repression or exploitation and that stresses sex as the only variable worth considering in women's history. The peculiar social problems of their sex did not seem to prevent many women of various ethnic groups and economic levels from engaging in activities that demanded personal assertiveness and strength of character, such as the management of small business, the administration of rural properties, or the provision of essential services to the community. Feminine institutions such as nunneries were of more than passing importance in the local economies. In the nineteenth and twentieth centuries the incorporation of a large body of women into the urban labor pool—even though not properly remunerated—has made women's work absolutely essential to maintaining certain sectors of the economy. Finally, there is the ironic situation of women using their sexual powers in a literal manner in order to obtain preferential treatment over other women and men. This use of sex may be regarded as a form of exploitation by many, but women who have used, and still use, their sex for gaining greater personal power rarely agree with this point of view. In other historical periods—and even today—the use of the specific "charms" of femininity or the appeal of motherhood has been considered acceptable. In Latin America the indications are that women have been reluctant to abandon traditional models of femininity, even in politics, because such models may give them access to power, in the home or in social activities.[22] Sexism in Latin America, thus, is an elusive, complex social and intellectual issue. The study of the effects of sexism on the historical experience of men and women in that area is a challenging subject that promises much fruitful debate.

Trying to determine if a factor such as class, race, or sex is more important than any other in defining women's status or role in history is not an easy task, and it might be an inconclusive one. The data unearthed by the contributions in this book suggest that a careful evaluation of period, geographic factors, and socioeconomic structures is absolutely essential before making any generalizations. Nevertheless, all the works in this volume carry an ultimate message: sex is a determinant in history that we cannot overlook no matter what weight we decide to give it.

The authors of these essays have tried to question the usual interpretation of Latin American history that virtually excludes half of the population from its narrative. Collectively, these essays also attempt to show a new way of seeing historical reality that will add an extra dimension and meaning to social and economic history. There will be less excuse in the future to continue to assume that women did not "exist" in Latin America until quite recently. A significant number of their deeds have been recorded and are available for analysis. Others that were not recorded may still be rescued by skillful reconstruction. As a social group, women are as worthy of study as merchants, slaves, priests, or miners. Certainly, they had just as much of a stake in their society. Although some might not be interested in the specific facets of women's personal lives, it is harder to deny the historical value of the study of women as essential parts of society and its mechanisms, whether political, cultural, or economic.

All goals have not been achieved, and more questions have been raised than answered. Some readers will remain dissatisfied because it is not yet possible to offer a smooth, compact, and chronologically continuous narrative of the participation of women in the historical development of Latin America. But these shortcomings should stimulate further studies to fill the lacunae that could not be covered by less than a dozen historians. In the future, as well as now, historians will continue to perceive women as playing many different roles due to the varied circumstances in which they have lived and still live. Some women have been involved in political struggles, while others have remained passively alienated from civic duties. Some have been economically marginalized, while others have been incorporated into the productive processes of their nations. Some still suffer cultural and economic repression, while others have learned how to use new forms of leverage in those areas. This variety of circumstances will continue to demand historical analysis and interpretation, not only for the sake of women, but for the sake of a better and more complete reconstruction of the past and a better understanding of the present.

Notes

1. William L. Schurz, *This New World: The Civilization of Latin America* (New York: E. P. Dutton, 1945), pp. 276-338.

2. See, for example, the works of James Lockhart, Asunción Lavrin, Susan Soeiro, Susan Socolow, Doris Ladd, Donald Ramos, Ann Pescatello, which will be cited in full throughout this volume.

3. See Charles R. Boxer, *Women in Iberian Expansion Overseas, 1415-1815* (New York: Oxford University Press, 1975); June E. Hahner, *Women in Latin American History: Their Lives and Views* (Los Angeles: UCLA Latin American Center Publications, 1976); Ann Pescatello, *Power and Pawn: The Female in Iberian Families, Societies and Cultures* (Westport, Conn.: Greenwood Press, 1976). Assuming an interdisciplinary approach to women are June Nash and Helen Icken Safa, eds., *Sex and Class in Latin America* (New York: Praeger, 1976); Ann Pescatello, ed., *Female and Male in Ibero-America: Essays* (Pittsburgh: University of Pittsburgh Press, 1974).

4. Recent works in social history have underscored the importance of marriage and family linkages in colonial society. See, as examples, Jacques A. Barbier, "Elites and Cadres in Bourbon Chile," *Hispanic American Historical Review* 52 (August 1972): 416-35 (hereafter cited as *HAHR*); Leon G. Campbell, "A Colonial Establishment: Creole Domination of the Audiencia of Lima during the Late Eighteenth Century," *HAHR* 52 (February 1972): 1-25; Mark Burkholder and E. S. Chandler, *From Impotence to Authority: The Spanish Crown and the American Audiencias, 1687-1808* (Saint Louis: University of Missouri Press, 1977); Stuart B. Schwartz, *Sovereignty and Society in Colonial Brazil: The High Court of Bahia and Its Judges, 1609-1751* (Berkeley and Los Angeles: University of California Press, 1973); Sherburne F. Cook and W. W. Borah, *Essays in Population History*, 2 Vols. (Berkeley and Los Angeles: University of California Press, 1971); Mary L. Felstiner, "The Larraín Family in the Independence of Chile, 1780-1830," (Ph.D. diss., Stanford University, 1970); Verena Martínez-Alier, *Marriage, Class and Colour in Nineteenth-Century Cuba* (New York: Cambridge University Press, 1974).

5. Magnus Mörner, *Race Mixture in the History of Latin America* (Boston: Little, Brown, 1967); Robert C. Padden, *The Hummingbird and the Hawk: Conquest and Sovereignty in the Valley of Mexico, 1503-1541* (New York: Harper Colophon Books, 1967), pp. 229-30.

6. Sylvia Arrom, *La mujer mexicana ante el divorcio eclesiástico, 1800-1857* (Mexico: SepSetentas, 1976), p. 50.

7. Donald Ramos, "Marriage and the Family in Colonial Vila Rica," *HAHR* 55 (May 1975): 200-225.

8. See works by Jane Jaquette, Morris J. Blachman, Vivian Mota, Michele Mattelart, and Ximena Bunster in Nash and Safa, *Sex and Class*, pt. 3. Many of the contributions to this volume also appeared in Spanish in *La mujer en América Latina* (Mexico: SepSententas, 1975). See also Jane Jaquette, "Women in Revolutionary Movements

in Latin America," *Journal of Marriage and the Family* 35 (May 1973) (hereafter cited as *JMF*); Elsa M. Chaney, "Women in Latin American Politics: The Case of Peru and Chile," in Pescatello, *Female and Male*, pp. 103-39; Nancy Caro Hollander, "Women: The Forgotten Half of Argentine History," in Pescatello, *Female and Male*, pp. 141-58. See also Meri Knaster, *Women in Spanish America: An Annotated Bibliography from Pre-Conquest to Contemporary Times* (Boston: G. K. Hall, 1977), section on "Politics and Twentieth Century Revolutionary Movements," pp. 534-60.

9. Evelyn Cherpak, "Women and the Independence of Gran Colombia, 1780-1830" (Ph.D. diss., University of North Carolina, 1975); Janet R. Kentner, "The Socio-political Role of Women in the Mexican Wars of Independence, 1810-1821" (Ph.D. diss., Loyola University, 1975).

10. Susan Soeiro and Asunción Lavrin, "Approaches to the History of Women in Latin America," in E. Bradford Burns, Eduardo Hernández, and Mary Karasch, eds., *Teaching Latin American History* (Los Angeles: University of California Office of Learning Resources, 1977), pp. 18-25. From the sixteenth through the late nineteenth century, whenever a woman succeeded in an intellectual or political career in Spain or Spanish America, she was dubbed "virile" (*varonil*) in character or endowed with the qualities of the male, thus denying any intrinsic capabilities to the female sex.

11. Louisa Hoberman, "Hispanic American Woman as Portrayed in the Historical Literature: Types and Archetypes," *Revista/Review Interamericana* 4 (Summer 1974): 136-47. Even though most educational and political leaders accepted the role of women as teachers without reservation, there were some conservative public men who opposed the idea. See, Heleith I. B. Saffioti, *A mulher na sociedade de classes: Mito e realidade* (São Paulo: Livraria Quatro Artes Editora, 1969), pp. 214, 222-24.

12. Feminism is here understood as the advocacy of legal and social changes in order to establish the political, economic, social, and personal equality of the sexes.

13. Cynthia Little, "Moral Reform and Feminism, *Journal of Interamerican Studies and World Affairs* 17 (November 1975): 386-97 (hereafter cited as *JISWA*). For an ambivalent position on the goals of feminism see Amanda Labarca H., *¿A dónde va la mujer?* (Santiago de Chile: Ediciones Extra, 1934). See also Hahner's and Macías's essays (chaps. 10-11) in this volume.

14. Many men served the cause of feminism in Latin America. See, for example, Genaro García, *Apuntes sobre la condición de la mujer* (Mexico: Cía. Limi de Tipografía, 1891); J. Margarito Gutiérrez, *La mujer: Defensa de sus derechos e ilustración* (Key West, Fla.: Imprenta El Cubano, 1888). Discussion of projects for the introduction of divorce in Latin American countries produced a number of writings for and against its adoption. Those who supported divorce usually buttressed their arguments with ideas that may be considered as feminist. See, for example, Guzmán Papini y Zas, *El divorcio ante la ciencia y el arte* (Montevideo: Tipografía Moderna, 1905); Enrique Dickman, *Emancipación civil, política y social de la mujer* (Buenos Aires, 1935); Knaster, *Women in Spanish America*, pp. 570-91.

15. Asunción Lavrin and Edith Couturier, "Dowries and Wills: A View of Women's Socio-Economic Role in Colonial Mexico" (Paper presented at the Ninety-first Annual Meeting of the American Historical Association, Washington, D.C., 1976). For a contemporary context, see Margo L. Smith, "Domestic Service as a Channel of Upward Mobility for the Lower-Class Woman: The Lima Case," in Pescatello, *Female and Male*, pp. 191-207. Some information on black women is available in Gonzalo Aguirre

Beltrán, *La población negra de Mexico* (Mexico: Fondo de Cultura Económica, 1972); Frederick P. Bowser, *The African Slave in Colonial Peru, 1524-1650* (Stanford: Stanford University Press, 1974), pp. 254-70; Manuel Acosta Saignes, *Vida de los esclavos negros en Venezuela* (Caracas: Editorial Hespéride, 1967); A. J. R. Russell-Wood, *Fidalgos and Philanthropists: The Santa Casa da Misericórdia of Bahia, 1550-1755* (Berkeley and Los Angeles: University of California Press, 1968).

16. See the titles cited in Knaster, *Women in Spanish America*, pp. 570-91.

17. Isabel Picó Vidal, "The History of Women's Struggle for Equality in Puerto Rico," in Nash and Safa, *Sex and Class*, pp. 202-13; Ignacio Torres Giraldo, *María Cano: Mujer rebelde* (Bogotá: Publicaciones de la Rosca, 1972). There are few studies of the connection between feminists and working-class women. There are also few historical works on the participation of women in the labor force and labor unions or on the evolution of women's work throughout time. See items 1360, 1368, 1428, 1436, and 1448 in Knaster, *Women in Spanish America*. See also Felicia R. Madeira and Paul Singer, "Structure of Female Employment and Work in Brazil, 1920-1970," *JISWA* 17 (November 1975): 490-96. See note 82 in Hahner's essay (chap. 10) in this volume.

18. See Ramos, "Marriage and the Family"; María Luisa Marcilio, "Tendances et structures des ménages dans la capitainerie de São Paulo (1765-1868)," in Frédéric Mauro, ed., *L'Histoire quantitative du Brésil de 1800 au 1930* (Paris: Centre Nationale de la Recherche Scientifique, 1973); Claude Mazet, "Population et société a Lima au XVIe et XVIIe siècles: La paroisse San Sebastian (1562-1689)," *Cahiers des Ameriques Latines* (1976): 51-102; Otilia Arosemena de Tejeira, *La mujer en la vida panameña* (Panamá: Editorial de la Universidad de Panamá, 1966), pp. 150-52; See also W. W. Borah and S. F. Cook, "Marriage and Legitimacy in Mexican Culture: Mexico and California," *California Law Review* 54 (May 1966): 995-99, 1002.

19. See Susan M. Socolow, "Religious Participation of the Porteño Merchants: 1778-1810," *The Americas* 32 (January 1976): 372-401; Marta Espejo-Ponce Hunt, "The Process of the Development of Yucatan, 1600-1700," in Ida Altman and James Lockhart, eds., *Provinces of Early Mexico* (Los Angeles: UCLA Latin American Center Publications, 1976), pp. 36-38; Nancy Farriss, *Crown and Clergy in Colonial Mexico, 1759-1821* (London: Athlone Press, 1968), p. 155. Further research on the endowment of chantries and loans of ecclesiastical institutions to laymen is likely to reveal the intimate ties between the Church and the influential families of each community. The influence of kinship and family in politics has been explored fruitfully, in particular in relation to *caudillismo* and control of local politics. See, for example, Billy Jaynes Chandler, *The Feitosas and the Sertão dos Inhamuns: The History of a Family and a Community in Northeast Brazil, 1700-1930* (Gainesville, Fla.: University of Florida Press, 1972); Linda Lewin, "The Pessoas of Paraiba" (Paper read at the Ninetieth Annual Meeting of the American Historical Association, Atlanta, 1975). See also Felstiner, "The Larraín Family."

20. Miguel León-Portilla, *Los antiguos mexicanos a través de sus crónicas y cantares* (Mexico: Fondo de Cultura Económica, 1972), pp. 150-54; Jacques Soustelle, *La vida cotidiana de los aztecas en vísperas de la conquista* (Mexico: Fondo de Cultura Económica, 1972), pp. 184-88; Colin M. MacLachlan, "The Eagle and the Serpent: Male over Female in Tenochtitlán," *Proceedings of the Pacific Coast Council on Latin American Studies* 5 (1975), pp. 45-56. See Lavrin's and Mendelson's essays (chaps. 1 and 7) in this volume. Recent studies on contemporary situations reflect the persistence

of a number of old attitudes. See Susan C. Bourque and Kay B. Warren, "Campesinas and Comuneras: Subordination in the Sierra," *JMF* 38 (November 1976): 781-88; Neuma Aguiar, "The Impact of Industrialization on Women's Work Roles in Northeast Brazil," in Nash and Safa, *Sex and Class*, pp. 110-28.

21. Evelyn P. Stevens, "*Marianismo*: The Other Face of *Machismo* in Latin America," in Pescatello, *Female and Male*, pp. 89-101; Elsa M. Chaney, "Old and New Feminists in Latin America: The Case of Peru and Chile," *JMF* 35 (May 1973): 331-43; Jorge Gissi Bustos: "Mythology about Women, with Special Reference to Chile," in Nash and Safa, *Sex and Class*, pp. 30-45; Nora Kinzer, "Priests, Machos and Babies: Or, Latin American Women and the Manichean Heresy," *JMF* 35 (May 1973): 300-12; Roberto Rodríguez Baños, Patricia Trejo de Zepeda, and Edilberto Soto Angli, *Virginidad y machismo en Mexico* (Mexico: Editorial Posada, 1973).

22. Lucy Cohen, "Women's Entry to the Professions in Colombia: Selected Characteristics," *JMF* 35 (May 1973): 322-30; Nora Kinzer, "Women Professionals in Buenos Aires," in Pescatello, *Female and Male*, pp. 159-90; Armand Mattelart and Michele Mattelart, *La mujer chilena en una nueva sociedad* (Santiago de Chile: Editorial del Pacífico, 1968); Evelyn P. Stevens, "The Prospects for a Women's Liberation Movement in Latin America," *JMF* 35 (May 1973): 313-21.

Asunción Lavrin

In search of the colonial woman in Mexico: the seventeenth and eighteenth centuries

Our knowledge of women in colonial Mexico has been fragmentary and inconclusive. Beyond the superficial historical treatment of several vicereines, only La Malinche (or Doña Marina), mistress and aide to Hernán Cortés, and Sor Juana Inés de la Cruz, the genial colonial poetess, have been considered worthy of the attention of historians. La Malinche has become, unfortunately, the embodiment of treason to her own people, an ironic fate for a woman who was sold as a slave by her family. Sor Juana, on the contrary, has been idolized and placed on a pedestal as the most perfect achievement of colonial womanhood.[1] Between these two female antipodes—the fallen woman and the apex of spiritual intellectuality—there is a vacuum. The question that this paper seeks to answer is how to fill that vacuum and restore some balance to a distorted picture of the past.

The search for the myriad of women who lived in New Spain is challenging, but not impossible. Archival records provide the raw material necessary to start uncovering the historical profile of the colonial woman, insofar as they have preserved the actions of thousands of them. At times such actions speak for themselves as specific examples of personal choices. In other instances they provide the bases for a collective analysis of women, as a group, within the family or in their social interaction with the opposite sex. In addition, a survey of the prescriptive literature pertinent to women is essential in order to define the role that they were expected to perform. The models provide forms of acceptable behavior. As a counterpoint, the actual behavior of women in several given circumstances helps to determine to what extent reality coincided with prescription or departed from it. This interplay of ideals and realities will hopefully produce a more reliable picture of colonial women than is so far available in most texts.

This study concerns itself mostly with white urban women, whose historical tracks are more accessible and easier to trace than those of the Indian or black women, but whenever possible, examples involving other social and ethnic groups have been included. Confining the treatment of women to the seventeenth and eighteenth centuries stems from the desire to deal with an established society that had already passed the formative and therefore more fluid years of the sixteenth century. In this settled society, fundamental patterns of behavior and social attitudes had jelled and thus can be analyzed with a greater degree of certainty. Many subtle and some not so subtle changes took place throughout this period. For example, Indian women were granted the right to profess in their own convents and were thus lifted to a fuller membership within the Church; educational institutions spread rapidly through the end of the eighteenth century and women became more literate than ever before. However, the general patterns of attitudes and behavior discussed in this essay did not change significantly.

Definitions of Women's Role in Society

Ideally, the study of what constitutes the role of women in society should be based on writings that reflect women's self-perception as well as men's vision of women. Prior to the nineteenth century, however, Spanish American women—with few notable exceptions—were not particularly articulate, not having the opportunities or encouragement to exercise their intellect. Insight into the personal thoughts of women are difficult to obtain due to the scarcity of such writings as diaries and letters.[2] While the majority of the women of colonial Mexico were illiterate, the largest group of literate females were nuns. Available writings by nuns tell a great deal about the religious experience, but they are not good indices for judging the experience of secular life.[3]

The best-known colonial nun is Sor Juana Inés de la Cruz, the woman whose literary genius remained unmatched by any other writer in the seventeenth and eighteenth centuries.[4] Yet, her figure remains alone in the category of great women. She had no imitators or successors in her religious order or among lay women. The basic isolation of her life in the cloisters, despite numerous social visitors, made of this woman a self-perpetuating myth. She advocated the right of women to learn and to express themselves freely. However, in her own life she followed many accepted social practices, perhaps for the lack of alternatives available to woman of her class. Ironically, the very Church to which she belonged and within which she had found shelter and fame eventually chastised her pursuit of knowledge and the exercise of her literary abilities, driving her to renounce them toward the end of her life. The value of Sor Juana as an example of colonial womanhood is restricted by the conditions of her life. The height of her achievements precludes comparison to any other woman and puts her in a category by herself. She cannot be said to exemplify colonial women, just as her contemporary, the seventeenth-century savant Carlos Sigüenza y Góngora, cannot be regarded as the epitome of colonial men. Sor Juana will remain the magnificent, but remote, North Star of colonial femininity.

In view of the scarcity of sources on women's role in society originating among women themselves, one must conclude that the image of woman in the colonial period was the creation of men. Women were told what was womanly and how to behave accordingly by men such as intellectuals, leading educators, or spiritual directors. The intellectual source of this role definition was in Spain. Through a process of cultural transfer, prescriptive literature and canons of behavior passed to Mexico and the rest of Spanish America. Although the printed sermons of priests and the advisory literature of bishops and archbishops contain normative prescriptions applicable not only to nuns, but to women in general, not a single work on feminine education was printed in colonial Mexico.

A lively feminist-antifeminist literary controversy existed in Spain since the late fifteenth century and continued through the period of the conquest. Debating the good and bad qualities of women and the relations between the sexes, these sources express commonly held views and opinions on women in those days.[5] They are often emotionally charged, however, and I have chosen to seek the image of the ideal woman in didactic authors such as Fray Martín de Córdoba, Fray Hernando de Talavera, Luis Vives, and Fray Luis de León. The works of these writers were specifically aimed at the education of women and contain well-outlined rules of female behavior.

Fray Martín de Córdoba was an Augustinian friar who wrote a small treatise on moral advice for the use of the future Queen Isabella the Catholic in approximately 1460. This work, entitled *Jardín de nobles doncellas*, was not published until 1500, but it was already reissued by 1542.[6] Addressed mostly to ladies of high birth, it defined the good and bad attributes of women, giving rules of behavior to preserve them as good and honorable beings. As good qualities he counted *vergüenza* (shyness), piety, and obsequiousness. Women's bad qualities were intemperance, loquacity, obduracy, and inconstancy. Fray Martín advised women to be ordered, restrained, shy, pious, and affable. Women's intemperance could lead them into pits of passions; thus, chastity and virginity were regarded as their highest accomplishments. Without chastity, virtues were nothing to him. Women were advised that although "female by nature they should strive to become male in virtue," a good indication that although he recognized high qualities in women, he assumed that men had higher moral qualities and were more accomplished than women. Although virginity was the most perfect state, women should marry to propagate the species. As wives, women should be faithful and remain in their homes, educating their children. Carnal passions were scorned as beastly. Married love should be more of the spirit than of the flesh. As one might expect of a man of his age, Fray Martín stressed spirituality and docility even though he was writing for a future queen.

Fray Hernando de Talavera, a Hieronymite friar confessor to Queen Isabella, wrote an essay on how married women should order and spend their time.[7] Although the essay is of a practical nature, it is based on a number of ideological assumptions about the character and nature of women. The most important one was that man was "in everything more perfect than woman," and thus it was reasonable for women to follow and obey man's judgment in all, except in that which could be venial or mortal sin. Since his work was addressed to the Countess of Benavente, Doña María de Pacheco, Fray Hernando defined the several degrees of social hierarchy that a woman of her class should bear in mind. The superiors of the countess were her husband, the king, and her confessor. Her equals were her kin in family and society. Her inferiors were her own children (under her authority until maturity), her younger relatives, her servants, and her vassals, male or female. Thus, Fray Hernando considered that a common man was socially inferior to a woman of high birth, a subtle definition that buttressed concepts of class and caste in Spain and its possessions. In the allocation of a woman's daily occupations Fray Hernando gave priority to prayer—one-tenth of her waking time—and work. The latter kept a woman occupied and consequently less susceptible to the temptations inherent in leisure. For a woman of high birth, work consisted in the good administration of her household and charitable work for hospitals or the Church. She was also allowed some honest recreation such as reading or the playing of music.

In Luis Vives, well-known educator of the sixteenth century, we find the sternest of all thinkers. His *Instrucción de la mujer cristiana* had a wide readership throughout the colonial period.[8] Vives lacked any sympathy for human passions and had very little of it for women. One of the first remarks in his book, first issued in 1524, was that "all the good and the bad in this world, one may unerringly state, are caused by women." Through the book he makes abundantly clear his belief that the bad outbalanced the good and that this situation was due mostly to the lack of a good education in most women. His educational suggestions aimed at keeping women away from evil in order that they learned only what was good, honest, and pure. For this purpose he prescribed a complete separation of the sexes at the earliest age and a complete indoctrination in the principal virtues of a woman—chastity, modesty, and strength of character.

Vives believed in the superiority of virginity over married life. Virginity made women similar to the Church and the Virgin Mary. As did many other men of his time, he regarded marriage as a social contract to be arranged by the parents, although he advised that parents not force their daughter's will on the subject. Marriage implied a sacrifice for women and was described as a yoke that could be light and easy if the husband were responsible and good. If husbands were unfaithful to their wives, wives should remain faithful to the husbands, since in Vives's opinion the loyalty of the wife sanctified the disloyalty of the husband. Double standards of morality were thus explicitly accepted. As housewives, women should remain at home, having as little contact as possible with the outside world. He showed an almost Arabic obsession with protecting women from being seen in the streets, advising a cover-all costume, "hardly uncovering one of their eyes in order to see their way."9 Learning was not forbidden, but, quoting Saint Paul, he was against women using their knowledge in public. The most important tasks for a woman were the care of her household and the preservation of her honesty. Luis Vives's essay on the education of women has long been extolled as a model in its genre. His work accurately reflects the ideas of his times. Despite his commendable goal of improving the intellectual and moral education of women, he explicitly endorsed their inferior social status and their subordination to men.

Fray Luis de León authored *La perfecta casada*, a manual for wives that first appeared in 1583 and was reprinted over twelve times during the next fifty years.10 This popular book was regarded as a healthy source of opinion and advice for young wives throughout several centuries. Fray Luis drew inspiration for its writing from the Bible and Luis Vives's writings. Faithful to these sources, he considered the state of matrimony inferior to virginity, but for practical purposes, perfection in each state was a desirable goal in life. Perfection for the married woman consisted in keeping herself pure and loyal to her husband, engaging in the duties of the home, and trying to be as valuable as a jewel to her husband. For the achievement of this kind of perfection he went into the details of how a woman should administer her husband's estate, love him and help him in times of stress, treat the servants well, nurse her own children, speak little, attend church often, and stay at home as much as possible. The general recognition of her virtues by man and God was woman's best reward. In conclusion, all these theologians and educators created a model world for women in which their purity and honor sustained and redeemed them and their families. The home and the Church offered protection and safety; the outside world, potential corruption and dishonor.

No challenges to these concepts were registered in the seventeenth century, despite the mild protests of an early feminist, María de Zayas y Sotomayor.11 However, in the first half of the eighteenth century an iconoclastic Benedictine friar, Benito Feijóo, reexamined some of these values. In his *Teatro crítico universal*, a multivolume encyclopedia that introduced many new ideas in Spain, Feijóo wrote "A Defense of Women," in which he rejected women's alleged intellectual inferiority.12 Nevertheless, although he praised women's superiority in private moral virtues, he was still persuaded that men had more aptitude for civic life, and he approved of the social and political submission of women to men. Feijóo's ideas contributed to some recognition of women's intellectual capabilities, but his writings did not remain unchallenged or lead to a widespread change in Spanish or Spanish American social attitudes toward women. However, building on the foundation established by Feijóo, several personalities of the Spanish Enlightenment proceeded to explore women's economic potential. The Count of Campomanes, adviser to Charles III, was the most outspoken endorser of a new outlook on female labor. Although not challenging the idea of women's dedication to household activities, he regretted seeing many women spending most of their lives in idleness that could be turned into profit for themselves and the State.[13] Campomanes was, above all, interested in the possible benefits that the nation might derive from the incorporation of women into the labor force. He also injected a moral issue into his argument: laziness led to corruption in feminine customs through irresponsible behavior. Feminine idleness, alien to the ancient roots of the Spanish people, was a habit introduced by the Moslems and thus more common in the south than in the north of Spain. For all his strong advocacy of female labor as a means to raise the family's and women's standard of living, Campomanes did not expect major changes to take place immediately. However, he placed great hopes in the improvement of women through intensive education.

Perhaps as a result of a more enlightened atmosphere during the reign of Charles III—a king who insisted that women be admitted in the Sociedad Económica of Madrid—it was possible for a woman, Doña Josefa Amar y Borbón, to make a public, printed defense of the intellectual capabilities of her sex and to write a treatise on the physical and moral education of women.[14] Doña Josefa, a member of the upper class, had the education, social standing, and strength of character necessary to undertake the task of speaking in the name of women. In her work on feminine education, she saw clearly that one of the major pitfalls in the upbringing of women was their being conditioned, since early childhood, to concentrate on making themselves beautiful and agreeable to men and society, with the ensuing belief that through such endeavors they would achieve complete happiness and satisfaction in life. Women lacked the social stimulus of reward for many occupations and especially for intellectual work. Despite her clear perception of some of the basic problems faced by women, Doña Josefa remained a reformer rather than an innovator. She respected tradition in the relationship between husband and wife in marriage. It was the man's obligation to sustain his family, while it was the woman's to take care of the children, the home, and the husband, trying to be a soothing influence in the life of the latter. Doña Josefa's most important contribution was to insist on a thorough education that paid greater consideration and respect to women as human beings and acknowledged the fact that the pursuit of beauty and social pleasures were not the only aims of a woman's life.

The ideas and opinions of these Spanish writers found their first echo in New

Spain in the work of José Joaquín Fernández de Lizardi, social critic and author of the first pedagogical novel written in Mexico on the education of women, *La Quijotita y su prima*.15 Although published in 1818, this work contains the ideas on women's role in society that were acceptable to an educated Mexican of the late eighteenth century. Lizardi started from the assumption that if women showed certain "defects" of character (vanity, pride, superstitiousness, and the like) more frequently than men, it was due to female ignorance bolstered by the neglect and callousness of men. He compared women to soft wax: easily malleable and thus corruptible by bad ideas. Lacking character of their own, women could be changed for the worst unless fathers and husbands provided them with responsible guidance and moral education. Thus, although sharing with Doña Josefa Amar y Borbón a concern for female education, he still assumed that women were only the reflection of men.

Although Lizardi tried to be objective on the topic of the equality of men and women, he still stated that "by natural, civil and divine law, woman, commonly speaking, is always inferior to man."16 He qualified this statement by explaining that this inferiority was not spiritual, but physical. Women had been created weaker by nature so that, being unable to perform masculine tasks, they could become the delight of men and the principal protagonists in the propagation of the species. Despite his effort to extol the role of women as wives and mothers, it is clear that women occupied a secondary and subservient place in the scheme of human affairs in Lizardi's ideal world. Altogether, Lizardi's ideas on women, although enlightened by concepts that were regarded as progressive for his time, offered little change in the image of womanhood accepted in Spain and its possessions in the seventeenth and eighteenth centuries. Women were to seek enclosure, modesty of behavior, and virginity until marriage, and after marriage they were to remain mothers and wives above all else. Although there was a gradual acceptance of women's intellectual potential and a greater interest in the social and personal need for feminine education in the late eighteenth century, the perception of women's role in society, by both men and women, remained traditional during the two centuries under consideration.

A Closer Look at Reality

Canons of feminine behavior were not necessarily followed by all women. The Spanish and Spanish American societies of the seventeenth and eighteenth centuries were far from conforming to such standards. As Robert Padden has stated, colonial baroque society was essentially contradictory in the establishment of ideals that were constantly denied in the daily actions of men and women.17 The models portrayed by colonial didactic writers supplied plausible goals of feminine conduct. They were adopted by influential ecclesiastical authorities and were transmitted as archetypes of behavior, via Sunday sermons or the confessional, to women of all social classes. Due to greater social pressure, women of the socioeconomic elite were likely to follow those ideals more closely than women of the lower strata of society. Social class was a key factor in the determination of the degree of adherence to ideal social or personal behavior. Women of the lower classes could not observe any enclosure etiquette, for example, since for economic reasons they were obliged to work outside the home. Even among the upper classes life was not conventlike for women, as attested by the travelers of the period and by contemporary records that will be cited throughout this study.

The assessemnt of the degree of acceptance of these ideals of womanhood poses a problem, but not an unsurmountable one. The acceptance or nonacceptance of such standards can be gauged by studying such indices as legislation regulating relations between men and women, social practices surrounding marriage, and records or men's and women's daily activities. The latter two, especially, have been overlooked as sources for understanding women's role in society.

A brief summary of the legal status of women in colonial Spanish America is essential to determine the boundaries that society set on women's behavior. The legal situation of women as daughters and wives was defined in codes such as the Siete Partidas, Leyes de Toro, Ordenamiento de Alcalá and the Ordenanzas de Castilla.[18] Women were under *patria potestad* (subject to their father's will) until they were twenty-five years old, when they gained complete personal independence if they remained unmarried. Under *patria potestad* women had some recognized rights, such as making their wills without parental interference, but this did not amount to much. Marriage required parental approval until age twenty-five, and once married, a woman was placed under the legal protection of her husband. She needed his consent and permission to make any legal transaction, but when this license was granted, the woman could act with complete freedom. Even the most superficial perusal of the notarial records of any colonial city throughout the seventeenth and eighteenth centuries provides ample evidence that the law was not a dead letter and that women were either active legal partners of their husbands or acted independently as legal persons. Thus, they bought and sold property, founded chantries, freed slaves, borrowed money, and took part in legal suits without any impediment from their husbands. Women could not be legally forced to act against their will, and in many documents they had to state that they had not been forced, compelled, or menaced by their husbands, fathers, or anybody else. If they could prove that their husbands were impeding their legal actions without any logical reason, they could obtain a license to perform any action.[19] After marriage women retained control over property acquired prior to it, and they also maintained ultimate control on their dowries and *arras*, as will be seen later. These were the basic terms of legislation framing the life of women in Spanish America. Women's activities were not determined exclusively by these legal standards, however. Beyond the boundaries set by the law there were a number of other determinants that were born out of the manner in which society itself developed in the New World and that exerted as much influence on women's behavior.

Like their male counterparts, the first immigrant women in the sixteenth century held a social status related to their role as conquerors and to their ethnic origins as a small group of white people in a predominantly Indian world. These women, and later their *criolla* descendants, enjoyed a high position in the social complex because as wives, mothers, or relatives, they were the kin of the conquistadors and their male children. The fact that they were to a considerable extent legally dependent on their husbands did not diminish their status before the majority of the conquered. As Fray Hernando de Talavera stated, the wife of the lord was the superior of the male vassal.

The scarcity of Spanish women in the initial period of the conquest, contrasted with the availability of Indian women, made them more desirable. Unions with Indians—especially those not belonging to the nobility—were largely consensual and added nothing to a man's social status.[20] The arrival of more women from Spain after the 1550s made marriage with equals in race more feasible.[21] As colonial society became more stable, the promiscuity of the first decades gave place to more orderly patterns of marriage. For the new elite—those who descended of conquistadors or *encomenderos* (receivers of Indian tribute) and had managed to succeed financially and those with newly acquired wealth—status was a combination of money, racial descent, and legal standing. Social supremacy was reinforced by the concept of racial superiority expressed as *limpieza de sangre*, or lack of blemish by mixture with other races. To this they added the concept of religious purity, which made Old Christians a privileged group, in contrast with those recently converted to Catholicism (New Christians), which in the seventeenth century included a significant number of crypto Jews. By the seventeenth century, the preservation of a high social status depended upon marriage between equals. Any union with elements of doubtful racial or religious origin could endanger the social standing of the family.[22]

Mixing of the white elite and *casta* members through legal marriage was not unknown, but it could be socially and economically detrimental.[23] There were social pressures against white women who married *castas*. A good example is provided by the regulation established by the Confraternity of Aranzazú, a Basque sodality, that gave dowries and pensions to marriageable women and poor widows. The confraternity stipulated that white women who married mixed-bloods (*hombres de color quebrado*) were not entitled to such dowries. However, widows of such men were eligible.[24] Social pressure against unequal marriages eventually produced a piece of legislation that theoretically amounted to infringement of the personal freedom of choice in marriage. The Real Pragmática de Matrimonios, issued in 1776, established punishment for those who married without parental consent. A person thus acting could be deprived of his or her share in the family's patrimony, an entailed property, a title of nobility, or the patronage of a pious deed. [25] The stress was clearly socioeconomic. However, the law also allowed challenge in court of any unreasonable parental pressure. The Church was requested to buttress this civil law by preaching and through spiritual advice. For practical purposes the enforcement of this law was restricted to white people and the Indian nobility. For *castas*, it was necessary only that the priest give a warning about the desirability of parental concent. This exception strongly suggests that the regulation of marriages, as stipulated by the Pragmática, was a device aimed at preserving the status quo of the dominant classes of society. Until proper demographic studies are carried out, it is difficult to state whether the Pragmática was the expression of a situation accepted by society or, conversely, a reaction to an increasing number of mixed marriages, or whether it ultimately had any significant effect on marriage trends.

It is apparent that many years of social tradition, reinforced by legislation, succeeded in creating a general distaste for unequal marriages, but among the social elite there are recorded cases of challenges and departure from tradition. In the early seventeenth century Josefa Oñate y Azoca, member of a distinguished family, was disinherited for having married Sebastián de Agüero, of whom her family disapproved. [26] Punishment could also be extended to men. The curator of the Pérez de Salazar entail sought to deprive José Pérez de Salazar of his entail for having married below his social level. [27] Available examples of legal reviews of marriage cases show that some parents were indeed tyrannical in their dominance and expected their offspring to accept their choices for marriage. When confrontations took grieved parties to civil or ecclesiastical authorities, the outcome was not always favorable to the parents. [28]

Although relatively few in number as yet, demographic studies on marriage trends in New Spain confirm the broader conclusions arrived at by qualitative studies and open new possibilities in perceiving the many behavioral nuances of social groups that otherwise would be difficult to grasp. These new data cast light on the affinities and disaffinities of certain ethnic groups for others and on the manner in which those groups mixed throughout time. Most of the results of these studies point to the general endogamy of white or near-white elites with a greater number of intermarriages taking place among the lower socioethnic groups. This conclusion is reached in the works of Edgar Love, Gonzalo Aguirre Beltrán, Patrick Carroll, Marcelo Carmagnani, and David Brading and Celia Wu. [29] The majority of white women preferred to marry white men, although they ventured outside their ethnic group, marrying mulattoes or *moriscos*, more often than their men. White men were conservative, hardly marrying outside their group. A possible explanation for this situation lies in the fact that men could maintain illicit relations with women of lower socioethnic groups and avoid legal commitment, a situation that was largely unacceptable for white women. *Moriscas* and *mestizas* rarely married men of darker skin, marrying whites, *mestizos*, or mulattoes.[30] Mulatto women married mostly within their group, but would also couple with *mestizos*, Indians, or blacks. Indian women were married mostly to Indian men, their second choices being mulattoes and *mestizos*.

Brading has found an increasing rate of intermarriage among the Indian women of León, mostly with mulattoes, in the late eighteenth century. The female slave married mostly black slaves, although Love has found that about one-third of them managed to marry free men. Marcelo Carmagnani has tied economic cycles with patterns of marriage in the seventeenth-century northern mining districts. He proposed that whites married outside their group more frequently in times of economic expansion than in times of economic stagnation or depression. However, he also stressed the general endogamy of this group. Undoubtedly, these demographic studies have made a significant contribution to a relatively unexplored social topic, although their results need further confirmation in more localities throughout the colonial period.

There is another social aspect of marriage that merits study, since it was a very important index of women's position in society: the dowry. Endowing a woman prior to marriage was a well-established custom in medieval Europe and Spain that can be tracked back to Roman law, although in Spain and Spanish America its usage had been modified by Gothic influences.[31] The dowry was a contribution made by the bride's family to help defray the expenses to be incurred during marriage. It was not a gift to the husband, but a form of financial security underwritten by the woman's family with the purpose of ensuring her well-being after her husband's death. Although the husband could administer the dowry during the marriage, he was obliged to take provisions in order that his widow would recover its full value. Most men's wills contained statements on the value of their wives' dowry, if they brought any. The man was also obliged to reimburse the value of the dowry to the woman's family in case the marriage was dissolved.[32]

The attractiveness of the dowry lay in the use that the husband, as its administrator, could give to it during his lifetime. The dowry could be a desirable asset if it consisted of property or cash, or both, that the husband could use as capital for investment and profit. On the other hand, dowries consisting mostly of clothing or furniture were not negotiable and were not an asset to the husband. Jewels were considered a safe investment, since they could be pawned or sold. In general, smaller dowries consisting mostly of clothing or furniture were not a basis for wealth consolidation. They fulfilled a social tradition as an aid to setting up the new home and as the bride's personal trousseau. Significantly, even though these goods were perishable, the husband was still legally bound to insure their value against his assets. The potential dangers of loss of the dowry through squandering or a bad investment did not materialize too often, as it seems apparent in the notarial records.[33]

Women in good social standing were expected to provide a dowry for marriage. Dowries could be concerted and settled prior to the wedding, but final settlement could take place after it or even after the death of the bride's father, when his estate was divided among his heirs. On some occasions, promised dowries were never delivered. Dowries were notarized in *cartas dotales*, meticulous lists of all the goods, properties, and cash brought by the bride. The size of the dowry varied according to the status of the bride's family and the number of the daughters to be endowed. Charitable institutions provided marriageable orphans with 300 *pesos* in cash. In provincial towns, where large dowries were not common, they ranged from one to several thousand *pesos*. In Mexico City the daughter of a wealthy merchant could be endowed with over 10,000 *pesos*. Among the nobility a single daughter could receive sums between 20,000 and 100,000 *pesos*, with some reaching 300,000.[34] These amounts were not all in cash. As suggested above, dowries consisted of cash, properties, jewels, clothing, art objects, furniture, and slaves. The wealthiest women had a representative sample of all, while the less affluent brides seem to have concentrated on clothing, jewelry, and some furniture.

Dowries were a very important asset for a woman. An attractive dowry was a helpful aid in negotiating an advantageous marriage that could strengthen or further her family's and her own social position. Throughout married life, a dowry could be used for backing a loan for the wife or the husband to help consolidate a business, to found a chantry benefiting a relative, or to improve a rural estate or other financial operation of advantage to the family.[35] The lack of a dowry, however, was not a social impediment for marriage. It has been argued that dowries were necessary to marry, but this proposition cannot be substantiated for all women of colonial Mexico—not even for all white women, and the others, we assume, were less affluent and less likely to follow this custom. There are enough examples of men who declared that their wives had brought no dowry to the marriage or fathers who stated that their daughters had not been endowed to dispel any doubts on the "need" of a dowry for the purpose of getting married. The dowry was a custom adopted by the Hispanic or Hispanicized segment of the population for the purpose of giving economic protection to their women and reinforcing social distinctions. It was not a prerequisite for marriage or a device to preserve morality among women.[36]

In addition to the dowry, women received another kind of financial security provided by the groom, the *arras*, which was legally defined as a sum of money equal to 10 percent of his assets at the time of marriage. This sum was added to the dowry to reinforce the woman's financial security. After her death it passed to her heirs at her will, since once it was granted, the husband lost control over his donation. In some instances a woman undowered by her family was endowed by her husband with the *arras* as a gesture of his desire to protect her financial future.[37] The wording of the *arras* also expressed the groom's regard for the virginity and honor of the bride and sometimes also for her social standing. For example, after listing the land, cattle, money, and Indian servants that his bride had brought, Juan de Loya, to be married to Ana de Solís in Monterrey in 1642, added a grateful acknowledgment to his in-laws, since he was "in the knowledge of the cleanliness and virtue of the said Ana de Solís, my wife . . . and the enhancement that I received with the said marriage due to the honor, good fame and reputation of the aforesaid in-laws for being conquistadors and in good standing."[38]

Dissolution of the marriage was a very difficult process and, as such, a rather infrequent incident. The suing party had to prove religious incompatibility, evidence of the partner's being a hidden Jew or a Protestant, flagrant adultery, or nonconsummation of marriage. Divorce suits were carried out in ecclesiastical courts, and the civil authorities dealt with the division of conjugal properties after the marriage was dissolved by the Church. The Church never accepted the concept of the complete dissolution of marriage. A divorce meant a legal separation (*separación de cuerpos*) in which the partners remained spiritually bound until the death of one or the other. While most men seeking a separation alleged adultery, most women recurred to allegations of physical and moral ill-treatment, economic stress due to abandonment, and, as a last resort, scandalous conduct due to open adultery. The law established that an adultery charge had to be brought against both offending parties, not just one of them. Double standards of morality, however, resulted in harsher punishment for female adultery. The idea behind this attitude was that an adulteress not only stained her husband's honor, but introduced the possibility of bastardy in the family. For a man only scandalous concubinage was regarded as meriting punishment. Abandonment of his family obligations, on the other hand, was considered more offensive to society than an occasional adulterous escapade.[39]

All charges in a divorce or separation suit had to be thoroughly documented, and the accusing party bore the burden of presenting the witnesses. Gathering evidence to support charges of mistreatment or abandonment did not seem too difficult a task since willing neighbors were usually available. Cases of adultery, however, were far more difficult to document, and many of them were based on circumstantial evidence. When a husband accused his wife of adultery, she would be temporarily interned in detention houses available in Mexico City and other major cities or in the home of a respectable family. This internment was called *depósito*. Women of the lower classes could be deposited in a private home, but if an internment house or *recogimiento* was available, she most likely would be sent to it. Some of these institutions sheltered all classes of women, including prostitutes. [40] The *deposito* was an imposition on women insofar as it restricted their movements and subjected them to social ostracism.

Some scattered evidence suggests that men were sometimes imprisoned during matrimonial litigation, but the extent of this practice needs to be gauged. Most of the evidence indicates that women were more penalized than men in all cases involving marriage settlements or divorce. [41] Soldiers and their wives, due to the special privileges of their corps (*fuero*), solved their marital suits with their military superiors. All the cases of divorce examined suggest that marital suits were raised not so much to obtain a legal separation as to obtain reformation of behavior in the accused party. Ecclesiastical and civil authorities quite often sought to reunite, rather than separate, the contending parties, unless the circumstances were very aggravating. [42] In addition to the persuasion of the authorities, women had to consider the economic implications of separation. Many women were willing to return to their officially contrite husbands because very few of them were in a position to support themselves, and it was very difficult to guarantee compliance with any maintenance award granted by the judges. Legal separation also carried undesirable social connotations for women. Consequently, only a very small number of women (and men) resorted to this solution.

Morality and the Protection of Women in Society

The family was regarded in Spain and Spanish America as the pillar of society, so the fostering and preserving of marriage and the family was one of the main concerns of the State and the Church. Within the family women had a preeminent role as wives and mothers. Their "predestination" to marriage was sanctioned by the Church and public opinion; their duties at home were elevated to the category of a fine art demanding all their dedication and providing them with all the rewards that they might desire. While the State provided legal protection to the institution that sheltered and ennobled women at the same time, the Church played a special role as supervisor of the moral aspects of marriage, the family, and women.

Marriage ensured legitimacy, which was the foundation of social acceptance and legal continuity of the family and a crucial factor in the preservation of status and patrimony. [43] Transgressors of the basic ethical rules dealing with marriage and sexual relations could expect to be punished by the Church, which reviewed all cases called to its attention. Self-appointed denouncers were not lacking, even in the smallest communities. Ecclesiastical concern had a mixture of social and religious motivations. Any couple not living in proper marital union was not only a source of scandal for society, but was also endangering its standing before God. *Con poco temor de Dios y gran daño de sus almas* (*"With little fear of God and great harm to their souls"*) was the usual formula used to support charges in the investigation of suspected violations of moral rules and behavior considered detrimental to society.

Ecclesiastical tribunals dealt with cases of marital abandonment by wife or husband, adultery, concubinage, bigamy, incest, or dispensation of consanguinity. Denouncements reached these tribunals via local priests or during the bishops' visits of their sees. Each case received careful attention; meticulous investigations were carried out and documented with the reports of many witnesses. When the attorney for the ecclesiastical tribunal gave his sentence, it was countersigned by the bishop and carried out by civil authorities. Any accusation involving a married woman in good standing or young women of respectable homes demanded the *depósito*. [44] Among the unfortunate circumstances surrounding many of these cases was that the woman on trial could have been accused by any kind of witness or an impassioned and vindictive marital partner. The process of sorting out dubious from reliable witnesses, and evidence from hearsay, could take a long time, and the accused could be imprisoned or deposited for months. Unproved cases were dismissed with some spiritual penalty such as prayers and the prohibition of further communication among the involved parties, even if they had been found innocent.

The records examined show a wide range of examples of moral wrongdoing that belies assumptions of the complete restraint of female sexuality. None of these examples is new in the catalogue of well-known human frailties, but they reveal that colonial women have been placed in stereotyped niches, either the guarded and pure female or the pious nun, that were not universally valid. The pressures to conform to accepted modes of behavior were great, but adherence was not as strict as it has been taken for granted, despite the constant supervision of the Church. The cases aired at the ecclesiastical tribunals reveal that promiscuity and callousness were not alien to the lives of colonial women, particularly and more often to those of lower classes. These records register girls already married at twelve; young women giving birth to illegitimate children in the open fields and placing them with older women who would raise them; women having relations with two men of the same family, or vice versa; girls who fell prey to their mothers' lovers or husbands. Criminal records involving such trespasses of colonial morality should not be misconstrued as setting the tone of general social behavior, but these samplings suggest that society was bawdier than it has been commonly acknowledged and that the concept of sheltered womanhood applied mostly to the upper classes. Even so, the assumption that *castas*, blacks, or Indians were more sexually permissive than whites needs further qualification, since many of the cases recorded involve the latter.

Since the sixteenth century, bigamy and fornication were the commonest moral transgressions practiced by the colonists, male and female, *castas* or whites. The cases surveyed by the Inquisition were probably a fraction of those actually taking place. The punishment for convicted cases was lashing and

exile from town, which did not seem inhibiting enough to deter potential "sinners." Punishment for adultery had the purpose of restoring the marriage and
removing the offending third party from the scene. Adulterous parties were
punished regardless of sex. Men running away from home or living with a
mistress were ordered to return home and support their legitimate wives.45
Single women living "scandalous" lives, especially in small towns where concubinage or prostitution was less acceptable or feasible than in the larger
towns or the capital, were sent to the site of the Sé or to Mexico City and deposited in the Casa de Misericordia or *recogimientos*, where they were expected to pay for their ill-behavior and to rehabilitate their lives under religious guidance or through sheer hard work. 46

The deflowering of women was also a common enough incident. Under
promise of marriage, men obtained the favors of women in advance of the religious ceremony. Later, a special permission for marriage could be obtained
from religious authorities. Many of these cases concerned couples with some
degree of consanguinity, which required dispensation from the Church. It is
possible that premarital sexual relations in many of the cases among relatives
were made easier by the fact that such socialization between male and female
might have received less vigilance from the family. It is important to note that
promise or pledge to marry (*palabra de casamiento*) exchanged by man and
woman, even in secrecy, carried legal weight with civil and religious authorities. A woman could argue that she had been given *palabra de casamiento* by a
man and sue him for nonfulfillment of the promise. Only mutual break of such
promise was acceptable before the law as breaking the agreement between a
couple. 47 The binding character of the pledge of marriage probably made the
loss of virginity acceptable for some women, who were confident that marriage
would eventually follow. After having seduced a woman, if a man wished to
marry her (or was compelled to do so), he requested authorization from ecclesiastical authorities. The argument most often used to support his petition was
that the woman would otherwise be left "exposed" in society. The wording
commonly used also implied that the man felt that he "owed" the woman her
virginity and was repaying her for its loss. After presumably "debasing" the
woman, the man would use accepted stereotyped arguments of a potentially
worse fate for the woman and assumed the role of her savior through marriage.
Thus, in these records we find evidence of how the moral canons established by
Vives, Fray Luis de León and others were broken and at the same time upheld,
subjecting women and men to contradictory situations of sexual enticement,
personal guilt feelings, and social shame. The Church almost always granted
requests for dispensations and blessed the marriage in order to redeem the
original wrong.48

It should be pointed out that the people who brought up their own cases for
ecclesiastical review and approval were those who felt moral or social pressures

compelling them to take such action. For the poorer or less educated members of society concubinage was not unusual. Marriage was often legalized only after many years of consensual union. Illegitimate relatives are frequently mentioned in records dealing with tailors, bakers, silk weavers, and similar urban artisans, for whom "natural" children were not as much a source of social concern as for the upper classes. Even among the upper classes, *hijos naturales* were by no means uncommon, most of the times stemming from men's illicit relationships. Through the seventeenth century the Counts of the Valley of Orizaba were notoriously involved in a long litigation over their title due to the existence of two illegitimate branches of the family, one of which originated in one of its female members.[49] A social problem difficult to explain is that of the orphans so frequently mentioned as adopted by rich and poor families alike, in the capital of the viceroyalty and in lesser towns. The possibility of their being the windfalls of illegitimate relationships is difficult to document, except with those declared as *hijos de iglesia*, or foundlings. One can only speculate that in many instances these children must have been born to "respectable" women and adopted by relatives or friends. As members of the extended family of their adopters, these foundlings or "orphans" were quite often provided for in the wills of their benefactors.[50]

The "endangering" situations from which men thought women needed protection were many, and such protection was provided by governmental, institutional, religious, or personal patronage. All socially respectable women came to expect that protection in times of distress, such as when they became orphans or widows or could not marry well. In the late sixteenth century and early seventeenth century numerous impoverished widows and spinsters, relatives of the marginal men who did not profit from postconquest colonial development, requested pensions from the Crown in order to get married, to raise their children, or simply to improve their living conditions, on grounds of being descendants of conquistadors or civil servants.[51] Although the Crown granted personal aid to many of them, this kind of patronage was not available to the many who wished or needed it.

The assignment of *encomiendas* (tribute in labor or an award in cash) to women, an established practice by the middle of the sixteenth century, should be regarded as another form of royal patronage for wives and daughters of conquistadors and early settlers. *Encomiendas* were used as dowries to facilitate the marriage of women with suitable men. This concept was reinforced by the legal proviso that both male and female recipients of *encomienda* marry within a year of the award. The Crown also bolstered the institution of marriage and the legitimacy of heirs by allowing *encomiendas* to pass only to legitimate children or wives. A woman *encomendera* could transfer the administration of her *encomienda* to her husband, but not the absolute right to own it, which legally reverted to her at the death of the husband-administrator.[52] In a closed and distant society such as that of Yucatán, the *encomienda* survived through the eighteenth century, and it was used as a form of endowment for women, providing them with some financial security for life.[53]

In the eighteenth century, governmental patronage in the earlier forms of *gracias* and *mercedes* (land and cash grants) seems to have been much reduced, to be replaced by *montepíos*. *Montepíos* are an eighteenth-century interpretation of state patronage for the female relatives and dependents of the officials of the Audiencia, Tribunales de Cuenta, Hacienda, and military corps. The *montepíos* drew their funds from compulsory deduction from the salaries of the employees of those governmental agencies. The Crown contributed to the fund with an annual sum; the royal treasury contributed one-sixth of the deceased employee's annual salary. Widows and children of the government officials covered by the *montepío* arrangement were entitled to one-fourth of the salary of their husbands or fathers as a pension. Widows received this pension as long as they did not remarry. In case of remarriage it passed to the children.[54]

Private or religious patronage took the form of *beaterios, recogimientos*, and nunneries, destined to those women who either had a religious vocation or needed a decent and safe retreat of a religious character. *Beaterios* were voluntary associations of *beatas*, pious lay women, under the supervision of the secular Church. The *beatas* devoted their lives to prayer and religious discipline, but did not profess as nuns. *Recogimientos* sheltered many kinds of women, as explained before, but some of them took only women of good moral standing. *Beaterios* and *recogimientos* were numerous, some evolving into nunneries or schools, others remaining as places of shelter.[55] They received mostly poor women, single or widowed, and married women who had been abandoned by their husbands, who were in the process of separating from them, or whose spouses traveled or were absent for a long time. These institutions received a limited number of women, due to their meager financial capabilities. For the most part, they would accept only whites or *mestizas* as full members. *Castas*, Indians, or black women were allowed only as servants. Nunneries, of which there were well over fifty in New Spain at the end of the eighteenth century, attracted women who felt they had a vocation for religious life or who, belonging to a large family, had a mixture of religious and economic motivations to profess. Profession as a nun meant a life of complete enclosure. Several of the largest convents of Mexico City had as many as one hundred professed nuns at certain times during the seventeenth century and an additional two or three hundred servants.[56] In the last decade of the eighteenth century there were 888 nuns and 732 servants in twenty convents of Mexico City.[57]

Women in Independent Roles

Independence of action is not usually associated with the image of colonial women. Yet, there were special situations that allowed women to act on their own, and they did—shattering the commonly held view of their passivity and docility.

The legal restrictions that placed women under the guardianship of men ceased when the latter died. Widowhood granted a great deal of freedom to women. A widow was not expected to return to her parents' house, even if she was relatively young. She acquired direct control of her dowry and *arras*, as well as half of her deceased husband's estate or the wealth that the couple had accumulated throughout marriage (*bienes gananciales*). As a rule, a widow also gained the tutorship of her children and the right to administer their inheritance until they became of age. Husbands could, however, appoint co-administrators or joint tutors to help their widows in the demanding task of supervising large estates or a large family.[58]

Whether they administered their wealth or simply enjoyed their incomes, widows wielded a great deal of power, especially if they belonged to the upper and richer segment of society. Many of the women of the propertied classes had the confidence of their husbands, as is evident in their wills. Women were thus entrusted with the task of preserving the family's patrimony, an undertaking that some performed with excellent results.[59] On the other hand, many widows were left with numerous debts to pay and had to face long legal suits (*concursos de acreedores*) and the eventual sale of their properties.[60]

As with many situations in life, the case with which a widow passed to living her new life depended on her social and economic circumstances. For the historian the most interesting group of widows are those who succeeded in continuing to manage their husbands' trades. The law allowed the widows of small artisans to take over their businesses, even if they remarried, as long as they maintained the obligations and standards of the craft. Many of the wives of these artisans had had experience in the management of their husbands' businesses through many years of collaboration. As a result, women are found to have been engaged in such occupations as hog dealers, gilders, owners of card factories, music teachers, money lenders, or partners with men in small stores. Although widows seemed to undertake such tasks more frequently than married or even single women, the latter two are also represented in the lively catalog of occupations revealed by the notarial records of most urban centers. Women owned sugar mills, mines, cattle *estancias*, textile sweatshops (*obrajes*), wine shops (*vinaterías*), and wax and cigar factories.[61]

The notion that colonial women did not work or had very little economic power needs to be revised. Economic power should not be defined in simple terms of earning a salary. This criterion is not enough to judge the economic capability of women. If economic power is measured in terms of access to wealth and property, women among the social elite gained considerable power as heiresses to their fathers and husbands. The socioeconomic power of rich heiresses depended on how their families used their marriage as a means to consolidate their wealth. Therein lies the significance of the dowries and the laws allowing women to retain control over their own property after marriage. Urban women of smaller economic means owned houses, plots of land, or stores that gave them an independent status in their communities. If output of work in nonsalaried situations is regarded as an economic asset, women of the lower classes were also quite valuable. In both rural and urban areas Indians and *casta* women engaged in a variety of occupations: they had stalls in the markets and sold almost anything from food to used clothing. They worked as maids, wet nurses, cooks, washerwomen, and peddlers, thus helping to sustain their families and themselves and, by providing these services, becoming an indispensable element in the local economy. 62

The importance of property ownership or engagement in some form of business for a woman can be gauged only when compared to the scarcity of "decent" employment for women who were not utterly poor, but needed economic help. *Obrajes* were run by forced labor; sugar mills employed slave women; mining towns required women as cooks, maids, or prostitutes; professional guilds were mostly closed to women. The traditional forms of occupation for women throughout the seventeenth and eighteenth centuries were those of teachers (*amigas*) or seamstresses, in which they earned very meager incomes. By the middle of the eighteenth century women were also employed as silk spinners and workers in candle and cigar factories. 63 As ideas of economic reform progressed in the eighteenth century, enlightened economists suggested the utility of women's work outside the home. Employment of women in textile industries or tobacco factories became acceptable and desirable. In 1779, in order to encourage female industrial work, Charles III abolished the guild rules preventing women from engaging in certain crafts, and in 1784 he issued an order permitting women to undertake any occupation compatible with their sex, decorum, and strength. This measure was extended to New Spain in 1798. 64 Most of the occupations suggested for women by Charles's ministers, however, were of an acceptable feminine character, such as hair stylists, lace makers, silk and wool weavers, and so on. 65 Some charitable institutions, such as hospitals, employed women as cooks and nurses. The Hospicio de Mujeres, for example, was completely supervised by women. 66 However, such forms of employment were numerically restricted. Tradition dies hard, and the notion that ladies did not work outside the home gave manual occupation or even early industrial employment a "lower-class" character. The fact remained that women worked in factories or in the streets only when forced by economic circumstances, and the vast majority of women so engaged were nonwhite. A lady remained at home.

The economic power of women property owners is more evident than other forms of economic influence so far treated. There are examples of women *labradoras*, or landowners of medium-sized rural properties, since the sixteenth century. Some of the earliest landowners exploited the land in a commercial sense, since they required *repartimientos* (labor allocations for landowners) of Indian labor. In the region of Chalco in 1618, the names of Ana de Zaldívar, Catalina and Juana Morante, and one Angelina appear in the list of *repartimientos*.[67] In the seventeenth and eighteenth centuries it was not unusual that women inherited large tracts of land of considerable value. Other women owned *trapiches* (sugar mills) and *molinos* (flour mills). It is possible to find examples of vigorous, business-minded women who maintained a close surveillance of their properties. Graciana de Velasco, fifth holder of the title of Count of the Valley of Orizaba (1702-39), managed the rural estates of the family, worth over half a million *pesos*, during the life of her husband, who had not proved efficient at that task.[68] In her will the countess showed considerable knowledge of the administrative issues of the properties, all debts and debtors, and the financial condition of the rural estates. She gave precise orders allocating all the properties according to the merits of her children. It is significant that she appointed her daughter Nicolasa as her executor and not her son, with whom she had had a legal suit in the Audiencia. Nicolasa also received the Pereda *mayorazgo* (entail) belonging to the family.[69]

It is difficult to assess the degree of responsibility assumed by women in the administration of large estates. Evidence suggests that, like men, many women entrusted their properties to majordomos or administrators and their legal affairs to *apoderados* (proxy attorneys). Although the limited education of most women possibly precluded them from taking complete charge of management, it would be misleading to assume that they did not count in decision making. Illiteracy was not an obstacle to carrying on practical business. Illiterate women entered into all sorts of contracts—as notarial records prove—such as the sale and purchase of cattle, land, houses, or slaves, having witnesses sign for them and thus solving the small inconvenience of not knowing how to write. Women of all social classes, from the owner of a small plot of land in town to the wealthiest heiress of the best family, also engaged frequently in litigation procedures related to their properties. The numerous cases of legal suits initiated by women over land boundaries, water rights, invasion of land by squatters, heritage rights, dispossession of land, and similar situations should dispel the notion that the colonial woman lacked any personality or strength. Even though the suits were carried out by lawyers, the women proprietors must have been aware of their rights and of the possibilities and liabilities of their claims and were, undoubtedly, a major driving force behind the legal processes.[70]

Women came into possession of land most frequently by inheritance from fathers or husbands and less often through their mother's legacy, direct purchase, or their own labor. However, the latter cases are by no means infrequent.[71] Another manner of coming into possession of property was through *mayorazgo* (entail). As a rule *mayorazgos* favored the firstborn and the male over the female, but they passed to women's hands when males were not available and when some founders specifically destined them to the female side of the family. Some fathers willed their entails to their daughters on purpose, as was the case with the fifth Countess of the Valley of Orizaba, mentioned before. The Peredo-Suárez entail held by the Counts of Orizaba had been founded by Diego de Peredo and María de Acuña expressly for their daughter Graciana. [72] Another interesting departure from the male lineage in a colonial entail was that of Sáenz de Sicilia, founded by Miguel Sáenz de Sicilia in 1774 over a estate valued at 60,000 *pesos*. He destined it for the particular benefit of the women of his family so that they would never be obliged to marry men of a lower social status for lack of personal means. [73]

An accurate assessment of the value of property held by women at a given time in any given region would be feasible through the study of property titles or censuses of properties when these are available. Although this kind of research remains to be done, a rehearsal exercise in its potential results was tried with a census of properties in the jurisdiction of Tlaxcala in the period of 1712 to 1716. The survey showed that 16 percent of the landowners were women, whose combined properties represented 17.2 percent of the total value of the real estate of this area (see Table 1.1). The lands belonging to women ranged from small *ranchos* to properties valued at over 30,000 *pesos*. [74] A 1712 census of Huichapa, predominantly a cattle region, showed nine women landowners out of a total of ninety-two. Although the value of the properties of the majority of these nine women was relatively small, one of them—the wealthy Doña María Teresa de Medina Saravia, wife of a Calatrava knight and sister of a *regidor* (councilman) of the city of Mexico—had one cattle *hacienda* and several *sitios* (small plots of land) with a total value of 100,000 *pesos*. Doña María Teresa's land was, in fact, the largest and most valuable property of the region. The total assessed value of the properties of Huichapa was 242,080 *pesos*; the properties of all the women, dominated by that of Doña María Teresa, was valued at 115,769 *pesos*, or nearly 50 percent of the total. [75]

Feminine religious institutions should also be taken into consideration as an important part of the property-owning class. In the late sixteenth and early seventeenth centuries, nunneries received properties as donations from patrons. Although these donations became less frequent as time passed, the nuns took an increasing interest in the purchase and sale of properties. Nuns were advised on investments by friends or administrators, and they had to request permission from their ecclesiastical superiors to buy and sell, but permissions were almost always granted if the investment looked sound. Due to their contemplative character, nunneries employed majordomos to collect rents and leases and to run their rural and urban properties, while the internal management of the income and expenses of the religious community rested in their hands. Nunneries owned *haciendas*, ranches, sugar and flour mills, sheep herds, cattle, and houses in the towns. The convents of Mexico City started to accumulate houses in the city in the late decades of the seventeenth century

Table 1.1

Property Owned by Women in the Jurisdiction of Tlaxcala, 1712

	Landowners			Women's Properties	
Partido	Total Number	Women	Total Value of All Properties (pesos)	Value (pesos)	% of Total Value
Huamantla	34	4	662,822	25,000	3.8
Hueyotlipa	10	4	143,100	40,000	28.0
Nativitas	34	8	421,965	131,500	31.2
San Felipe Santa Clara	23	4	191,900	37,500	19.5
Chiautempan	26	1	140,275	600	0.4
Tlaxco	13	2	255,325	52,800	20.7

Source: Isabel González Sanchez, *Haciendas y ranchos de Tlaxcala en 1712* (Mexico: Instituto Nacional de Antropología e Historia, 1969).

and, for all practical purposes, gave up investments in land in the eighteenth century. This was possibly due to the problems inherent in the administration of a rural property through intermediaries. Provincial convents retained rural estates, but they also invested in houses. Nunneries were also important as banking institutions, using the numerous pious donations that they received and the profits of some of their investments as loans to merchants and property owners. As a result, women's convents developed a close association with the socioeconomic elites of the viceroyalty that made them an important economic factor in colonial society.[76]

Property conferred economic and social status. Women with property could act as bond agents for their husbands or sons, using their dowries, conjugal property, or their own property.[77] Backed by property, women could ask for and receive loans, thus gaining access to credit and acceptance within the economic elite.[78] Loans granted to women by ecclesiastical sources, for example, varied from small sums to thousands of *pesos*. In the second half of the eighteenth century, when it was not unusual for a religious institution to lend 30,000 or 40,000 *pesos* to some individuals, the amounts lent to women increased similarly, especially those lent to the female members of wealthy families. Ana María Erijar Montecino, sole heiress of her father and owner of over fifty *caballerías* of land in the valley of Toluca and houses in Lerma, offered her properties as collateral in order to obtain a loan of 10,000 *pesos* from the Juzgado de Capellanías in 1774. She had brought the land as her dowry to her first marriage and used it to support her second husband's financial affairs. [79] In 1786 the Countess of San Mateo Valparaíso returned a loan of 30,000 *pesos* to the Confraternity of Aranzazú. [80]

The question of how women were involved in the mechanism of transmission of property and the conservation of the socioeconomic colonial system has not been properly studied. Although the topic can only be broached here, it is worthwhile to point out its relevance. Since women could retain separate property of their own and could bequeath it freely, the allocation of the maternal inheritance could make a great difference to the heirs, particularly among the economic elite. But even among people of very small means, the inheritance of the maternal plot of land or a small house worth only several hundred *pesos* was of great significance. Theoretically, a widow commanded her personal property, a dowry and *arras*, and half of her husband's estate. It was not until her death—unless other arrangements were made—that the children received their total share. Add to this the control that a widow had over the minor childrens' share of the paternal inheritance, and a picture of considerable power emerges.

The family and the Church were the usual recipients of a woman's property. Most wills of women, whether rich or poor, show equal concern for their souls and their immediate relatives or protégés. In order to exemplify these two concerns I have chosen the wills of two women of different economic situation. In 1696, Anna Clara Mejía disposed of a medium-sized fortune of about 15,000 *pesos*. She devoted 7,430 *pesos* to various pious deeds such as masses, celebrations of saints' feasts, purchase of bulls, and donations to religious institutions. She left 300 *pesos* to be distributed among the poor and 6,325 *pesos* for various protégés and one foundling; and she left undisposed the fate of one slave. In the same year a poor widow, owner of a plot of land and a few animals in Metepec, carefully allocated several *pesos* to each of the confraternities of the town and a mass for her soul. She left her home and housewares to four female orphans; an ox, a cow, and a mare to two others; and an ox to a boy orphan. [81] Examination of numerous testaments of women in Puebla and Guadalajara in the seventeenth and eighteenth centuries offers a fascinating variety of personal situations, but they do not depart from the general pattern exemplified above.

Women's financial contribution to the Church and the family defines them as a basically conservative economic power. They strengthened the vested interests of society, tending to consolidate rather than to diversify. Further analysis of women's share in the maintenance of the colonial socioeconomic structure will confirm this. The relationship between women and ecclesiastical institutions is of particular interest. In the seventeenth and eighteenth centuries the records of the foundation of chantries, religious feasts, and convents are crowded with women's names. [82] Thus, the relationship was not exclusively spiritual, educational, or moral: its economic implications were manifold and broad. The main assets of numerous families could pass through women's hands to the Church. The evolution and extent of this process deserve further attention. For example, sixteen nunneries in Mexico City were founded by widows or single women, either acting singlehandedly or encouraging others to make donations. Two other convents were founded by young rich orphans who later professed. [83]

Beyond the direct control of property and money, women had another kind of economic impact—also usually neglected—as consumers of items such as furniture, clothing, jewels, carriages, and the like. Whether women belonged to the economic elite or not, their consumption of nondurable goods was the basis upon which many trades owed their existence and many merchants made their profits. The rise of the merchant class in the seventeenth century spurred a pattern of consumption that did not change significantly during the rest of the colonial period. Mining booms could only enhance it. The consumption traits of the population reflect, to a large extent, the consumption demands of women, especially of products designed to provide material comforts or a measure of social status.

Dowries and inventories of deceased women provide direct information on the kind of products consumed and their estimated prices. Among the wealthy, the signs of conspicuous consumption are unmistakable. Dresses were very expensive items in the seventeenth century, and their prices did not decrease significantly in the following century. Prices ranged from 70 to 150 *pesos* or more. A dress costing 150 *pesos* equaled the annual income of a 3,000-*pesos* chantry—on which some priests lived—and was half the price of a healthy slave in the seventeenth century. [84] Silverware, jewels, fine furniture, and pieces of religious art were other items purchased by or for women in direct proportion to their acquisitive power and social status. Sumptuary laws against excesses in dress were enacted in Spain during the sixteenth century. In 1679, 1691, and 1716, royal *cédulas* against luxury reached New Spain, but there is no evidence that they changed the dressing habits of the upper class. Thomas Gage, well-known seventeenth-century traveler, remarked on the fine clothing and jewels worn by the ladies and their slaves. In the mid-nineteenth century another European traveler made similar remarks on the dressing customs of Mexican ladies and was particularly critical of their habit of wearing diamonds in the morning. [85]

Conclusion

The various sources consulted have given many different views of women. Each provides information on important aspects of their lives and suggests the multiplicity of roles played by women in colonial society. Legal sources show that although legislation was restrictive, it was not repressive. It limited women's actions in certain spheres, but left others open for meaningful activities. Legal sources help to define the perimeter of personal behavior and to reflect men's attitude on how women fit into the social order. Yet, legislation by itself is a static source, like anatomy in comparison to physiology. Other sources of daily activities have provided the functioning rhythm of women's existence. Wills and dowries reveal women's importance as heiresses and controllers of property and the role they played in cementing kinship nets among the upper classes or in buttressing the assets of even those with much more limited financial capabilities. This view of women's economic importance is extended by the consideration of the labor of the lower-class woman, which, although almost totally neglected by historians, was a dynamic element in certain areas of the economy. The role of women as consumers—hinted at, but not yet fully explored—is another new angle suggested by the sources, putting women in direct relation to market demands, the movement of merchandise, and the subtler topic of material culture.

The most personal view of women's status and private life was gleaned from records of litigation or other conflicts with the secular or ecclesiastical authorities. Although the gap left by the lack of personal writings by women cannot be filled by these records, they nonetheless allow us to come close to baring the sinews of male-female relationships and the manner in which these relations were linked to the social and religious mechanisms regulating them. These records have uncovered a variety of personal situations that defy many previous assumptions about women. Altogether, the most important result of this search for the colonial women has been the discovery of women as individuals capable of carrying out independent activities that affected their families and society. Women had for so long been cast in the role of shadows within the house or assumed to have been submerged under the wills of husbands and parents that their very humanity had been almost forgotten.

There are many threads still loose, and the picture we have is still far from complete. The possibilities for future research are wide. Topics such as the internal migration of white women from the center to the frontiers or of Indian women from Indian towns to the cities (in the first instance as carriers of Spanish culture and social stability, and in the second instance as members of the labor pool) should be investigated. The quality of life of the upper and lower classes, criminality among women (objects or perpetrators?), the manners of raising children (since motherhood was such an overwhelming theme)—all are to be explored. The economic activities of women at the local and regional levels, the relationship between women and the Church, and the many nuances of the relations between the sexes are also topics that deserve attention.

Women, marriage, and the family (which implies motherhood) were a tightly knit trilogy, highly cherished by colonial men. Women were the physical entities embodying the other two. As a result, they became the guarded guardians, the protected protectors, of marriage and the family. Protection is the key word for understanding the relation of male to female and of society to women. Even nonelite women came under the broadly protective character of civil and ecclesiastical legislation in matters regarding those two important subjects. The State protected women as individuals, and marriage and family as institutions. To some extent, the Church overlapped in those functions, although stressing the moral and spiritual aspects. The duality involved in the protector-protected relationship explains the contradictions seen in women's historical roles as actors and objects. Women were both. Their personal and social lives involved a pendulum movement from one to the other or, perhaps more accurately, an ambiguous course between both extremes. Historians will have to learn how to follow that course in all its delicate variations. The more we learn about women, the more complex they become as subjects of historical study and the more relevant they appear as members of past societies. Eventually, we will come to the realization that it is not possible to write valid social history without consideration of the role of women.

Notes

ABBREVIATIONS

ACLDS	Archives of the Church of the Latter Day Saints
AGN	Archivo General de la Nación, Mexico
AGN/BN	Archivo General de la Nación, Mexico: Ramo Bienes Nacionales
AHHM	Archivo Histórico de Hacienda, Mexico
AINAH	Archivo del Instituto Nacional de Antropología e Historia, Mexico
AIPG	Archivo de Instrumentos Públicos de Guadalajara
ANM	Archivo de Notarías de Mexico
ANP	Archivo de Notarías, Puebla
ASMG	Archivo de la Sagrada Mitra, Guadalajara
ASSA	Archivo de la Secretaria de Salubridad y Asistencia, Mexico
exp.	*expediente*; legal case
leg.	*legajo*; a batch or bundle of manuscripts

1. The enumeration of published titles on La Malinche and Sor Juana would fill several pages of notes. See Meri Knaster, *Women in Spanish America: An Annotated Bibliography from Pre-Conquest to Contemporary Times* (Boston: G. K. Hall, 1977), pp. 456-58 for titles on La Malinche and pp. 55-58 and other entries listed in the Subject Index for Sor Juana. For more specific titles of works available on colonial women, see notes to this essay and those of Sister A. M. Gallagher (chap. 5) and Edith Couturier (chap. 4). The most quoted and often no more than trivial sources of information about colonial women are the remarks of the few travelers who visited New Spain in the seventeenth and eighteenth centuries. Mostly, they consist of the description of the physical attributes of women and some of their social habits. See Thomas Gage, *A New Survey of the West India's* (London: R. Cotes, 1648), pp. 56-57, 59; Gemelli Careri, *Viaje a la Nueva España*, 2 vols., Biblioteca Mínima Mexicana, 13-14 (Mexico: Libro Mex, Editores, 1955), 1: 108, 161, 164; Juan D. Vieira, *Breve compendiosa narración de la ciudad de Mexico* (1777; Mexico: Editorial Guaraní, 1952); D. P. E. P. [Pedro de

Estala], comp., *El viagero universal, O noticia del Mundo Antiguo y Nuevo*, 39 vols. (Madrid: Impresora de Espinosa, [179-]-1801), 26: 301, 306, 340.

2. A number of letters of colonial men and women have been discovered in the archives and printed. See Enrique Otte, "Cartas privadas de Puebla del siglo XVI," *Jahrbuch für Geschichte von Staat, Wirtschaft und Gesselschaft Lateinamerikas* 3 (1966): 10-87. Translations are available in James Lockhart and Enrique Otte, eds., *Letters and People of the Spanish Indies: The Sixteenth Century* (New York: Cambridge University Press, 1976).

3. There are numerous writings by nuns, some printed and some not. For an analysis of several, see Asunción Lavrin, "Values and Meaning of Monastic Life for Nuns in Colonial Mexico," *Catholic Historical Review* 58 (October 1972): 367-87.

4. Her complete literary work is available in *Obras Completas* (Mexico: Editorial Porrúa, 1969).

5. Julia Fitzmaurice-Kelly, "Women in Sixteenth Century Spain," *Revue Hispanique* 70 (June-August 1927): 557-632; Barbara Matulka, *An Anti-feminist Treatise of Fifteenth-Century Spain: Lucerna's Repetición de Amores* (New York: Institute of French Studies of Comparative Literature Series, 1931); Jacob Orstein, "La misoginía y el profeminismo en la literatura castellana," *Revista de Filología Hispánica* 3 (January-March 1941): 219-32; María del Pilar Oñate, *El feminismo en la literature española* (Madrid: Espasa-Calpe, 1938); Edna Niecie Sim, "El antifeminismo en la literatura española hasta 1560" (Ph.D. diss., Catholic University of America, 1970).

6. Fray Martín de Córdoba, *Jardín de nobles doncellas*, Colección Joyas Bibliográficas (Madrid, 1953). The fact that this and the following works were written mostly for the nobility or upper-class women does not detract from their value as prescriptive literature for women of other social classes. Compliance with norms of behavior is discussed elsewhere in this work.

7. Fray Hernando de Talavera, "De como se ha de ordenar el tiempo para que sea bien expendido. Avisación a la . . . muy noble señora Doña María Pacheco, Condesa de Benavente," *Escritores Místicos Españoles* 1, Nueva Biblioteca de Autores Españoles (Madrid: Casa Editorial Bailly-Ballière, 1911), vol. 16, pp. 93-103.

8. Juan Luis Vives, *Instrucción de la mujer cristiana* (Buenos Aires: Espasa-Calpe, 1940).

9. This kind of costume suggests that used by the women of Lima since the seventeenth century, which made them well known as *tapadas* (covered up).

10. Fray Luis de León, *La perfecta casada* (Mexico: Editorial Porrúa, 1970).

11. Carmen Martín Gaite, *Usos amorosos del dieciocho en España* (Madrid: Siglo Veintiuno de España, 1972), 203-30.

12. Benito G. Feijóo y Montenegro, "A Defense of Women," in Seymour Resnick and Jeanne Pasmantier, eds., *An Anthology of Spanish Literature in English*, 2 vols. (New York: Federick Ungar, 1958), 2: 333; Oñate, *El feminismo*, 157-98.

13. Pedro Rodríguez, Conde de Campomanes, *Discurso sobre la educación popular de los artesanos y su fomento* (Madrid: Imprenta de B. Antonio de Sancha, 1775), pp. xxxi-xxxiii, 150-63, 241-48. Campomanes hoped that the Church and the *sociedades económicas* would join in a campaign for feminine education. He stated that "no other goal is more urgent to the *sociedades económicas* than that of examining the means of solidly establishing feminine education in the provinces of our Spain." It should be pointed out that while Campomanes urged the incorporation of women into the labor force, he did not want them to encroach on occupations suitable only for men. He also

remarked that women's labor was much cheaper than skilled men's work, implicitly accepting the exploitation of female work.

14. Josefa Amar y Borbón, *Discurso sobre la educación física y moral de las mujeres* (Madrid: Imprenta de D. Benito Cano, 1790), pp xxxi-xxxiv. Doña Josefa, like many of the social reformers of the late eighteenth century in Spain, endorsed the concept of equality of women, but was interested in returning to the simple and "healthy" values of the moralists of the Renaissance. She quoted Fray Luis de León, Vives, and the French educator and theologian François de Salignac de La Mothe-Fénelon. The resurrection of traditional feminine virtues and the reform of the social "vices" of the period were the essential objectives of the education of women. See *Discurso*, pp. 150-63, 170-72, 241; Jean Sarrailh, *La España ilustrada de la segunda mitad del siglo XVIII* (Mexico: Fondo de Cultura Económica, 1957), pp. 515-19. For the ideas of Fénelon, see *Oeuvres choisies* in *Tous les chefs d'oeuvres de la littérature française* (Paris: E. Mignot, 1913), p. 44.

15. José Joaquín Fernández de Lizardi, *La Quijotita y su prima* (Mexico: Editorial Porrúa, 1967).

16. Ibid., chap. 3, p. 27. See also chaps. 4, 9-13.

17. R. C. Padden, ed., *Tales of Potosí: Bartolomé Arzáns de Orsúa y Vela* (Providence: Brown University Press, 1975), p. xxxiii.

18. Marcelo Martínez Alcubilla, *Códigos antiguos de España*, 2 vols. (Madrid: López Camacho, 1885); José María Manresa y Navarro, *Comentarios al código civil español*, 9 vols. (Madrid: Imprenta de la Revista de Legislación, 1908), 9: 23-61; Rafael Gibert y Sánchez de la Vega, *El consentimiento familiar en el matrimonio según el derecho medieval español* (Madrid: Instituto Nacional de Estudios Jurídicos, 1947); José María Ots Capdequí, "Bosquejo histórico de los derechos de la mujer en la legislación de Indias," *Revista general de legislación y jurisprudencia* 132 (March-April 1918): 161-82; Woodrow W. Borah, "Marriage and Legitimacy in Mexican Culture: Mexico and California," *California Law Review* 54 (May 1966): 946-1008.

19. AGN/BN, leg. 230, loose papers, "Doña María de Salazar ante el Ldo. Manuel de Madrid y Luna" (1620). This woman, owner of four *sitios* (small plots of land) in Mascaltepec, filed a complaint stating that her husband and her mother were pressing her to sell the land for less than its value. She refused to be coerced and made a legal deposition declaring that if she acceded to the sale, it should be understood that she had acted under pressure and the contract should be invalidated. Further examples may be found in ACLDS, AIPG, Tomás de Orendaín and Diego P. de Rivera (mid-seventeenth century); Felipe de Silva, García de Argomanis, Blas de Silva, Manuel de Mesa Mayor, José A. Sánchez de Lara, and Antonio de Morelos (eighteenth century), among others.

20. Magnus Mörner, *Race Mixture in the History of Latin America* (Boston: Little, Brown, 1967). Although it has been pointed out that in the sixteenth century in particular and throughout the colonial period in general many *criollos* classified as whites or *españoles americanos* must have had some Indian ancestry, the relevant question is not the absolute purity of the race, but the accepted standards of whiteness and the fact that once a person was regarded as white, he or she became part of the racial elite.

21. Peter Boyd-Bowman, "Patterns of Spanish Emigration to the Indies until 1600," *Hispanic American Historical Review* 56 (November 1976): 580-604 (hereafter cited as HAHR).

22. Spain discovered the New World immediately after recovering the peninsula from the Moslems and in the same year that Jews were expelled from its territory. Many

of the latter settled in the Indies as converts. During the sixteenth and seventeenth centuries there was a strong feeling of prejudice against New Christians. This prejudice was enhanced by persecution from the Inquisition and the theoretical exclusion of New Christians from bureaucratic positions. Thus, the concept of *limpieza de sangre* had both racial and religious implications. *Castas* or *casta* refers to mixed-bloods. See Seymour B. Liebman, *The Jews in New Spain* (Coral Gables, Fla.: University of Florida Press, 1970), p. 147; Martin Cohen, ed., *The Jewish Experience in Latin America*, 2 vols. (Walton, Mass.: American Jewish Historical Society, 1971); Henry Kamen, *The Spanish Inquisition* (New York: New American Library, 1965); J. I. Israel, *Race, Class and Politics in Colonial Mexico: 1610-1670* (London: Oxford University Press, 1975). Apparently a few converted Moslem women traveled to New Spain. See "Una morisca en el Santo Oficio de Mexico," *Boletín del Archivo General de la Nación* 18 (October-December 1947): 461-516 (hereafter cited as BAGN); Doris M. Ladd, *The Mexican Nobility at Independence, 1780-1826* (Austin, Tex.: University of Texas Press, 1976). Ladd offers numerous examples of endogamous marriage among the nobility in Mexico.

23. The *patronato de legos* (lay patronage) for masses founded by the Bishop of Oaxaca, Juan de Bohórquez, in 1624 stipulated that the holders could not marry any woman who was not a descendant of *hidalgos*, or Old Christians. See Guillermo S. Fernández de Recas, *Mayorazgos de la Nueva España* (Mexico: Universidad Nacional Autónoma de Mexico, 1965), p. 457. See also in the same work, p. 356, the testament of Rui Díaz de Mendoza (1615), founder of an entail in Atlixco, in which he established legal disinheritance for any member of the family contracting an unequal marriage. Even the open-minded Josefa Amar y Borbón advised "equality of circumstances" as a basis for a happy marriage. See her *Discurso*, p. 272.

24. AINAH, Microfilm Collection, Vizcaínas, reel 36, Libro de Obras Pías de la Cofradía de Aranzazú (1773-1805).

25. Richard Konetzke, ed., *Colección de documentos para la historia de la formación social de Hispanoamérica, 1493-1810*, 3 vols. (Madrid: Consejo Superior de Investigaciones Científicas, 1953-1962), vol. 3, bk. 1, pp. 401, 406, 438.

26. Fernández de Recas, *Mayorazgos*, p. 438.

27. Ibid., p. 333; ACLDS, ASMG, Guadalajara, Matrimoniales, loose papers, no. 165 (1678), no. 95 (1692); ACLDS, AIPG, Antonio de Berroa, vol. 20 (1776), fol. 139. In this instance, María Manuela de Acuña y Ayllón, wife of an Audiencia lawyer, stated in her will that an orphan whom she had raised should be disinherited if the girl married against the advice of her appointed tutor or of María Manuela's husband. Although the husband's advice should be regarded as uncontestable, the tutor's advice could be disputed in the tribunals.

28. AGN/BN, leg. 543, "María Josefa Sánchez vs. su hija María Josefa Jiménez"; José Bravo Ugarte, *Historia sucinta de Michoacán*, 3 vols. (Mexico: Editorial Jus, 1962-63), 2: 145. The daughter of José Antonio de Peredo, a rich family in Valladolid, had twice rescinded her engagements under pressure from her father. The third suitor started legal proceedings to force the father to release the daughter, while the Bishop of Michoacán threatened Peredo with excommunication if the young woman's will continued to be forced. See also Ladd, *the Mexican Nobility*, p. 235, for the case of the Audiencia-approved marriage between a man of the upper class and a mulatto woman. For data concerning the military, see AGN/BN, leg. 1086, exp. 22; Konetzke, *Colección*, vol. 3, bk. 1, pp. 214, 294, 420, 433.

29. Edgar F. Love, "Marriage Patterns of Persons of African Descent in a Colonial Mexico City Parish," *HAHR* 51 (February 1971): 79-91; Gonzalo Aguirre Beltrán, *La población negra de Mexico* (Mexico: Fondo de Cultura Económica, 1972), chaps. 12, 13; Patrick J. Carroll, "Mexican Society in Transition: The Blacks in Veracruz, 1750-1830" (Ph.D. diss., University of Texas, 1975). See also his "Estudio sociodemográfico de personas de sangre negra en Jalapa, 1791," *Historia Mexicana* 23 (July-September 1973): 111-25; Marcelo Carmagnani, "Demografía y sociedad: La estructura social de los centrol mineros del norte de Mexico, 1600-1720," *Historia Mexicana* 21 (January-March 1972): 419-59 (this study does not include persons of African descent); David A. Brading, "Los españoles en Mexico hacia 1792," *Historia Mexicana* 23 (July-September 1973): 126-44; David A. Brading and Celia Wu, "Population Growth and Crisis: León, 1720-1860," *Journal of Latin American Studies* 5, no. 1 (1973): 1-36; David A. Brading, "Grupos étnicos, clases y estructura ocupacional en Guanajuato (1792)," *Historia Mexicana* 21 (January-March 1972): 460-80. Also of interest are Elsa Malvido, "Factores de despoblación y de reposición de la población de Cholula (1641-1810)," *Historia Mexicana* 23 (July-September 1973): 52-110; Claude Morin, "Population et epidémies dans une paroisse mexicaine: Santa Inés Zacatelco, XVIIe-XIXe siècles," *Cahiers des Amériques Latines* 6 (July-December 1972): 43-73.

30. *Moriscos* were individuals with three Spanish and one black ancestor; *mestizos* were the offspring of Indian and white; mulattoes were the descendants of white and black. For a recent reinterpretation of racial mixtures, see Isidoro Moreno y Navarro, *Los cuadros del mestizaje americano: Estudio antropológico del mestizaje* (Madrid: Editorial José Porrúa Turanzas, 1973).

31. Martínez Alcubilla, *Códigos*, 1: 496-501; Manresa y Navarro, *Comentarios*, 9: 23-24, 33.

32. In 1650, Gaspar de Castro, *oidor* of the Audiencia, was obliged to return 30,000 *pesos* to his former wife, Doña Leonor de Canzueta. Of this sum, 20,000 were the income of his office, which had been part of the dowry provided by the bride. In Spanish America it was possible for the father of the bride to buy governmental office for his future son-in-law. See Andrés de Guijo, *Diario, 1648-1664*, 2 vols. (Mexico: Editorial Porrúa, 1952), 1: 112. See also p. 92 for the reimbursement of 25,000 *pesos* by Sebastián Báez Acevedo to Lorenza Esquivel. Báez had been condemned by the Inquisition in 1650 and was sued for divorce by his wife (Konetzke, *Colección*, vol. 2, bk. 1, p. 402).

33. Evidence to support these statements was gathered in the notarial records of Guadalajara, Puebla, and Mexico City and through a synthesis of those of Monterrey. Samplings cover the period 1650 to 1800. Dowry deeds as well as testaments of men and women have been examined. Among the notaries sampled are Nicolás del Castillo (late seventeenth century); Jose A. Sánchez de Lara (mid-eighteenth century); Antonio de Berroa of Guadalajara (late eighteenth century); Agustín González de Santa Cruz (mid-eighteenth century) and José Benítez de Zárate (late eighteenth century) in Puebla. See also Israel Cavazos Garza, *Catálogo y síntesis de los protocolos del archivo municipal de Monterrey, 1599-1700* (Monterrey: Instituto Tecnológico y de Estudios Superiores, 1966), pp. 68, 94, 97, 114, 231, 281.

34. ANM, José de Anaya (1669), fol. 225v. AINAH, Microfilm Collection, Vizcaínas, reels 4, 8; AGN/BN, leg. 281, exp. 3; leg. 667, exp. 10; leg. 1265, exp. 2. The wife of the Marqués de Altamira, Pedro Sánchez de Tagle, who was also his cousin, brought a dowry of 50,000 *pesos*. The Condesa de Peñalva, Luisa Urrutia de Vergara, had a dowry of 80,000 *pesos*, although only 20,000 *pesos* were in cash. When her daughter married

Francisco de Valdivieso, a wealthy merchant, she had a dowry of 30,000 *pesos*. See ANM, Antonio Alejo de Mendoza (1728), fol. 214; José de Anaya y Bonilla (1715), fol. 163; AGN/BN, leg. 643, exp. 6. Other examples will be found in AGN/BN, leg. 1029, exp. 8; Ladd, *Mexican Nobility*, p. 23; ACLDS, ANP, José Benítez de Zárate (1779), fols. 40-44; ACLDS, AIPG, Nicolás del Castillo, vol. 3 (1695), fol. 259v; AGN, Tierras, vol. 412, exp. 6; John Super, "Querétaro: Society and Economy in Early Provincial Mexico: 1590-1620" (Ph.D. diss., University of California, Los Angeles, 1973).

35. AGN/BN, leg. 605, nos. 3, 12, 13, 18, 20; leg. 1906, exp. 43. ACLDS, AIPG, Felipe de Silva, vol. 4 (1705), fols. 12, 18; Antonio de Morelos, vol. 7 (1727), fol. 239v; Tomás de Orendaín, vol. 8 (1652-54), fol. 117; vol 10 (1667), fol. 8. ANP, Agustín González de Santa Cruz (1737), fol. 210; Benítez de Zárate, "Testamento de José Severo Romero," 3 October 1780. ANM, Andrés Delgado Camargo (1748), fol. 17; (1750), fol. 25; Antonio Alejo de Mendoza (1724), fol. 21v. AIPG, García de Argomanis, vol. 9 (1715), fol. 257v; Sánchez de Lara, vol. 1 (1758), fol. 99; Cavazos Garza, *Catálogo y síntesis*, pp. 100, 131, 165, 168, 248, 255.

36. In a survey of 380 marriages taking place in Puebla, Guadalajara, Monterrey, and Mexico City in the seventeenth and eighteenth centuries, 15 percent were nonendowed and 64 percent were endowed. There was no information for the rest. See Asunción Lavrin and Edith Couturier, "Dowries and Wills: A View of Women's Socio-Economic Role in Colonial Mexico" (Paper presented at the Ninety-first Annual Meeting of the American Historical Association, Washington, D.C., 1976). I disagree with the conclusions of Josefina Muriel, *Los recogimientos de mujeres: Respuesta a una problemática social novohispana* (Mexico: Universidad Nacional Autónoma de Mexico, 1974). Russell-Wood's interpretation of the dowry in Brazilian society still implies a certain degree of honor protection. The Brazilian situation might have differed from the Mexican. Further research on this subject will elucidate this point. See Russel-Wood's essay (chap. 2) in this volume.

37. Ots Capdequí, "Bosquejo histórico," pp. 162-83. Almost all dowries contained statement of *arras*, but this practice was not universal. The law prescribed that no more than 10 percent of the man's estate could be allocated for *arras*. However, in many instances the groom did not specify what percentage of his estate was the *arras*. Assessment of the former, unless declared, is nearly impossible using available sources. For an example of a man endowing his undowered bride, see document EOG-P12 in the Edmundo O'Gorman Collection at the University of Texas and ACLDS, ANP, Benítez de Zárate, "Testamento de José Severo Romero." See also Edith Couturier's essay (chap. 4) in this volume.

38. Cavazos Garza, *Catálogo y síntesis*, pp. 30, 58; AGN, Tierras, vol. 412, exp. 6. A usual phrase was *"en honra de la virtud, nobleza y virginidad de la dicha mi mujer"* ("in honor of the virtue, nobility, and virginity of my wife").

39. Bancroft Library, University of California, "Rescriptos reales sobre asuntos eclesiásticos," MM 208, fol. 101; Martínez Alcubilla, *Códigos*, 2: 494-96; José Ignacio Rubio Mañé, "Gente de España en la ciudad de Mexico, 1689," *BAGN* 7 (January-March 1966): 275; Fernández de Lizardi, *La Quijotita*, chap. 24, pp. 189-90; AIPG, Miguel de Vargas, vol. 9 (1734-36), "Declaración de Don Nicolás Gil de la Sierpe." This man had been sent to jail and later held within the limits of the city of Guadalajara after his wife started a divorce suit against him. She was the daughter of a lawyer.

40. See Muriel, *Recogimientos*.

41. AIPG, Blas de Silva, vol. 20 (1776-77), fol. 90v. Don José de Munguía had a suit

against his wife for adultery. She was imprisoned in the *Casa de Recogidas* of Guadalajara while her assumed correspondent was jailed in the royal prison; Pedro Agundis Zamora, vol. 1 (1696), fol. 12. Don Gerónimo Ramírez de Arellano was imprisoned for living with Juana de la Fuente. He was released from jail after presenting a bondsman who guaranteed that he would arrange the marriage of the couple.

42. AHHM, Juicios, leg. 491-24, 491-63, 492-5, 492-15; ACLDS, ASMG, Matrimoniales, loose papers; these records contain many examples of divorce suits and allegations from the seventeenth and eighteenth centuries. See also Muriel, *Recogimientos*, pp. 61-68. Compare with nineteenth-century data on the same topic presented by Sylvia Arrom, *La mujer mexicana ante el divorcio eclesiástico, 1800-1857* (Mexico: SepSetentas, 1976).

43. There were only two desirable "states" for women in life: marriage to man or marriage to God, and both were marriage. Spinsterhood was not a desirable choice. However, single women were not socially rejected. For a demographical consideration of household and family, see Sherburne F. Cook and W. W. Borah, *Essays in Population History* (Berkeley and Los Angeles: University of California Press, 1971), vol. 1, chap. 3.

44. The archival sources used for statements on marriage and morality throughout these pages are in AGN/BN, leg. 406, 442, 596, 655; ACLDS, ASMG, Matrimoniales, loose papers. See also AGN, Clero Regular y Secular, vol. 92, "Marqués de San Clemente vs. José de Bustos"; Muriel, *Recogimientos*. For comparative purposes, see Verena Martínez-Alier, *Marriage, Class and Colour in Nineteenth Century Cuba* (New York: Cambridge University Press, 1974).

45. AGN/BN, leg. 596; there are several unnumbered cases against men in this *legajo*; Richard E. Greenleaf, *The Mexican Inquisition of the Sixteenth Century* (Albuquerque: University of New Mexico Press, 1969), p. 100. It is also true that when justice was not pursued through official channels, the families of the "injured" parties could take its execution into their hands. Many men sought marriage because they felt endangered by the active physical pursuit of the woman's family. ACLDS, ASMG, Matrimoniales, cases of Nicolás de Cortázar (1691), Benito Gutiérrez (1692), and José Manuel Marín (1692). Also Cavazos Garza, *Catálogos y síntesis*, p. 59. Spanish laws, although allowing a wider margin of freedom to men, did not grant automatic immunity to them for all sorts of transgressions. For example, men who willingly allowed their wives to prostitute themselves were punishable with public exposure and galley work. However, it is obvious that even in these instances punishment was inflicted because it affected the morality of women. See *Pragmática y declaración sobre los que permiten que sus mujeres sean malas* (Madrid, 1575) in the Hispanic Law Collection of the Library of Congress, Washington, D.C.

46. Julián Gutiérrez Dávila, *Vida y virtudes del siervo de Dios, el venerable D. Domingo Pérez de Barcia, fundador de la casa y voluntario recogimiento de mujeres de San Miguel de Belén* (Madrid: N. R. Francos, 1720); Muriel, *Recogimientos*.

47. AGN/BN, leg. 406, 442, 596, 655; ACLDS, ASMG, Matrimoniales, loose papers; Antonio de Robles, *Diario de sucesos notables, 1655-1703*, 3 vols. (Mexico: Editorial Porrúa, 1946), 3: 271, for the case of General Domingo de Tagle; Aguirre Beltrán, *La población negra*, p. 255. In his novel *La Quijotita y su prima*, Lizardi comments that one of the most common mistakes among young women was to believe those men who gave them *palabra de casamiento* and then took their virginity (p. 160). For the origin of this obligation, see discussion of *esponsales* (bethrothal) in María Gabriela Leret de

Matheus, *La mujer: Una incapaz como el demente y el niño* (Mexico: B. Costa-Amic Editor, 1975), p. 31.

48. See note 47 for archival sources.

49. Patricia Seed, "A Mexican Noble Family: The Counts of the Orizaba Valley, 1560-1867" (Master's thesis, University of Texas at Austin, 1975); Fernández de Recas, *Mayorazgos*, pp. 155-68, 306; Rubio Mañé, "Gente de España," pp. 7, 282; ACLDS, ANP, González de Santa Cruz (1737), fols. 17, 23. AGN/BN, leg. 85, "Profesión de Juana de Sandoval," leg. 156, exp. 5, 18; Cavazos Garza, *Catálogo y síntesis*, pp. 141, 203, 208, 215, 265.

50. ANM, Andrés Delgado Camargo (1749), fol. 11; José de Anaya y Bonilla (1715), fol. 94; Antonio Alejo de Mendoza (1723), fols. 136, 138. In the latter source, Pedro Sánchez de Tagle, Marqués de Altamira, left 1,000 *pesos* each, in cash, to three orphan boys and one girl who were being raised in his house; two others girls received 300 *pesos* each. AINAH, Microfilm Collection, Notarías, reel 8, José de Anaya, "Testamento de Ana María Orozco" (1669). AGN/BN, leg. 634, exp. 6; leg. 396, exp. 12; leg. 213, packet 2, exp. 29-32, 35. ACLDS, AIPG, Diego P. de Ribera, vol. 11 (1664), fols. 138, 190; vol. 12 (1665), fol. 222v; Tomás de Orendaín, vol. 9 (1660), fol. 60. Thomas Calvo is also of the opinion that many foundlings were simply "natural" children: "Démographie historique d'une paroisse mexicaine: Acatzingo (1606-1810)," *Cahiers des Amériques Latines* 6 (July-December 1972): 22.

51. "Catálogo de pobladores," *BAGN* 12 (July-September 1941): 271, 737, passim; 13 (January-March 1942), 97, 657, passim; 14 (July-September 1943), 416-17. See other examples in AHM, Salarios, leg. 423-48, 423-93, 424-48, 424-73, 425-98.

52. Juan de Solórzano y Pereira, *Política Indiana*, 4 vols. (Madrid: Compañía Ibero-Americana de Publicaciones, 1930), vol. 2, bk. 3, chap. 17, pp. 190, 205-6, 215; chap. 22, pp. 246-56; chap. 23, pp. 260-65; chap. 24, pp. 271-78; Francisco A. de Icaza, *Diccionario autobiográfico de conquistadores y pobladores de Nueva España*, 2 vols. (Madrid: Imprenta de "El Adelantado" de Segovia, 1923), 1: 110, 115, 128; 2: 30, 90. Some parents gave half of their *encomiendas* to their daughters when they married. See Icaza, 1: 119; 2: 137.

53. Manuela Cristina García Bernal, *La sociedad de Yucatán, 1700-1750* (Seville: Escuela de Estudios Hispano-Americanos, 1972), pp. 61-71, 89-90, Appendix I; Library of Congress, Washington, D.C., Microfilm Archives, Colección Medina 0350, reel 239, no. 11, *Pleito de encomienda de Casimiro Osorio Rubín de Celis* (ca. 1690).

54. Library of Congress, Microfilm Archives, Colección Medina 0350, reel 47, *Reglamentos para el gobierno del monte pío de viudas y pupilos de ministros de Audiencias, Tribunales de Cuentas y oficiales de Real Hacienda . . . de Nueva España* (Mexico, 1781). I am indebted to Professor D. S. Chandler for information and advice on the role of the *montepíos* in Mexico.

55. Asunción Lavrin, "Religious Life of Mexican Women in the XVIII Century" (Ph.D. diss., Harvard University, 1963), chap. 4; Cavazos Garza, *Catálogo y síntesis*, p. 3. *Recogimientos* for honest women should not be confused with similarly named institutions for prostitutes, adulterous women, and such others, which were meant to "correct" the latter types.

56. Asunción Lavrin, "Ecclesiastical Reform of Nunneries in New Spain in the Eighteenth Century," *The Americas* 22 (October 1965): 182-203; "El convento de Santa Clara de Querétaro: La administración de sus propiedades en el siglo XVII," *Historia Mexicana* 25 (July-September 1975): 76-117.

57. Alexander von Humboldt, *Ensayo político sobre el reino de la Nueva España* (Mexico: Editorial Porrúa, 1966), p. 574.

58. AGN, Tierras, vol. 412, exp. 6. AGN/BN, leg. 697, "Will of Anna Mejía"; leg. 643, "Will of Anna Urrutia de Vergara"; leg. 773, "Manuel Cano por Juana Micaela de Ledos." ACLDS, AIPG, Tomás de Orendaín, vol. 9 (1660), fol. 12; Pedro Agundis Zamora, vol. 1 (1692, 1694), fol. 158; Antonio de Morelos, vol. 7 (1726), fol. 6v. Library of Congress, Microfilm Archives, Colección Medina 0350, reel 47, no. 71; reel 195, no. 13. Rubio Mañé, "Gente de España," p. 86.

59. In medieval Spain women had gained direct control over their children and household after their husband's death. See Rafael Gibert y Sánchez de la Vega, *El Consentimiento familiar*, pp. 40, 49; Pierre Bornassie, "A Family of the Barcelona Countryside and Its Economic Activities Around the Year 1000," in Sylvia Lettice La Thrup, ed., *Early Medieval Society* (New York: Appleton-Century-Crofts, 1967), pp. 103-23; Charles Boxer, *Women in Iberian Expansion Overseas, 1415-1815* (New York: Oxford University Press, 1975), chap. 2; ACLDS, AIPG, García de Argomanis, vol. 15 (1718), fol. 184v. See also Edith Couturier's essay (chap. 4) in this volume.

60. AGN/BN, leg. 213, packet 1, exp. 17; leg. 1884, exp. 7, 29; AGN Tierras, vol. 2512, exp. 41; vol. 2718, exp. 17; Cavazos Garza, *Catálogo y síntesis*, pp. 42, 47, 78, 245, 261, 289.

61. AHHM, Anatas, leg. 269-82. ANM, Andrés Delgado Camargo (1774), fol. 483; here María Francisca Martínez lent 12,000 *pesos* to two merchants. ANM, Antonio Alejo de Mendoza (1724), fol. 561 (1720), fol. 56v; in one example a widow provided 2,000 *pesos* to the owner of a textile sweatshop, who provided 2,500 *pesos* himself. They agreed to form a company that would last for three years and to divide the profits equally at the end of that period; ANM, José de Anaya y Bonilla (1715), fols. 85, 91v. Cavazos Garza, *Catálogo y síntesis*, pp. 65, 149, 156, 189. Silvio Zavala and María Castelo, comps. *Fuentes para la historia del trabajo en Nueva España*, 8 vols. (Mexico: Fondo de Cultura Económica, 1939-46), 6: 142; 7: 34. Eduardo Báez Macías, "Planos y censos de la ciudad de Mexico, 1753 (Segunda Parte)," *BAGN* 8 (October-December 1967): 485-1156, passim. ACLDS, AIPG, Protocolos de José María Vicente de Berroa, vol. 18 (1775), fol. 63; Protocolos de Antonio de Morelos, vol. 7 (1726), fol. 6v. ASMG, Testamentos, loose papers, "Testamento de Doña María Teresa González de Cosío, 1779;" ANP, Joaquín Pérez de Aguilar (1763), fol. 71; Urbano Ballesteros, vol. 21 (1794), fols. 203, 254v.

62. AHHM, Anatas, leg. 267-233, 267-216. AGN/BN, leg. 592, "Dean of the Juzgado de Capellanías to María Teresa de Vera," a single woman who requested 500 pesos to establish a tannery in her house. ACLDS, AIPG, Tomás de Orendaín, vol. 10 (1669), fol. 22; Enríquez del Castillo, vol. 4 (1654), fol. 48. ACLDS, ASMG, Testamentos, loose papers, "Inventario de doña Teresa de Contreras," 1660. Báez Macías, "Planos y censos," records women registered as beggars. The number of females in a list of thirty-five "occupational" beggars is twenty-two. In the lists of tenants of houses belonging to nunneries of the city of Mexico, there is a substantial number of women referred to as head of household, without reference to any husbands. See Asunción Lavrin, "La riqueza de los conventos de monjas en Nueva España: Estructura y evolución durante el siglo XVIII," *Cahiers des Amériques Latines* 8 (2d semester 1973): 91-122; Juan Manuel de San Vicente, "Exacta descripción de la magnífica corte mexicana, 1768," *Anales del Museo de Arqueología, Historia y Etnografía* 17 (1913-14): 9-40; Zavala and Castelo, *Fuentes*, 7: 493, 305, 509; Isabel González Sánchez, *Haciendas y*

ranchos de Tlaxcala en 1712 (Mexico: Instituto Nacional de Antropología e Historia, 1969), for examples of *mujeres labradoras*, or landowners.

63. Báez Macías, "Planos y censos." The number of washerwomen recorded in this census was forty-five. There were thirty-two female silk spinners out of a total of thirty-three. This form of employment could be performed at home, and it was, like that of seamstress, a popular one; Luis Chávez Orozco, *La educación pública elemental en la ciudad de Mexico durante el siglo XVIII* (Mexico: Secretaría de Educación Pública, 1936), pp. 19-24, 90-92.

64. Sarrailh, *La España ilustrada*, pp. 517-19; Campomanes, *Discurso*, pp. 301, 358-61; James Clayborn La Force, Jr., *The Development of the Spanish Textile Industry, 1750-1800* (Berkeley and Los Angeles: University of California Press, 1965), pp. 100-1; Konetzke, *Documentos*, 3: 767.

65. Carmen Martín Gaite, *Usos amorosos*, pp. 203-30.

66. Archivo de la Secretaría de Salubridad y Asistencia, "Cuaderno de borradores de sueldos, gratificaciones . . . de este Hospicio hasta el 31 de agosto de 1822." The directress received 10 *pesos* monthly from 1821 through 1823. The midwife in charge of "secret" births received 13 *pesos* monthly.

67. Zavala and Castelo, *Fuentes*, 6: 95, 137, 215, 240.

68. Seed, "A Mexican Noble Family."

69. AGN/BN, leg. 396, exp. 12. See David M. Szewczyk, "New Elements in the Society of Tlaxcala, 1519-1618," in Ida Altman and James Lockhart, eds., *Provinces of Early Mexico* (Los Angeles: UCLA Latin American Center Publications, 1976), pp. 137-54, for remarks on women in sixteenth-century Tlaxcala.

70. ACLDS, AIPG. The notarial records consulted for samplings of these activities were those of Tomás de Orendaín, Diego P. de Ribera, José A. Sánchez de Lara, Felipe de Silva, Blas de Silva, García de Argomanis, Manuel de Mesa Mayor, Antonio de Berroa, and Antonio de Morelos, among others. Similar records can be found in the notarial records of any colonial city and in the AGN, Tierras (for land litigation). See also Edith Couturier's essay (chap. 4) in this volume; González Sánchez, *Haciendas*, pp. 67, 127, 132, 162; AGN, Tierras, vol. 587, exp. 4; vol. 403, exp. 6; vol. 2712, exp. 17, 18, 19.

71. See notarial sources in note 70. Also Cavazos Garza, *Catálogo y síntesis*, pp. 164, 189, 224, 240, 246.

72. Fernández de Recas, *Mayorazgos*, p. 141. This entail eventually passed to the family of the Counts of the Valley of Orizaba. See also pp. 5, 108, 149, 158, 193, 229, 234, 266; Ladd, *Mexican Nobility*, pp. 71 ff.; AGN, Tierras, vol. 788, exp. 1; Carlos Sánchez-Navarro y Peón, *Memorias de un viejo palacio* (Mexico: Cía. Impresora y Litográfica Nacional, 1951), pp. 172-78; Jesús Amaya, *Los conquistadores Fernández de Hijar y Bracamonte: Ensayo biogeneográfico* (Guadalajara: Gráfica Editorial, 1952), p. 116.

73. Fernández de Recas, *Mayorazgos*, pp. 289-97; Josefina Muriel, ed., *Fundaciones neoclásicas: La Marquesa de Selvanevada: Sus conventos y sus arquitectos* (Mexico: Universidad Nacional Autónoma de Mexico, 1969).

74. González Sánchez, *Haciendas*.

75. AGN, Tierras, vol. 1430. Doña María Teresa left her property to her brother, who founded an entail. Her property had liens for over 70,000 *pesos*, and she advised him that 30,000 *pesos* should be spent in helping to bring the agonizantes Order to New Spain. See Fernández de Recas, *Mayorazgos*, p. 95.

76. Lavrin, "La riqueza de los conventos de monjas." "El Convento de Santa Clara

de Querétaro;" "Problems and Policies in the Administration of Nunneries in Mexico, 1800-1835," *The Americas* 28 (July 1971): 57-77; "Mexican Nunneries from 1835 to 1860: Their Administrative Policies and Relations with the State," *The Americas* 28 (January 1972): 288-310. Also William B. Taylor, *Landlord and Peasant in Colonial Oaxaca* (Stanford: Standord University Press, 1972), pp. 164-194.

77. AGN/BN, leg. 405, packet 1, exp. 1; leg. 605, nos. 1, 18; leg. 1844, exp. 16. AINAH, Microfilm Collection, Serie Porrúa, reel 14, Censos del convento de San Lorenzo (1801). AGN/BN, leg. 566, "Cuentas de la Cofradía de Nuestra Sra. del Rosario" (1791-92).

78. AGN/BN, leg. 405, packet 1, no. 4. Library of Congress, Microfilm Collection, Colección Medina 0350, reel 47, no. 71. *Regidor* Lugo y Terrenos of Mexico was the heir of this mother's estate and the recipient of a dowry valued at 80,000 *pesos*; ACLDS, AIPG, García de Argomanis, vol. 15 (1718), fol. 90. Cavazos Garza, *Catálogo y síntesis*, p. 213.

79. ANM, Andrés Delgado Camargo (1744), fol. 494v. A *caballería* was 105.7 acres of land. See also ACLDS, AIPG. José A. Sánchez de Lara, vol. 1 (1758), fol. 99; Blas de Silva, vol. 30 (1789), fols. 9, 10, 20, 73, 80; Felipe de Silva, vol. 18 (1704-7), fol. 18, AHHM, vol. 2168. AGN/BN, leg. 566, "Cuentas de la Cofradía de Nuestra Sra. del Rosario"; leg. 592, Loans from the Juzgado de Capellanías; leg. 605, nos. 10, 13; leg. 1844, exp. 16, ASSA, Convento de Jesús María, 17-8-9, 17-8-19.

80. AINAH, Microfilm Collection, Vizcaínas, reel 4.

81. AGN/BN, leg. 697, "Testamento de Anna Clara Mejía" and "Testamento de Felipa de la Vega." Further documentation is available in Lavrin and Couturier, "Dowries and Wills."

82. AGN/BN, leg. 396, exp. 12; leg. 592, "Testamento de Anna de Quiroga"; leg. 605, nos. 3, 5, 8, 14, 18; leg. 634, exp. 6; leg. 733, Petición de Miguel Aguilar; leg. 1096, exp. 43. AINAH, Colección Lira, vol. 65A, no. 57; vol. 179, portfolio 2, no. 2. AGN, Templos y Conventos, vol. 23, exp. 22; vol. 84. See also Lavrin and Couturier, "Dowries and Wills."

83. Ann Miriam Gallagher, R. S. M. "The Family Background of the Nuns of Two *Monasterios* in Colonial Mexico: Santa Clara, Querétaro; and Corpus Christi, Mexico City (1724-1822)" (Ph.D. diss., The Catholic University of America, 1972); AGN/BN, leg. 634, exp. 6. The Countess of Peñalva, Luisa Urrutia de Vergara, left 31,666 *pesos* to charities in 1678, which were still being distributed in the late eighteenth century.

84. Prices have been obtained in dowry letters and inventories of Guadalajara, Puebla, and Mexico City. Merchants' bills of lading and stores' inventories are potential sources of information for prices of numerous articles. See, for example, Peter Boyd-Bowman, "Early Spanish Trade with Mexico: A Sixteenth Century Bill of Lading," *Studies on Latin America*, Buffalo Studies, vol 4 (August 1968), pp. 45-56. Men's clothes were never as expensive as women's. See also the suggestive comment of Fernand Braudel on costumes, fashions, and the economic process in his *Capitalism and Material Life, 1400-1800* (New York: Harper & Row, 1974), pp. 226-43.

85. Frances Calderón de la Barca, *Life in Mexico* (Garden City, N.Y.: Doubleday & Co., n. d.), p. 96. See pp. 99 and 145 for description of expensive costumes. See also Couturier's essay (chap. 4) in this volume for information on the expenses of women of the upper class.

2   A. J. R. Russell-Wood

Female and family in the economy and society of colonial Brazil

Introduction

The role of women in Portuguese America in the colonial period from 1500 to 1822 was contradictory. Crown, Church, and colonist viewed womanhood as the repository of the virtues and moral qualities of the Portuguese people. On the other hand, she was hidebound by civil and canon law, and the role prescribed for her both in continental Portugal and overseas was restricted to domestic and religious spheres. If this contradiction intrigues rather than daunts the potential inquirer, further study reveals two obstacles. The first lies in the sources available, published or unpublished, and in Brazilian historiography. The second is born of a medley of legal, religious, and social components that have created an attitude that today is sometimes described as a "machismo cultural complex." These two obstacles are interrelated. A major problem is to locate females in an age whose documentation reflected the widely held belief that females performed functions, for example, bearing children, managing a household, that were not worthy of official recognition. Moreover, in colonial Brazil, regardless of personal talents, the female remained an appendage of her spouse. The husband had the potential to perform deeds that merited official reward or Crown favor and would therefore be recorded. Moreover, in a drum-and-trumpet historiographical tradition (from which colonial Brazil is only now being mercifully liberated) there was little place for the female.

Both her contemporaries in the colony and later students of Brazilian history ignored the basic fact that females formed part of a larger society. Current protagonists of women's history, black history, or gay history face the very real danger of performing a disservice to their themes by adopting too parochial a perspective and abstracting the objects of their scholarly attentions from the social matrix. In colonial Brazil the role of the female and her contribution to the economy and society were determined by a code of ethics, by theological doctrine, by canon and civil precepts, and by social and religious attitudes that had comprised the ethos of Catholic countries of Western Europe. This had been transferred to the New World, there to be preserved, strengthened, or modified to meet the needs of colonizing societies. The female, no less than the male, had been affected by social mores and economic change in Brazil. No less than the male, she experienced the stresses and strains within a society in transition and within an area characterized by regional differences and economic imbalance. In short, it is as impossible as it is unrealistic to dissociate the position of the female from general social and economic developments in Brazilian history.

This essay has a twofold purpose. It will be argued that the female played a significantly more important role in the ideological, economic, and social development of colonial Brazil than has been acknowledged. The second purpose is to focus attention on potential sources for the history of women in colonial Brazil, which have not been adequately used or have been ignored by scholars. Insofar as we know, memoirs, diaries, or chronicles written by females in the colony have not survived, if they were written at all. This lacuna can be partly filled by wills, inventories, municipal licensing ledgers, brotherhood and conventual records, and fiscal registers extant in private and public archives. Such evidence was gleaned from Rio de Janeiro, São Paulo, Bahia, and Minas Gerais.

These sources prompt three *caveats*. The first is that such was the human and ecological heterogeneity of Portuguese America that regional variations may well differ from the picture here depicted. The second is that class and racial perspectives, then as now, have tended to divide the female experience in Brazil. My sources will tend to portray the role of the female in an urban environment rather than in the countryside. Furthermore, although every effort has been made not to succumb to writing an account of the position and functions of the elite, inevitably such sources better reflect life-styles and value systems of white females than of blacks or Amerindians. Thus, my discussion will be limited to the white female. The third *caveat* is prompted by latter-day adulation of Clio and resulting high expectations of a quantitative solution to problems besetting historians. The welter of recent publications on family history, especially those based on a quantitative approach, has yet to embrace Brazil. While the sources I have used would be susceptible to econometric study, the materials are so partial and unevenly distributed as to make any general conclusions based on quantitative analysis alone speculative. The exception may lie in highly localized studies at the parish level or within a limited time frame.1 At present the historian writing about women in the colony lacks data on such fundamentals as numbers of migrants, female composition of the overall population for an extended period of time, incidence of marriage or remarriage, and mortality and natality. The present study is intended to throw new light on the position of females in the domestic, economic, and social life of colonial Brazil and to suggest possible avenues of further inquiry in the long overdue reassessment of their contribution to the building of Portuguese society in the tropics.

Crown Policy and Colonial Demography

Demographic factors played an important part in determining the role of the white women in Portuguese America. Although urban, rural, and regional variations existed, there was imbalance between the number of white women and white men in Brazil for much of the colonial period. Migrants to Portuguese America were predominantly bachelors, especially before the mid-eighteenth century. Even married men, who came in search of fame or fortune, left wives and families in Portugal or the Atlantic islands of Madeira and the Azores with the avowed intent of returning after a short period in the tropics. This imbalance was aggravated by the fact that many fathers preferred daughters of marriageable age to enter a convent, rather than contracting a socially disadvantageous marriage in the colony.2 Girls, with their consent or against their will, were a regular feature on ships traveling from Brazil to Portugal in the colonial period. Finally, many white men preferred irregular sexual alliances with Amerindian or black women to the stability of marriage.

From the outset the Crown was acutely conscious of social and demographic problems caused by a shortage of white women of marriageable age in Brazil. Furthermore, the Crown was sensitive to the moral evils and adverse repercussions on colonial society resulting from the solution chosen by the colonists, namely, concubinage with Amerindian or black women and an apparent preference for them even if white were available.

The Crown was not willing to turn Brazil into a haven for white female undesirables, even if the cost were to be a smaller white population. It took up the twofold challenge of trying to make available to the colonists white women of marriageable age and of increasing the number of white married couples in Brazil. In the sixteenth century the Crown had attempted to increase the population of "Portuguese India" by sending "orphans of the king" to Goa and other way stations. A half-hearted attempt was made to extend this policy to Brazil, but it failed for much the same reasons: the numbers of such women were too few; many died in childbirth; inducements to potential grooms were inadequate.[3] The Crown also adopted the policy of placing restraints on white women wishing to leave Brazil. These fell into two categories: first, women who of their own volition or at the command of their parents left Brazil to enter convents in Portugal or the Atlantic islands and, second, widows or wives and daughters who wished to return to Portugal.

Such measures were inadequate, and comparatively few white marriages took place in the colony in the early eighteenth century. The result was minimal demographic increase in the white sector of the population, although this varied from region to region. In 1717 the municipal council of Salvador informed the king that between eight and ten white women left the city on each fleet to enter convents overseas.[4] In the hinterland the dearth of white marriageable women was more serious. The Count of Assumar (governor of Minas Gerais, 1717-21) was vociferous in his complaints about the shortage of white women in his captaincy. His successor, Dom Lourenço de Almeida (1721-32), reported that although there had been an improvement, nevertheless fathers in the mining areas used their newly gained riches to endow their daughters and send them to convents in Portugal and the Atlantic islands, often against their will. He recommended that the king should prohibit any woman from leaving Minas Gerais to be a nun and suggested that this should be extended to all Brazil.[5]

Crown reaction was as unexpected as it was draconic. Faced by the reality of zero demographic increase in the white population of Brazil as a direct consequence of the exodus of women of marriageable age from the colony, by a decree of 1732, Dom João V forbade any female to leave Brazil without royal permission. If a young woman wished to enter a convent in Portugal, civil and ecclesiastical authorities were to conduct investigations to ensure that she was taking this step of her own free will, and not as the result of parental opposition to her marrying in Brazil. A ship's captain infringing this decree would be jailed for two months and fined 2,000 *cruzados* for each female found on board.[6]

In the face of outcry by the colonists, a royal resolution of 6 February 1733 allowed that this decree did not apply to women who had come to Brazil with their husbands. Such were free to return, provided they were accompanied by their spouses. This did not assuage the colonists' concern.[7] The Count of Galvêas asked for guidance concerning men from Portugal and the Atlantic islands who had married local women before the prohibition. He reported that men who would otherwise never have dreamed of leaving Brazil were now considering this step and that many engagements that would have led to marriages had now been broken. The governor reminded his sovereign that no man was willing to lose his freedom twice—by marriage and by exile. Although Dom João ruled that his order was not susceptible to interpretation, he acknowledged that no reasonable request would be refused.[8] Granting of permission was not automatic, and bureaucratic delay was endemic. Married women had to be accompanied by their husbands. Petitions citing age or sickness were invariably granted. There is evidence to suggest that by the late 1750s, population quotas and the number of white marriages were considered adequate, and restrictions became less rigorous, although remaining in force.[9]

The Crown attempted to increase the white married population of colonial Brazil in three manners: by offering inducements to bachelors to leave their concubines and marry white women; by encouraging Crown employees to bring their families to the colony; and by a policy of sponsored migration of married couples and their families from the Atlantic islands.

The Crown and governors in Brazil encouraged marriages, either by closing posts to all but white married men whose wives were also white or by favoring married men over bachelors for minor bureaucratic offices, honorary positions in militia regiments, and grants of land. The most flagrant example of Crown intervention concerning married whites occurred in 1726. Because of a shortage in Minas Gerais of white candidates for positions on town councils, mulattoes had occupied such posts. In 1726 Dom João V ordered this tolerance to cease, because there were now enough whites with families to be potential candidates. By a resolution of 26 January 1726, the king ordered that in the future nobody could be elected to the office of municipal councillor "who is mulatto within the four degrees in which mulattism [*mulatismo*] is an impediment and likewise that nobody can be elected unless he be married to a white women or be a widower of the same." The king expressed the hope that such restrictions would induce aspirants to public office to marry white women.[10] In the 1740s when Dom João V ordered a new township to be established in Mato Grosso, he insisted that only married men should be eligible to hold law enforcement posts.[11]

The Crown was keenly aware of the need to populate—as well as to cultivate—Brazil. Land grants were made to suitable applicants, preference being given to those who had wife and family.[12] The Crown also attempted to make overseas service less onerous. Contracts were drawn up for dragoons who were married, guaranteeing discharge after reduced tours of duty in order to return to wives and families. Family allowances were made to Crown employees in Brazil, such as clerks in the royal mints. Senior Crown judiciary officials were allowed to bring their wives to the colony, but were forbidden on pain of suspension from contracting marriages without royal permission.[13] Advantages accruing to white married couples in the colony were not restricted to official favors. In the social life of Brazil, to be unmarried or to be married to a mixed-blood woman could be a bar to social advancement.[14]

The Crown also instituted a sponsored migration policy. In the seventeenth century, families had been encouraged to migrate from the Azores and Atlantic islands to Brazil. The response had not been as great as had been anticipated, and the majority of such migrants had settled in Rio Grande do Sul and Santa Catarina. In the eighteenth century Dom João V and his successors pursued this policy more vigorously in an attempt to populate the hinterland. In 1721 and 1731 the governor of Minas Gerais advocated the introduction of families from Terceira, the Azores, and Madeira in an attempt to provide white women of marriageable age.[15] Evidently, migration did increase, because in 1742 the governor of Rio de Janeiro, Gomes Freire de Andrada, reported that no official financial aid was necessary because families were migrating of their own free will from the Atlantic islands. The cost of their passages and immediate expenses for transportation from Rio de Janeiro to Minas Gerais were often met by relatives already settled in the mining areas.[16] After the arrival of the royal court in Brazil in 1808, further incentives were provided to encourage migration from the Atlantic islands. Migrants were given lands to cultivate, farming tools, and seeds in addition to a house and draft animals. Furthermore, such families received financial aid for the first two years, until their crops were ready. By a decree of 16 February 1813, Dom João VI exempted such families and their offspring from military service in the troop of the line and ruled that they could not be forced to serve in the militia against their will. Such families were distributed among the captaincies of Rio de Janeiro, Minas Gerais, Espírito Santo, São Paulo, and Pôrto Seguro.[17] Obviously, the effectiveness of this migration policy varied from region to region.

Royal concern to increase the number of white females in the colony and the pious hope that they would marry and multiply was less the fruit of humanitarian considerations than a hard-nosed assessment of the needs of Brazil. The Crown's policy represented a melding of preconceptions, premises, and projections, which were economic, political and racial in nature. Large tracts of land in Brazil were underpopulated, uncultivated, and consequently unproductive. Settlement by family groups would advance the frontier of civilization, improve the quality of the land, raise crops, and provide a return to the Crown in the form of taxes. Furthermore, such communities would, in time, be incorporated into townships. As such, they would represent a Portuguese presence in the hinterland and extend the arm of Crown authority. Economic factors were allied to considerations concerning law and order and defense. Lacking familial responsibilities, a bachelor society was mobile, evaded civic and military duties, and provided a continual challenge to effective law enforcement. King and governors believed that married men not only would work harder, but also would defend their communities against Indian attacks and assume civic responsibilities.[18]

The Crown was also deeply conscious of the adverse social, legal, and moral repercussions on the colony of a society whose offspring were for the most part the by-blows of sexual liaisons with black, mulatto, and Amerindian concubines. Kings, governors, and colonists lived in constant fear of a black revolt. There can be no doubt that the Crown strove to implant and preserve in Brazil the Christian values, social mores, and national institutions of Portugal. An increase in the number of white marriages was seen as the panacea for all evils.

Stereotypes, Ideologies, Values, Attitudes, and the Legal Position of Women

No character in Brazilian history has been the victim of so stereotyped a treatment as the white female. Traditionally the white *donzela* (maiden) and the mistress of the "big house" have been depicted as leading a secluded existence, be it in the innermost recesses of their homes or in conventual cells, immune to the harshness of life and safe from brash overtures by male pretenders. Of the white woman it was said that during her lifetime she left her home on only three occasions: to be baptized, to be married, and to be buried. In short, the position of the white woman was seen as essentially passive, the victim of the demands of an overbearing and frequently unfaithful older husband to whom she would bear children or of a domineering martinet of a father.

Such a stereotype owes much to narratives by European visitors to Brazil. The Frenchmen Froger and Frézier, both homeward bound from the Straits of Magellan, put into Salvador for brief stays in 1696 and 1714, respectively. Both commented on the seclusion of white females, the unrestrained jealousy of the Portuguese male, and the manner in which the female found ways to escape from the watches of father or husband, despite his vigilance, to engage in amorous intrigues. Froger attributed this to the "extravagant and free manners" of the irresistible French male, whereas Frézier more modestly suggested the effects of climate combined with human desire for the forbidden fruit. [19] English visitors in the first two decades of the nineteenth century repeated these earlier observations, but made more pointed commentaries on the white Brazilian female. Thomas Lindley described (1802-3) white females as having poor complexions of an "obscure tawny colour," wearing their hair long and twisted up on the head and being sloppily dressed in a loose, transparent chemise with a petticoat and slippers. This was normal dress for the home. Elsewhere, Lindley remarked, European styles of dress were finding increasing acceptance with Brazilian women. Writing in 1812, John Mawe described Paulista women as being elegant, enjoying dancing, and offering sprightly conversation. The last, however, was limited to trivia, which he attributed to their staying at home and only sewing, embroidering, and making lace. Their "almost universal debility" was caused by inadequate nutrition, lack of exercise, and an excess of warm baths: "they are extremely attentive to every means of improving the delicacy of their persons, perhaps to the injury of their health." Mawe contrasted their appearance at home with that in the street and was impressed by English influence in fashion. He opined that although Bahian women were less industrious than those in the south, nevertheless the ladies of top society in Bahia outshone their counterparts even in Rio de Janeiro. [20]

John Luccock, who resided in Brazil from 1808 to 1818, had little good to say about white females. Their lack of education, course manners, boisterous conversation, poor carriage, and coquettish airs were but some of the attributes he found disagreeable. Among females of thirteen and fourteen he noted their pleasing physical appearance and happy and frank demeanor. Attaining maturity at eighteen, the Brazilian female was corpulent and stooping by twenty. Luccock attributed this to seclusion at home and indolence. Henry Koster, who made two extended journeys for reasons of health to Brazil between 1809 and 1815, commented favorably on the physical appeal of the white female, but withheld his highest accolades for the mulatto woman, imbued with "more life and spirit, more activity of mind and body" than the white female. In his travels in the interior of the northeast he noted the seclusion of women and their slovenly dress, but praised their excellent riding skills. In São Luís the lack of education of females impressed him unfavorably, but Koster noted that female reserve was broken down when it came to gaming, to which they were addicted. In view of their domestic existence, Koster was surprised that "so many excellent women should be found among them." As had Lindley and Mawe, Koster noted the "spirit of alteration" in styles and customs. In Recife the womenfolk of a few families from Lisbon and England had exerted considerable influence. The former walked to mass in broad daylight, whereas the latter took strolls in the late afternoon. In both cases the example was being adopted by local white females.[21]

Such comments cannot merely be dismissed as reflecting male bias. Two English females had illuminating things to say about the Brazilian women. Mrs. Kindersley, who wrote from Salvador in 1764, must be taken *cum grano salis* because of her virulent anti-Catholic and anti-Portuguese bias. She praised the good features of young women, but commented on their poor complexions and premature aging. At home they were dressed in a loose garment, had braided hair, and wore a profusion of gold ornaments. As had Frézier and Froger, she commented that because females were "brought up in indolence, and their minds uncultivated, their natural quickness shows itself in cunning . . . and, to speak the most favorably, a spirit of intrigue reigns amongst them." She hinted that if she were to tell of the goings-on in the darkness of night, "it would look like a libel on the sex." Less bitter and more observant was Maria Graham in the early 1820s. In Bahia she was appalled by the slovenly dress in their homes of Brazilian women, their disheveled hair, and unwashed appearance. She commented on their absence of physical appeal, but caustically observed: "But then who is there that can bear so total a disguise as filth and untidiness spread over a woman." However, at an evening ball at the consul's residence, Mrs. Graham had difficulty in recognizing the fashionably dressed ladies as the slatterns of that morning. Lacking education, these women had conversational skills limited to the beauties of Bahia, dress, children, and the more lurid aspects of diseases. Endogamous marriages stifled contact outside of a small circle. Unlike Mawe, Maria Graham maintained that the ladies of Bahia could not hold a candle to those of Rio de Janeiro, polished by the presence of the court. But she, too, hinted that at a musical evening many of the women carried notes for their gallants. On this she made the perceptive observation that whereas in Europe a mother, governess, or maid kept an eye on single girls to check any excess, in Brazil the slave females saw themselves in an adversary position to their owners and assisted, rather than prevented, any amorous intrigue. Nevertheless, it was in the highest levels of Rio society that Maria Graham met highly educated and sophisticated women. One Brazilian woman, well versed in botany and widely read, drew from her visitor recognition as being "a true blue stocking." [22]

Attitudes of male colonists in Brazil toward women did not differ markedly from their counterparts in Portugal. Male-oriented, male-dominated, patriarchal societies, both ascribed a marginal role to the female, isolating her from the mainstream of developments in the colony. Antifeminist and even misogynic writers from the sixteenth to eighteenth centuries were widely read in Portugal, their works reflecting not only unshakable beliefs in the innate superiority of the male, but corresponding disparagement for the female. At first sight such attitudes appear wholly negative, humiliating the female by relegating her to an inferior position. But such an interpretation is not the whole story. Ideals and precepts that nowadays have come to be characterized as restrictive and male-chauvinistic were regarded in the Lusitanian world as the normal outcome of theological teaching and were unreservedly accepted as such in Portugal and colonial Brazil.

In practice, the colonists' attitudes toward women depended on their social position and color. They did not look on a white woman with those same eyes with which they looked on black or Amerindian women. However, rather than a double standard of values, there was a double standard of expectations and of enforcement. Expectation of deviation from behavioral ideals demanded of the white woman varied inversely with the decreasing degree of whiteness and financial means of the woman. While it was accepted that the white woman was sexually unassailable and that sexual promiscuity on her part could result in death at the hand of her husband or father, for the black slave it was conceded that she was in no position to repel sexual advances by an owner and that she might resort to prostitution to buy her freedom. Such was the sexual mystique enshrouding black and mulatto females that infidelity and promiscuity on their part were regarded as inevitable.

Once an antifeminine stance has been acknowledged, one may discover yet another apparent contradiction: balanced against this attitude was a strong current of opinion that accorded unusually high regard to the female. Seclusion of women, which variously taunted and intrigued European travelers to colonial Brazil, led to observations couched in less than flattering terms on the excessive jealousy of Portuguese menfolk, female social gaucheness, or absence of feminine physical appeal. Explanation for pathological obsession with the seclusion of their wives and daughters by white colonists may in part lie elsewhere. Seclusion of the female was generally held to be an ideal state for womanhood and derived not from any desire to humiliate the female, but rather to isolate her from the harshness and potential temptations of everyday life. Exaltation of the female, inseparable from her undisputed chastity and virginity, may have owed much to another cultural legacy from the Old World to the New: Marianism, or the cult of the Virgin Mary, which had been popular in Spain and Portugal from at least the fourteenth century. The large number of brotherhoods dedicated to the Virgin was evidence enough of the veneration in which she was held by colonists in Brazil. [23]

Some of this veneration may have been transferred into everyday attitudes toward lay women. In colonial Brazil the female was a possession to be cherished and protected against coarseness, sexual advances, or any act that might tarnish her purity. This explains in part why colonial fathers were so willing for their daughters to enter convents. If the girls were to choose marriage, no effort was spared to ensure that the transition to her new role should be as painless and effortless as possible. Rare was the girl who came to the altar without being endowed within the financial means of her parents, who tried to ensure that the groom should be his bride's social equal. In this ideological context the closing of certain avenues to the white woman—sexual, social, or economic—may be viewed as a positive aspect of colonial society in Portuguese America.

The most explicit contemporaneous commentary on the position of the white female in colonial Brazil and her relations to her family is in a moralistic tract authored by Nuno Marques Pereira and entitled *A Narrative Compendium of the Pilgrim in America*. [24] A journey to Minas Gerais provided the pretext for a commentary on the evils of the colony. At each stop the "pilgrim" took the opportunity to moralize and to gloss that commandment most relevant to his host's situation. In this general context there is no reason to suppose that Pereira was moved by antifeminism in his comments on the female, but rather it seems that he was reflecting the attitudes of contemporaries.

The pilgrim advocated that ideally marriages should be between partners of about the same age and of similar social and financial standing. Once married, the woman was to shun the company of clerics and women of questionable repute because of their propensity for sexual alliances and malicious gossip. The ideal wife dressed modestly, did not aspire beyond her means or social station, and never spoke disparagingly of her husband. In short, "married women must be strong, discreet, and prudent. Within their homes, they should be diligent. Outside their homes they should be retiring. And at all times they should be exemplary in their conduct and mien and be reputed as long-suffering rather than spendthrifts."

That the wife should be totally subordinate to her husband was the sine qua non of any marital relationship. The pilgrim expressed this succinctly: "By divine ordinance the wife is obliged to obey her husband, especially in matters

concerning the service of the Almighty. And even in the civil code it is stated
that a wife may not cut the hair of her head without the consent and permission
of her spouse."

While describing the obligations of a wife to her husband, the pilgrim
emphasized the responsibilities of a husband toward his wife. Many wives were
"mal cazadas" ("badly married") and had wearied of the married state because of their husbands' inconsiderate behavior. It was the Christian duty of
the husband to mend his ways and accord to his wife the attention and respect
that she deserved. He was not to take concubines, whom the pilgrim compared
to turtles who emerged from the water, deposited their eggs on the beach, and
then returned to immerse themselves in an ocean of sin. Nor was the husband
to place temptation in the way of his wife. He should not take young men to his
home nor exhibit his wife to male friends as he would a sample of cloth. He was
to be vigilant over the company she kept, forbidding her from visiting female
friends whose composure or conversation might be injurious. In sexual matters
he was to be moderate and not overly demanding.

As *paterfamilias* the father was responsible for the physical, spiritual, and
economic well-being of his household, which embraced wife, children, and servants. Pereira emphasized the importance of a father's good example and a
constant vigil over his offspring, whom he should not hesitate to punish. On no
occasion should the father allow a daughter from his sight. She should not
keep the company of slave females of dubious morals, and her teachers should
be rigorously screened. Pereira quoted one mother's dictum that she preferred
her daughters to be less knowledgeable and more secluded. Selection and approval of a marriage partner were the final responsibility of a father to his
daughter. Pereira cited the adage that "a father need not lose a moment's rest
in marrying off ten sons, but the marriage of a virtuous daughter is the labor of
a decade," and he gave a final warning against fathers who married off daughters against their will.

Dearth of documentation makes assessment difficult on white females' reaction toward such attitudes and the manner in which they perceived their own
role in colonial society. From their testaments and rare letters it appears that
white females did not challenge the position ascribed to them by society. In
fact, even if women had wished to rebel, it would have been difficult for them to
find adequate channels for self-expression. Wills made by females and other
sources constitute only a small number of those dating from the colonial period, but these are sufficient to illustrate attitudes of white women on certain
issues. Five such themes, basic to an understanding of colonial society, may be
singled out for further study: attitude toward manual labor, treatment of
slaves, religiosity, marriage, and vanity.

The dependence of the white female on slaves for the running of her household was unquestioned. That the delegation of responsibility to female slaves
was allied to scorn for manual labor by white females was documented only

when they faced the possibility of being deprived of slave labor. Two examples, both taken from institutions, will illustrate this. The Retirement House of the Most Holy Name of Jesus in Salvador (opened in 1716) provided a haven for girls of middle-class families who were of marriageable age and whose honor was endangered by the loss of one or both parents. When the issue of menial labor had first been raised, Dom Pedro II had ordered in 1702 that the inmates should care for themselves and cited the precedent set by convents in Lisbon where even noble recluses had no servants. In 1721 the inmates revolted, alleging that the female warden "treated them as if they were slaves . . . ordering them to wash crockery and scale fishes and dealing with them harshly despite the fact that they were white women and wards [of the Misericórdia]." The inmates presented their case to the all-male governing body. The warden was dismissed and the number of slaves increased to such excess as to be the subject of a royal enquiry in 1754.[25] Slaves were also employed for general duties in the Convent of the Poor Clares in Salvador (founded in 1677). Nuns were permitted to have personal servants, but only after petitioning for an apostolic brief. The petition had to be supported by a document signed in secret by the members of the conventual community favoring such an addition and by a letter from the family saying that it would meet the additional costs. This directly contravened the brief of Clement IX (13 may 1669), which had authorized fifteen servants for general duties, but had expressly stated that no nun should have a slave for her particular needs.[26] Many nuns came to have not only one, but two servants. Some petitions were made less from necessity than from social consideration. In 1701 the two daughters of Manuel Álvares Pereira urged their father to purchase two black female slaves not only to satisfy the daughters' domestic needs, but also to enhance the daughters' standing in the conventual community.[27]

In the attitudes of white females toward slave women, distinctions of class, color, and civil standing precluded any feeling of common cause. It was alleged that slaves were accorded varying degrees of treatment depending on whether their owner was male or female and whether they were in Portugal or Brazil. The Count of Assumar observed that "these Americans venerate their black slaves as they would demigods." Pereira noted that women in Portugal were less tolerant toward black domestics than were their Brazilian counterparts, who would go so far as to condone misbehavior or even criminal behavior committed by a female slave. In the early nineteenth century, Henry Koster wrote, "It is said that women are usually less lenient to their slaves than men."[28] In their treatment of female slaves, white women ran the gamut from Christian charity to sadistic cruelty. Many left legacies of dowries for slaves to be married, together with household linen and even furniture. Such legacies often included a clause granting the slave her freedom. At the other extreme were white women who prostituted slaves for personal gain or were spurred by jealousy to acts of cruelty.

In their attitudes toward marriage, white women followed the precepts of colonial society. White female testators recognized their responsibility to assist unmarried nieces, more distant relations, or the daughters of friends to make suitable marriages. Clauses in wills specifically allocated substantial sums of money for dowries. Many followed the example of Joana Fernandes and Maria de Leão, Bahian ladies of the seventeenth century, who provided capital to establish trust funds to provide orphans of the city and the surrounding region known as the Recôncavo with dowries to enable them to marry. [29] By such generosity the white female not only recognized her obligations to society, but also was moved by a profound feeling of Christian charity.

Works of social philanthropy were but one aspect of religious conviction. Equally indicative of colonial attitudes were testamentary provisions for funerals and the saying of masses. In these the wills of female testators differ only in minor points from those of their male counterparts. Pomp and piety melded to ensure that the funeral would be worthy of the social standing of the deceased and that her soul would be provided for by the saying of masses. Catharina de Silva, who died in São Paulo in 1694, ordered that her body be buried in the Church of St. Francis. Her cortège was to be accompanied by the brothers of the Misericórdia and by representatives of other brotherhoods. Masses were to be said for her soul. The wealth of Maria de Leão (who died in 1656) enabled her to order that ten masses be said over her body and that a further twenty be said in the church of the parish of the Destêrro; rents from two houses should meet the cost of the saying of two masses weekly and one mass monthly. [30]

In such provisions there was not a little of that vanity and mania for nobility that pervaded colonial society. Male aspirations are easily documented in the endless flow of petitions to the Crown for the concession of knighthoods in the military-religious orders or of largely honorary pseudomilitary posts. Such evidence is lacking for female pretensions, but the white female was no less vulnerable to the trappings of office. In 1725, Dom João V warned the governor of Minas Gerais to scrutinize the social standing and capabilities of candidates because it had come to the royal notice that unsuitable people were obtaining such posts, "dazzled by the honor that such posts bestow on the incumbent, to which their wives are no less susceptible." [31]

If such attitudes and behavioral norms shown by the white female in colonial Brazil did not set her apart significantly from her male counterpart, when it came to the legal position of the female in Portuguese America, she enjoyed less protection than the male. Canon, civil, and consuetudinarian law made her subordinate to the male. Whatever chasm there may have been between the letter and the practice of the law in Brazil, there can be no doubt that custom and tradition contributed to buttressing restrictions placed on the female. Her potential for gaining legal redress depended largely on extrajudicial factors, namely, social standing, financial means, color, and parentage. Political participation, even at the local level, was an exclusively male privilege, and females were excluded from the "good folk of the Republic" permitted to vote in municipal elections. Nevertheless, despite evident antifeminine bias in legislation and in custom, this has been exaggerated by commentators to the point of portraying the female as devoid of any standing in law and of denying to her any form of legal redress. Closer scrutiny reveals that the female was entitled to due process of law and, if this failed, could appeal directly to the Crown. She could serve as executrix of a will, could inherit and possess land and properties, and could and did hold the legally recognized position of head of household. She could conduct trade and commerce in her own name and could bring legal charges against others. It was not even unknown for a daughter to prosecute her father, if he were reluctant to further her hopes of marriage, and to demand payment of a dowry. 32

It was in matters concerning marital relations that the female was likely to receive less than justice and that discrimination in the law and in the enforcement of the law was most blatant. A double standard of expectations of marital fidelity by husband and wife prevailed. Courts looked leniently on crimes of passion in which a husband had beaten or killed a wife who was adulterous or whom he merely suspected of infidelity. Proven adultery was sufficient cause for a man to divorce his wife, but the onus was often placed on a wife to provide evidence of a second cause—such as cruelty, desertion, or forced prostitution—for her to obtain a divorce. In such cases a lien was placed on all possessions of the defendant, who was responsible for making financial arrangements for the upkeep of an estranged wife and any offspring. During the period of legal separation the estranged wife was placed in the home of a respectable relative or citizen on the order of the vicar-general. After six months the wife could file for divorce, and final judgment would be made by the vicar-general. In some cases it would appear that the ecclesiastical authorities overstepped their jurisdiction. In the 1750s one such divorced woman, Thereza de Jesus Maria, alleged that she was being held against her will in the Retirement House of the Misericórdia in Salvador on the personal orders of the archbishop while her good-for-nothing bookkeeper husband fled to Portugal with her wealth. She charged that she had been the victim of collusion and that the Crown judge in Salvador, bowing to heavy archiepiscopal pressure, had refused to hear her appeals or order her release. 33

This was not the only instance, when it came to matters of heart or body, in which any sexual impropriety by the female resulted in her effectively being denied her legal rights or due process in a court of law. Not infrequently the viceroy or governor general and the ecclesiastical authorities decided without recourse to a court of law what would be the most appropriate action to protect a female's virtue, real or imagined, or to quell potential scandal. Numerous examples could be cited from the colonial period in which an unfaithful wife was deposited in a convent or retirement house against her will by virtue of a royal or viceregal order or archiepiscopal edict. Appeals were ignored. Amorous intrigues with clerics or friars met with especially harsh treatment. The unusual case of Dona Helena de Lima and her two daughters has been told elsewhere. An even more bizarre case at the beginning of the nineteenth century involved Dona Luiza Francisca do Nascimento e Oliveira, a proven adulteress. Her businessman husband had requested that she be placed in the Retirement House of São Raimundo in Salvador. On the royal order she had been transferred to the Convent of the Lapa, where it was shown by a legal inquiry that she had entertained male visitors, including the prior of the Calced Carmelites, friar Manuel da Piedade Valongo. Without going through the normal legal channels, the governor, the Count of Ponte, and the archbishop ordered that she be placed in the Retirement House of the Misericórdia. [34]

It must be pointed out that the female was not always the victim of extralegal measures in dealing with marital or sexual problems. When João de Couros Carneiro, secretary of the city council of Salvador, beat his wife, kept her locked in a room with a ration of flour each day, and brought his concubine to live in the house, it came to the notice of the viceroy and the archbishop. The viceroy reported the incident to the king in 1728 and ordered the wife to be placed in the Retirement House of the Misericórdia. [35] Such a proceeding circumvented normal legal channels, but provided a form of safety valve against potential miscarriages of justice by an exclusively male judicial bureaucracy, whose members often had familial or business interests in the community.

Social Role of the White Woman

THE SINGLE WOMAN

The role accorded to the single white woman was no other than that of preparing herself *tomar estado* (to take state), that is, to enter either a convent or marriage. In either case, until final documents were signed, parents lived on tenterhooks of doubts and fears. A woman's childhood and adolescence were passed in seclusion to remove any doubt as to her virtue. Sometimes family pressures were exerted on her either to marry or to enter a convent. The parents' financial circumstances could be a critical factor, as in the following instance. In 1740, eighteen-year-old Quiteria Teixeira of Vila do Carmo petitioned the Crown for permission to travel to Portugal to enter a convent and take her vows. Inquiry made by the local Crown judge showed that she had made a vow of chastity and had rejected her parents' wishes that she marry. The judge noted that the parents were opposed to their daughter's entering a convent because with their limited financial means they would be better able to help her if she were to marry in Brazil than if she were to become a nun in Portugal. But for the most part the concern of the parents was no more than that she should "take state." Testators left legacies to daughters, nieces, and the female offspring of friends for this purpose, without specifying marriage or convent. In 1732, Dom Lourenço de Almeida waspishly commented that "it was very fitting for people of low birth to have their daughters take the veil," but there is nothing to suggest that this practice was more prevalent in any one class of colonial society. Even if the outcome were in defiance of parents' wishes, a rare event, nevertheless there was a feeling of relief once the decision about a daughter's future had been taken.[36]

Should the young woman choose to enter a convent, the question arose as to whether this would be in Portugal or Brazil. The outcome was decided by three factors: the proximity of a convent, the color of the intending nun, and the financial resources of the parents. By 1750 most cities in Portuguese America counted at least one convent. Such foundations were the fruits of public and civic pressures, but could not meet the demand for places. Black and mulatto women were not admitted to convents in Brazil and were compelled to go to Portugal or the Atlantic islands where they were accepted. The expense of sending a young woman to Portugal, paying the fees for her to enter a convent, and meeting the cost of her upkeep was substantial. Such considerations led the "native citizens and good men" of the city of São Paulo to remind the Crown in 1736 of a royal favor permitting the Retirement House of Santa Thereza de Jesus to become a convent under the initial supervision of an abbess and nuns from Portugal. Their petition informed the king that thirteen potential nuns from that city alone had raised 56,000 *cruzados* for such a foundation, and a further fourteen people from Minas Gerais had expressed interest.[37]

Judging by the petitions asking for royal permission to send or accompany young women to Portugal to enter convents, there was no shortage of fathers willing to meet such costs. Some fathers were prominent figures in the colony. In 1725 the Lisbon agent of the powerful landowner Manuel Nunes Viana gained royal approval to come to Portugal "to make nuns of his daughters." In 1726 he placed his six daughters in the Convent of São Domingos das Donas in Santarém and returned to Bahia. Nunes Viana deposited 16,000 *cruzados* with the friars of São Vicente de Fora in Lisbon, the annual interest to meet the costs of upkeep and maintenance of his daughters. In the 1750s the daughters who had taken the veil brought legal action against their brother, Dr. Miguel Nunes Viana, charging him with fraud and embezzlement of the capital. This was the subject of a royal inquiry, culminating in a ruling upholding their claim.[38] Other fathers had aspirations beyond their financial means. Despite financial straits, António Rodriguez Silva, who served for five years in the Arassuahí mines in the 1730s, placed his two daughters as novices in the Calvário Convent in Lisbon. He petitioned the king for payment of arrears of his salary so that he could meet the additional costs of their taking the veil and of sustaining them. Dom João V ordered payment to be made at the yearly rate of 300$000 *reis*.[39]

Many colonists were unable or unwilling to meet such financial costs. In

Salvador in the early eighteenth century, they could choose between the Convent of the Poor Clares or the Lapa Convent. The demand for places in the former was such as to lead the city council in 1717 to petition the king for an increase in the number of places to 100 from the original 50 authorized in 1665. 40 Some fathers entered their daughters as "pupils" (*educandas*) in the hope that as such they would be favored when a vacancy occurred among the quota of nuns. Other hopeful, but frustrated, fathers followed the example of Manuel de Almeida Mar, who asked the king to intervene so that his niece could be admitted to the convent, or of another prominent Bahian, Domingos Pires de Carvalho, who made a similar appeal on behalf of his daughters. In fact, the granting of such favors fell outside the royal jurisdiction, and no places were reserved for royal nominees. Those who were successful in gaining admission often placed all their daughters in the convent. João de Couros Carneiro, whose physical abuse of his wife was later to come to the royal notice, had earlier gained the abbess's permission for entry of his three daughters in 1686. The guarantee of protection and seclusion was not cheaply bought. In 1684 master of the field Pedro Gomes paid 600,000 *reis* and fees for each of his two daughters to be admitted as novices. Such "dowries" were not refundable, should the girls fail to take their final vows. In 1751 the "dowry" for a girl wishing to take her vows as a nun was 1,600$000 *reis*. Nevertheless, for their own peace of mind the citizens of Bahia did not balk at such expenditures. 41

Marriage was an option more available to young females. Choice of groom was predicated on the assumption that marriage did not represent the fulfillment of a woman's desires or wishes, but was rather an instrument for bettering the financial and social position of the family. Legacies revealed this consciousness of enhancing prestige. The last instructions of the Paulista Pedro Vaz de Barros to his widow were that she should marry off their two daughters "as quickly as possible with worthy men who have the ability to follow an honorable career." Jorge Ferreira, a wealthy property owner who died in Salvador in 1641, bequeathed the fruits of his labors to his niece Jerónima Ferreira as a dowry "so that the husband whom she marries may be the more ennobled thereby." 42 Final choice was made from a small circle of acceptable suitors, selected and approved by her parents. For the rural aristocracy of Pernambuco and Bahia endogamous marriages served the double purpose of strengthening family ties among this elitist group and improving their economic position and landholdings. As plantation families fell on hard times, potential suitors from the rising and prosperous urban merchant class were courted to bolster the family position by the infusion of new capital.

The female was aided in her quest for marriage by the institution of the dowry. So important was the dowry that it served as a microcosm for attitudes and ideals and illustrated the interplay of social and economic pressures in colonial Brazil. A dowry was both a symbol of social status and a palliative. On the one hand, the social and economic standing of a doting father could only be

enhanced if it were to become common knowledge that his daughter was endowed well. On the other hand, a substantial dowry could offset lack of charm
or beauty on the part of its owner. Such an institution was open to abuse. Many
a man married a dowry rather than a bride. So prevalent was this mercenary
practice that one petitioner for a royal favor claimed in support of his appeal
that he had married his wife for love and not for her dowry. Some women fell
victims to the wiles of unworthy opportunists. The example of the bookkeeper
of low birth who married a rich Bahian widow, Thereza de Jesus Maria, and
then absconded to Portugal with her wealth was not unique. Whatever the evils
of the tradition, for the daughter of a wealthy family it was never doubted that
she would be endowed. For the daughter of a middle-class or poorer family, a
dowry was no less a prerequisite for marriage. For the daughter of poor parents
or an orphan, a dowry could mean the difference between an honorable marriage and prostitution.

The function of the dowry was not limited to helping a young woman find a
husband or saving her from prostitution. In colonial Brazil, where widowhood
and desertion were common, the dowry had an important protective function.
Facing the impending marriage of a daughter, parents tacitly acknowledged
such eventualities. The degree of acknowledgment may have depended on
class differentiations, and cases must be examined on an individual basis. But
such thinking may explain in part why dowries frequently took the form of possessions rather than outright cash payments. Economic circumstances such as
the shortage of currency in certain regions at different periods, the prevalence
of a barter rather than a monetary economy, or familial pressures to maintain
an estate intact may have been important factors in such parental decisions.
But recognition that possessions afforded a hedge against inflationary trends,
were not subject to embezzlement, and could not be disposed of by an unscrupulous husband as easily as cash may have weighed no less heavily in the
minds of parents endowing a daughter. Such dowries in kind did on occasion
include estates, plantations, cattle corrals, and houses, as well as livestock,
farming equipment, black and Amerindian slaves, bales of cotton, tobacco,
and sugar. But regardless of differences of class or financial means, more frequently dowries included domestic items, tableware, beds, tables, chairs, bed
linen, or cotton towels.

An interesting variation on the theme of dowries in kind was the dowry that
took the form of a public office or a promise of a habit in one of the religious-
military orders. Francisco Zorilla, who had seen military service and held
minor posts including that of *procurador dos Indios* (procurator, or protector,
of Indians), exacted from the king in 1620 the favor that this post should be
granted to his widow in trust for the man who married their only daughter. For
his part Afonso do Pôrto Poderoso was granted royal permission in 1673 to retire as clerk to the High Court in Salvador, a post that he had held for three
decades. The king ordered that, at the discretion of Pôrto Poderoso, this post

was to pass to his eldest son or to the man who took his daughter in marriage. [43] Alleged deeds of prowess in overcoming Indians, establishing homesteads and settlements, and discovering gold in Minas Gerais in the eighteenth century provided the basis for a spate of petitions to the Crown for recognition of these services. One such petitioner was António Pereira Machado, one of the first colonists and miners in the area that was to be the site of the future Vila do Carmo. He had given to the fledgling municipality a land grant made to him by Governor António de Albuquerque (1702-10). Later Machado petitioned Dom João V for the *mercê* of the proprietary post of secretary to the town council of Carmo and a habit in the Order of Christ. Being too old to hold the post himself, the father asked that this be transferred to his legitimate son, Pedro Duarte Pereira. The habit and a pension of 12$000 *reis* were to go to his niece Thereza de Souza as her dowry. The king conceded all the requested favors in 1731. [44] One of the more bizarre instances of habits in the Order of Christ being given as dowries involved a petition to the Crown in the early nineteenth century by Manuel José de Oliveira Sampaio. A century earlier, in return for services in Minas Gerais, the king had granted Romão Gramacho Falcão the benefice of two habits of the Order of Christ for him to give to his nephew and to whosoever should marry his niece. One habit was inherited by a nephew-once-removed, Gaspar Fernandes da Fonseca. It fell to Manuel José to claim the other due to his cousin and wife Maria Rosa do Nascimento de Sampaio, daughter of Gaspar Fernandes da Fonseca and consequently grandniece of Gramacho Falcão. This extraordinary claim was upheld by a report in 1809. [45]

Other dowries were given in recognition of the fact that without them daughters or female relatives would stand little chance of getting married. This was acknowledged by Marcelino Vieira Machado, captain of Monserrate fortress in the Bay of All Saints. In 1809 he petitioned the Crown for promotion to the rank of sergeant major, citing thirty-eight years in the royal service. He was moved to make this request because on an annual salary of 10$000 *reis* it was impossible for him to endow his three daughters. Promotion would almost double his salary and permit him to provide dowries for his girls, thereby enabling them to find suitable husbands. [46] That it was essential to bring a dowry to marriage was recognized not only by anxious fathers who made special bequests to daughters. Colonists, many of whom had no children of their own, made testamentary provisions for dowries to be given to their nieces, their godchildren, the daughters of their executors, or simply the unmarried female offspring of friends. In an age in which personal legacies were comparatively few and testators preferred to leave their fortunes for the saying of masses or charity, legacies for dowries afforded a notable exception.

Orphan girls were perhaps the most in need of dowries. Loss of a father or of both parents placed the girl's virtue and future in jeopardy. Concern for a girl's moral well-being provoked a strong response on the part of colonists. Foundlings left on doorsteps were adopted and provided with dowries. This generosity extended to dowries for female slaves and even their offspring. Many testators preferred that the Misericórdia should minister dowries for orphan girls. These fell into two categories: specific sums were left to the Misericórdia for immediate allocation to deserving cases, or legacies were made to the Misericórdia for the capital to be placed on loan and a number of dowries to be financed each year from the interest. [47]

THE MARRIED WOMAN

To separate the position of the white woman in colonial Brazil from her role in marriage would be to ignore the social, ideological, and religious context of an age and country. It was unquestioned that her *raison d'être* was to be virtuous as a girl, honorable as a bride, loyal as a wife, and loving as a mother. It was in marriage, with its multiplicity of obligations and responsibilities, that the white woman made her major contribution to society. Moreover, only through marriage would a girl become a woman in her own right and in the eyes of others.

Despite societal recognition of marriage as a highly desirable behavioral norm, recent research suggests that comparatively few church marriages occurred in colonial Brazil in proportion to the overall population. Extortionate demands for inflated fees by churchmen, especially in more remote regions, or the bureaucratic hassle of providing documentation and proof of being single may have been deterrents. But, more tellingly, it appears that incidence of unions sanctified by the Catholic church was related to the social standing of the partners. There were fewer marriages between slaves than freedmen, fewer between blacks than whites, and fewer in the lower orders of white society than in the upper echelons. Although unavailability of suitable white female partners may have been a factor until the mid-eighteenth century in some regions, there is every indication that by the end of the century there were plenty of eligible females for marriage. Nevertheless, among the free population of a sample parish in São Paulo the nuptial coefficient was 10.6 per 1,000 between 1780 and 1799, decreasing to 7.5 per 1,000 in the early nineteenth century. From 1820 to 1850 only 31 marriages were recorded in an average year. [48]

The age at which a woman was "marriageable" depended in part on her parents' financial position and social standing. That females matured earlier than males had been recognized by canon law, which permitted males to marry at fourteen years, whereas females could marry at twelve or earlier in special circumstances. The census of 1776 classified males from seven to fifteen as boys (*rapazes*), whereas the upper age for girls (*raparigas*) was fourteen. Furthermore, whereas old age was considered to start for a female at forty, only on reaching his sixtieth year did a male fall into this category. To judge by conditions imposed by the Misericórdia for dowries, the age span for first marriages was between fourteen and thirty years of age. [49] Parents encouraged daughters to marry early. The relief expressed by Catharina de Araújo, "who rejoices greatly at seeing her daughter protected and made mistress of her own household as she desires" on the occasion of the marriage of her fourteen-year-old Bernarda to a Bahian blacksmith, was typical of the reaction of many parents. Although the evidence is too partial to be conclusive, it appears that a higher proportion of females under twenty were married than males of that age category. Marriage registers did not record the age of the female partner, but data for Vila Rica from the third quarter of the eighteenth century show an approximate median age of twenty-two years for a female's first marriage, whereas her partner was some seven or eight years older.[50]

Marriages may have been contracted against some women's will, but less frequently than popular mythology and folk literature would suggest. The custom existed that female orphans in convents and retirement houses were provided for by wealthy benefactors until they came of an age at which their elderly protectors would claim them in marriage. This practice met with the consent and approval of the authorities. That women should marry much older men was commonplace. Parents viewed with approval the suit of a man old enough to be their daughter's father or even grandfather because of the financial security and social position such a marriage would provide. Some child-wives may have accepted such a fate with resignation, but horrifying pictures have been painted of young women being forced into marriages with tubercular septuagenarians.

At the present state of research, conclusions on the fertility of white couples in the tropics must be tentative. There is evidence to support the hypothesis that many white marriages in colonial Brazil did not result in children. Whether this was due to physiological, psychological, or environmental factors is unclear. The answer may lie in a combination of all three influences. Repeatedly, testaments of white property owners in the colony asserted the absence of offspring, and, in default of these, bequests were made to the Church or to religious orders.

There is no reason to believe that such a situation was restricted to testators whose wills have survived or who were careful enough to make a will—not a widely practiced custom in the colony. This is not the whole story, and the numbers presented in Figure 2.1 may give a more representative picture of family compositon in Portuguese America. This chart was prepared from data obtained from a sample of 142 married couples in São Paulo in the seventeenth century. Much information is lacking, but membership in the Misericórdia or Third Orders suggests that such couples were white and of middle- or upper-class background. Children registered are the offspring of first marriages only. All told, there were 731 legitimate children, which, divided among the 142 families, gives an arithmetic mean of 5.15 children per family. But to assert that the average white family comprised parents and 5 children is misleading,

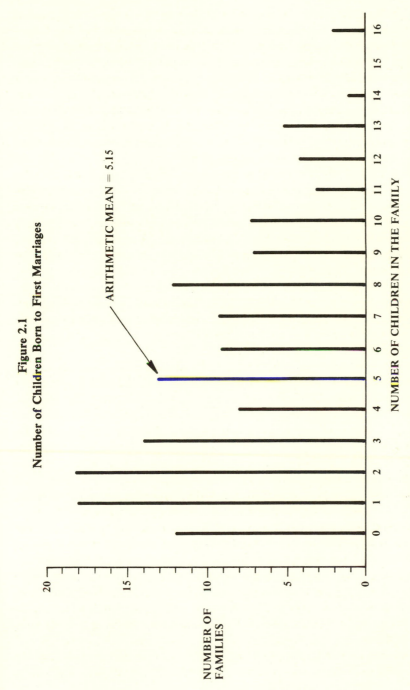

Figure 2.1
Number of Children Born to First Marriages

Source: Departamento do Arquivo do Estado de São Paulo, *Inventarios e testamentos; papeis que pertenceram ao 1º cartprio de órfãos da capital: Documentos da secção do arquivo histórico*, 50 vols. (São Paulo: Typ. Piratininga, 1920).

because of the asymmetrical distribution of the data. Some families counted as many as 16 children, but the most frequent value, or mode, is 1 or 2 children.

The white woman of colonial Brazil has been depicted as a matronly figure at twenty, worn out by successive pregnancies and lack of exercise. Evidence on frequency of childbirth is scanty. Testators often failed to mention the ages of deceased children or of married offspring no longer living under the parental roof. Some few examples tend to bear out the view of repeated pregnancies. Isabel Gomes, who died in 1628 in São Paulo, bore her husband ten children whose ages at the time of her death were as follows: twenty-three, twenty, eighteen, twelve, ten, eight, six, three, and one; the tenth was not listed. The offspring of another Paulista mother were aged nineteen, seventeen, fifteen, twelve, ten, nine, four, and two. Although one married child of Ignez da Costa was not listed by age, the recorded ages of the remainder of the family were twenty, nineteen, eighteen, sixteen, fifteen, ten, eight, seven, and two years. [51] Infant mortality among whites was high, but not as high as among offspring of black families. The belief that higher black infant mortality was offset by larger numbers of offspring was challenged in 1821 by the German mining engineer von Eschwege. Based on observations made in Minas Gerais he concluded that white women were more fertile than mulatto women and that the fertility of a black woman depended on whether she were free or slave. A survey for the Passo parish of Salvador in 1799 suggests a mortality coefficient of 172.4 per 1,000 for "innocents" of white parentage. Although wills rarely specified the age of a child at death, there is no doubt that whether it resulted from infant mortality or later sickness, many white children failed to survive their parents. Such productivity was not without its risk to the health of the mother. Several wills mention that the wife was pregnant at the time of making her last dispositions, "sick in bed and in fear of death." The inference is irresistible that her death resulted from complications during pregnancy or in childbirth. [52]

Of interest to students of women's history and family history is information on the disparity of ages among offspring with the same parents. In extreme cases, this difference of age between oldest and youngest was as much as a generation (generally taken to be about twenty-five years). Of the seven children of the Paulista Agostinha Rodrigues her eldest son was thirty, whereas her youngest was only five. The sixteen children of another Paulista family ranged from thirty-four to eight. [53] Such large families provided a form of security, especially in agricultural areas, against the death of a breadwinner. Then, as now in Brazil, children joined the labor force at a tender age, and many a dying father could take solace in the fact that his widow would be helped by their already adult offspring.

A survey of 165 testaments made in São Paulo in the seventeenth century provides information on first and multiple marriages (Table 2.1). Such basic information as the causes resulting in the termination of a marriage—for ex-

Table 2.1
Incidence of Marriage and Remarriage in São Paulo in the Seventeenth Century

Number of Marriages	Male		Female	
	Number	*%*	*Number*	*%*
0	2	2	—	—
1	99	87	43	84
2	12	10	7	14
3	1	1	1	2
	114	100	51	100

Source: Departamento do Arquivo do Estado de São Paulo, *Inventarios e testamentos; papeis que pertenceram ao 1º cartorio de órfãos da capital: Documentos da secção do arquivo histórico*, 50 vols. (São Paulo: Typ. Piratininga, 1920).

ample, migration, widowhood, desertion—is lacking. Conclusions based on such partial evidence can be only tentative, but may be applicable elsewhere in the colony in the seventeenth century. It was unlikely that white females of marriageable age would remain single. Alternatives open to the male—cohabitation or promiscuity—were barred to her. From the data for São Paulo in this period, a higher incidence of white females than males contracted second or third marriages. The shortage of white women placed a premium on the eligible widow. Furthermore, early first marriages by females often led to widowhood at a comparatively young age. Finally, the female's own search for the financial security and social position afforded by marriage may have been a factor in remarriage by a greater number of females. Changing economic, demographic, and social circumstances may have contributed to a tilt in the opposite direction in the urban area in the eighteenth century. Marriage records for the parish of the Sé in São Paulo suggest that between 1728 and 1770, 9.6 percent of males remarried in contrast to 8.0 percent of females. In the period 1771 to 1809 the disparity was more noticeable: 14 percent of males and only 7.0 percent of females.[54] Much research has yet to be done, but further consultation of standard genealogies may throw light on this fascinating aspect of colonial mores.

The Woman as Head of Household: Social Aspects

The commonly held view that the family was an unshakable pillar in the social life of Portuguese America and that the patriarchal extended family prevailed in the colony has come under challenge as the result of recent research. Analysis of the 1804 census of Vila Rica has revealed that matrifocal families accounted for 45 percent of all households. Significantly, 90 percent of identifiable female heads of household were mulattoes and blacks, but the fact that even 10 percent were white suggests that a reassessment of the role of the white female as head of household is in order.[55] Vila Rica at a time of economic decline was scarcely representative of all regions of the colony throughout the colonial period, but these surprising data do suggest new lines of inquiry. Factors contributing to the female's assuming the position of head of household were divorce, desertion, and widowhood. To judge by the paucity of references, rarely did estranged couples go to the length of formally filing for divorce. In those few recorded cases the property of the couple was divided by the legal authorities, and the female received half of the value at which the property and possessions were assessed. Custody of children was invariably granted to the mother, and the father was liable for maintenance of mother and children. The only exception was when the wife was the guilty party. In 1782, Manuel Nicolau, a native of Crete living in Salvador, was granted permission to return to Portugal with his three young daughters. Custody of the children had been granted to him after his wife had been found guilty of adultery and had been jailed, as had her lover.[56]

Far more frequently, the wife was thrown into the position of effective head of household as the result of desertion. Sometimes she was the victim of circumstances; on other occasions such desertion was intentional. In a highly mobile and essentially opportunist society, the woman not only exerted a stabilizing influence on the family, but had to shoulder the responsibility of bringing up children during their father's absence.

Conditions in the colony were not conducive to a secure family life. A head of household, with his wife's consent, would leave a family in Portugal or a Brazilian coastal city rather than endanger their lives in the interior. Few followed the example of one doughty character who traveled from the hinterland of Pernambuco to Minas Gerais in the 1730s accompanied by his wife and eight children.[57] Wives and families were often the victims of vengeance born of jealousies and rivalries. Furthermore, arbitrary Crown policy did little to imbue settlers with a sense of security. Orders in the eighteenth century banishing goldsmiths from the captaincy of Minas Gerais or expelling settlers from the diamond-bearing rivers of the Distrito Diamantino threatened the livelihood of many families. When it came down to the line, the king was more concerned with increasing the wealth of the royal coffers than with furthering the welfare of individual families. Throughout Brazil during the colonial period threats of attack by Amerindians or groups of runaway slaves were constant. White females were victims of rape, mutilation, and murder. To such hazards could be added unsanitary living conditions, the usual gamut of tropical diseases, and inadequate medical attention.

Against such a background, breadwinners could scarcely be criticized for not wishing to expose families to such hazards. Many a father who left wife and family in Portugal with promises to return died in the colony. Some committed bigamy or took a concubine; others simply lost contact with relatives. Soldiers in the dragoons often served terms of ten years in Minas Gerais before petitioning the Crown for leave of absence of one year to return to their families in Portugal. Royal approval for such leaves and increased family allowances failed to prevent the disintegration of family ties. Petitions by widows for the discharge of soldier sons were invariably granted.[58]

Cases of desertion were not limited to wives and families in Portugal. In Brazil, men left home for long periods while on expeditions to the *sertão*. In default of any news of their whereabouts, they were presumed dead. Soldiers who had married in the colony and whose tours of duty were over preferred to desert their wives rather than return with them to Portugal. Black and mulatto women, whether or not their unions with a white partner had received the blessing of the Church, were especially likely to be the victims of such neglect.

The emphasis placed on marriage tended to conceal the inescapable fact that the majority of them would end in widowhood. It was more usual for the white female to outlive her spouse than the opposite. For the woman who chose not to remarry, the alternative was not only a struggle for her own survival, but also the burden of being guardian of her children and, frequently, owner of property. The widow became a true head of household with extensive responsibilities. Relatives and older married children rallied around at times of need, but success or failure for the widow and her family lay in her hands. The difficulties that she was likely to face were acknowledged by husbands who made special clauses in their wills to support their widows.

The first hurdle to be faced by the widow was bureaucratic. This was especially the case if the husband had died intestate or if the offspring were below twenty-five years of age. The local authority responsible for the "dead and absent" (*provedor*) not only made an inventory of the possessions of the deceased, but also placed a lien on them and all currency holdings. Given the mobility of colonial society, it was not unusual for a person's possessions to be distributed throughout Brazil. Delays were inevitable, prejudicing heirs because of devaluation of plantations and death of cattle as the result of neglect. Heirs in Brazil often lost their inheritances because of a ruling that no *provedor* should release the possessions of the deceased without written authorization obtainable only in Lisbon. This absurd ruling was relaxed in 1719, but three years later the town council of Vila Rica informed the king that rich men were buried as paupers and many a young widow was made destitute because of restrictions placed by *provedores*.[59] Despite reforms and Crown intervention in specific cases, delays and abuses were endemic. Heirs in Portugal making claims in Brazil were ignored by local *provedores*. Delays of twenty to thirty years were not infrequent.[60] In 1813 the populace of Xique Xique asked for the status of township (*vila*) to be conceded to their village. This appeal alleged that only thus could a remedy be found to the present situation whereby widows and orphans were left destitute, lost properties, and were unable to collect debts because their nearest legal recourse was fifty leagues distant.[61]

Arrangements made by the deceased for his widow and family varied. The simplest arrangement derived from the time of marriage when a "division of properties" was made, enabling the wife to maintain legal possession of her half. Where this was not stated in so many words, the customary practice was for an inventory to be made of the possessions of the deceased. The wife received half of the proceeds derived from the sale of such possessions. Debts and legacies were made from the husband's portion and the residue subdivided. In some cases the deceased had set aside one-third of his portion for the saying of masses for his soul. In other instances this was left to a favorite niece or daughter or even to his wife. The remaining two-thirds were usually divided among his sons and heirs. Matters became complicated when, for example, a testator ordered that his third (terça) should be divided equally between legitimate and illegitimate children and then that the respective halves should be further subdivided so that each child would be a beneficiary.

In some instances the legacies made to the widow were substantial enough to guarantee her security and enable her to bring up children without undue financial strain. But all too many testators left their survivors with no more than their blessing, "heirs to the poverty I possess." Sometimes the sum realized by the sale of the deceased's properties and possessions was insufficient even to meet the liabilities and debts that he had incurred during his life. Rather than being beneficiaries, the heirs and widow had to realize their own capital investments to pay these debts. Such straits led the Archbishop of Bahia to grant licenses to widows and donzelas to ask for alms in public.[62]

The widow was often the executrix of the terms of her husband's will. In this she was usually assisted by a male relative or friend of the deceased. Should the widow die soon after her husband, such a relative became the guardian of the orphaned children. Certain testators placed limitations on the role of the mother as guardian, should she remarry. One Paulista in the seventeenth century made his wife guardian (curadora) of their children only as long as she did not remarry. Francisco Pedroso Xavier left his widow Maria Cardoso his third in addition to the half of his property that she had received as his widow. This supplementary legacy was conditional, "only for as long as she does not remarry because I trust that she will behave honorably towards our children, and when and if she should remarry, then my 'third' is to be divided among my sons and daughters."[63]

The widow was helped in her task by two factors: first, those benefits derived from larger families and, second, specific bequests made to her by the deceased. Older offspring were exhorted by dying fathers to help their widowed mother. Bequests to provide the widow with the means of fulfilling such responsibilities included placement of money in trust for dowries to female offspring, supplementary legacies to the widow, and a home or a small-holding to provide income and sustenance. This assistance could not detract from the awesome responsibility to be shouldered by the widow. Many widows faced the task of bringing up younger children and then providing boys with basic skills or ensuring that girls were suitably married. Maria Rodriguez, widow of Manuel da Cunha Gago, to whom she had borne twelve children and by whom she was pregnant at the time of his death, confronted a household of children aged twenty years to one year. The duties of the widow were not directed merely to supporting herself and her family. Her prime obligation was toward the physical and spiritual welfare of her children. Hers was the responsibility of teaching the children Christian doctrine and "ensuring that they are taught good habits and behavior, the girls to sew and perform domestic tasks and the boys to read, write and count."

For boys several options were open to the widowed mother. A son could take over the estate or small-holding when he came of age. Other male offspring were induced to sign up for military service or were apprenticed to a trade. Few widows were able to meet the costs of a university education, but some still entertained the hope of most parents in the colony that at least one of their sons might enter the Church. It was not uncommon for fathers or relatives to make legacies specifically for boys wishing to follow such a vocation. The expenditure was substantial, involving travel to Europe and study there over a period of years. Thus, the dedication and sacrifices demanded of one Paulista widow, Euphemia da Costa, cannot be underestimated: four of her sons took holy orders. For daughters the hopes of widows were centered on marriage, and fathers made bequests for the realization of such hopes. [64]

The responsibilities of the widow were not limited to her immediate family and offspring. Concubines and extramarital relationships were prominent features of colonial life. If a mistress were to be discarded or to die, it was customary for the man to bring the children home to his legitimate wife to be cared for, reared, and educated alongside their legitimate children. Foreign travelers to Brazil never ceased to comment on such children, often of darker hues than the legitimate offspring, seated at the family table and treated on a basis of equality with children born within wedlock. Attitudes by fathers to such illegitimate offspring were ambivalent. Many simply deserted mother and child, so there may have been grounds for the Crown's insistence on a correlation between concubinage and the number of foundling children, whose upkeep was a financial drain on town councils in Brazil.

But this was only one side of the story. Other fathers acted most responsibly toward offspring born on the wrong side of the blanket. Diogo de Cubas, a Madrileño living in São Paulo, exhorted his wife and daughter to look after his illegitimate daughter by a slave. They were to not only care for her well-being, but also were to "indoctrinate her, teach her good customs and make her pray." António Pedrozo de Barros asked his widow to find a suitable spouse for his illegitimate daughter and made a bequest for this purpose. [65] Female slaves received not only their freedom, but also household linen, domestic utensils, and even, on some occasions, a dowry.

The Woman as Head of Household: Economic Aspects

The role of the white female in the country's economy could not match her vital contribution to the formation of Brazilian society. Social mores and the institution of slavery stifled any initiative that the white woman might have been spurred to take. Even at the domestic level, slaves were charged with the day-to-day provisioning and maintaining of the household. Those few "cottage industries" that may have existed were performed by blacks or Amerindians. The contribution that the white female made to the colonial economy came less by dint of her own efforts than as the result of circumstances that she could not avoid. As the widow was forced to assume the position of head of household, so too was death to be instrumental in placing the white woman in positions in which she was compelled to take decisions on financial matters and the management of estates. In this regard she belied her traditional image of being divorced from the commercial life of the colony.

Some dodged this responsibility and were content to abrogate the administration of estates or inherited properties to sons or distant relatives. Such trust was open to abuse. Luzia Freire, a widow living in Bahia, refused to make any legacy to her sons-in-law in her will of 1685. Both had cheated her in the management of a sugar plantation and cattle corrals, had misappropriated animals, and had stolen her slaves. Other widows followed the example of Magdalena da Silva, widow of Manuel Thomé da Cunha and a native of Mathoím in Bahia. On her husband's death, she rented out her cane plantation for a guaranteed yearly income of 25$000 *reis*. Other widows or daughters who had inherited estates assumed responsibility for their management by themselves or in partnership with a relative or another male. Catharina Paes, after the death of her husband, André Lopes, continued to manage their estate, divided between two major areas in São Paulo. Total holdings comprised 224 cows, 4 oxen, 31 heifers, and 97 bullocks. That such examples were not merely a few entrepreneurial widows was shown by a seventeenth-century description of Pernambuco and Alagoas, which listed twenty-four women as cane growers. They comprised 17 percent of the total number of sharecroppers in that area. [66]

An outstanding example of a white female assuming control of her family's legal and financial affairs was Izabel Maria Guedes de Brito. She was the daughter of António Guedes de Brito of the house of Ponte, one of the "big five" landowners of the northeast in the seventeenth century, and the widow of António da Silva Pimentel, descendant of a leading Bahian plantation family. Development of the *sertão* as the result of the gold rush to Minas Gerais in the 1690s brought her landholdings under official scrutiny. Certain lands had been granted to her predecessors on the express condition that they should be cultivated. Failure to comply would lead to their disappropriation and redistribution. Governor António de Albuquerque Coelho de Carvalho charged that she had failed to cultivate lands that she owned in the Rio das Velhas area. His successor, Bras Balthazar da Silveira, claimed that her lands fell under his jurisdiction as governor of Minas Gerais rather than Bahia. Lengthy enquiries and lawsuits ensued. A French cleric, Felippe de LaContria, tried to usurp some holdings and threatened Dona Izabel's tenants. The powerful landowner Manuel Nunes Viana and his cousin Manuel Rodrigues Soares intervened nominally on behalf of Dona Izabel, but in reality sought to extend their own influence. Over several decades Dona Izabel firmly maintained that she had inherited these lands from her father, to whom they had been granted by the Crown in 1663 and 1684 in recognition of his having discovered and colonized them at their own cost, despite Amerindian attacks. Her determination triumphed. In 1718, 1720, and again in 1723 Dom João V ordered restitution of her property to Dona Izabel. Future colonization and settlement in that area were to respect her rights, and on no account were her tenants to be harassed by tax collectors.[67]

Occasionally, white women acted independently. In 1726 one league of land near the "new road" was granted to Izabel de Sousa at her request. Being recently widowed and having children, she had slight financial resources and intended to establish herself and support her family by raising cattle. Others maintained small-holdings and small stores and may even have engaged in black-market activities. In the 1760s Dona Ana Maria Barboza de Penha de França, a widow in Minas Gerais, revealed in a petition to the governor a thorough understanding of the economics of operating a gold mine that employed some seventy slaves. She asked that restraints be placed on trespassers cutting wood on her lands on the banks of the Rio das Velhas. She needed wood for making boxes, wheels, and axles as well as for working the placer mines in the river and for reconstructing aqueducts bringing water from as much as four leagues away.[68]

Economic interests and landholdings involved their female owners in such topical issues as land grants, division of judicial districts, and taxation. During the 1730s there was hostility throughout Minas Gerais at the collection of the royal "fifths" (*quintos*) by means of a capitation tax. In Papagaio in the hinterland of the Rio das Velhas this culminated in a revolt and an attack on the local judge. The evidence indicated that the revolt was the outcome of a conspiracy by powerful landowners and leading Paulista families with business interests in that area, rather than a truly popular uprising. Cited as conspirators in the official enquiry were Dona Maria da Cruz and her son Pedro Cardozo, the nephew of Domingos do Prado. In 1737 she and her son were arrested by the intendant of the royal treasury in Sabará, Dr. Manuel Dias Tôrres, who journeyed into the *sertão* accompanied by thirty dragoons. Family connections involved the leading families of Vila Rica and Sao Paulo, and one conspirator fled to the ranch in Jacobina of Dona Joanna Cavalcante, who came from a prominent family and was sympathetic to the cause.[69]

The White Female and Brazilian Colonial Society

In the absence of literary sources, diaries, chronicles, or personal correspondence it is difficult to assess the value systems of a society. Colonial Brazil is no exception to this rule and has been categorized as male dominated and patrilineal. New evidence suggests that in this mobile and precarious society the white female was regarded as a stabilizing factor and as the guardian of values that had originated in Europe, but had undergone modification in the tropics.

In their wills male testators gave preference for a variety of reasons to female survivors, be they widows, daughter, or nieces. Many such testators were not legally married or, if so, had no offspring. Frequently they had lost contact with wives and children, to say nothing of more distant relatives. When the time came to make their wills, "in fear of death," they were acutely conscious of two factors: the possibility of scurrilous claims being made against their wills and an abhorrence of the possibility (very real in a multiracial society) that a son or heir might have bastard children by a slave woman and that these should inherit. In preambles and dispositions of their wills many testators responded first to ideological precepts derived from Europe concerning "purity of blood" and second to a realistic assessment of the prevalent social mores in the colony. Even where there was a legitimate son to inherit, a testator would insist that inheritance of his possessions should be restricted to female descendants only. This favoring of the distaff side of a family casts the role of the woman in colonial Brazilian society in a wholly new dimension, as will be seen from the following examples. Diogo Fernandes (who died in 1621), a tertiary of Saint Francis and brother of the Misericórdia of Salvador, insisted in his will that only descendants on the distaff side should inherit his wealth or possessions. Another Bahian of the early seventeenth century, the bachelor Francisco Dias Baião, also disqualified the sons of his descendants from benefiting from his will and stipulated that only the daughters of such descendants could inherit. Another Bahian bachelor of the seventeenth century, António Dias de Ottões, allocated his considerable wealth for a variety of charitable purposes and for the saying of masses. While making legacies of 200$000 *reis* to each of his three sisters and allocating 200$000 *reis* for his nieces if they were legitimate and alive, he specifically ruled that no legacy should be made to his nephews. Felippe Correia, owner of a sugar plantation in Pituba, ruled in his will of 1650 that a trust be established so that dowries of 400$000 *reis* be available for the female offspring of his sisters. Beneficiaries were limited to female offspring of the distaff side only. Fear that a male descendant might dishonor the family was well expressed in the will of Jerónimo de Burgos and his wife, who instituted a charitable trust in 1664. Any sums left from such a trust were to go to their son, the Crown Judge Cristóvão de Burgos, and his descendants on the male side and, failing such, the female side. This legacy was made on the express condition that they should "not marry anybody tainted by the blood of the prohibited races." Such clauses suggest that the female was seen not only as the guardian of the social prestige of the family, but also as the preserver of ideals of purity of blood that were deeply rooted in white colonial society. [70]

Such considerations may in large part explain the enthusiasm shown by white colonists for the building of convents and retirement houses. That such convents housed sanctity, piety, and devotion is indubitable, and present-day historians ignore at their peril the strength of religious attitudes and practices prevailing in the colony. But the justification for such expenditures and the impetus leading to their construction were wholly secular. The townfolk of São Paulo requested in 1736 that the Retirement House of Santa Thereza de Jesús be given conventual standing. [71] In 1738 the governor and city council of Rio De Janeiro insisted how important it was that the city have a convent. Completion of the Convent of Nossa Senhora da Ajuda had been delayed because royal consent had contained a clause ruling that intending nuns would have to secure the approval of the Overseas Council in Lisbon. The local worthies had seen this as an insuperable barrier to gaining admittance for their daughters, and enthusiasm had waned. In 1736 two Capuchin friars had asked the king to allow them to occupy the empty and uncompleted shell. This spurred the city council to ask Dom João V to reject this request and throw his royal support behind the early completion of the building and its occupancy by Capuchin nuns. On his visit to Minas Gerais in 1743 the Bishop of Rio de Janeiro collected alms for this purpose. [72]

Equal enthusiasm was shown in the founding of retirement houses. Although wholly secular, such foundations were motivated by Christian sentiments and an awareness of the need for social charity. Best known was the Retirement House of the Most Holy Name of Jesus, opened in Salvador in 1716 under the auspices of the Misericórdia, and made possible by an endowment of 80,000 *cruzados* by the local philanthropist João de Mattos de Aguiar in 1700. This was exceptional, and most retirement houses were more modest. After the death of her husband, Sebastiana Pereira da Conceicão lived with her sister and two nieces in cloistral seclusion in a house in the parish of San Antônio além do Carmo in Salvador. Encouraged by promises, she petitioned the king for permission to establish a retirement house with fifteen girls. In 1757 the viceroy dampened such hopes in a report to the effect that the promised financial aid would never be forthcoming. He asked the king to refuse permission "especially because this city already has a great abundance of convents and retirement houses." [73] Finance was not the problem of the Italian Jesuit Gabriel de Malagrida, who founded a retirement house next to the Soledade Church in Salvador for poor women, prostitutes, and girls whose honor was endangered.

With entry fees ranging up to 3,000 *cruzados*, financial resources of the enterprise topped 90,000 *cruzados* by 1739. Granted conventual status, this institution was thereafter known as the Convent of the Ursulines. Wealthy colonists endowed such foundations. In 1787 the queen accepted a proposal by the miner António de Abreu Guimarães to set up a trust fund in the district of Sabará: this was destined for the building of three charitable institutions—a leprosarium, a seminary to bring up poor children, and a retirement house for needy girls. [74]

Both convents and retirement houses admitted paying residents for varying periods of time under the names of *educandas, recolhidas*, and *porcionistas*. Young girls of good parentage were placed in convents until they married or decided to take the vows. Retirement houses catered more to orphan girls of middle-class parentage whose honor might otherwise be jeopardized. Husbands also placed their wives in retirement houses while journeying to Portugal or making an expedition to the interior. Some husbands preferred to place a wayward wife in a retirement house rather than make a public issue of her adultery. Seclusion thus became an alternative to the finality of divorce. Finally, many widows or divorced women adopted such institutions as more or less permanent homes. Benefactors of retirement houses invariably ruled that the occupants should be "white, honorable, poor, and Old Christians." This also applied to convents. This makes all the more significant the request to Queen Maria by Anna Joaquina do Coração de Jesús, a mulatto (*parda*) native of Bahia, asking for royal approval to establish a Convent of the Immaculate Conception of the Mother of Christ for mixed-bloods. The queen ordered an enquiry in 1797, but there are no records to indicate the outcome of this petition. [75]

Convents and retirement houses afford an instance of collective female behavior, both in domestic affairs and in business management. For their patrimony such institutions depended largely on legacies or fees paid by the incumbents. This capital enabled them to engage in business operations. No banks existed in the colony, so it was to such convents that businessmen would come to request loans to finance their commercial ventures. One such businessman was José Ricardo Gomes, a Bahian who secured a loan of 7,000 *cruzados* from the Convent of the Poor Clares in 1793. By making such capital available, the convents played a vital role in the economy of the colony. Some convents traded in tobacco, sugar, and other commodities. Frequently these were the produce of plantations acquired as legacies or as the result of foreclosure for debts due to the conventual community. Retirement houses did not usually have so secure a financial base, but the Retirement House of Our Lady of the Conception of Macaubas near Sabará had cultivated so diligently a land grant on the banks of the Rio das Velhas granted by Governor Dom Bras Balthazar da Silveira (1713-17) that by 1725 the twenty recluses asked for a further six leagues of land in order to expand their cattle-ranching interests. [76]

The lay brotherhoods afforded another example of collective female action. Although women were not permitted to join such brotherhoods, governing bodies looked more favorably on applications by males when they were married. Barred from holding office, wives performed charitable works and helped in the decoration of the brotherhood's church at major festivals. Some brotherhoods followed the example of Nossa Senhora da Boa Morte in Salvador and reserved the title of "judge" (*juiza*) for female benefactors or ladies of noble birth. [77] In all cases brotherhoods assisted, to the best of their financial ability, the widow and offspring of a brother. A wife or widow was also entitled to the privilege of a funeral accompanied by members of the brotherhood and the saying of masses for her soul in the brotherhood's church.

It may well have been that it was in such convents and retirement houses that white females in the colony received an education and cultural upbringing otherwise denied to them. Opportunities in Brazil to gain an education were minimal for the male, let alone the female. Female offspring of wealthier families received private tuition in music and learned to read and write. But even at the highest levels of white society, illiteracy among women was not unusual. Henry Koster, who visited Brazil in the early nineteenth century, attributed this situation to the

ignorant state in which they are brought up; they scarcely receive any education, and have not the advantages of obtaining instruction from communication with persons who are unconnected with their own way of life, of imbibing new ideas from general conversation. . . . Bring these women forwards, educate them, treat them as rational, as equal beings; and they will be in no aspect inferior to their countrymen; the fault is not with the sex, but in the state of the human being. [78]

The stifling of intellectual curiosity and the lack of interest in cultural matters were matched by a similar indifference to personal appearances on the part of the white woman. From Johan Mauritz onwards, European visitors commented unfavorably on the sedentary life of the white woman in Brazil. On those rare occasions when she did leave her home, she was carried by slaves in an enclosed *palanquin*. Nor did the average white woman show any flair for fashion or for her own dress. Social and financial standing of women could lead to reservations concerning this generalization, as too could the standpoint of the individual observer. But no researcher can fail to be impressed by the small amount of personal clothing recorded in inventories of deceased females of good birth and of financial means. Apart from everyday wear of an embroidered chemise or smock, items listed in inventories might include a taffeta cloak, a burlap skirt, a loose or a sleeveless jacket, and cheap silk and satin petticoats. Any judgment must take into account two factors. The first was climate. Tropical heat, humidity, and the fact that the white woman was usually secluded in her home were inducements enough to wear the minimum of formal clothing. Furthermore, limitations were imposed by sumptuary laws (1749) intended to reduce expenditure on luxury items and to protect the Portuguese textile industry.

Conclusion

The role of the white female in colonial Brazil and her contribution to the life of the colony were circumscribed, and to some extent preordained, by tradition, law, and religious beliefs. But at no time was she divorced from the mainstream of colonial existence and reduced to mere marginality. Every aspect of colonial life was pervaded by a consciousness of her presence. Physically secluded she may have been and unable to realize her potential in the intellectual or political life of the colony, but she contributed to the building of Portuguese America despite such limitations.

The king, ecclesiastical authorities, viceroys, governors, town councillors, and colonists were perpetually concerned for the well-being of the white female. To each she held a particular importance. The Crown saw her presence as a stabilizing factor, the preserver of Lusitanian traditions and language, and a catalyst to curb the wanderings of restless and opportunist males. Moreover, the white woman was seen as the instrument of populating the vast expanses of Portuguese America, offsetting to some extent countless numbers of slave and free blacks. For the colonist, the white woman was wife and mother of his children, guaranteeing him a certain respectability within colonial society by the mere fact of being married. Moreover, marriage made him eligible for certain official positions denied to bachelors. To every Portuguese, be he king or colonist, the white woman was an object to be cherished and protected.

The idealism surrounding the white women did not mean that she was denied a decision-making capability independent of the male or that she was unable to set her own course of action. While not contravening the tenets of Pereira's moral treatise, some white females acted beyond the limits prescribed for them by the pilgrim. The evidence supports attribution to the white woman of a role that did not match the female stereotype so beloved of European visitors to colonial Brazil. As head of household she took up the reins of authority, raising and educating children and finally ensuring that they had a trade, vocation, or respectable position when the time came for them to leave home. Women managed estates and properties, involving themselves in the day-to-day workings of gold mines, cattle ranches, and sugar plantations. Thus did the white female make significant contributions to the society and economy of the colony.

The position of the white woman in Portuguese America differed from that of her counterparts in Spanish and English-speaking America. This was partly the result of different patterns of migration. Although there was a numerical predominance of males migrating from Spain to the New World, even during the first decade of the sixteenth century some 10 percent of all licenses granted were to women and wives accompanying their husbands.[79] Passenger lists in the Archivo General de Indias reveal an increase in the numbers of females migrating to the Spanish Indies, reaching 28.5 percent in the years 1560 to 1579 before declining in the last two decades of the sixteenth century.[80] Although miscegenation did occur in Spanish America no less extensively than in colonial Brazil, Spanish America possessed a larger proportion of white women than did Portuguese America for much of the colonial period. In the English colonies in North America—once allowances have been made for differing migration patterns between New England and Virginia or the Carolinas—the customary form of colonization was the family unit. It appears that in Spanish and English America the larger number of white women guaranteed a cultural continuity less in evidence in Portuguese America. Spanish and English were more widely spoken in the home, and the custom of handing over a child to a black nanny was less prevalent than in Brazil. It is possible that because of a less absolute dependence on slave labor, the Spanish- or English-born wife was more likely to champion the continuation of European customs, albeit in a New World environment. Finally, it appears that there was a lesser tendency on the part of the English or Spanish colonists in the New World to permit their cultural and linguistic heritage to become assimilated with, or dominated by, African and Amerindian life-styles and languages. In short, as the colonization and development of Portuguese America were to differ from other European colonies in the Americas, so too were the role and contribution of the white female in Portuguese America to be unique and distinctive.

Notes

ABBREVIATIONS

ACDB	Archives of the Convent of the Poor Clares, Salvador
AMB	Municipal Archives, Salvador
ANRJ	National Archives, Rio de Janeiro
APBOR	Public Archives of Bahia, Register of Royal Orders
APMCMOP	Public Archives of Minas Gerais, Registers of the Municipal Council of Vila Rica
APMSG	Public Archives of Minas Gerais, Registers of the Secretaria do Govêrno
ASCMB	Archives of the Santa Casa da Misericórdia, Salvador
BNRJ	National Library, Rio de Janeiro

This chapter is an expanded version of "Women and Society in Colonial Brazil," which appeared in *Journal of Latin American Studies* 9, no. 1; pp. 1-34. ©1977 Cambridge University Press.

1. On roles of Amerindian and black females, see Gilberto Freyre, *The Masters and the Slaves: A Study in the Development of Brazilian Civilization* (New York: A. A. Knopf, 1946). On black sources, see A. J. R. Russell-Wood, "Black and Mulatto Brotherhoods in Colonial Brazil: A Study in Collective Behavior," *Hispanic American Historical Review* 54 (November 1974), especially pp. 574-75 (hereafter cited as *HAHR*). Emilio Willems has discussed the Luso-Brazilian family in "The Structure of the Brazilian Family," *Social Forces* 31 (May 1953): 339-45, and "On Portuguese Family Structure," *International Journal of Comparative Sociology* 3 (September 1962); 65-79. Pioneering studies are by Maria Luiza Marcilio, *La Ville de São Paulo: Peuplement et population, 1750-1850* (Rouen: University of Rouen, 1972), and by Donald Ramos, "Marriage and the Family in Colonial Vila Rica," *HAHR* 55 (May 1975): 200-25.

2. A further factor was European-born Portuguese antipathy for Brazilian-born subjects, noted by Maria Graham in 1821: "The European Portugueze are extremely anxious to avoid intermarriage with born Brazilians, and prefer giving their daughters and fortunes to the meanest clerk of European birth, rather than to the richest and most meritorious Brazilian"; *Journal of a Voyage to Brazil and Residence there during part of the Years 1821, 1822, 1823* (London: Longman, 1824), p. 126.

3. In the early seventeenth century young women from the Retirement House of Madalena were sent to Bahia; *Documentos historicos da Bibliotheca Nacional do Rio de Janeiro*, 120 vols. (Rio de Janeiro, 1928-), 15: 250 (hereafter cited as *DHBNR*).

4. The council noted an overall two-thirds increase in the population of the city since 1665; Senado to King, 25 August 1717, AMB, 176, fols. 119v-20. Dom Pedro II rejected without explanation the governor-general's suggestion in 1695 that there be a royal ban on the practice of sending women from Brazil to Portugal or to the Atlantic islands of Madeira and the Azores to be nuns; APBOR, 4, doc. 108.

5. APMSG, 23, fols. 109-10; 32, fol. 105.

6. *Alvará* of 1 March 1732 and accompanying letter of 14 April 1732 to Governor of Rio de Janeiro, ANRJ codex 952, vol. 26, fols. 398, 400-1.

7. APMSG, 18, fol. 3A; 35, doc. 129.

8. Galvêas to King, 23 August 1733, APMSG, 35, doc. 129; and royal reply of 6 July 1735, AMPSG, 10, fol. 8.

9. APMSG, 10, fols. 75, 75-A; 38, fols. 10-11v.

10. ". . . q' não possa daqui em diante ser elleito vereador ou Juiz ordinario, nem andar na governança das villas dessa Capitania homen algum q' seja mullato dentro nos quatro graos em q' o mullatismo hé impedimento, e q' da mesma sorte não possa ser eleito, o q' não for cazado com mulher branca, ou viuvo della"; King to Dom Lourenço de Almeida, 27 January 1726, APMSG, 29, doc. 17. Similar prohibitions extended to military posts. In 1784 the Crown approved the governor of Bahia's dismissal from his post in the city's artillery regiment of Second Lieutenant António Gomes Viana, "por haver cazado com huma Mulher Preta, de costumes perversos, e escandalozos" ("because he has married a black woman, of perverse and scandalous behavior"); APBOR, 77, fol. 77. See A. J. R. Russell-Wood, "Colonial Brazil," in David W. Cohen and Jack P. Greene, eds., *Neither Slave Nor Free: The Freedmen of African Descent in the Slave Societies of the New World* (Baltimore: Johns Hopkins University Press, 1972), pp. 111-15.

11. APMSG, 50, fol. 46.

12. APMSG, 1, fols. 128, 192, 193, inter alia.

13. On dragoons, see APMCMOP, 6, fol. 18. Clerks in mints and smelting houses were similarly favored; APMSG, 13, fol. 33. On officers of the magistracy, see APMSG, 35, doc. 21, and Stuart B. Schwartz, "Magistracy and Society in Colonial Brazil," *HAHR* 50 (November 1970): 715-30.

14. Ruling of the Venerable Third Order of St. Dominic of Salvador, Tombo, vol. 2, fols. 208v-10, consulted in the order's archives. On brotherhoods, consult A. J. R. Russell-Wood, *Fidalgos and Philanthropists: The Santa Casa da Misericórdia of Bahia, 1550-1755* (Berkeley and Los Angeles: University of California Press, 1968), pp. 135-45; "Class, Creed, and Colour in Colonial Bahia: A Study in Prejudice," *Race* 9 (October 1967): 133-57; and "Black and Mulatto Brotherhoods."

15. APMSG, 23, fols. 101, 109-10; 32, fol. 105.

16. Andrada to Secretary of State, 23 August 1742, replying to an inquiry of 26 March 1742, APMSG, 78, fols. 33-34, 88-89.

17. APBOR, 115, fol. 120.

18. This opinion was often expressed; consult APMSG, 4, fols. 177-78; 11, fols. 40-41, 200-1; 23, fols. 6, 109-10; 32, fols. 86-88. In 1743 the king suggested that newly arrived colonists from the Atlantic islands be sent to the southern captaincies to provide foodstuffs and manpower in case of attack; APMSG, 81, doc. 42. Cf. APMSG, 78, fols. 33-34, 88-89; 82, fols. 88-89.

19. F. Froger, *Relation d'un voyage fait en 1695, 1696, & 1697 aux Côtes d'Afrique, Détroit de Magellan, Brezil, Cayenne & Isles Antilles*, 2d ed. (Paris: Nicolas Le Gras, 1700), pp. 136-37; Amédée François Frézier, *Relation du voyage de la mer du Sud aux côtes du Chily et du Perou, fait pendant les années 1712, 1713 & 1714* (Paris: Chez Jean Geoltroy, 1716), p. 275.

20. Thomas Lindley, *Narrative of a Voyage to Brazil* (London: J. Johnson, 1805), pp. 55, 138, 271-72; John Mawe, *Travels in the Interior of Brazil* (London: Longman, 1812), pp. 82-83, 281.

21. John Luccock, *Notes on Rio de Janeiro and the Southern Parts of Brazil* (London: S. Leigh, 1820), pp. 111-17, 189-90; Henry Koster, *Travels in Brazil* (London: Longman, 1816), pp. 24, 28, 48, 144-46, 181-82, 188-90, 388-89.

22. Mrs. Nathaniel Kindersley, *Letters from the Island of Teneriffe, Brazil, the Cape of Good Hope, and the East Indies* (London: J. Nourse, 1777), pp. 25-26, 31, 41-43; Maria Graham, *Journal*, pp. 135-37, 142, 166, 225-26, 308.

23. Fray Agostinho de Santa Maria, *Santuario Mariano, e historia das imagens milagrosas de Nossa Senhora*, 10 vols. (Lisbon: Officina de A. P. Galvão, 1707-23). On Marianism, see Charles R. Boxer, *Women in Iberian Expansion Overseas, 1415-1815* (New York: Oxford University Press, 1975), pp. 97-112, and Evelyn P. Stevens, "*Marianismo*: The Other Face of *Machismo* in Latin America," in Ann Pescatello, ed., *Female and Male in America: Essays* (Pittsburgh: University of Pittsburgh Press, 1974), pp. 89-101.

24. Nuno Marques Pereira, *Compendio narrativo do peregrino da America* (Lisbon: Officina de Manuel Fernandes da Costa, 1728). My account is based on chaps. 13, 14, and 19. In 1803 Lindley read this book and described it disparagingly as "merely an old moral tour in Brazil, conveying scarcely any real information"; *Narrative*, p. 139. For bibliographical details, consult Rubens Barba de Moraes, *Bibliografia brasileira do período colonial* (São Paulo: Instituto de Estudos Brasileiros, 1969), pp. 279-82.

25. King to Governor-General, 6 April 1702, APBOR, 7, doc. 15; ASCMB, 14, fol.

129; BNRJ, 11, 33, 24, 45, chap. 29.

26. ". . . e nenhuma Freyra possa ter Escrava que a ella particularmente sirva," ("and no nun may have a slave exclusively for her own needs"); ACDB, case 1, portfolio 1(i).

27. ACDB, case 3, portfolio U. Further details on this family and the daughters, one of whom (Maria de São Raimundo) became abbess in 1753, are in A. J. R. Russell-Wood, "Educação universitária no impêrio português: Relato de um caso luso-brasileiro do século dezassete," *Studia* 36 (July 1973): 7-38.

28. ". . . porq' estes Americanos reputão os seus negros por semiDeoses" ("because these Americans regard their blacks as they would their demigods"); Assumar to Crown Judge of Rio das Velhas, 1 January 1721, APMSG, 13, fol. 13. Koster, *Travels*, pp. 388, 390.

29. ASCMB, Tombo, vol. 1, fols. 167-68; Tombo, vol. 2, fols. 46-47.

30. Departamento do Arquivo do Estado de São Paulo, *Inventarios e testamentos; papeis que pertenceram ao l° cartorio de orfãos da capital: Documentos da secção do arquivo histórico*, 50 vols. (São Paulo: Typ. Piratininga, 1920-), 23: 227-307; ASCMB, Tombo, vol. 1, fols. 44-45; Tombo, vol. 2, fols. 46-47.

31. King to Dom Lourenço de Almeida, 9 July 1725, APMSG, 20, doc. 113.

32. Pereira, *Compendio narrativo*, p. 180.

33. APBOR, 58, fols. 315-440; Luis Edmundo da Costa, *Rio in the Time of the Viceroys* (Rio de Janeiro: J. R. de Oliveira, 1936), pp. 319-21.

34. Russell-Wood, *Fidalgos and Philanthropists*, p. 332; APBOR, 109, fols. 151-53.

35. APBOR, 23, doc. 109; 25, doc. 36.

36. ". . . e como se achão as cabeças de familias com dinhr^o. p^a dotes de suas filhas, não cuidão em outra couza senão em as mandarem p^a freyras, ou p^a as Ilhas, ou p^a Portugal e por nenhum cazo as querem cazar, porq' he m^{to} proprio da gente de baxo nascim^{to} o fazer as filhas freiras" ("and once the heads of the families have funds enough with which they could endow their daughters, their only thought is to send them to Portugal or to the Atlantic islands to be nuns. Under no circumstances do they wish their daughters to marry, because among people of humble birth, it is held very fitting for their daughters to become nuns"); Governor to King, 5 June 1731, APMSG, 32, fol. 105. On Quiteria Teixeira, see APMSG, 77, doc. 148 and acc docs.; 78, fol. 63v.

37. Petition of 4 August 1736, APMSG, 63, docs. 20, 21. On the refusal to admit blacks, see Russell-Wood, "Women and Society," n. 23, and "Colonial Brazil," pp. 111-12.

38. APBOR, 19, docs. 159, 159a; 22, doc. 29; 54, fols. 225-32v; 57, fol. 342; 75, fol. 188.

39. APBOR, 37, docs. 13, 13a; 38, doc. 92; 69, doc. 33.

40. Senado to King, 25 August 1717, AMB, 176, fols.119v-20.

41. APBOR, 46, docs. 1, 1a, 1b; ACDB, case 1, portfolios 4, 32, 36. In order to help evaluate the cost of these dowries, compare this sum to the annual salary of some employees of the Santa Casa de Misericórdia in Bahia. In 1690, a priest earned 40$000 *reis*; a lawyer, 70$000 *reis*; and a nurse, 16$000 *reis*. See Russell-Wood, *Fidalgos and Philanthropists*, p. 380. See also Harold B. Johnson, "A Preliminary Inquiry into the Money, Prices, and Wages in Rio de Janeiro, 1763-1823," in Dauril Alden, ed., *Colonial Roots of Modern Brazil* (Berkeley and Los Angeles: University of California Press, 1973), pp. 231-83.

42. *Inventarios e testamentos*, 24: 13-67; ASCMB, Tombo, vol. 1, fols. 143v-53.

43. *DHBNR*, 16: 142-48; 26: 451-53.

44. APMSG, 30, fols. 104v-5.

45. APBOR, 105, fols. 205-7.

46. APBOR, 107, fols. 312-15.

47. Russell-Wood, *Fidalgos and Philanthropists*, pp. 173-200.

48. Ramos, "Marriage and the Family," 207-9, 212-15, 218; Marcilio, *La Ville de São Paulo*, pp. 170, 187 (figures based on the overall free population).

49. APMSG, 38, fols. 13-14; Resolution of the governing body of the Misericórdia of 1 November 1653, ASCMB, Livro 1 de Acórdãos, vol. 1, fol. 42. See also Dauril Alden, "The Population of Brazil in the Late Eighteenth Century: A Preliminary Survey," *HAHR* 43 (May 1963): 173-205.

50. ASCMB, Acórdãos, vol. 4, fols. 30v-31; Marcilio, *La Ville de São Paulo*, pp. 125-26; Ramos, "Marriage and the Family," pp. 209-11.

51. *Inventarios e testamentos*, 7: 376-78; 10: 99-134; 17: 93-111.

52. Thales de Azevedo, *Povoamento da Cidade do Salvador* (São Paulo: Companhia Editora Nacional, 1955), pp. 204-6; Marcilio, *La Ville de São Paulo*, p. 204.

53. *Inventarios e testamentos*, 9: 89-105; 24: 245-93.

54. Marcilio, *La Ville de São Paulo*, pp. 191-92. This refers to all recorded marriages, regardless of color or civil status.

55. Ramos, "Marriage and the Family," pp. 207, 215-16, 218-21. On his arrival in Rio de Janeiro, Luccock cited 4,000 females at the head of families; *Notes on Rio de Janeiro*, p. 41.

56. ASCMB, Tombo, vol. 2, fols. 108v-9v; APBOR, 17, docs. 14, 14a, 14b, 75, fols. 281-86.

57. APMSG, 54, fol. 129.

58. APMSG, 46, docs. 42-45; 10, fol. 28; APBOR, 22, docs. 24, 24a.

59. APMSG, 4, fols. 222v-24; APMCMOP, 9, fols. 5v-6v, 9v-10v, 57-62; 37, fols. 2-3, 46, 59-60, 81, 82, 99-100v.

60. APBOR, 78, fol. 50; APMSG, 20, doc. 82. On 19 June 1793 the Crown sharply reprimanded the *provedor* of Sabará for unjustifiable delays in settling estates; APMSG, 19, doc. 149.

61. APBOR, 115, fols. 97-107v.

62. APBOR, 3, doc. 81.

63. *Inventarios e testamentos*, 7: 427; 19: 293.

64. *Inventarios e testamentos*, 16: 370; 19: 231-41, 262.

65. *Inventarios e testamentos*, 19: 5-39; 20: 6, 354. Russell-Wood, *Fidalgos and Philanthropists*, pp. 182-84.

66. ASCMB, Tombo, vol. 2, fols. 85v-87v, 248-51; *Inventarios e testamentos*, 24: 245-93; Stuart B. Schwartz, "Free Labor in a Slave Economy: The Lavradores de Cana of Colonial Bahia," in Alden, *Colonial Roots*, pp. 178-79.

67. The case is exhaustively documented in APMSG, 4, fols. 37, 215-18, 224, 225v, 229v-31; 5, fols. 69, 84v-85; 11, fols. 58, 86-91, 94-99v, 136v, 277-78, 285v-86; 14, fol. 68; 20, doc. 73; APBOR, 17, doc. 35; 18, doc, 1a; 21, doc. 29.

68. APMSG, 28, fol. 150; 60, fols. 59-60v.

69. APMSG, 44, fols. 126-27v, 149, 151-56v; 57, fols. 52v-53; 61, fol. 13.

70. ASCMB, Tombo, vol. 1, fols. 23v-28v, 28v-33v; Tombo, vol. 2, fols. 24-29,

97v-98v; Acórdãos, vol. 3, fols. 243v-45.

71. APMSG, 63, docs. 20, 21.

72. Ibid., 66, fols. 159-62v; 82, fols. 162-63.

73. Russell-Wood, *Fidalgos and Philanthropists*, pp. 320-36. Viceroy to King, 20 October 1757, APBOR, 58, fols. 563-65. A resolution of the Overseas Council of 24 September 1738 had forbidden admittance of further novices in the Province of St. Anthony of the Capuchins until the numbers of friars was down to 200. On the recommendation of the viceroy, this order was relaxed by a resolution of 20 May 1740, placing the limit at 400; APBOR, 37, doc. 63; 52, fols. 34r-36r.

74. APBOR, 48, fols. 184-85; 54, fols. 14, 46-47; 78, fols. 36-43.

75. Ibid., 83, fol. 272v.

76. ACDB, case 1, portfolio 37; APMSG, 28, fols. 142-43; 59, fol. 22v-23. See Susan Soeiro's essay, chap. 6 in this volume. See also her article "The Social and Economic Role of the Convent: Women and Nuns in Colonial Bahia, 1677-1890," *HAHR* 54 (May 1974): 209-33.

77. Agostinho de Santa Maria, *Santuario Mariano*, vol. 9, bk. 1, title 13, pp. 38-39.

78. Koster, *Travels*, p. 388; see also Luccock, *Notes on Rio de Janeiro*, p. 111.

79. Magnus Mörner, *Race Mixture in the History of Latin America* (Boston: Little, Brown, 1967), pp. 15-16; James Lockhart, *Spanish Peru, 1532-1560: A Colonial Society* (Madison: University of Wisconsin Press, 1968), p. 163, inter alia.

80. The high percentage of single females is significant. See Peter Boyd-Bowman, "Patterns of Spanish Emigration to the Indies until 1600," *HAHR* 56 (November 1976): 596-601.

Elinor C. Burkett

3

Indian women and white society: the case of sixteenth-century Peru

Andean colonial history as written by modern authors has been pitifully devoid of the stamp of the common people. In the maze of earthshaking events, from the discovery to the rebellion of Manco Inca, and in the tangle of such famous names as Pizarro and Atahualpa, the tramps and dreamers, the foot soldiers and small farmers, and even the working people have been lost. Only recently has any effort been made to fill this void, as historians attempt to humanize our view of slaves, artisans, and little people of all stripes.[1] But even as the common man begins to take shape and claim his rightful place in Andean history, the common woman, indeed, even the uncommon woman, remains faceless.

What writing has been done about women is both sexist and shallow. Women have been shunted aside as insignificant by authors whose prejudices are now becoming clear as we realize that insignificance often lies more in the eyes of the beholders than in the reality that they seek to recapture. This study is an attempt to discern the impact of Spanish colonization on the indigenous female and the impact of the indigenous female on Spanish colonization. In so doing I am not only introducing new material, but also exposing old material to a new subjectivity, one with a clear bias toward the forgotten female. I am trading the traditional prejudice that all women, but especially Indian women, had relatively little impact on colonial development for the bias that women, despite (or perhaps because of) their exploitation by the white male-dominated society, were major actors on the stage of colonial Peru.[2]

The material on which this study of indigenous women facing Hispanic colonization is based is part of a larger work including all groups of women in that society. Since the Andean women most involved in the colonial experience were urban, primary attention will be given to those females who left their traditional communities. The sources range from notarial records to court cases, from royal licenses to inquisition papers. While the data involve all of Peru, the focal center is Arequipa. This was a deliberate choice made in the belief that Lima, the most atypical urban center, has too long dominated the historical scene and too long been virtually the sole focus of studies that purport to deal with colonial Peru.

Andean Women in Their Traditional Society

The position of women in preconquest Andean society was determined by the forms and culture of that society as a whole.[3] Under Inca rule, Andean peoples were organized into a rigid social order in which positions were assigned by the political aristocracy. There was little escape. A person was born in a village, was raised in the traditional manner, worked as ordered by the local elite and central bureaucracy, contributed the allotted tribute of goods and services, married at the designated age, reproduced, was provided for in her or his old age, and died, all according to ritual, custom, and order.

Despite the much-discussed collective nature of landholding in Inca society, it is more appropriate to consider that land (the means of production) was controlled by the central state and subdivided into parcels allotted to clan-like organizational units, the *ayllus*. Individuals gained access to the land through membership in the community, and in turn the community members had the obligation to pay tribute to the central state and the aristocracy by cultivating the lands of the Inca and the Sun, by giving their service to the State, and by paying assigned taxes in goods. Rights and obligations were key in this situation; "the two factors are linked: in accordance with the principle of reciprocity, the tributary obligation and the right to communal land are inseparable."[4]

In all agricultural areas there were three basic types of tribute payments: tribute in agricultural goods, in service, and in textiles. It is clear that in the first two types of tribute, women had no obligation since such work was primarily the responsibility of men from twenty-five to fifty. However, the status of women vis-à-vis the textile tribute is somewhat more difficult to assess, since spinning and weaving were primarily female occupations.

Because tribute was assigned to able-bodied men over the age of twenty-five, it is too easy to conclude that women were not considered citizens, were denied access to the means of production, and thus occupied a decidedly inferior position. In this discussion the concept of tribute payments is the fundamental issue, though one frequently misunderstood.[5] We might approach a clearer understanding of indigenous society by considering tribute as a household— rather than an individual—obligation, with the male viewed as its representative. Viewing the household as the basic economic unit of Inca society, in terms of both rights and obligations, we must then conclude that individual rights and obligations were subordinate. All households of common people were equal. Any differentiations between male and female labor can be made only from an examination of the internal division of labor within the household.

Male activities included service to the State and major agricultural work, while female activity consisted of spinning and weaving for household use and for tribute; gathering of fuel, herbs, and fruits; preparing food; bearing and raising children; caring for animals; and participating in planting, harvesting, and selling grains and other produce. There was a sharp sexual division of labor within the productive unit of the household: activities were decidedly different. The relative importance of these tasks is in a sense irrelevant, since they were all critical and interdependent. In such "primitive" societies the "basic problem is survival, and to achieve this end the combined efforts of man and women are equally required. . . . Although it may be true, as Margaret Mead says, that whatever tasks are assigned to the menfolk of the community are by common consent considered more important, the fact remains that all tasks are essential and everyone knows it."[6]

Marriage customs have been viewed by modern anthropologists as important indicators of the position of women in society. Traditionally, they have advanced the culturally narrow interpretation that the existence of bridewealth (marriage payment from groom to bride's father) is evidence that women were bought, that they were considered to be little more than chattel. However, modern scholars, primarily Ester Boserup and Jack Goody, have contended that bridewealth is indicative of active female economic participation, while the existence of a strong dowry system demonstrates a low evaluation of the economic importance of female activities.[7] Bridewealth payments must be seen as acknowledgment of the value of women, of the importance of their economic and practical contribution to their families, and thus as compensation to the natal family for the loss of an economically active member of that productive unit. Thus, the fact that the payment of bridewealth was an integral feature of Andean American customs suggests an implicit societal recognition of the importance of female economic activities.

Discussion of inheritance customs also suggests an important perspective on the situation of women, for they are key indicators of class patterns and transmission of the ownership of the means of production. But in this arena Andean society stands apart from a classic Western scheme due to the unusual type of land ownership. Because there was no private property, there was nothing to be transmitted. The only major type of inheritance involved political positions, which never passed to women despite the fact that lineage was traced through them.[8] Analysis of inheritable offices is outside the bounds of this discussion.

The roles and responsibilities of females, as of males, were assigned by the central bureaucracy, and individuals had virtually no control over their social and economic movement. Alternatives for both sexes were extremely circum-scribed. For men, alternatives were based on particular heroism or talent in military arts; for women, the avenue was beauty.

Beauty meant the chance to be selected to enter one of the *casas de recogi-miento* of the empire.9 There were several orders of houses, divided both by the class of the inhabitants and by the degree of their beauty. The women lived controlled and isolated lives, dedicating themselves to domestic chores and food preparation for themselves and members of the royal family. These wo-men were especially reserved as property of the Inca himself. The highest cate-gory consisted of something akin to the personal concubines of the Inca and his favorites. The other houses contained women destined to be given as rewards to governors, soldiers, *curacas*, and other servants of the emperor. The Inca thus rewarded a vassal not only with beauty, but with another economically active adult for his household.

The women who occupied a totally unique position were the Virgins of the Sun, the royal nuns of the empire, selected for their special beauty. These women were brought from all four provinces of the empire at a very young age in order to ensure their virginity. They were dedicated to the service and wor-ship of the supreme god, the Sun, and prepared clothing for idols and food and drink for sacrifice. They were not cloistered, despite the importance of chas-tity, for they were said to have been so revered that no one would dare touch them.10

This type of life, however, was in no sense a real alternative, because the in-dividual woman exercised no control over it. Either she was born beautiful or she was not; either she was selected or was not; she had no option to refuse. This role, as all other roles in Inca society, was determined by the State.

The position of the women of the Inca royal family is difficult to assess. Padre Murúa, like most of the chroniclers, contends that while the *ñustas* and *pallas* were politically influential, they were nonetheless legally powerless.11 Yet other documentation raises doubts about these conclusions. Inés Huayllas Yupanqui, consort of Francisco Pizarro, brought suit for return of an *en-comienda*, claiming to be mistress of the Indians of the province of Guaylas.12 In support of this claim, she cited her mother, Contargache, one of the wives of Huayna Capac, as mistress of this province at the time of the Spanish arrival. The control that Contargache exercised over Guaylas was exhibited by her ordering indigenous troops to Lima in support of the Spanish during the revolt of Manco Inca. It is unclear whether this provincial political power dated only from the Spaniards or whether it was part of her Inca traditional position.13

Finally, we need to consider the sexual balance in the pre-Columbian popu-lation. Demographic studies of this region have been attempted during recent years, but there is, as yet, no study as complete and accurate as that done by Woodrow W. Borah and the "Berkeley group" for the central valley of Mex-ico.14 However, preliminary figures indicate that there was a serious demographic imbalance. Among the Aymaras and Urus of the Lake Titicaca region there were approximately four times as many women as men in the population over forty-five years of age. In the coastal and low mountain region of southern Peru, adult females outnumbered males by more than two to one.[15] The indications are that there was an extraordinarily high number of widows. The reasons for such imbalance are extraneous to this discussion, but its implications for the postconquest period are enormous.

Inca society was clearly patriarchal, for power was concentrated in the hands of an all-male political elite, dominated by a male ruler. Yet among those who wielded no influence, the common people, women were economically active in trading, herding, spinning, weaving, gardening, and farming. The Andean female, as the Andean male, was assigned a role in her world by custom and political decision that made her work an essential and integral part of community survival.

The Conquest

Discussions of the initial relationships between the Spanish conquerors and indigenous women are usually confined to the lack of prejudice on the part of the Spaniards and the sensual nature of the women. Magnus Mörner, one of the few historians to reject these myths, rather says: "The satisfaction of a natural instinct should not be confused with social and aesthetic attitudes."[16] Yet even Mörner does not carry the analysis far enough, for the relationship between Spanish men and Indian women must be viewed as part of the total conquest and, indeed, part of the very meaning of conquest.

An intrinsic part of conquest—the act of overcoming or gaining possession and control of a people and the territory that they inhabit—is violence. It is in this light that the rape of indigenous women must be seen, as a type of violent behavior intended to subjugate and oppress. The act of rape implicitly says: I am your master; you must submit to me, or I will force my will upon you. In that, it is symbolic of the very conquest itself. To view the individual case of rape as a desperate action of a sex-starved man, as does Mörner, is to miss the point, for viewed collectively, the rape of Indian women was an integral part of the drive for submission that characterizes all conquest.

This is not to deny the existence of willing women, although it is impossible to know the extent to which willingness was based on general submission to the conquerors as conquerors rather than to the conquerors as individually attractive men. Nor is this to deny the fact that there were instances in which local leaders gave their daughters or members of their communities to the Spaniards as tokens of friendship. Indeed, these actions would seem to extend the point, for they are exemplary of tribute paid to new masters.

The conquerors also used their relationships with Indian women, and even marriage to them, to consolidate and confirm the hegemony acquired through their violence. Indeed, the Spaniards quickly realized that through marriage to Inca *pallas*, their children would gain position of leadership in indigenous society for themselves and thus, by extension, for the Spanish. The extent of this realization is obvious when one notes that Spanish conquerors married every daughter of Huayna Capac, the Inca who died on the eve of the Spanish conquest. The specific advantages of such a policy emerge from individual case studies.

Mancio Sierra de Leguizamo took as his mistress Beatriz Huayllas Nusta, daughter of Huayna Capac and thus sister to Manco Inca. Diego Fernández noted that in the 1550s "in Cuzco, where she resided, there was no surviving lord, male or female, as important as she." In 1555, Spanish Viceroy Don Andrés Hurtado de Mendoza enlisted her aid in ending the Indian rebellion begun by her brother Manco Inca in 1536 and continued by her nephew, Sayri Tupac Inca. With her assistance, as well as that of her son by Mancio Sierra, negotiations were undertaken with the rebel leader and Sayri Tupac was convinced to surrender.[17] As a *mestizo*, with direct relationships to both sides, Doña Beatriz's son had been the perfect intermediary. Thus, the new generation created through Spanish-Indian relationships was of basic political importance in the contacts between the two societies.

The advantages were based on material rewards as well as influence, for indigenous noblewomen claimed control over extensive territory and Indians. The example above of Inés Huayllas Yupanqui is a case in point. After bearing two children in free union with Francisco Pizarro, she married Francisco de Ampuero, a conqueror who later was both city councilman (*regidor*) and mayor (*alcalde*) of Lima. As her husband, Ampuero claimed the right to control the Indians of Guaylas—*her* Indians—as their *encomendero*. He lost this claim when Pizarro granted those Indians instead to his daughter by Inés, Francisca Pizarro. But the lands and Indians still were not lost to direct Spanish control, for Hernando Pizarro, half-brother of Francisco, married his niece Francisca, thus consolidating all Pizarro family holdings in Peru and gaining control over the Guaylas Indians for himself and the Spanish.[18]

Such political calculations were not reserved to the Spaniards, but formed a part of Indian strategy as well. Indigenous reasoning seems to have been that through establishment of kinship relationships with the conquerors, either through marriage or through bearing of children in free union, the Indians would thus improve their position. Garcilaso de la Vega described one side of the situation: "In those early times when the Indians saw an Indian woman giving birth to the child of a Spaniard, all her relatives joined together to respect and serve the Spaniard as an idol because he had become their kin."[19] The other side of the coin was, of course, the expectation of equal respect on the part of the Spaniard. This was the weakness of the Indian strategy, for while the indigenous peoples saw kinship as based on equality and mutual respect, the Spanish appear to have adopted such an attitude only when the kin concerned were white.

Such calculations around marriage were confined to the upper echelons of indigenous society and thus had little impact on the average woman. These women, however, were politically crucial to the Spaniards as well. It was through close contacts with Indian women that the Spaniards began their understanding of local languages and acquired translators; it was from such women that they learned about the social and political organization of local communities, of fights and weaknesses that facilitated both conquest and consolidation of control. It was through relationships with these women that the Spaniards ate and traveled and were guided.[20]

But the gains were not totally one-sided, and it would be naive to believe that indigenous women provided multiple services to the Spanish from pure love and altruism. Selfish motives cannot be forgotten as one considers the benefits accrued by association with the white rulers: escape from confining situations, sense of importance, material reward. And one wonders whether there were not political motives as well, for if the Spaniards could learn about Indian society through association with indigenous women, then Indian women could also gain considerable knowledge of Hispanic society and customs that might prove advantageous to their society.

The Early Colony

With the benefit of hindsight, we can look back on the period of Spanish conquest and consolidation and note the enormous changes wrought in the fabric of native society. Many Indians died and whole villages were destroyed, reconstituted, and moved; new crops and agricultural techniques were introduced; a new religion and its ethical and moral code were implanted and pushed and often enforced; changes in tribute demands, coupled with demographic disaster, modified the pattern of life and social organization throughout the Andes.

But the impact of these changes was uneven. For some who remained in traditional villages, life might well have appeared to continue in remarkable continuity, although for others the world became a totally new experience. Indigenous women fell largely into the latter category. The point should not be overstated: there were many men whose lives changed considerably under the new regime, and many women whose lives changed very slightly. But on the whole the conquest appears to have been considerably more disruptive for rural females than for rural males.

There were two major reasons for this difference. The first involved modification of tribute requirements under the Spanish. The Inca tribute system had been based on the household unit, apparently taking into consideration the internal division of labor within the household that allowed the male the freedom to undertake major agricultural work almost exclusively because of the household, herding, and textile activities of female household members. For most individuals the system changed little under the Spaniards, modified perhaps in content, but not in form. However, this was not the case with widowed women, a group that was disproportionately large, as we have seen above.

The tribute obligations of these women under the Incas are unclear. Such women, as others of both sexes who were old or infirm, were provided for by the *ayllu*. Thus, if they were subject to tribute obligations, such labor did not interfere with their work to maintain themselves, since this was a community responsibility. However, during the period of Spanish consolidation, the *ayllu* system of maintenance of the aged and infirm broke down in many regions, as men were forced into the mines and the population declined rapidly. Under the Spanish tribute system, widows had heavy obligations in cloth, animal, and even agricultural produce and labor. Because these women were no longer supported by the community, such tribute assessments were burdens added to their struggle for basic maintenance.

The situation, of course, varied from village to village. But the case in Canchapara is illustrative of the general pattern. According to the 1562 census of the province of Huánuco, the village had thirteen tributary households, seven of which were headed by widows. One woman had no yearly tribute obligations because of advanced age. Another provided four two-ounce balls of cotton thread, and the third provided an equal amount of thread as well as an occasional chicken. The fourth provided these same items and six *ycangas* of potatoes, while the fifth provided one ball of thread, one chicken, and some potatoes. The sixth woman wove one *pierna* of cloth and gave nine *almudes* of corn, half a *fanega* of potatoes, and a chicken. The last woman contributed five balls of thread, three chickens, and four to six days of work in the fields. To make the weight of those obligations clear, one needs to measure them against those of males. For themselves and their wives the four married men were each assessed one and one-half pieces of cotton clothing, one-half *fanega* of corn, an equal amount of potatoes, one chicken, and approximately sixteen days of agricultural work. The only widower in the village contributed one piece of cotton clothing, one-half *fanega* of corn, one and one-half *fanegas* of potatoes, and three days of labor. Thus, widowed women, who made up just over 40 percent of the adult labor force, were providing three-quarters of the corn, one-half of the footage of cloth, about one-third of the potatoes, two-thirds of the chickens, two-thirds of the thread, and a small portion of the day labor. [21] While this was clearly a village with an exceedingly high number of widows, the percentage of the tribute that they provided, considering their numbers, was not unusual.

In 1575, Viceroy Toledo modified this tribute system, taking much of the pressure off these women. On 11 November he ordered that women married to tributary Indians not be required to pay tribute because they needed to work to serve their families. All taxation of widows was abolished. [22] However, by this time the basic harm had been done. Excessive tribute demands not only oppressed the women saddled with them, but also succeeded in forcing a disproportionate number of indigenous women off the land and into urban centers.

The second major change in the lives of village women was in the character of the labor demands, both legal and illegal, made by the *encomenderos*. [23] Traditional labor levies in Inca society were confined to males, who were used in road building, construction, maintenance, and the like. Thus, Spanish demands for women for personal service were a new element in that society. A key question, of course, is the meaning of personal service. On a legalistic basis, such service meant cooking, cleaning, sewing, and performing other household tasks. Yet it would appear, if from no other evidence than the number of children whom Indian women bore by these masters, that service included sexual duties as well.

While the lives of most men and many women in traditional villages continued on as only slightly changed from their preconquest patterns, those of both males and females who ceased to work in such traditional settings were severely disrupted. Individuals were displaced and found themselves in cities that appeared alien, walking among beings whose physical presence was foreign, whose manners and thoughts were senseless, and whose tongue was unknown. The extent of the movement away from villages is virtually impossible to calculate, at least at this state of historical demographic knowledge. It is clear only that at least as many indigenous women as men, if not more, entered the Hispanic urban world. [24]

What is more accessible is the motives behind such mobility among females. The reasons for leaving were compelling: the population balance of sexes was poor, and thus opportunities for marriage were limited; tributes were exceedingly burdensome, especially prior to 1575; the cities offered new opportunities and new horizons that, if in hindsight appear poor, nonetheless were appealing at the time.

The concept of a woman's leaving her village, her family, and her security to head off across the mountains to an alien city seems terrifying to many a modern female; it might well have provoked similar emotions at the time. The fact that hundreds of women did just this is testimony to the burdens of village life and the lure of the cities. The change, however, was probably not so totally abrupt as it might seem, for it was unlikely that a woman in Guayaquil decided to leave and travel to Potosí. Migration was probably gradual, and the immediate goal was usually to a nearby city. The pattern might have been similar to that of modern-day migration, in which movement from village to town is then followed by further movement from town to city and then perhaps even from city to city. Undoubtedly, many of these female migrants traveled along with groups of Spanish explorers and travelers. We must also consider that much of this emigration was involuntary and that many women were simply carried along by traveling Spaniards.

The most outstanding, if atypical, example of such involuntary movement was enslavement. Much has been written about Spanish attitudes toward slavery and about the realities thereof. However, little mention is made of the royal prohibition on enslavement of women.[25] Further, historians appear to have concluded that Andeans were not enslaved. The information is extremely scanty, but there are indeed records in the Archives of the Indies in Seville that demonstrate the existence of such slavery. The most striking feature of this data is that all the slaves mentioned were female. They were enslaved in the 1530s and 1540s and taken by Spanish men to Seville. Some were sold and others were retained in the personal service of their captors until the mid-1550s, when the prosecutor of the Council of the Indies began to press for their emancipation.[26] It is significant that the emancipation was not general, but was granted individual-by-individual in court actions. The numbers of women involved were extremely limited; there are less than a dozen such cases extant. However, it is reasonable to assume that many slaves were freed without court action and that many, especially those living outside of Seville, were not freed at all.

But this is an extreme example, and clearly the mobility of Indian women in Peru was in no sense so totally involuntary. More common indeed was the situation of the woman taken by a Spaniard to the city, or sent into his service from a tributary village, and then prevented or discouraged from leaving. In some instances the prohibition was tantamount to enslavement; in others the attitude of the Spaniard coupled with the situation of the indigenous women—alone, far from her village, and penniless—made leaving difficult.

This situation was of great concern to the Crown since it involved both the issue of virtual enslavement of Indians and, tacitly, the issue of sexual exploitation. Thus, as early as October 1541, the king noted that he had been informed that Spaniards "have a large number of Indian women in their houses in order to carry out their evil wants with them" and ordered that "no Spaniard may have in his house a suspicious or pregnant Indian or Indian mother," except those necessary for cooking and service.[27] The ineffectiveness of such decrees is witnessed by their reiteration throughout the period.

A particularly marked aspect of this question is the geographical range of mobility. Entries in notarial records mention the place of origin of each Indian. In such records for sixteenth-century Arequipa, it is not uncommon to find an Indian woman from Guayaquil, Chicapoyas, or Quito, thousands of miles away, not to mention those from the closer regions of Cuzco, Huánuco, and Chucuito. And one should recall that Arequipa was no huge urban center, no great magnet of wealth and adventure. The records of Potosí are even more marked in this respect, and it is clear that the mines were a lure for Indians from all over the viceroyalty. [28]

There were, then, large numbers of indigenous women who abandoned their villages and traditional life to cast their lots with the Iberian-dominated urban society. The picture of them reflected in modern histories is of a few women serving the Spaniards as domestics and, perhaps, prostitutes. This is extremely deceiving, however, for it portrays the female Indian as a marginal person, as a person living on the fringes of society and contributing little, if anything, to economic activities. Indigenous women, then as now, supplied the bulk of the household labor force as cooks, maids, and nursemaids. They dominated the marketplace and ran numerous small shops and businesses, dispensing groceries and prepared foods, selling silver objects and wax. The importance of these activities and the impact that they had on that society should not be underestimated.

The household servants were a diverse group ranging from resident mistresses (often existing alongside a Spanish wife) to contract laborers. This last group is the most visible to the historian, for the contracts are extant in notarial records of that period. [29] In an average year in the late sixteenth century, eighteen or nineteen such contracts appear in the book of each of the three major notaries of Arequipa. There were probably about five hundred Spanish households in the city by that time, each with at least one and, in most cases, several servants. Thus, it appears that less than 10 percent, and probably as few as 5 percent, of the indigenous servants were legally contracted for. Remuneration for service always included room, board, medicine, religious instruction, and two sets of woolen or cotton clothing per year. Annual salaries were fixed by law at twelve *pesos corrientes* for domestics under eighteen years of age and eighteen *pesos corrientes* for those over eighteen. [30] However, actual pay ranged from six to thirty *pesos corrientes*, with the high salaries usually going to wet nurses (in constant demand) or women of royal descent; the usual salary was twelve *pesos*. The worth of such salaries is thrown into some perspective when one notes that two thirteen-ounce loaves of bread cost one-eighth of a *peso*; a *fanega* of corn, three to five *pesos*; and a llama, two and one-half *pesos*. There are no instances of contract renewals in the notarial records of Arequipa, and it is probable that service continued on the same terms without legal renewal.

In these contracts, responsibilities and obligations were rarely spelled out. In virtually all instances the contract mentioned only that the worker would serve the employer in and out of her or his household. Only in the cases of women being hired specifically as nursemaids or wet nurses is the exact nature of the job made clear. It is important to note that this was true of the contracts for personal service of Indian men as well and that salaries for both sexes were virtually identical. [31]

The Crown was apparently quite concerned about the treatment of female household servants. Proclamations were issued continually dealing with their freedom, their separation from their husbands, the importance of their Christian education, and their general treatment. One issued in Madrid on 18 October 1569 and directed to the Audiencia of Quito is particularly revealing. The king stated that the custom in Quito appeared to be for local aristocrats and their wives to keep twenty to thirty young female Indians as servants in their homes. The monarch considered the treatment of these women to be especially disgraceful because "in order to have the service of female Indians, they allow them to be in sin and single, refusing to let them marry so that their husbands will not take them away; it is a type of enslavement."32

The king cited the particularly grave example of the behavior of a judge of the Real Audiencia of Lima (royal high appellate court). His twenty-year-old Indian servant wished to marry, and the judge opposed the idea. She ignored his wishes and went with her intended spouse to the bishop, who ordered them to return the following Sunday. When they did so, a slave belonging to the judge followed them, threw them on the floor, and kicked them. The bishop called on the judge to punish his slave, and, far from so doing, the judge "responded with words undignified for a minister of our justice . . ." and threatened to order the bishop not to perform the marriage.33

A considerable number of Indian women were in positions of more independence and thus less subject to the direct abuses of Spanish males than were the household servants. The activities of these women were socially vital on an immediate and material level because indigenous women controlled the preparation and distribution of food to a very large extent. The major exceptions were grain and meat, which were municipal monopolies, and the imported food items found on the shelves of the Spanish-owned stores.

Perhaps the most visible of these women were the hawkers. They walked through the streets and squatted around the plazas, selling small, prepared food items to residents and travelers. For the most part, they were vending *chicha* (corn beer), cheese, breads, and fruit. However, in larger towns, especially in Potosí, many of these women also sold soups and meals in the plaza and the market, especially to the Indian community.34

Economically more important, however, were the women of the marketplace. Market women were licensed and had small stools or squatted on the ground with their goods spread out on cloths before them. The market itself was divided into separate sections for each type of produce, so no individual was likely to sell more than one type of food: fruit, vegetables, eggs, cheese, prepared food, and so on. It would appear then that, as today, there was a tension of hierarchy within this scene, for new market women, especially non-Indians, complained bitterly that the established vendors harassed them and prevented them from selling. Many of the women sold their own or their family's produce and thus came to the market on an irregular basis. There were, however, others who were permanent and had arrangements to buy the produce of other Indians living in or near the city.

The importance of these activities is obvious: Indian women were responsible for provisioning the cities. The women who lived on the outskirts of town planted truck gardens, raised chickens, and prepared food to supplement the family income, while their husbands were involved in *mita* (forced labor) or contract labor. They then sold these items either by themselves or through intermediaries, who were also indigenous women, to *mestizos*, whites, and other Indians.

The indigenous women who actually owned stores were the elite of woman traders since their business operations involved considerable capital outlay in rent and stock. Examining only the records of Potosí, one finds Indian women with stores selling pastry, candy, silver items, groceries, bread, prepared food, and general articles of necessity.35 Potosí, the booming mine town, was somewhat exceptional in the opportunities that it provided to Indian women. In Arequipa, for example, where the Indian population was proportionately smaller and the economy less spectacular, it would have been unheard of for an indigenous female to be involved in selling silver.

Many Indian women were employed as clerks and workers in various Spanish-owned establishments. In the principal bakeries of the cities (which were run by white women), there were many indigenous female employees involved in both preparation and sale. In grocery stores and small shops, these women were employed as clerks and assistants. Examination of royal restrictions on female Indian labor throughout this period indicates other areas in which they were actually working. They were barred from working in heavy labor, from kneading bread, and from hauling.36

Perhaps the most vehement prohibition was against woman's work in mining. In a variety of pronouncements the crown made clear its opposition to such work in any aspect of mining.37 However, such regulations were often ignored. Oviedo described the following scene at Potosí: "For the most part, those who wash [the mineral] are Indian or black women. These women, or washers, are seated by the water and have their legs in the water up to their knees, or almost, according to the site or water level."38 Since women were exempt from the *mita*, and since such exemptions appear to have been respected, one can conclude that the washers were working as contract laborers of some sort.

At times it is impossible to discern the reasons for these restrictions. That is especially true for the prohibition against Indian women's kneading bread (although one might speculate that the whites feared poisoning). At other times the rationale is more apparent. In a prohibition against hauling, the justification was presented clearly: "female Indians who were hauling killed the infants whom they carried at their breasts and said that they could not handle them and the load and that they did not want their children to live to suffer the work that they were suffering."39

The other area of work from which Indian women were largely excluded was the Church. While no legal impediment prevented Indian women from entering convents as nuns, there was a virtual social prohibition. Ots Capdequí noted that there were special convents for Indian women because the Spanish nuns did not want to live with them.40 In Arequipa, Quito, and Potosí there were no such convents in the sixteenth century, and thus Indian women were effectively barred from religious life. However, there was a small convent established for them in Cuzco, although it appears that it was primarily a refuge for Indian noblewomen.41

It is perhaps worthwhile to note that while Indian women participated in a wide variety of economic activities, there is no information to sustain the notion that they engaged in prostitution. In every case in which I found specific mention of individual prostitutes, such women were either Spanish or *mestiza*. The myth that they were in fact engaged in such activities was frequently propagated by colonial chronicles such as Padre Ocaña who mentions: "And these princesses are like public women to the Spaniards." But even Ocaña, noteworthy for his sexism and racism, continues on to say: "I am not saying that they live from this, but that with their facility in dealing with the Spaniards, they are honored to have a Spanish consort."42

The amount of formal education among indigenous women of all classes, economic levels, and ages throughout the century was apparently negligible. I have found one Indian woman who was able to sign her name.43 However, it is interesting to note that in the ability to speak Spanish, indigenous females were more proficient than indigenous males, with the latter group needing translators to make up public documents 50 percent more frequently than the former.44 The lack of education can be seen as a result of both sex and race. Few Spanish women were formally educated during this period, and the only Indian men whom the Spanish saw fit to educate were the sons of political leaders. In the cases of women of all races, especially those of non-Christian Indians, education had a total moral and religious emphasis, to the exclusion of practical or useful training.

Such education was largely confined to Church attempts at conversion, baptism, and catechism. However, because of social belief in the sexual promiscuity of Indian women, further attention was paid as well to moral education. In October 1551, the king responded to information he had received from Francisco Pizarro and Bishop Valverde of Cuzco about Spanish men who kept indigenous women in their houses, "saying that they have them for service, but the malice is very clear." He ordered that those women be put "in the power of some Spanish matrons where they might be above suspicion, in order to learn good customs and leave married, and serve God."45 Such gathering up of

Indian women, especially noblewomen and their children, was frequent in Cuzco and Lima.

The question of marriage of indigenous peoples was a major concern of the Spanish monarchs in their capacity as both heads of states and heads of the Church. The immediate problem during the conquest and consolidation was the recognition of existing marriages. While there was an across-the-board recognition, special provisions were necessary to deal with polygyny, marriage between relatives, and marriages based on force. Pope Paul III declared that in cases of polygyny, the legal wife was the first with whom the husband had had sexual relations. [46] Ascertaining this information was far from simple, and in 1550 the Synod of Lima ordered that while baptizing Indians, priests should attempt to trick them into divulging such details. However, recognizing the difficulties implicit in this matter, the synod ended by requiring only that the man legally married one of his wives. The choice was left entirely to the man, and there is no indication that women were given any voice in such selection. [47]

At the same time, the synod also temporarily ratified marriages between siblings, pending papal decision. They permanently approved existing marriages with aunts, sisters-in-law, and blood nieces. All of this legislation was expressed from the point of view of the husband, and, indeed, the only instance in which attention was directed toward the woman herself was in the nullification of marriage by force or sale. [48]

The question of marriages taking place after the conquest was more complex, as the Crown was beset by conflicting demands. The centralized Church-State apparatus pushed marriage strongly. To a certain extent this policy was clearly religious in origin. The Church was particularly concerned that Indian couples were living together before marriage and that indigenous women were thus bearing children out of wedlock. Marriage was seen as the solution to this problem. The policy had political implications as well, for the authorities believed that marriage itself contributed to political stability by discouraging rebellious behavior by the males. [49] But this policy ran counter to the tacit belief and the religious law providing for freedom of marriage, which meant not only freedom in choice of mate, but also freedom not to marry at all.

These policies and beliefs. emanating from Spain, however, often conflicted with the interests of local Spaniards in Peru. As we have seen above, in many instances Spanish men attempted to prevent their female servants or tributary Indians from marrying at all. These actions were the result of an attempt not only to maintain these women for sexual duties, but to maintain other kinds of control over them as well. When an Indian woman married, she became a resident of her husband's village and so was lost as tributary to the *encomendero* of her original village. Similarly, if a servant or employee in town or city married, her employer had to give her freedom to leave with her husband or at least to spend time with him.

Such conflicts of interest came even more often over the question of whom the woman would marry. Marriage between two Indians of his *encomienda* was definitely in the interest of the *encomendero* since the birth of children increased his tribute. Thus, these men often attempted to force such marriages, arranging them while the Indians concerned were still children. A decree by Phillip II on 17 April 1581 ordered that *encomenderos* engaging in such practices be fined 100 *pesos* and be deprived of their Indians.[50] The fact that the records show no grants being revoked or fines being paid for this reason is probably a commentary more on enforcement than compliance.

Legally, Indian women, like Indian men, were free to marry whomever they chose. This right of free choice was expressly granted by Ferdinand V in 1515 when he stated that "my will is that male and female Indians have full freedom to marry whomever they wish, be they Indians or natives of these parts [Spain]."[51] Studies of marriage patterns are, sadly, few in number, since the work of Edgar Love for a parish in Mexico City has yet to be followed for cities in Peru.[52] However, some preliminary findings on Arequipa are useful.

Of eighty Indian women mentioned in notarial records in the late 1590s, the marital status of forty-five is recorded. Two-fifths of these women were not married at all. Eight of the forty-five, almost one-fifth, were married to Spaniards; twenty, a little less than half, were married to Indians; and one was married to a mulatto.[53] These statistics would seem to demonstrate that despite royal policy, a very large number of Indian women did not marry (although it could also be interpreted as meaning that these women were more controlled by their Spanish masters and thus less free to marry or that the women who decided to leave their villages for the city were more likely to remain on their own). The actual pattern of marriage is not surprising since it demonstrates that, for the most part, these women married men of their own race. This marriage pattern explains the high number of single indigenous women, since there were far more female than male Indians.

Thus, while there was legally freedom of choice, social convention restricted intermarriage to a great degree. It is difficult to judge the extent to which this was a result of pure and simple racism. Critics of this conclusion can point to the marriages of Spaniards to Indian noblewomen and to the one-fifth in disproof. Wealth and status clearly did serve to "whiten" some indigenous females into a degree of social acceptability. But it is important to note that even the most important noblewomen did not marry Spanish men of comparable importance. Indeed, the women themselves were very conscious of this difference in status. Garcilaso de la Vega told the story of a daughter of Huayna Capac who refused to marry a man named Diego Hernández, saying that it was unjust to wed the daughter of the Inca to a common tailor.[54]

So it seems that we are dealing more with a lack of interclass marriage than a lack of interracial marriage. This has been obscured to a certain degree by the social mobility of many individuals during this period. Thus, for example, one might say that a man of social standing did indeed marry an Indian noblewoman: as mentioned above, Francisco de Ampuero married Inés Huayllas Yupanqui, daughter of Huayna Capac. However, it is important to note that Ampuero was not a man of distinction when they married and only later became wealthy enough to become councilman and mayor of Lima. It would appear generally true that elites married each other and, since elites were invariably white, that important people rarely married interracially. The individuals of the lower echelons of society married within their circle as well. The fact that this circle was composed of whites, blacks, Indians, and *mestizos* accounts for virtually all of the interracial marriages.

It is clear that Indian women occupied a significant position in the Spanish world of the early colony, as wives and concubines, maids and traders. But what is missing from the picture thus far delineated is an assessment of the impact on the women themselves of their situation in this world. Such an assessment is part of the larger question of the response of the Indian population, both male and female, to the conquest and continued presence of the Spaniards in Peru. It is not sufficient for historians to limit such examination to rebellions, population decline, and migration, for that would beg the question. A more generalized and human view is called for.

In recent years, anthropologists and sociologists have discussed the character of the "*chola*" in Andean towns and cities. She is depicted as a strong, willful woman, either Indian or *mestiza*, aggressive economically and socially. She stands in sharp contrast to her "*cholo*" brother who is seen as drunk, bumbling, meek, and not very bright. The sources of such differences (for they do not seem to exist only in the minds of scholars) have provoked little analysis. Most scholars avoid the question or facilely point their finger to the latest and easiest explanation for everything: modernization.

But reading through records of the sixteenth century, researchers are struck with the similarity in the picture of that era to modern times. The Indian man appears infrequently, and when he does, it is as criminal, fieldhand, drunkard, or lackey. Yet the indigenous female emerges in an aggressive stance. Not only does she appear very often as servant, wife, or concubine, but also as author of a detailed will, prosecutor in a civil court case, and defender of her rights. The difference between the sexes is striking.

In Arequipa's notarial records, there are less than half a dozen wills of Indian men during the sixteenth century, while there are usually four to ten wills of Indian women per year. In the books of royal licenses to travel to Spain from Peru, there are no licenses granted to indigenous males, although there are a dozen or more to indigenous females. In court cases preserved in Arequipa, Lima, and Seville, the same pattern emerges. The picture of indigenous women defending themselves, making contracts, fighting in court, and disposing of considerable property emerges clearly.

There are explanations for this phenomenon in each individual area. The petitions for royal licenses to go to Spain are all involved with the Indian woman as mother of *mestizo* children. In March 1559, Ysabel, an Indian from Peru, was licensed to take her young *mestiza* daughter to Spain because she had explained her inability to contract an honorable marriage for her at home. In July a different Isabel, native of Xaquixaguana and resident of Lima, requested a license, stating that Alejo González Gallego, father of her children, planned to take them with him to Spain. The Crown accepted her argument that her daughter was too young to be separated from her and granted her a license.[55] It appears that Indian women used the existence of their *mestizo* children and Spanish attitudes toward these children to their own advantage. Obviously, indigenous males lacked this type of leverage.

It is also possible to attribute much of this difference in stance to the greater involvement of the Indian women in Spanish society. Indigenous females were in much more intimate contact with Spaniards of both sexes than were their male counterparts.[56] Just through their presence in Hispanic households as servants, they learned Spanish and became acquainted with Spanish customs, attitudes, and ways of dealing with the world. This information was vital in the creation of an aggressive stance in the face of white domination. An Indian male who lived on the outskirts of a Spanish city and worked for Spaniards in the fields or in urban construction, but who lacked both that sort of intimate daily contact with whites and the freedom of movement of Indian women, could not easily have fought for his rights or defended himself, for he was likely to be ignorant of what his rights were.

The greater involvement of Indian women in Spanish society provided them not only with information, but with material resources as well. A survey of the wills of Spanish men in sixteenth-century Peru shows how they strengthened the position of Indian women. The bequests were rarely based on the service rendered by many indigenous females; Spanish law dictating inheritance provisions would have prevented great generosity.[57] Mostly they were sums of money from 20 to 150 *pesos corrientes*: a vast sum of money for these women, although a pittance to a wealthy Spaniard. Many bequests took the form of immovables: a small plot of land just outside the city or the use of a shack or small house rent-free for her lifetime. The relationships between the individual women and their benefactors were rarely spelled out. In some few cases, the will states that she was the mother of his children, but in the majority the reason given is the love and the good service that she had rendered. Indigenous women probably received other money and goods through their positions in the Spanish world. In some cases they were supported by Spanish men and perhaps given gifts of money, clothing, and food. Undoubtedly, there was a fair amount of theft, especially among household servants.

While these goods and moneys must have lightened the burden of individual women and made their lives more comfortable, there is a more important aspect to this question. It is difficult for an individual or group to defend herself or himself from a position of weakness: strong stances can really be taken only when information and resources are available. Through their relationships with Spaniards, particularly with Spanish males, indigenous females were able to gain access to economic resources that were comparatively closed to Indian males. Despite a strong ideology of male supremacy and dominance in Hispanic society, control of economic resources put some Indian women in an independent and viable position from which they could act for their own interests. While Indian males controlled some economic resources, their wills, and lack thereof, indicate that particularly in Spanish-controlled areas, they were able to accumulate little surplus or to gain direct control over a means of production.

It is, however, insufficient to confine this analysis of the differing impact of the conquest on indigenous females and males in sixteenth-century Peru to the presence of *mestizo* children and the advantages of proximity. While these factors were important in shaping reactions, they are insufficient explanations for those reactions. A comparison of preconquest and postconquest role possibilities is crucial to broaden our perspective.

The conquest and early colonial periods were akin to a "frontier" era: social divisions were remarkably fluid compared to the preconquest and the later colonial situations; the new Hispanic-controlled economy was being built and was expanding rapidly; confiscation of Inca and Indian religious properties and the demographic disaster opened up vast tracts of land to settlement and cultivation. After studying pre-Columbian and Spanish societies, one can only conclude that this situation offered wider role possibilities to many, if not most, individuals involved than were previously available. This is not to say that their positions were better, but just that they often had more alternatives.

The group that stands apart from this generalization is the indigenous males. While women had an important economic position in Inca society, they were clearly living under a male-dominated regime: males wielded the political and military power and filled all positions of leadership. For the Indian male the conquest could be only an emasculating experience. Despite the fact that most individual males had exercised little or no power prior to the conquest, they nonetheless had been part of the dominant group. From this position of dominance, they fell to a position of subservience. They were stripped of their power, of their prestige, and thus, in many respects, of their masculinity. While in prior meetings with new groups, contact had been man-to-man, the meeting of Indians with Spaniards was heavily female-to-male. Their women were sought out, carried away, and attended to; in most cases the men themselves were sought out only as pack animals. While their sisters and daughters and wives found entry to the society of the whites as servants, traders, concubines, and even wives, the men found no such open doors.

The totality of such changes—of loss of position, lack of opportunity, and limited access to information and economic resources—left the indigenous male in a weak situation in which his choices were essentially limited to obedi-

ence or flight. The changes evoked by the conquest left the Indian woman in a
considerably different position. Her sex and Spanish attitudes toward females
and female roles allowed her greater involvement in the Hispanic world. As a
result of this involvement she had some few opportunities, based largely on her
access to information and to economic resources. She exploited these opportunities forcefully, defining herself and her culture, much as her *chola* descendant does today.

Such a bifurcation in the positions of male and female Indians could not but
change the human relationships within the indigenous community. Indeed, it
led to a distinct split in that community in urban areas along sex lines. Indian
men and women lived in two separate worlds that, while touching each other in
many areas, were nevertheless remarkably isolated from one another. Social
networks were overwhelmingly forged along sex lines.

Perhaps the most concrete indication of this split comes from the wills of the
Indian women. As a primary source of information, the testaments are useful,
although their main shortcoming is that they are based on a very small group of
people. Yet they are reflective of general patterns that corroborate the impres-
sions coming from other sources.

The sections of the wills most relevant to this discussion are those dealing
with debts and minor bequests.[58] Debts were recorded meticulously despite
the illiteracy of the Indian women. In most instances, they were extensive.
Lucia de Santa Cruz, a single Indian from Asangaro, was owed 547½ *pesos* by
fifty-two different people.[59] She was exceptional. Francisca Bisca, Indian
from the Valley of Tambo, was more typical: she was owed 169½ *pesos* by sixteen individuals.[60] The remarkable aspect is the sex of the debtors rather than
the size of the debts. Of Lucia's fifty-two debtors, forty-three were other Indian
women, four were mulatta women, one was a white woman, and only three
were indigenous males. In Francisca's case, eleven were Indian women, and
only four were Indian males.

Small bequests indicate a similar pattern. In her will of August 1599, Madalena Amanca, Indian from Cayma, bequeathed the corn that she had at home
to her sister María Guancha and three boxes that she owned to her friend Magdalena López.[61] Francisca Vispa, from the *encomienda* of Diego de Cáceres,
left a basket of garlic and some clothing of her choice to Francisca, an Indian;
one blue *lliquilla* and a white cotton skirt to Ysabel, wife of Martín; and one
cotton skirt and a wool *lliquilla* to María Nuso.[62] Lucía de Santa Cruz wished
to express her gratitude to her niece María for eight years of faithful service
and thus instructed her executors to allow María to choose one outfit and one
pair of shoes from her wardrobe and to live permanently in her shack.[63] Virtually every Indian woman included these small legacies in her will. The recipients were rarely male.

The general view provided by wills is that while there were many Indian
women married to indigenous men, their activities divided them. Further,

there was a large block of indigenous females living in towns and cities who had few connections with men of their own race. This is apparent from the large number of Indian women who were either unmarried or married to non-Indians, from the almost total absence of debt relationships between indigenous males and females, and from the rarity of small bequests from Indian women to Indian men.

But while the public documents indicate considerable distance between Indian women and Indian men, they nonetheless demonstrate the existence of strong relationships within the indigenous female population. The extensive network of debts shows close economic links; the bequests reflect strong personal ties. Wills frequently mention that the author was living in the house of a woman friend or that a female neighbor had been caring for her during her illness.

The explanations of this phenomenon are varied. It undoubtedly was related to the demographic balance, the type of women who were making wills, and many other minor variables. But the key to understanding the social networks within the urban Indian community lies in the nature of male and female economic activities.

The work of Indians was largely segregated by sex. Males were primarily involved in group and gang labor in agriculture, construction, and mining. Their work kept them isolated from the mainstream of everyday city life and severely limited their interaction with other groups. Indian women, on the other hand, worked in the midst of the urban scene: they were buying, selling, and working in active Spanish homes. Their economic activities gave them stronger connections with other groups in the cities than with their male counterparts. Further, a large percentage of the women were living in Spanish households in which they were isolated from men of their own race. The business of living and working minimized contacts between Indian men and women since their spheres of activity and the very location of their activities were so different.

At the same time these economic activities not only facilitated, but actually necessitated, contacts between indigenous females. They spent their time buying and selling in the market, securing goods from each other, or waiting on customers in their stores. Theirs was the type of economic activity based on cooperation, credit, and short-term loans. This is exemplified by the system of debts found in their wills. The debts reflect the commercial network that linked indigenous females, a network that was a basic tie between them.

The commercial network not only connected Indian traders to one another, but linked them to other females as well. Their primary association was with other Indian women, especially the female indigenous servant population. These women clearly had close relationships with each other as groups of them worked, ate, and slept in Spanish homes. Their links to women engaged in commerce were based largely on trading ties centering in the marketplace.

But while the primary relationships maintained by Indian women were with other indigenous females, their economic activities linked them to non-Indian as well. In their roles as servants, they worked for and/or were supervised by Spanish women; they lived in their homes, they cooked for them, and they helped to raise their children. In their commercial activities, they sold food to mulattas, traded with *mestizas*, and worked alongside black women.

The financial network detailed in their wills strongly indicates that their economic activities provided and, indeed, required closer contact between Indian women and non-Indian women than between indigenous females and males. The number of non-Indian women who were in debt to them was almost always higher than the number of Indian men. While the economic activity of indigenous women strengthened their position within Hispanic society, it nonetheless broke down the relationships between these females and indigenous males, tying the women into a sex-based, rather than a race-based, social network.

Conclusion

It is apparent, then, that the conquest and colonization was a markedly different experience for indigenous men and women. While the majority of the Andean peoples remained in their traditional villages living much as their foreparents had, the Indians who were in more direct contact with the Hispanic world experienced changes in their lives that were determined to a remarkable degree by their sex.

In searching for explanations for this phenomenon, the frequency with which nonwhite women appeared in the documents as though they were white seemed significant. The most outstanding instance involved a woman named Juana Leyton who was married to an important Arequipeño, Francisco Bosso. Her name appeared frequently in records in Arequipa, and there was no reason to believe that she was anything other than the usual white woman of position in a provincial city. It was only in a court case found in the Archives of the Indies that she was mentioned as an Arab who had been brought to Peru as a slave and wore a brand of that status on her forehead.

There were numerous less outstanding examples as well. In all documents the Spanish notaries mentioned the race of any individual who was not white. Yet women who were mentioned as Indian in some documents frequently appeared as white in others. Seeing such "passing" by so many nonwhite, particularly Indian, women and virtually none by nonwhite males, one could not but wonder what it was about being female and about Spanish attitudes toward women that allowed this to occur in a society as race-conscious as Spanish America. Indeed, the documents seemed to show that in certain instances Spanish sexism tended to mitigate Spanish racism, thus allowing the indigenous female more opportunity than the indigenous male.

In this, the scarcity of white women was a decisive factor; there were more than ten white male immigrants to every white female. With women of their own race in short supply, Spanish men fell back on the available Indian females, allowing them to fill roles and positions that would ordinarily have been reserved for white females. This had the effect of widening the alternatives and increasing the mobility of indigenous females. It was a classic market situation wherein the scarcity of white women increased the value placed on Indian women. This is particularly borne out by the fact that by the late sixteenth century and thereafter, when a demographic balance of the sexes had been achieved with the birth of a new generation, the mobility of indigenous females became more circumscribed. [64]

General attitudes of men toward women also contributed to the disparity in male and female experiences. Men are traditionally considered more violent, more hostile, and thus more dangerous than women. Females are seen as passive and submissive. Men are thus viewed as a potential threat, while women are not feared. Given these attitudes, it is understandable that in a conquest situation, a situation of precarious control by a numerical minority, the conquerors would keep men at arm's length. The group of twenty Indian women living in a Spanish household in Quito was not perceived as a threat, for women were not considered to be hostile and rebellious. A group of twenty men in the same position would have been viewed as a dangerous basis for rebellion.

Attitudes toward female activities had similar results, reserving for women positions in household work, sewing, and small trading, while isolating men in gang labor in mining, construction, and agriculture. In this instance, traditional "women's work" placed indigenous females in positions of closer contact with Spaniards, thus helping them to strengthen their economic and social position.

These factors combined to permit the Indian woman to play roles radically different from contemporary social ideas of the position of nonwhite females in societies dominated by white men. Our vision has been one of double oppression, of double jeopardy, of women victimized both by the brutality of racism and by the strength of sexism. [65] This view has been represented graphically by sociologists who depict society as a hierarchical ladder with nonwhite women on the bottom step.

It is easy to envision such a ladder of sixteenth-century Andean society with the Indian woman sitting next to her black sister in the inferior position. As an Indian, she was relegated to the most menial tasks, treated as an inferior for the color of her skin and her non-European ways. As a woman, she was raped, treated as a prostitute, and abandoned. As a victim of poverty (for in a world dominated by a white, male power structure, poverty is almost an inherent characteristic of nonwhite females), she was kept on the outskirts of the city, despised for her tattered clothing, and treated with contempt. But if this view conformed well to reality, then the indigenous woman would have had few alternatives in her life: some doors would have been closed to her because of her race, others because of her economic status, and most of the rest because of her sex. Yet as we have seen, a different picture of Indian women emerges from colonial documents.

The explanation for this divergence from contemporary social ideas does not lie in some strange inherent characteristic of Andean society or Hispanic mentality. The repetition of this same situation in many eras and many societies implies a universality of causation. In considering the position of nonwhite women, we have too frequently viewed racism as a single oppressive reality and then added to that the burdens of sexism, as if they were two static and separate forces. [66] What is missing in this analysis is a comprehension of the interplay between racism and sexism. The dynamic created between these two forces is the key to understanding the realities of the position of indigenous women in Spanish American society.

Notes

This essay is a revised version of "La mujer durante la conquista y la primera época colonial," which appeared in *Estudios Andinos* 5, no. 1 (1976): 1-35.

1. Most noteworthy in this attempt is the work of James Lockhart, *Spanish Peru* (Madison: University of Wisconsin Press, 1968), and Frederick P. Bowser, *The African Slave in Colonial Peru, 1524-1650* (Stanford: Stanford University Press, 1974).
2. In the sixteenth century, Peru comprised not only the modern-day nation of that name, but Ecuador, Bolivia, Chile, and Argentina as well. For purposes of this paper, however, I am speaking of Peru primarily as the heartland of colonial Peru—Peru itself and Bolivia.
3. In speaking of traditional Andean society, I am limiting myself to the core of the Inca empire.
4. Nathan Wachtel, *La vision des vaincus: Les Indiéns du Pérou devant la Conquête espagnole, 1530-1570* (Paris: Ed. Gallimard, 1971), p. 116. In the original this reads: ". . . les deux fait sont liés: conformément au principe de réciprocité, l'obligation au tribut se confond avec le droit á la terre communautive."
5. There are many works that the reader might consult for examples of this discussion of tribute and for general information on Inca society. For information from the point of view of the Spanish conquerors, see Pedro de Cieza de León, *The Incas*, trans. Harriet de Onis (Norman: University of Oklahoma Press, 1959). For works written by Indians and *mestizos* after the conquest, see Garcilaso de la Vega, *Royal Commentaries of the Incas and General History of Peru*, 2 vols., trans. Harold V. Livermore (Austin: University of Texas Press, 1965), and Felipe Huamán Poma de Ayala, *La nueva crónica y buen gobierno*, 3 vols. (Lima: Ed. Cultura, 1956-66). For a traditional and very complete historical source, see Padre Bernabé Cobo, *Obras* (Madrid: Ediciones Atlas, 1956). For a modern survey, see John Alden Mason, *The Ancient Civilization of Peru* (Baltimore: Penguin Books, 1957). An especially fine survey of Inca culture at the time of the conquest is John Rowe, "Inca Culture at the Time of the Spanish Conquest," in Julian H. Steward, ed., *Handbook of South American Indians*, 7 vols. (Washington, D.C.: Smithsonian Institution, 1946), 2: 183-330.

6. Eva Figes, *Patriarchal Attitudes* (London: Faber and Faber, 1970), pp. 66-67.

7. For their discussions, see Ester Boserup, *Woman's Role in Economic Development* (London: George Allen and Unwin, 1971), and John Rankin Goody, in John Rankin Goody and S. I. Tambiah, *Bridewealth and Dowry* (Cambridge: Cambridge Papers in Social Anthropology no. 7, 1973).

8. Clement Markham, *Narratives of the Rites and Laws of the Incas* (London: Hakluyt Society, 1973), as most other authors, contends that inheritance was traced through women, but that offices never passed to them. However, José María Ots Capdequí, *El sexo como circunstancia modificativa de la capacidad jurídica en nuestra legislación de Indias* (Madrid: Tip. de la Revista de Archivos, 1930), implies the opposite when he contends that Viceroy Toledo was recognizing local tradition by declaring that in the absence of eligible males, daughters could inherit local political positions. See note 5, above.

9. *Casas de recogimiento*—literally, houses of withdrawal or seclusion—were centrally controlled institutions scattered throughout the Inca realm. For further information, see sources mentioned in note 6 or Markham, *Narratives*, p. 52.

10. Padre Martín Murúa, *Historia general del Perú*, 2 vols. (Madrid: Editora Manuel Ballesteros-Baibros, 1964), 2: 79-80.

11. Murúa, *Historia*, 2: 64-65. *Pallas* were noblewomen not of royal blood, while *ñustas* were royal princesses.

12. An *encomendero* was an individual who was given a grant of an *encomienda* by the Spanish Crown. This grant gave the individual a degree of control over a specific group of Indians, especially the right to collect tribute from them. In turn, the *encomendero* had the obligation to Christianize the Indians and to hold himself ready to serve the Crown with men and arms. While there were females who held such grants in inheritance from their fathers or husbands, the administration thereof passed to their husbands upon marriage or remarriage, although they remained the legal owners. I will refer to *encomenderos* as masculine throughout. For a full description of this institution, see Lesley Byrd Simpson, *The Encomienda in New Spain* (Berkeley and Los Angeles: University of California Press, 1950). See also James Lockhart, "Encomienda and Hacienda: The Evolution of the Great Estate in the Spanish Indies," *Hispanic American Historical Review* 49 (August 1969): 411-29 (hereafter cited as *HAHR*); Robert G. Keith, "Encomienda, Hacienda and Corregimiento in Spanish America: A Structural Analysis," *HAHR* 51 (August 1971): 431-46. Keith also discusses aspects of encomienda in his book *Conquest and Agrarian Change: The Emergence of the Hacienda System on the Peruvian Coast* (Cambridge: Harvard University Press, 1976), pp. 27-54.

13. Archivo General de Indias, Sección 5, Audiencia de Lima, leg. 204, Probanza de Francisco de Ampueros (hereafter cited as AGI).

14. See Woodrow W. Borah and Sherburne F. Cook, *The Population of Central Mexico in 1548*, Ibero-Americana no. 43 (Berkeley and Los Angeles: University of California Press, 1960); Sherburne F. Cook and Woodrow W. Borah, *The Indian Population of Central Mexico, 1531-1610*, Ibero-Americana no. 44 (Berkeley and Los Angeles: University of California Press, 1960); Woodrow W. Borah and Sherburne F. Cook, *The Aboriginal Population of Central Mexico on the Eve of the Spanish Conquest*, Ibero-Americana no. 45 (Berkeley and Los Angeles: University of California Press, 1963).

15. C. T. Smith, "Depopulation of the Central Andes in the Sixteenth Century,"

Current Anthropology 11 (October-December 1970): 453-64, for figures on Aymaras and Urus; Alejandro Málaga Medina, "La población de Arequipa," *El Pueblo* (Arequipa), 15 August 1972, for figures on southern Peru.

16. Magnus Mörner, *Race Mixture in the History of Latin America* (Boston: Little, Brown, 1967), p. 22.

17. AGI, section 5, Lima, leg. 205, Probanza de Juan Sierra de Leguizamo; Diego Fernández, *Primera y segunda parte de la historia del Perú* (Madrid: Ediciones Atlas, 1963), pt. 2, bk. 2, chap. 4, para. 76; pt. 2, bk. 3, chap. 4, para. 77.

18. See note 13 for sources and AGI, Sección Escribanía, leg. 496-A.

19. Quoted in Mörner, *Race Mixture*, p. 24.

20. The best-known illustration of such assistance comes from Mexico and involved La Malinche, who was given to the Spaniards with a group of slaves in Tabasco. As Cortés's mistress, she aided considerably in his conquest of the Aztecs. Malinche's importance exemplifies the central role that indigenous women played in the conquest of Peru as well as Mexico.

21. John V. Murra, ed., *Visita de la provincia de León de Huánuco en 1562* (Huánuco: Universidad Nacional Hermilio Valdizán, 1967), pp. 94-101. A *fanega* was 2.58 bushels or 90.8 liters, although *fanegas* varied in several regions. One *almud* was 6.8 dry quarts or 7.5 liters. One *pierna* may be translated as a length of cloth. The equivalence of the *ycanga* remains unsolved by ethnohistorians and historians.

22. Roberto Levillier, ed., *Gobernantes del Perú: Cartas y papeles, siglo XVI*, 14 vols. (Madrid: Sucesores de Rivadeneyra, 1921), 8: 346.

23. The New Laws of 1542 began a reform of the institution of the *encomienda*. In 1549 the payment of tribute in the form of personal service was officially outlawed. See Richard Konetzke, *América Latina: La época colonial* (Madrid: Siglo XXI de España, 1972), p. 176.

24. Population figures for urban Indians are extremely unreliable. However, they generally confirm this impression. Antonio Vázuquez de Espinosa, *Compendio y descripción de las Indias Occidentales* (Madrid: Ediciones Atlas, 1969), quotes the figures from Toledo's 1575 census, showing the number of Indian women in the *cercado* (outskirts) of Lima to be 922 and the number of men to be 645. The figures for La Plata in 1610 were 300 tributaries, 300 old and young men, and 1,000 or more Indian women.

25. *Recopilación de leyes de los Reynos de Indias*, 4 vols. (1681; Madrid: Ediciones Cultura Hispánica, 1973), 2: 196.

26. AGI, Sección Escribanía, leg. 952.

27. AGI, Sección 5, Lima, leg. 566, vol. 4, fol. 260v. The original reads: ". . . que tienen en sus casas cantidad de yndias a efectuar con ellas sus malos descos y que para lo remediar convenia mandesemos que ningun español tuviese en su casa yndia sospechosa, ni parida, ni preñada. . . ."

28. This is clear from data shown to me by Judith Bakewell, University of Michigan, whose work on Potosí is as yet unpublished.

29. Archivo Histórico Nacional, Arequipa, Protocolos of Gaspar Hernández (hereafter cited as AHNA).

30. *Recopilación de leyes*, 3: 267.

31. This section is based on work contracts found in the notarial records of Arequipa, housed in the AHNA, for the period 1540 to 1610.

32. Richard Konetzke, ed., *Colección de documentos para la historia de la forma-*

ción social de Hispanoamérica, 1493-1810, 3 vols. (Madrid: Consejo Superior de Investigaciones Científicas, 1953-1962), 1: 447-48. The original reads: ". . . para tener servicio de indias consienten que estén en pecado y sin casarse por no les dar lugar a ello, porque los maridos no se las lleven, que es manera de esclavonía."

33. Konetzke, *Colección*, 1: 447-48. The original reads: ". . . respondió palabras no dignas a ministro de nuestra justicia. . . ."

34. Real Academia de la Historia, Madrid, Colección Muñoz, vol. 39, "Relaciones Geográficas," fols. 240-53. This is further confirmed by the data of Judith Bakewell, mentioned in note 28, above.

35. AGI, Sección Escribanía, leg. 965B.

36. *Colección de documentos inéditos relativos al descubrimiento, conquista y organización de las antiguas posesiones españolas de América y Oceanía sacadas de los archivos del reino, y muy especialmente del de Indias*, 42 vols. (Madrid, 1864-84), 11: 243.

37. Ibid.

38. Domingo Amunátegui Solar, *Las encomiendas indígenas en Chile* (Santiago de Chile: Imprenta Cervantes, 1909), p. 115.

39. Rafael Altamira y Crevea, *Historia de España y de la civilización española*, 5 vols. (Barcelona: Sucesores de Gil, 1900-30), 3: 232. The original reads: ". . . yndias que iban cargandas mataban las criaturas que llevaban a los pechos y decian que no podian con ellas y con la carga, y que no querian que viviesen sus hijos a pasar el trabajo que ellas pasaban."

40. Ots Capdequí, *El sexo como circunstancia*, p. 73.

41. Ibid.

42. Fray Diego de Ocaña and Fray Arturo Alvares, *Un viaje fascinante por la América Hispana del siglo XVI* (Madrid: Studium Editores, 1969), p. 259.

43. This is based on the notarial records of Arequipa, housed in the AHNA, for 1540 and 1610.

44. Ibid.

45. AGI, Sección 5, Lima, leg. 566, vol. 5, fol. 260v; decree dated October 1542. The original reads: ". . . diciendo que las tienen para su servicio y que . . . la malicia es tan clara . . . en poder de algunas mujeres españolas casadas donde no se pueda tener sospecha para que alli tomen buenas costumbres y puedan salir casadas y sirvan a Dios. . . ."

46. Ots Capdequí, *El sexo como circunstancia*, p. 27.

47. Ibid., p. 37.

48. Ibid., p. 28.

49. This attitude was openly stated in regard to blacks. See AGI, Indiferente General, leg. 421, vol. 12, fol. 151. There was a similar push toward marriage of Spaniards. See AGI, Audiencia de Mexico, leg. 1088. vol. 3, fol. 165v. See also essay by Lavrin (chap. 1) in this volume.

50. *Colección . . . América*, 18: 530.

51. *Colección de documentos inéditos relativos al descubrimiento, conquista y organización de las antiguas posesiones españolas de Ultramar*, 25 vols. (Madrid: Sucesores de Rivadeneyra, 1855-1932), 4: 52. The original reads: "Mi voluntad es que las dichas yndias e yndios tengan entera libertad para se casar con quien quisieren, asi con yndios, como con naturales destas partes."

52. Edgar F. Love, "Marriage Patterns of Persons of African Descent in a Colonial Mexico City Parish," *HAHR* 51 (February 1971): 79-91.

53. This is based on three books of notarial records of Arequipa, housed in the AHNA.

54. Garcilaso de la Vega, *Royal Commentaries*, 2: 1229.

55. AGI, Sección 5, Lima, leg. 568-69, fols. 35v-36, 63v, 231v (1559).

56. There were, of course, Indian men who were very closely tied to the Spanish society. For a view of the situation of the Kurakas, see Karen Spalding, "Social Climbers: Changing Patterns of Mobility Among the Indians of Colonial Peru," *HAHR* 50 (November 1970): 645-64.

57. The inheritance laws dictated that no more than one-fifth of the estate could be bequeathed to persons other than the heirs recognized by the law.

58. Only minor bequests are considered, since major bequests were governed by law.

59. AHNA, García Muñoz (1601), fol. 15.

60. AHNA, García Muñoz (1599), fols. 247v-48.

61. AHNA, García Muñoz (1599), fols. 407v-11.

62. AHNA, Diego de Aguilar (1581), fols. 117v-320. *Lliquilla* is a piece of clothing; its meaning is obscure.

63. See note 60, above.

64. See Peter Boyd-Bowman, "Patterns of Spanish Emigration to the Indies Until 1600," *HAHR* 56 (November 1976): 580-604.

65. Such a view pervades much contemporary literature. One example is F. M. Beal, "Double Jeopardy: To Be Black and Female," in D. Babcox and M. Belkin, eds. *Liberation Now* (New York: Dell Publishing, 1971), pp. 185-96.

66. My point is that in the United States we too frequently try to isolate problems like racism and sexism from one another so that they become separate issues. We thus often see social problems or actions in one category or the other without understanding their interrelationship. I recently had an experience that well typifies this tendency. A reader of this paper took issue with my section on the moral education of indigenous women and my interpretation of the incident in that section. The reader found "this incident more suggestive of attitudes of Spanish males vis-à-vis all women than a specific slur on indigenous females." Thus, despite the facts that similar actions were never taken against Spanish women and, in fact, that Spanish women were trusted to help deal with the problem, the reader saw no elements of racism.

Women in a noble family: the Mexican counts of Regla, 1750-1830

The family offered women members of elite colonial Mexican society opportunities for power and participation in economic activities. Their conception of
family included residence and business as well as relatives. Public office and
ecclesiastical appointments could be incorporated into the familial interest.[1]
Within this framework some wealthy women entered into arranged marriages,
while others remained single or entered convents. They saw to the education
and training of children and through their various actions could contribute to
the increase or decrease of family fortunes. Financial and, to some extent,
social independence was possible for the colonial woman as a result of her legal
right to inherit and manage property and to hold aristocratic titles.

This study of eight women over four generations in the powerful Regla
family will highlight the activities of four women who were noteworthy for their
economic and social independence and four who filled more traditional roles
as wives, mothers, consumers, and spenders of capital.

The Regla family won its status through the extraordinary entrepreneurial
skills of Pedro Romero de Terreros, the first Count of Regla, who was one of
the initiators of Mexico's mid-eighteenth-century silver-mining boom.[2] In
1756, at the age of forty-six, he married the youngest daughter of the relatively
impoverished family of the Counts of Miravalle. His mother-in-law, the third
Countess of Miravalle, only eight years older than he, then became the archi-
tect of an informal alliance between the two families that financially strengthened her family and established social position for the Romero de Terreros.

Intelligent, literate, active, and ambitious, the Countess of Miravalle became one of eighteenth-century Mexico's most influential women. Although she proudly traced her origins to sixteenth-century conquistador stock, her titles and entailed estates dated only from the years between 1690 and 1717. Even then, family position rested on insecure economic foundations of an inherited public office and scattered agricultural *haciendas*.[3]

Her generation produced no male heirs, and, as she was the oldest child, the future countess's education received her parents' special attention. Her handwriting is clear; she had some knowledge of bookkeeping; and she composed a poem that won a contest in 1729. Married in 1720 at age nineteen to a Spanish officer, she bore eight children who survived to maturity. Her husband died some time before 1743, leaving extensive debts.[4]

Her duties as a widow and heir to her family's entail spanned both "masculine" and "feminine" pursuits; while contesting and initiating lawsuits and administering *haciendas*, she supervised the health and education of her children and grandchildren and managed several households. She emerged at this time as one traditional "type" of female personality: the *mujer fuerte*, or powerful woman. Her own image of herself was as a "good captain," in command of an extensive family.[5]

Providing for eight children might well have strained the resources of a far wealthier family, but the Countess of Miravalle arranged their futures with considerable skill. Two sons held official positions, while a third son administered the family's outlying properties before he also received a government job through family contact.[6] Of her five daughters, one entered a convent; for this her mother spent more than 7,000 *pesos*, portioned out with difficulty over a long period of time. The money paid her religious novitiate and the dowry required to support her and supplied her with a "cell" or small residence.[7] Another daughter, Angela, received 6,000 *pesos* in cash plus the value of her jewelry and clothing when she married an officer attached to the viceroy's palace in Mexico City. After this marriage, because of her straitened finances, the countess and her six unmarried children lived in her son-in-law's house while she rented her own in order to pay debts and receive extra income. Her youngest daughter, María Antonia, who married Pedro Romero de Terreros, received no cash dowry, although her mother later claimed that the value of her personal possessions reached 16,000 *pesos*.[8] While Pedro Romero de Terreros made no acknowledgement of this sum, he did issue a document providing 50,000 *pesos* in *arras*, or a jointure, for his wife if she should be widowed.[9] Two daughters remained unmarried and lived with their mother.

During the twenty years between 1746 and 1766, the countess turned a debt-ridden inheritance into a series of apparently profitable enterprises. She invested heavily in *hacienda* improvements, rented other properties, paid off both her father's and husband's debts, and vigorously disputed claims to her lands. When the government tried to take away the public office that she had inherited as a part of her entail, she organized a series of noisy protests until

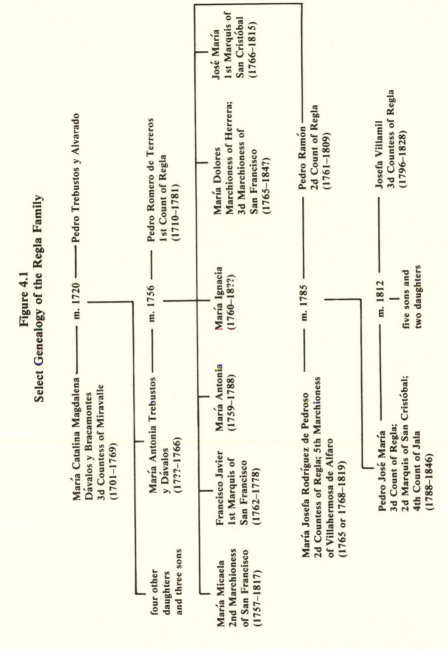

Figure 4.1
Select Genealogy of the Regla Family

María Catalina Magdalena Dávalos y Bracamontes 3d Countess of Miravalle (1701–1769) — m. 1720 — Pedro Trebustos y Alvarado

four other daughters and three sons

María Micaela 2nd Marchioness of San Francisco (1757–1817)

Francisco Javier 1st Marquis of San Francisco (1762–1778)

María Antonia Trebustos y Dávalos (17??–1766) — m. 1756 — Pedro Romero de Terreros 1st Count of Regla (1710–1781)

María Antonia (1759–1788)

María Ignacia (1760–18??)

María Dolores Marchioness of Herrera; 3d Marchioness of San Francisco (1765–184?)

José María 1st Marquis of San Cristóbal (1766–1815)

María Josefa Rodríguez de Pedroso 2d Countess of Regla; 5th Marchioness of Villahermosa de Alfaro (1765 or 1768–1819) — m. 1785 — Pedro Ramón 2d Count of Regla (1761–1809)

Pedro José María 3d Count of Regla; 2d Marquis of San Cristóbal; 4th Count of Jala (1788–1846)

Josefa Villamil 3d Countess of Regla (1796–1828) — m. 1812

five sons and two daughters

her demands were settled. When she added the last codicils to her will in 1766, she felt good reason to be gratified.[10]

The countess enjoyed a warm friendship with her son-in-law Pedro Romero de Terreros, which was cemented when she became the godmother and ritual coparent (*comadre*) of his first child, María Micaela, in 1757. By becoming a coparent, the countess reinforced a link in a chain of affinity with her son-in-law. In the next years, the countess, her sons, and one of her daughters acted as godparents to all of the children of Pedro and María Antonia. Like most elite families, they chose only relatives as baptismal sponsors, as it welded families closer together and also avoided the obligation of mutual assistance with outsiders.[11]

Her business and political activities on behalf of the Miravalles were extended to include Pedro's interests. She acted as his purchasing agent in Mexico City, sending him commodities as diverse as iron bars and cloth, as well as remitting and receiving money and silver either through her agents or his own. She frequently purchased slaves from various sources and arranged for their transport to Pedro for working his mines and refineries at Pachuca and Real del Monte. With characteristic business acumen, she investigated the character of male slaves, advised on their potential capabilities, and even suggested employment for their wives.[12]

Other Miravalle connections were also useful to Pedro. His brother-in-law, Joaquín, important in the viceroy's court, kept him politically informed through his mother. In one court case challenging Pedro's ownership of a mine in Pachuca, the Miravalles went to great trouble to arrange that their second cousin be assigned as judge and then to try to conceal the relationship.[13]

While the countess's letters to Pedro reveal a keen awareness of the problems of mining, *hacienda* administration, politics, and finance, they also disclose more conventional interest in shopping for calicoes, fine linens, sewing materials, and other items requested by her daughter. She had a lively concern with medicine, and her letters include perceptive descriptions of illnesses—the health of family members was a constant preoccupation. For ten of the thirteen years in which she wrote to Pedro, María Antonia was pregnant or suffered poor health. She described María Antonia's physical condition in her first pregnancy. During the early weeks, she suffered from vomiting and pain, and then in the later months she told of swollen feet, inability to walk, fears, more pains, headaches, sleeplessness, and a fall. Finally, at 3 A.M. on 9 May, 1757, these discomforts ended as, the countess wrote, María Antonia had had a "fat and healthy" baby girl.[14]

Views on the education and behavior of women emerged occasionally in the correspondence. The countess's five daughters were literate, and she impatiently waited for news that her granddaughter and godchild, María Micaela, had learned to read. However, she was cautious and conservative in the ways that she felt her youngest daughter should behave. Married women were expected to spend most of their time in their houses; even attendance at mass, if too frequent, was frowned on. Fearing gossip because María Antonia had gone to mass three times in different places in one day, the countess wrote to Pedro: "She continues to go out of the house, and I fear that people will talk, and it is necessary that you return, as somebody might insinuate something."[15]

Her basic conservatism combined with her strong personality might well have discouraged her daughters' aspirations for personal and economic independence. With three brothers in line to inherit the entail, there was little possibility that the two single Miravalle women would have substantial economic resources. Moreover, the countess's specific power had been achieved only through widowhood, traditionally the time when colonial women had their greatest influence.[16]

In a family so dominated by the enterprising countess and a husband at least twenty years her senior, María Antonia appeared relatively powerless. Beyond the fact that she gave birth to five girls and three boys (almost the same ratio produced by her mother), there is hardly any information in official archives about her. We do not even know the date of her birth. The little that we can glean of her personality comes from her mother's letters and in forty-two fairly brief letters that she wrote to her husband in Pachuca between 1757 and 1759. After 1759 she seems to have been almost continuously resident at Pachuca with her husband and children, returning to Mexico City only when she was very ill.

María Antonia's letters display great affection for her husband. Even though her mother had probably arranged the marriage, on the basis of Pedro's large fortune, a genuine fondness soon emerged. She wrote often of missing him, noting that her loneliness was assuaged only by a visit of her mother or sisters. She hoped that "he would come out of [his] cares" and "that he would not look for another treasure [silver mine] in Pachuca," as she would be content "to live only on chiles and tortillas" with him there. She playfully regretted her poverty. Her head "heated up at the thought that [he] would come to [Mexico City]." With these letters, María Antonia sent cakes she had baked, cigars, pomegranates, and sometimes jars of honey. Once when the inquisitor brought her a cargo of pears, she tried to find a way of sending Pedro some. Her letters express the emotions of a young woman concerned with love, family, children, religious holidays, and visits from relatives, priests, and friars.[17]

In almost all of the letters, she thanked Pedro for a specific amount of money sent for personal and household use—usually 500 *pesos*, which could also cover the purchase of expensive fabrics. On one occasion, she rejected his gift of a bracelet because it was overpriced.

Another theme dominating the letters is her acute physical suffering from chronic poor health. She complained of constant headaches and the demands of several pregnancies. She noted that she looked for the skin of an animal "so that it would not be so easy to have children."[18] The countess's letters after 1758 indicate that her daughter's health continued to deteriorate; after 1764 she was almost continually ill until she died in 1766, a month after childbirth.

Despite continuing poor health, María Antonia appeared devoted to raising her children. She nursed her oldest daughter, María Micaela, for several months; then, because of acute trembling whenever she began to feed her,.it was decided that she should not continue. Several of her letters describe the quest for a satisfactory Indian wet nurse. When she was in Pachuca, her orders for clothing, fabric, and shoes were mainly for the children.19

In almost all of her letters, she mentioned religious matters—from saying her rosaries to celebrating special feast days. Her biography, as it is sketched in letters, describes a young woman who passed rapidly from the delights of a young bride to life as a sacrificing, devout, suffering wife and mother.

Years after her death, when the Count of Regla was dying, he wrote a letter to his daughters, regretting that their mother had had so little time to influence them. He praised her "discreet character, virtuous soul, [and] pious, moderate, and benign heart," 20 characteristics that he apparently wished his daughters to emulate and that also are reiterated in eighteenth-century literature as the ideal behavior of women. 21

We know little about the education of the four Regla daughters who survived to adulthood. They lived principally at their father's *hacienda* at San Miguel, supervised by a widowed aunt, Angela Díaz Labandero, who had been assigned by their grandmother to help care for them since their infancy. The Count of Regla's funeral eulogy mentions that his daughters were taught "to sew, weave [and] embroider to perfection . . . which were their constant occupations when not reading devout books." 22 As the inventories record the value of family books at a relatively low price, the manual skills might have been emphasized.

When the count died in 1781, his daughters emerged briefly from obscurity in the two years it took to settle the estate. A review of the arrangements made by the count for his children helps to indicate the position of women in legal and financial matters.

In the 1770s, Pedro, who had become the Count of Regla between 1767 and 1769, arranged his family's future. He obtained two additional titles for his younger sons, the Marquises of San Francisco and San Cristóbal, and organized the bulk of his property into three *mayorazgos*, or entails, one for each of his sons. In the entail attached to the title of the Count of Regla, he placed all of the mines and refining *haciendas* and a large number of agricultural estates. In the other two entails, he placed additional *haciendas* that he had purchased from the former estates of the Jesuits. In the *bienes libres*, or unentailed estates, which could be sold or mortgaged, there were silver objects and silver bars, furnishings, and various houses as well as *haciendas*. He instructed his executor to divide the bulk of the *bienes libres* among those children (his daughters) who had not received entails, although his sons still had certain undefined rights to these possessions. 23

Under the provisions of his will, the count had granted preference in the inheritance of entails to male over female and to older over younger. Thus, when the second son died in 1778, María Micaela, the oldest daughter, was to inherit the least valuable entail. At the count's death, her brothers were in Spain. Her father's oral instructions and the inability of the other males to agree upon an administrator made it possible for her to be appointed executrix, even though she had not quite reached twenty-five, the age of legal majority. After the customary ten days of mourning had passed, she journeyed to Mexico City to assure her own appointment. The viceroy placed himself in overall charge of the settlement of the disputed issues, but gave María Micaela the titular role, which she exercised in alliance with her father's former advisers and agents. She also acted as the guardian of her younger sisters.[24]

For the next two years, María Micaela "continued the business operations of the Count of Regla, as they had been before his death."[25] She became the custodian of a enormous estate of more than five million *pesos*, the rich mines of Pachuca and Real del Monte, three large refining mills, and agricultural *haciendas* that extended in a wide arc around the mining region, south toward Mexico City and north in the direction of Querétaro. The philanthropic commitments ranged from pledges to construct a convent to duties as guardian of the Franciscan college of Propaganda Fide in Pachuca.[26]

In her role as executrix, María Micaela borrowed money, renewed rental contracts, supervised inventories, and worked closely with the bookkeeper on the complex matters included in closing the estate. Her decisions influenced the final disposition of disputed properties and money. At least two of her father's business allies were permitted to collect substantial payments. The decision on borrowing 500,000 *pesos* to pay for additional former Jesuit *haciendas*, which the count had purchased shortly before his death, committed family resources for years in the future. While experts argued that some of the lands were not even worth the interest to be paid on them, María Micaela and her advisers believed that the honor of her father demanded that the sales be carried out and the money paid.[27]

Nearly all money required to settle the estate came from the unentailed properties that were to become the property of María Micaela's younger sisters. The royal official assigned to protect the younger daughters' interests opposed these payments. He also suggested that María Micaela forego the 30,000 *pesos* (a percentage of the value of the estate) that executors received for their work.[28] This interference with her conduct was the first factor in an apparent estrangement between María Micaela and her sisters. She had inherited an entail and they had not; her decisions reduced the size of their inheritance.

María Micaela promoted her own interests and refused to relinquish her pay as executrix, arguing that she had been diligent in protecting her sisters' rights and had incurred heavy costs. She took an additional 668 *pesos* for her validated expenses and utilized her position in order to assure receipt of the second most valuable entail, that of San Francisco (appraised at 607,356 *pesos*). This consisted mainly of properties in the wealthy agricultural region of the Bajío, where she went to live sometime between 1783 and 1786. [29]

Only a few of her letters have survived. They are brief and formal, all but two being written to her brother, Pedro Ramón, the second Count of Regla. The letters allude to social and family events or exchanges of land titles and receipts. [30]

Throughout her life she displayed her capacity to defend her rights and to oversee her *haciendas*. When the villagers near her *hacienda* of Tiripetio, in Tuzantla, Michoacán, built a dam on her property, she ordered it destroyed. When the villagers sued her for damages, she won a partial victory by having her titles to most of the disputed lands confirmed, but she had to repair the dam. [31] A few years later, at a time when María Micaela had no administrator, she sent a representative to arrest seven men in a nearby village because they owed her money. A local official brought suit against her in Mexico City and accused her of practicing debt peonage, illegally maintaining a jail on her *hacienda*, and issuing her own coinage. On the last two charges she pleaded that the preliminary administration of justice, such as the right to punish workers and the circulation of token money on *haciendas*, was the prerogative of ownership. To the charge of debt peonage, her lawyer responded that a large sum of advance money had been given and that the plaintiff had failed to work on the *hacienda* in order to pay the debt. In an able defense of the rights of a landowner, the marchioness's lawyer pleaded that only the ability to punish crimes prevented petty pilferers from becoming full-fledged thieves and allowed the owners to manage large numbers of workers. Her lawyer had his defense printed in order to "salvage her reputation" and appealed the adverse decision of the viceroy that she pay a fine and remove the jail. Her personal defense to the charges was ambivalent: on the one hand, she lacked an administrator, and on the other, she could not be responsible for the actions of her minor employees. [32] It is certain that her practices as a *hacienda* owner followed contemporary patterns.

Between 1792, when the case against her was initiated, and 1800, María Micaela had established a residence in Mexico City and was engaged in a law case on the location of a *pulquería* (tavern) next to her house in San Cosme. Her philanthropies included large sums to the Colegio de Propaganda Fide in Pachuca, of which she was the guardian and for which she purchased the relics of Santa Colomba. When she died in 1817, she left her estates to her only surviving sister in compliance with her father's will, despite a serious legal dispute over money in 1807. [33]

María Micaela is an example of an unmarried woman who displayed business acumen. She derived her capacity to function independently in this masculine-dominated world perhaps from her grandmother's special interest in her godchild, surely from her position as the oldest child of the Count of Regla. A wish expressed by a prominent cousin at her birth—"that she would have landed properties for a *mayorazgo*"—reveals a contemporary attitude toward the firstborn, regardless of sex, which encouraged her to be independent.[34]

Surviving records for the three daughters of the count are far less complete than María Micaela's; we know only about the property that they inherited. The unentailed inheritance was to be divided equally among them. Since there was no way each sister could be given absolutely equal units, the *junta* juggled the appraised values of many items to approximate equal treatment. Since much of the addition is incorrect, it is possible that the experts felt obligated to have each sister receive an estate of about 300,000 *pesos*, as their father had declared in 1778.[35] (Table 4.1 illustrates the divisions.)

As they had not yet reached their majority when the estate was settled, their brother, Pedro Ramón Romero de Terreros, the second Count of Regla, replaced María Micaela as their guardian when he returned from Spain at the end of 1783. For the next two and one half years, he kept account of their expenditures, which provide us with clues to the lives of three wealthy, unmarried women under the age of twenty-five living in Mexico City in the 1780s. The two younger sisters, Ignacia and Dolores, lived in their own house; Antonia, the older sister, lived temporarily with her brother. He charged her for food, her servants, and other expenses.

The furnishings and household effects for the two younger sisters cost nearly 6,000 *pesos*. The house was staffed by a housekeeper and cook, who each received 6 *pesos* a month; a dressmaker, who received 2 *pesos* 4 *reales* a month; and a kitchen assistant and a manservant, who received, respectively, 2½ *pesos* and 3 *pesos* a month. Their greatest expenses were for a coach, mules, and salaries and clothing for a footman and coachman, which amounted to 2,274 *pesos* in slightly over a year. The purchase of four mules alone cost 500 *pesos*. The total expenses for the thirty months that the two sisters lived together was 8,729 *pesos*. In addition to the money for salaries and furnishings, the second count gave his sisters a daily allowance (presumably for food), of 10, 20, or 30 *pesos* a day. For thirteen months this alone amounted to 5,218 *pesos*. Their individual expenditures, also paid from their estates, ranged from clothing, special diets, and medical bills to gifts and charities. One of the sisters was charged nearly 1,000 *pesos* over a two-year period for the maintenance of her four slaves on her brother's *hacienda*.[36]

Since we have no price indices for Mexico in the late eighteenth century, it is difficult to evaluate these accounts. If we were to note that the dowry and fees needed to enter a convent ranged from 3,000 to 6,000 *pesos* and that this money was intended to produce enough income at 5 percent interest to support a woman frugally for the rest of her life, the quantities spent by the Regla

Table 4.1

Properties Inherited by the Three Younger Regla Sisters, 1783

Name	Properties	Assessed Value[a]	Final Value[b]
María Antonia (1759–1788)	Hacienda de Ajuchtitlán el Grande (house in Querétaro and Descubridora mine)[c]	133,562 9,776	147,159 ?
	Hacienda de San Francisco	90,532	132,772
	Hacienda de Tenería (house in Huichapán)*	43,088	43,274[d]
	*All properties were in Huichapán and vicinity	———	
			323,206
María Ignacia (1760–1800?)	Hacienda de Provincia[e] (Colima?)	105,541	79,528
	Hacienda de Cuyutlán (Colima; included salt mines)	83,704	83,707
	Hacienda de Tecajate (and a *pulquería*)	133,892	134,377
	4 additional *pulquerías*	?	18,520
	Money added from other sources	———	7,063
			323,607
María Dolores (1765–18??), later Marchioness of Herrera and of San Francisco	Hacienda de San Pedro de las Vaquerías (Acatlán and Tulancingo)	132,223[f]	147,111
	Hacienda de San Juan Hueyapán (Huasca and Acatlán)	47,480	50,779[g]
	Hacienda de San Antonio and San José (Tula)[h]	87,783	89,036
	2 *pulquerías*	?	11,460
	House in Querétaro	?	9,866[i]
	Mesón (inn)	?	2,000
	Money added from other sources	?	12,953
			302,166

This table illustrates the range of possibilities in the valuations of *haciendas*. The valuations were made extrajudicially, without the usual participation of local officials, in order to save the Regla estate a great expense, since the count had not divided up his entailed property before his death. All values are adjusted to the nearest peso, and the incorrect additions are in the original source, AMRT, "Testamentaria del Conde de Regla."

Apparently at some later time, other properties and commercial credits were added to the sisters' estates. Working with family papers deposited at Washington State University in Pullman, John Tutino noted that the value of each estate was 604,685 pesos, which included urban real estate and commercial credits. John Tutino, "Creole Mexico: Spanish Elites, Haciendas, and Indian Towns, 1750–1810" (Ph.D. Diss., University of Texas, 1976), p. 79.

[a] The assessed valuations were made by Crown-appointed officials during 1782, and they are bound as a part of a leather volume called "Albaceazgo de María Micaela Romero de Terreros," Archivo de Manuel Romero de Terreros (hereafter AMRT).

[b] The final values were determined by a *junta* held at the *cabildo* in Mexico City and are bound in a book called "Cuaderno de Juntas" in a section called "Junta de Menores." These values are also included in the "Testamentaria del Conde de Regla," vol. 2.

[c] All of her agricultural *haciendas* were in Huichapán and vicinity.

[d] Minor differences in price can usually be accounted for by the objections of Lucas Lasaga, who was in charge of defending the interests of the minor children.

[e] This *hacienda* was purchased for 150,000 *pesos* in 1780–81, around the time of the death of the first count. He had instructed his representatives to purchase agricultural *haciendas* for him at auctions. The representative at Colima was overly enthusiastic and paid too much for the *hacienda* of Provincia. At the Junta de Menores, they assumed that the

assessed valuation should be 105,000 *pesos*, but that the ture value was 79,528, in order to bring the value of María Ignacia's share into line with the other two.

f In an earlier evaluation made in 1782 by Francisco Antonio Villaverde, the *hacienda* of San Pedro de las Vaquerías was valued at 93,034 *pesos*. AMRT, "Los segundos condes de Regla."

g. In 1780, just three years before the final division, San Juan Hueyapán had sold for 40.000 *pesos* at an auction and included a house in Real del Monte, "Archivo de la Dirección General de Terrenos Nacionales, Departamento Agrario; Expediente San Juan Hueyapán."

h These *haciendas* were purchased by the Count of Regla on 11 December 1769 for 90,831 *pesos*, 3 *reales*, AMRT, "Libro de Caja," fol. 124 r.

i Whether Dolores or Ignacia received the house in Queretaro is uncertain. It may be the same one that Pedro Romero de Terreros received through his uncle's estate, although that is not proved. In 1733 it was valued at 8,000 *pesos*; AMRT, "Testimonio del Testamento de Juan Vázques de Terreros."

sisters seem large. However, if we were to compare them to their mother's probable expenditures in the 1750s—approximately 500 *pesos* a month—then these costs appear appropriate to the habits of aristocratic women.

It appears that these accounts are honest and are based on the customary receipts. Most of the prices seem reasonable. For example, the cost of a carriage and mules was somewhat less than their father had spent for two carriages and the mule teams for his wedding.[37] Costs of clothing, medical expenses, and servants are about equal to other prices in various Regla accounts. The one startling expense is the 10 to 30 *pesos* given daily to the two sisters. This might have been an allowance for food, since it is not included elsewhere—but in that case the figure is preposterous. The Count of Regla had paid between 20 and 27 *pesos* a month for the daily expenses of a household of seven children and their caretakers in 1769.[38] It is possible that the sisters spent the money for some purpose unknown to us. Or we might also speculate that years later, when the second Count of Regla or his widow might have been called upon to account for money spent between 1783 and 1785, not all of the receipts could be found. A daily expenditure might seem plausible.

We do not know the income that the sisters received from their estates. Contemporaries observed that in order to produce an income for their owners, properties had to be carefully and honestly administered. It is probable that their lands, apparently rather marginal, could not continue to support them at this level, even if the sisters had been trained *hacienda* administrators.

Their brother, Pedro Ramón, still very young himself, apparently feared that their patrimonies might soon disappear and that he would be held accountable. He used the occasion of María Antonia's twenty-fifth birthday to divest himself of their guardianship. He wrote to the viceroy that even he had difficulty overseeing his administrators and that his "sisters, by their sex, and their natural submissiveness, their prudent upbringing and education . . . are incapable of administering their business skillfully."[39] Each sister then chose an agent to administer her affairs.

María Antonia Romero de Terreros, the second eldest daughter, lived for only two and one-half years after reaching her majority and taking charge of her estates. She reduced her living expenses to under 1,000 *pesos* a year by not residing with her brother's family, but countered this frugality by constructing a house in Pachuca that cost 9,222 *pesos*. Her correspondence with her agent,

Manuel Ramón de Goya, portrays her as unable to make the smallest decision alone, for example, the choice of a present for her niece and godchild. At her death in 1788, her agent confiscated her jewelry in order to collect money that he claimed was owed him. [40] Her will specified a number of charitable bequests, including chaplaincies for her cousins, for which there were no longer funds. [41] Either she was victimized or thoughtless in handling her property. The few records of her life leave us with the impression that she was incapable of managing money and improvident. She fulfilled her brother's prediction of her sisters' incapacity. Of the third sister, María Ignacia, little is known so far, except that she lived for forty years.

There is more information on María Dolores, the youngest surviving daughter, born in Mexico City on 18 February 1765. She appeared as a maid of honor at her brother Pedro Ramón's wedding in May 1785. The witness was Vicente Herrera, regent of the Audiencia, who was the effective ruler of New Spain between the death of one viceroy and the arrival of the next. [42] Not quite two years later, on 18 March 1787, María Dolores married Herrera. He was then forty-seven years old, and she was twenty-two. Her brother arranged the marriage. After the ceremony she disappeared for two days and was discovered on the roof of her brother's house. His authority triumphed over her reluctance, and shortly afterwards she left for Madrid with her husband. [43]

While in Madrid, she rarely wrote to her brother Pedro Ramón and visited infrequently with her younger brother, Jose María, who was a resident there from 1787 to 1792. Whether this partial alienation from her brothers resulted from disputes over inheritances or over her marriage is unknown. However, her husband acted from time to time as a family representative. [44] In 1794, at the age of fifty-five, Vicente Herrera died. Five years later, María Dolores, at the age of thirty-four, married Manuel de Pedreguera, a Creole officer from Jalapa who was ten years her junior. [45]

In 1807, finances might have been rather tight, as María Dolores began to request a pension from her older sister as the holder of the entail that her family would inherit. Although there were many disputes over the properties of María Dolores, these seemed to have been on her administrator's initiative, rather than on her instructions. [46] However, her need for funds may have impelled her administrators to guard *hacienda* lands more diligently. María Dolores inherited the title of Marchioness de Herrera from her first husband and the title of Marchioness de San Francisco from her sister María Micaela in 1817. Her husband died in Mexico City in 1830, but she was still alive in 1840. [47]

In view of the limited alternatives open to women in the late eighteenth century, it is curious that none of the Regla sisters chose entry into a convent, either because they lacked religious or intellectual "calling" or because their father might have decided that they should remain single. Marriage was apparently forced upon one sister. Only the eldest daughter, María Micaela, exerted any significant economic power.

In contrast, the wife of the second Count of Regla, María Josefa Rodríguez de Pedroso, was a woman who enjoyed a high social status in her own right, married one of the wealthiest men in the colony, and, when widowed, controlled the family fortunes for more than a dozen years.

The second Count of Regla, Pedro Ramón Romero de Terreros, heir to the mines and the substantial agricultural properties of the main entail, returned from Spain at the end of 1783. He was returning to a land that he had not seen since he was fourteen and was warmly welcomed by the Count of San Bartolomé de Jala, Antonio Rodríguez de Pedroso, who intended to arrange a marriage between him and his older daughter, María Josefa.

On the surface this union appeared to join two of the greatest fortunes in New Spain of the 1780s. The Jala entail included valuable *pulque* (an intoxicating beverage) *haciendas* on the outskirts of Mexico City, as well as outlets for its sale in the city. The patina of prosperity was deceptive. The Count of Jala claimed that his estates were in bad repair in 1773 when he inherited them, and a luxurious style of living further diminished his resources. [48] The marriage of Josefa, the Count of Jala's daughter, to the second Count of Regla united her somewhat depleted fortune to his large one, resolving the family's fiscal crisis. Special concessions and arrangements had to be made before the count could get permission to marry, as he was still under twenty-five. Holders of entails often favored early marriages for their children, as it helped to assure the continuity of family property.

María Josefa's dowry, consisting of jewelry, household effects, clothing, slaves, and a country house at San Agustín de las Cuevas, was valued at 163,000 *pesos*, of which only 37,000 *pesos* came from her father. The bulk of the dowry derived from her mother's family. In March 1784, the second Count of Regla gave his fiancée 50,000 *pesos* in *arras*, which was added to her dowry in a document issued by the Count of Regla in April 1785. Wording in this donation protected the legal and property interests of the Jala family beyond the minimum standards imposed by law. The value of much of María Josefa's dowry was determined by the inventories made in late 1783, after her mother's death. In order to increase the registered size of the dowry that he was giving to his daughter, the Count of Jala added one-third to one-half to the value of most of the objects. [49] He might have argued, although he did not do so, that changing the values placed upon goods by experts was not unknown. After all, the year before, a group of the most respected men in the kingdom of New Spain had juggled the values of certain *haciendas* in order to assure an equitable distribution of wealth among the Regla daughters. But when the second Count of Regla and his wife discovered this alteration, they felt cheated. They later observed that they had not received any productive estates beyond the country house. The second count refused to cooperate with his father-in-law in agricultural matters, and relations between them cooled. Writing years later, the Countess of Regla claimed that she and her husband had overlooked the fraud in the dowry letter because of family loyalty. [50]

We have only details of the married life of the second Countess of Regla. She gave birth to four children, but only a son, Pedro, survived infancy. As late as 1807, she had a child, who died shortly before her husband in 1809. The family of the second count had an enormous household, including four clergymen, two of whom enjoyed the chaplaincies from María Antonia's estates. The family was on intimate terms with the viceregal court and was especially friendly with the family of José Iturrigaray, who was viceroy from 1803 to 1808. One of the Iturrigaray sons became a *compadre*, or coparent, of the Reglas at the birth of their son in 1807. After the Iturrigarays were banished in 1808, Inés Jáuregui de Iturrigaray corresponded with the Countess of Regla.

As a family, the Reglas engaged in the pleasures of the aristocracy in Mexico, which included rides in the country, outings at the old Jala house in San Agustín de las Cuevas, bullfights, visits to convents, both to see the younger sister of the Countess of Regla and to visit other nuns, and periods of time in the *hacienda* of San Miguel Regla, with its beautiful lake and supply of fresh fish. In 1788 both of the Reglas appeared before the notaries to grant freedom to four slaves, at least one of whom had purchased his liberty from the countess, although the manumission statement does not note this. In 1802 they received the right to have masses said in all of their residences through a special dispensation from Pius VII.[51]

It was not until the death of her husband in 1809 that Josefa emerged as an independent personality. The widowed Countess of Regla met the challenge of administering the estates of the two entails of Regla and San Cristóbal and other properties with considerable enthusiasm, administrative capacity, and skills in agricultural management, continuing a tradition among women in this family. She organized her household to oversee these affairs, setting up books to regularize the payment of interest due on various chaplaincies. She had an amanuensis copy each of her letters into a bound volume so that a permanent record could be kept.[52]

Shortly after the assumption of the guardianship of the estates and of her twenty-year-old son, Pedro José María, the Independence Wars broke out. Destruction caused by contending armies crippled her efforts to improve production on her lands near Huichapán, which were apparently the only ones she managed directly, rather than renting. She wrote frequently to her creditors about the damage inflicted to the Regla lands by the insurgents and claimed her inability to repay capital. As soon as she learned that the fighting had ended, she wrote to her administrators telling them that she had heard that the area was free of enemies and that they could now begin to adopt her plan for the government of *haciendas*, "which is my hope for the redemption of the house of Regla."[53]

In 1812, at the age of twenty-four, her son, Pedro José María, married Josefa Villamil, despite the vigorous resistance of his mother. She went to the judicial authorities to oppose it, as he was still legally a minor, being under twenty-five. The viceroy intervened in his behalf, and the mother's opposition became ineffective. The widowed countess explained her antagonism by asserting that the Reglas' financial crisis meant that the family could not support a new household.[54] It is interesting to observe that the second Countess of Regla had failed to prevent or postpone the marriage of her minor son, while years before, one of the Regla daughters had been married against her will by her brother. The countess did have as her adversary the "Güera" Rodríguez, the mother of the bride, an influential woman who wanted to marry her oldest daughter to the third Count of Regla, one of the most eligible bachelors of his time.[55]

Shortly after the marriage of her son, the countess moved from the house on San Felipe Neri, in which she had lived for more than twenty-five years, to permit Pedro and his new wife to live alone. She asked for a loan of 12,000 *pesos* from the Inquisition to facilitate the change. In her new home, she had six paid male servants: a caretaker, a coachman, two lackeys, a cook, and a kitchen scullion. Presumably, she also had female servants. She lost no time before informing her correspondents that she alone remained in charge of family affairs.[56]

After the marriage of Pedro, the widowed Countess of Regla effectively lost her titles, as her daughter-in-law became the Countess of Regla. Therefore, when an opportunity arose to inherit the title of the Marchioness of Villahermosa, she seized upon it, explaining that one of her son's children might want to inherit it. Since impecunious candidates were not permitted to inherit titles, her son guaranteed the value of her dowry letter to be 213,000 *pesos*, which indicates how a woman could use her dowry, even if it were exaggerated in value, to add to her social status.[57]

The second Countess of Regla died suddenly in March 1819. Her son immediately inherited all of her property and the considerable responsibilities of the Regla, San Cristóbal, and Jala entails.

Married at the age of sixteen or seventeen, Josefa Villamil, the third Countess of Regla, gave birth to seven children between 1815 and 1824. At the time of her marriage, her mother-in-law described her as a beauty "of much prudence and modesty," and ten years later, despite her numerous pregnancies, foreign visitors continued to comment on her appearance and charm.[58] An active life included serving on charitable boards, taking promenades in the Alameda (large public park), attending the theater and *tertulias* (salons), visiting country houses, discussing politics, and with her husband arranging such functions as a baptismal ceremony for the daughter of the British minister and hosting a dinner afterwards.[59]

As might have been anticipated from a daughter of Güera Rodríguez, known as the western Madame de Staël, the Countess of Regla also entered politics. She enjoyed the confidence of Guadalupe Victoria, the first president of Mexico, and on one occasion almost succeeded in a plot to change cabinet officers. As well as beauty, the countess possessed shrewdness and political skills.[60]

Her life as an elite woman ended abruptly for the countess in February 1826, when she left for New York, where she died two years later, at age thirty-two. A growing estrangement from her husband, too close ties with Guadalupe Victoria, poor political choices—all might explain her surprising departure from Mexico.

It is difficult to evaluate the third countess's power in the family. A request that her husband not act as executor of her will was ignored, and her views on the education of her sons did not prevail.[61] But she died before she reached an advanced age or the state of widowhood at which her opinion might have been respected. Her efforts to expand her interests outside the family failed.

This study of the Regla women illustrates the variety of personalities within this one family—from the very strong to the very weak. It also indicates the ways in which the demands on resources made by women could affect the destiny of the family. A conclusion to be drawn is that widows and single women exercised substantial influence as executors of estates, guardians of minor children, or inheritors of property. The experiences of the Countess of Miravalle, of her granddaughter and godchild, María Micaela Romero de Terreros, and of the second Countess of Regla demonstrate how these possibilities were used by colonial women. When such women were given the opportunity, their strength of character is revealed in their letters, business deals, and legal suits. They belie stereotypes of subservience and lack of control over the economic aspects of their family. However, their lives, even at the most active, were bounded by limits of the extended family. Even such an enterprising woman as the Countess of Miravalle had a barely significant extrafamilial role, although her actions in defense of her family interests had political consequences.

As women were circumscribed by family ties, it is important to observe that a network of similar obligations often dominated the lives and influenced the economic activities of their male relatives. But if women could exert influence and power in the preservation of the family and appeared to play a role far greater than our previous knowledge has indicated, they were nonetheless far from free of accepted mores—forced marriages or prohibitions on excessive outings.

As the eighteenth-century family was significant both politically and economically in New Spain, the role of marriage had to be a crucial one. Marriages provided both wealth and children: the marriage of María Antonia Trebustos, the daughter of the Countess de Miravalle, to the first Count of Regla gave the older man the chance to establish a family and to gain social status even though he sacrificed a dowry. The marriage of the second Count of Regla into an equally prestigious family supplied him with no productive wealth and only one child, but with a capable wife who can be credited with the preservation of the Regla family interests. The third Countess of Regla, by mothering many children, provided the family with an opportunity to contract favorable marriages and to exchange their name and family properties for political and economic position in the emerging elite of the nineteenth century.

Far from simply being enclosed behind the high walls of their houses, women were pivotal in the fate of their families as marriageable pawns, child-bearers, heiresses, advisers, and administrators. The dimensions of their influence are only beginning to be fully perceived, but the complexity of their roles warrants further inquiry and a reassessment of their power and authority.

Notes

ABBREVIATIONS

AGI   Archivo General de Indias
AGN   Archivo General de la Nación, Mexico
AINAH   Archivo del Instituto de Antropología e Historia
AMRT   Archivo de Manuel Romero de Terreros
ANM   Archivo de Notarías de Mexico
PCR   Papeles del conde de Regla, Manuscript Collection at the State University of Washington in Pullman
UT   University of Texas, Manuscript Collection

The research for this paper was carried out with the assistance of a grant from the Penrose Fund of the American Philosophical Society. I am indebted to Doña Concepción Romero de Terreros for her kind assistance. The pioneer historical works on the history of the family were carried out by Manuel Romero de Terreros, who explored new ground in this, as in so many fields.

An earlier version of this paper was delivered at the First Berkshire Conference of Women Historians at Rutgers University. Asunción Lavrin, Virginia Hardman, and Anna Macías read this paper and offered valuable suggestions.

1. Doris M. Ladd, *The Mexican Nobility at Independence: 1780-1826* (Austin, Tex.: University of Texas Press, 1976). Mary L. Felstiner, "The Larraín Family in the Independence of Chile, 1780-1830" (Ph.D. diss., Stanford University, 1970), pp. iii-iv. Diana Hernando, "Casa y Familia: Spatial Biographies in Nineteenth Century Buenos Aires" (Ph.D. diss., University of California, Los Angeles, 1973).

2. Manuel Romero de Terreros, *El Conde de Regla: Creso de la Nueva España* (Mexico: Ediciones Xochitl, 1943). Recent works on the Count of Regla include Robert Randall, *Real del Monte* (Austin, Tex.: University of Texas Press, 1972), pp. 10-14, and Alan Probert, "Pedro Romero de Terreros: The Genius of the Vizcaína Vein," *Journal of the West* 14 (1975): 51-78. See David Brading, *Miners and Merchants in Bourbon Mexico, 1780-1810* (London: Cambridge University Press, 1971).

3. On the history of the Miravalles and the biography of the countess, see the following: Manuel Romero de Terreros, "La Condesa de Miravalle," in *Apostillas Históricas* (Mexico: Editorial Hispano-Mexicana, 1945), pp. 83-85; Artemio Valle Arizpe, *Calle vieja y calle nueva* (Mexico: Editorial Jus, 1949), pp. 197-215; Jesús Amaya, *Los conquistadores Fernández de Hijar y Bracamonte* (Guadalajara: Gráfica Editorial, 1952), pp. 84, 107, 122; Ricardo Ortega y Pérez Gallardo, *Histórica genealógica de las familias más antiguas de Mexico*, 3 vols., 3d ed. (Mexico: A. Carranza, 1908), vol. 2, "*Condado de Miravalle*"; AINAH, Colección Antigua, "El derecho de Hidalguía de la

familia Bracamontes y Terreros," vol. 31; Edmundo O'Gorman Collection at the University of Texas, nos. 3, 4.

4. Romero de Terreros, "La Condesa de Miravalle," p. 84. AGN, Vínculos, vol. 87, exp. 2; vol. 93, exp. 3. ANM; José Manuel Arroyo (1743), fol. 541.

5. AMRT, "Miravalles," Letter from the Countess de Miravalle to Pedro Romero de Terreros, 5 March 1761.

6. Eduardo Báez Macías, "Planos y censo de la ciudad de Mexico, 1753 (Segunda Parte)," *Boletín del Archivo General de la Nación* 8 (October-December 1967): 833; Valle Arizpe, *Calle vieja*, p. 197; Guillermo S. Fernández de Recas, *Mayorazgos de la Nueva España* (Mexico: Universidad Nacional Autónoma de Mexico, 1965), p. 194; AMRT, "Miravalles," Letters from Vicente Trebustos.

7. AGN, Vínculos, vol. 93, exp. 3. In the case of the Miravalle family, there seems to have been only a small difference in cost in placing a daughter in a convent or providing a dowry for her marriage.

8. AGN, Vínculos, vol. 93, exp. 3. In the section of her will written after María Antonia's death, the countess recalled that she had supplied the cost of the wedding. She probably meant some of the feasts and clothing, as Pedro spent 50,000 *pesos* on wedding costs, which included clothing of all male attendants, coaches and mules, and gifts. AMRT, "Cuentas Sueltas."

9. ANM, Ambrosio Zevallos, 26 June 1756. PCR, folder 94. For a further discussion of *arras*, see the article by Lavrin (chap. 1) in this volume, and also the collection of laws in Marcelo Martínez Alcubilla, *Códigos antiguos de España* (Madrid: López Camacho, 1885); the article on *arras* in *Enciclopedia Jurídica de España*, 30 vols. (Barcelona: F. Seix, 1911-23), 3: 310-11 and the discussion in A. H. de Oliveira Marques, *Daily Life in Portugal in the Late Middle Ages* (Madison: University of Wisconsin Press, 1971), pp. 166, 324.

10. AGN, Vínculos, vol. 93, exp. 3; Media Annata, vol. 153, exp. 1; Correspondencia de los Virreyes, 16 March 1758 and 24 October 1760; Vicente Riva Palacio, ed., *Mexico a través de los siglos*, 5 vols. (Mexico: Ballesca, n.d.) 2: 811. It appears that a year later she suffered financial difficulties, as she borrowed 8,000 *pesos* from the Count of Regla, and shortly before her death in 1769 an additional 6,000 *pesos* was borrowed; AMRT, "Libro de Caja," fol. 102.

11. *Compadres* (coparents) become equivalent to siblings through this ritual. Mary Lowenthal Felstiner, "Kinship Politics in the Chilean Independence Movement," *Hispanic American Historical Review* 56 (February 1976): 60 (hereafter cited as *HAHR*).

12. AMRT, Letters of the countess to Pedro Romero de Terreros. The purchases of slaves are discussed in letters of 26 January 1757, 8 November 1761, 13 December 1761, and 19 April 1762. Business affairs are described in letters of 8 November 1761, 2 February 1764, and 1 November 1765.

13. AGN, Vínculos, vol. 210, "Cuaderno Secreto. . . ."

14. AMRT, "Miravalles," Letters of 24 March, 28 and 29 April, 9 May 1757.

15. AMRT, "Miravalles," Letter of 16 June 1757.

16. See article by Lavrin (chap. 1) in this volume, and José María Ots Capdequí, *Manual de historia del derecho Español en las Indias* (Buenos Aires: Editorial Losada, 1945), p. 424.

17. AMRT, "Miravalles," Miscellaneous letters of 1757, and letters of April and May 1757, July 1758, and July 1759.

18. AMRT, "Miravalles," Undated letter of 1758.

19. AMRT, "Miravalles," Letters of 15 July 1757 and August 1757; Letters from 1759 to 1763.

20. This letter, allegedly written to his children, was published as part of his funeral oration and is quoted in full in Manuel Romero de Terreros, *El Conde de Regla*, p. 152.

21. See article by Lavrin (chap. 1) in this volume.

22. José Ruiz de Villafranca y Cárdenas, *Llanto de la religion derramado, en la muerte del Señor Don Pedro Romero de Terrerois* . . . (Mexico: Zúñiga y Ontiveros, 1796).

23. Under Spanish law, unless a special entail or *mayorazgo* was made, all legitimate children shared equally in the estate. Establishing *mayorazgo* permitted the oldest son or another designated heir to inherit the third and fifth part of the estate. These *mayorazgos* were inalienable, the properties could not be mortgaged, and the founder could set up specified conditions for succession. He or she designated the properties that were to be included in the entail, the order of preference in inheritance, which was usually such as male over female and older over younger, and other provisions such as Christian names of heirs. In the inheritance of entails, the rights of females were well protected in law. See article on *mayorazgos* in *Enciclopedia Jurídica de España*, vol. 22, pp. 105-220; Bartolomé Clavero, *Mayorazgo: Propiedad feudal en Castilla, 1396-1836* (Madrid: Siglo XXI Editores, 1974). On the Count of Regla's entails and his will, see PCR, folder 94; AMRT, "Testamentaría del Conde de Regla"; AGN, Correspondencia de los Virreyes, 1st ser. vol. 112 (1778), fols. 439, 455-60.

24. AGN, Minería, vol. 48, fols. 483-89; Vínculos, vol. 145, exp. 1; AMRT, "Testamentaría."

25. Ruiz de Villafranca, *Llanto*.

26. Ibid.

27. The question of the amount of money that the Reglas did pay for all of the former Jesuit *haciendas* purchased between 1776 and 1781 has been vexing lawyers, bureaucrats, and historians for nearly two hundred years. In 1782, when María Micaela and her representative, José Marrugat, borrowed 500,000 *pesos* from various church and sodality funds, they stated that the money was to complete the purchase price of *haciendas* in the north of Mexico, especially Tetillas. Their assumption was that the properties purchased in 1776 had been paid for by the 700,000 *pesos* deposited by the first count; ANM, Jacinto de León, 17 May 1782, fols. 164-183. University of Chicago, Mexican Confraternity Papers, Miguel Domínguez, *Manifiesto del derecho que asiste al Conde de Regla, al Marqués de San Cristóbal, a la Marquesa de San Francisco sobre el remate de varias haciendas de las temporalidades de los ex-Jesuítas, hecho a favor del Conde de Regla, padre de aquellos* . . . (Mexico: Zúñiga y Ontiveros, 1796). Modern scholars so far have not found evidence that more than 700,000 *pesos* were paid for all the *haciendas* together. Ladd, *Mexican Nobility*, p. 238.

28. AMRT, "Testamentaría" and "Cuaderno de Juntas," Statement by Rafael Molina, 3 December 1783.

29. AMRT, "Los segundos condes de Regla"; "Cartas de María Micaela."

30. AMRT, "Cartas de María Micaela."

31. AGN, Tierras, vol. 1153, exp. 3.

32. Fernando Fernández de San Salvador, *Defensa jurídica de la Señora Doña María Micaela de Terreros* . . . (Mexico: Zúñiga y Ontiveros, 1796).

33. Luis Azcúe y Mancera, *Catálogo de construcciones religiosas del estado de Hidalgo*, 2 vols. (Mexico: Talleres Gráficos de la Nación, 1940), 2: 56. Manuel Romero de Terreros, "Los hijos menores de los primeros Condes de Regla," *Memorias de la Academia Mexicana de la Historia* 3 (April-June 1944): 191; AGN, Vínculos, vol. 145, exp. 7; PCR, 1868 folder.

34. UT, García Collection, no. 183, Letter from Fr. Alonso Giraldo de Terreros, 12 February 1758.

35. AMRT, "Junta de Menores"; AGN, Correspondencia de los Virreyes, 1st ser., vol. 112 (1778), fols. 455-50.

36. AMRT, "Libro de Censos," no. 2.

37. AMRT, "Libro de Cuenta." The mule team cost 600 *pesos*, and the two carriages cost 2,529 *pesos*.

38. AMRT, "Libro de Cuenta." Another series of accounts placed in the same book documents expenses in 1768-69. It might also be noted that the official rate of support of a minor, or for payment to a beneficiary of an estate while it was being settled, was four reales or one-half *peso*, daily; Archivo de Notarías de Puebla, Josef Antonio Saldaña (1752), Will of Blas Clavijero, fol. 159.

39. AMRT, "Junta de Menores," May 1786.

40. AMRT, "María Antonia Romero de Terreros," is a collection of receipts and letters exchanged between Goya and María Antonia, which were submitted by Goya as proof of payments made. Goya may in fact have taken large amounts of her money, as he was in serious financial trouble and was accused of misappropriating money from another mining family. Brading, *Miners and Merchants*, pp. 116, 202, 207. Also, see his "Mexican Silver Mining in the Eighteenth Century: The Revival of Zacatecas," *HAHR* 50 (November 1970): 665-81.

41. PCR, folder 120; ANM, Manuel Puertas, 16 October 1788, fols. 255-64. For history of the will, see AGN Bienes Nacionales, 1767; Consolidación, vol. 5, fols. 267-68; Temporalidades, vol. 13, exp. 8; AMRT, "Recibos de la obra pía que instituyó Antonia, 1810-1812."

42. Archivo del Antiguo Ayuntamiento, Nobiliario, IV-6; vol. 3301.

43. Manuel Romero de Terreros, "Los hijos menores," pp. 193-94.

44. AMRT, "Cartas de los menores hijos. . . ."

45. Manuel Romero de Terreros, "Los hijos menores"; AMRT, Carta de Manuel Pedreguera (hijo), written in 1847.

46. AGN, Vínculos, vol. 145, exp. 7; and PCR, 1868 folder; Edith B. Couturier, *La Hacienda de Hueyapán: 1550-1936* (Mexico: SepSetentas, 1976), pp. 81-84.

47. Howard T. Fisher and Marion Hall Fisher, eds., *Life in Mexico: The Letters of Fanny Calderón de la Barca* (Garden City, N.Y.: Doubleday, 1966), pp. 218, 713.

48. Ladd, *Mexican Nobility*, p. 55. She gives various values of the properties in this entail. See also AGN, Vínculos, vol. 59, cuaderno no. 6, fol. 10v; vol. 58, passim; AMRT, "Cartas al Conde de Jala . . . ," Various letters of 1785. The Count of Jala received a marriage gift from both his mother's and father's estate in 1761 of 216,313 *pesos*, which included the hacienda of Ojo de Agua, evaluated at 171,200 *pesos*; ANM, Josef de Molina, 14 March 1761, fols. 94-116, which indicates that the hacienda was in fairly productive condition.

49. PCR, Carta Dotal de la Segunda Condesa de Regla; Manuel Romero de Terreros, ed., *Una casa del siglo XVIII en Mexico, la del Conde de San Bartolomé de*

Xala . . . (Mexico: Universidad Nacional Autónoma de Mexico, 1957); this book contains the list of values given by the appraisers for most of the objects in Josefa's dowry.

50. AMRT, "Los segundos condes de Regla," 12 May 1810, 1807; AMRT, Cartas al Conde de Jala, 16 April 1787, 12 June 1788, 4 December 1787, February 1793.

51. ANM, Manuel Puertas, various dates in November 1788; PCR, Carta Dotal de la Segunda Condesa de Regla, clause 536; AMRT, "Los segundos condes de Regla."

52. Some of these letters have been published by Manuel Romero de Terreros with an introduction, "La Condesa escribe," *Historia Mexicana* 1 (January-March 1952): 456-67.

53. AGN, Minería, vol. 29, 23 July 1811; AMRT, "Borrador de Cartas," April 1812 and passim.

54. Manuel Romero de Terreros, "El tercer Conde de Regla," *Memorias de la Academia* 2 (July-September 1942): 297-99; AGN, Minería, vol. 29, 23 July 1811; AMRT, "Borrador de Cartas" has another copy of this letter; Letters on 16 April 1812 to Marqués de San Cristóbal and on 12 June 1812 to Pedro Sierra.

55. Artemio Valle Arizpe, *La Güera Rodríguez* (Mexico: Editorial Porrúa, 1950).

56. AMRT, "Borrador de Cartas," 1812.

57. AMRT, "Los terceros condes de Regla," no. 37; AGN, Temporalidades, vol. 157, exp. 1. Ladd, *Mexican Nobility*, p. 264.

58. AMRT, "Borrador de Cartas," Letter to Inés Jauregui, 4 July 1812. Poinsett, *Notes on Mexico* (London: J. Miller, 1825), p. 77.

59. Poinsett, *Notes on Mexico*; Henry Ward, *Mexico in 1827* (London: Henry Colburn, 1828). See also Fisher and Fisher, *Calderón de la Barca*, for the best description of social life several years after these events.

60. U.S. National Archives, General Records of the Department of State, vol. 2, 12 October 1825, dispatch no. 24 from Joel Poinsett.

61. Information from Alan Probert, who is working on a paper on the Reglas in the 1820s; Manuel Romero de Terreros, "D. Pedro Romero de Terreros: Count of Regla" (Mimeographed copy of a translation made by the Cía Real del Monte y Pachuca in late 1909 or early 1910), pp. 38-39; I am indebted to Alan Probert for this copy. AMRT, "Los terceros condes de Regla." For a description of her death in New York, see F. R. Pleasants, "Museum Acquires Collection of Colonial Mexican Portraits," *Brooklyn Museum Bulletin* 14 (Spring 1953): 12.

5

Ann Miriam Gallagher, R.S.M.

The Indian nuns of Mexico City's *Monasterio* of Corpus Christi, 1724-1821

An attempt to write an essay on Indian women living in Mexico during the last century of the colonial era may suggest a certain degree of presumption on the part of an author, especially since there have been remarkably few studies published on Indian society in general for the period.[1] However, an examination mainly of a private collection of manuscript sources has made it possible to look into the lives and family backgrounds of a very select group of Indian women—the nuns of Mexico City's *monasterio* (nunnery) of Corpus Christi, founded in 1724.[2] Although these women constituted only a fragment of the total female Indian population of New Spain, this study will serve to shed light on the social values held by the Indian community in the capital of the most important viceroyalty of the Spanish empire in the eighteenth century and to suggest the relationship between these women and the Church, an institution that so greatly influenced the lives of all social groups in Spanish America.

Almost from the beginning of the Spanish occupation of Mexico, the Church manifested concern for the welfare of native women, particularly in seeing to their preparation for the role of Christian wife and mother. Just a few years following the conquest of Mexico City in 1521, Indian girls were attending classes in Christian doctrine in the "patio schools" located in the church courtyards of the Franciscan friars.[3] Within a decade of the conquest, Spanish female teachers were on the scene, partly in hopes of alleviating the work of the friars and partly in the belief that they could better instill some of the principles of Christian womanhood in the indigenous women. Thus in 1529, owing largely to the efforts of Mexico's first bishop, Juan de Zumárraga, the Spanish matron Catalina Bustamante was operating a boarding school for Indian girls in Texcoco. During the next few years similar schools were established in several other places.[4]

While these institutions continued to function, another educational plan was introduced, that of employing *beatas*, or Third Order Franciscan women, as teachers, with six arriving from Spain in 1530 and three more in 1535.[5] But having become convinced that the matrons and *beatas* lacked the kind of dedication necessary for such an important task, Zumárraga founded the *monasterio* of La Concepción in Mexico City in 1540, believing that Spanish nuns who had taken the solemn vows of poverty, chastity, obedience, and cloister would be the best teachers.[6] In this foundation, the bishop initiated what he hoped would become a network of female *monasterios* to serve as teacher training centers for Indian women who would leave them and instruct other native women—a system not unlike the one employed by the friars for the Indian male population. However, Zumárraga and his successors were to find themselves more occupied with the needs of different women, the *criollas*, or Spanish women born in the New World. While the education of Indian women was rapidly neglected, La Concepción became identified with meeting the various interests of *criollas*, as did the other thirty-eight feminine *monasterios* established in Mexico up to the eighteenth century. Only occasionally were Indians admitted into them for educational purposes, to be instructed either by individual nuns as private tutors or else by nuns who taught in the *colegios*, or schools, annexed to some of them.

Although not greatly benefiting from a formal education, many Indian women were active in the affairs of the Church: they taught catechism, prepared their people for the reception of the sacraments, ministered to the sick and dying, looked after the upkeep of churches, and even directed *cofradías*, or confraternities, associated with them. When the religious drama was utilized as a teaching method, they were on hand, portraying saints and sinners alike.[7] Some of these women were regarded as important enough to have their names recorded in history. An examination of old chronicles reveals such names as Ana de la Cruz of Santiago Tlaltelolco, who spent much of her time collecting alms for the friars; Juana de Motolinía, who opened her home in Cholula to needy Indian girls whom she raised; Juana de San Jerónimo, whose model behavior as a servant in the *monasterio* of Santa Catalina in Mexico City was a source of edification to the nuns and secular women living there; and the shepherdess Salvadora de los Santos, whose virtuous life as a young girl in San Juan del Río later facilitated her gaining admittance as a servant into Querétaro's *beaterio* of San José de Gracia. Her apostolic activities there brought fame to the institution.[8] Some of these Indian servants made private vows, especially of chastity, and pursued something of a religious life in their respective institutions, in which they were usually classified as *donadas*. But as far as is known, until after the foundation of Corpus Christi in 1724, no Indian woman other than Luisa de Tapia of the Real Monasterio de Santa Clara de Jesús in Querétaro took the solemn vows of religion that made her a professed nun.[9]

How do we explain the absence of Indian nuns in Mexico prior to that time? Early experiments of the Franciscans in receiving Indian men into their order failed; Indians were generally regarded as lacking the mentality to comprehend the true meaning of religious life.[10] Apparently Indian women were excluded from religious life on similar grounds. In fact, this attitude appears to have been prevalent among the Indians themselves: some Indian men in Mexico City took the first steps for the founding of the *monasterio* of San Juan de la Penitencia in 1598 for Spanish women and not for their own; and several years later (1607), when Diego de Tapia founded the above-mentioned Santa Clara, he did not open its doors to Indian women other than his daughter.[11] It is possible that the Indians, at least during those times, did not consider their women ready for and perhaps even worthy of embracing the religious life.

Around the middle of the seventeenth century, Juan Palafox y Mendoza, bishop of Puebla de los Angeles, tried to explain the lack of Indian nuns in Mexico, stating that "[Indian] women do not become nuns because, owing to the misery and poverty in which they live, they have no dowries."[12] All feminine *monasterios* in Mexico at that time exacted dowries from their professed-elect.[13] However, dowries were not the primary factor barring the Indian women from the religious life, because it was evident that even the ability to provide one would not have gained their entrance into a *monasterio*. Racial considerations were more relevant. Before being received in a convent, as aspirant had to give proof of her *limpieza de sangre*, or pure Spanish ancestry. This usage had originated in mid-fifteenth-century Spain as a political weapon for depriving Jews of officeholding.[14] When feminine monasteries were founded, the Spanish founders ordinarily specified that they were for Spanish girls. The rules, constitutions, and ordinances of these institutions—as well as the legislation of general, provincial, and local chapters of the male religious orders that had jurisdiction over some of them—insisted on the quality of *limpieza* for its members. In Spain, in order to prove her *limpieza*, an aspirant had to give evidence that she and her family had never been engaged in lowly offices, that they had not been investigated by the Inquisition, and that they were *cristianos viejos*, or Old Christians, free from any taint of Jewish or Moorish blood. In America, while these same matters were explored, greater emphasis was placed on searching out any possible Indian ancestry that would disqualify an aspirant. Exemptions to the *limpieza* requirement could be obtained by *breves* (apostolic briefs) or royal *cédulas*, but I found no sources to show that they were resorted to in Mexico.[15]

Instead of seeking exceptions for Indians, New Spain's viceroy, Baltasar de Zúñiga, the Marquis of Valero, proposed in 1719 a unique foundation, offering 40,000 *pesos* to carry it out—a *monasterio* in Mexico City exclusively for

Indian women.[16] Since he was aware of the large number of Indian women in New Spain, he determined to reserve it for the daughters of *caciques* and *principales*, the members of the upper and lower nobility of Indian society. Despite this concession to elitism, this innovative idea was not exactly welcomed by all. From the beginning, some Jesuits and members of Mexico City's Audiencia opposed the project, arguing that even this privileged group could not be trusted with fulfilling the obligations of a nun. They made serious charges against all Indian women: they were very prone to incontinence and therefore should not be permitted to make a vow of chastity; they were unstable; they were slow in learning; and their melancholic temperament would hinder them from living in community as religious.[17]

When these accusations were made public, the nuns and chaplains of *monasterios* where some Indian women lived as servants and students and the priests in several Indian parishes volunteered to speak on their behalf. They attested that Indian women manifested a high regard for chastity, and many had even lived as consecrated virgins for most of their lives. Indian women, they stated, had the ability to persevere in seeking religious perfection in the religious state; some were so educated that they could read and write Latin better than their native languages.[18] In the light of this information, civic and Church officials agreed that a "chance" could be taken with the foundation. Meanwhile, the royal authorization arrived, and the *monasterio* of Corpus Christi was founded on 16 July 1724.[19]

Corpus Christi was placed under the jurisdiction of the Franciscans of the Province of the Holy Gospel, who entrusted the formation of the new community and its government to several white nuns of Mexico City's *monasterios* of San Juan de la Penitencia, Santa Clara, and Santa Isabel. At the end of twenty years, if the Indians showed themselves capable, they would take over the various administrative positions. Since it was of the strict Order of the Clares of the First Rule, Corpus Christi was mendicant, requiring no dowry from members and depending on the alms of benefactors for maintenance. As was customary in mendicant orders, the size of the community at any time was never very large. The founder set the number of religious between 18 and 20, but provincials periodically allowed a few more than 20. A *breve* in 1760 permitted as many as 33 members.[20] All told, from the foundation to the end of the colonial period in 1821 there were 147 women admitted into the novitiate.

To become a novice an aspirant had to meet certain requirements not unlike those met by *criollas* or white nuns. The Corpus Christi novice had to be a full-blooded Indian of legitimate birth and the daughter of *caciques* or *principales*; she and all her family members had to be free of ever having exercised "vile offices"—such as working as animal slaughterers, vendors of alcoholic beverages (like *pulque*), and cooks in public eating houses—and all had to be innocent of participation in ceremonies of an idolatrous nature. She was also expected to be of good health; to be at least fifteen years of age;[21] to be able to read Latin for the Divine Office; to be trained in sewing, embroidering, and other domestic arts; to be unmarried and not engaged to marry; and, in general, to have followed a virtuous life.

The procedure for investigating these requirements was a very formal and uniform one. After an applicant's petition for entrance into Corpus Christi was received with her baptismal certificate, the Franciscan provincial appointed a friar as a *comisario* to conduct an inquiry on her. The *comisario* was assisted in this by a *notario*, or notary, usually another Franciscan. The inquiry consisted of two parts. The first was the *información secreta* (secret information) for which several *testigos*, or witnesses (men or women), acquainted with the applicant and her family were called one at a time before the *comisario* and the *notario* and revealed what they knew of them. In the case of adverse personal information the questioning ceased, and the applicant was no longer considered for the novitiate. When no such evidence was given, then the second part of the inquest was carried out, namely, the *información pública* (public information). For this, ordinarily six witnesses (usually the same ones who took part in the *información secreta*, but never women[22]) came individually before the *comisario* and the *notario* and answered the *comisario*'s questions on the aspirant's qualifications.[23]

The entire process was the applicant's *información de limpieza de sangre* (a term that had now taken on the new meaning of pure Indian ancestry), *nobleza, legitimidad, vida y costumbres*. Gathering these data took anywhere from a few days to a year or more. The length of the report varied from several to thirty or more pages, and the material that it contained ranged from what was only general in nature to that which was minutely detailed. Almost always the applicant's family surrendered additional documentation—baptismal and marriage certificates, *informaciones* made on particular members, copies of titles of nobility, and the like—either on a voluntary basis because they wished to "push" their case in getting her accepted, or else at the request of the *comisario*, who needed to strengthen or clarify points in his own investigation. The applicant's complete *información* along with any supplementary material were forwarded to Corpus Christi where the abbess and her council examined their contents and determined from them whether or not the applicant qualified for membership in the community. These documents are the sources consulted for this study.[24] They have provided detailed information about the women of Corpus Christi: their place of origin; their racial, social, and economic background; their education; and finally, the forces that impelled them to seek the religious life.

Unlike many founders who demanded that nuns be from geographical areas under the same ecclesiastical jurisdiction as their respective *monasterios*, the Marquis of Valero founded his for Indian women of the entire viceroyalty of New Spain. As would be expected, however, many of the nuns were from the diocese of Mexico, in which Corpus Christi was located. Table 5.1 gives data on the place of origin of 143 of the 147 who were received from 1724 through 1821. It shows that 106, or 74 percent of them, were from that diocese, with the various subdivisions of Mexico City—especially the Indian *parcialidades* (districts) of San Juan Tenochtitlán and Santiago Tlaltelolco—supplying more than half that number, while others came from the cities of Toluca and Querétaro and from thirty-one Indian pueblos dispersed throughout the diocese. The diocese of Puebla de los Angeles provided 26 (18.1 percent); Oaxaca, 6 (4.2 percent); Guadalajara, 3 (2.2 percent); and Michoácan, 2 (1.5 percent). The more remote regions like Sonora and Yucatán had no representation.

Information on the racial background of the aspirants was thoroughly tested because *limpieza* was such an important requisite for admission. Witnesses often went to great lengths in their efforts to prove that the aspirants for whom they were testifying were truly Indians. A few examples will illustrate this. For one aspirant, the following points were elaborated on to make clear why she had been baptized in a Spanish parish, a circumstance that would have been cause to question her *limpieza*: as a newborn infant in Santiago Tlaltelolco, she was very ill; her Spanish godmother took her into the city to be cured. Rising waters between the two areas caused floods, and the godmother was forced to have the baptism performed in her own church.[25] For two others, all witnesses mentioned that they had "white-skinned" grandfathers, but swore they were nevertheless Indians: they dressed and conducted themselves like Indians; they actively participated in Indian *fiestas*; and they had perfect command in speaking and understanding the native dialects of their towns.[26]

On the other hand, there were three denied the habit mainly because they lacked *limpieza*. The *informaciones* showed that some of their ancestors were Spaniards. Although the Franciscan *comisario* would have admitted at least one of them, the Indian nuns in Corpus Christi, exercising their right to decide who joined them, made the final decision: they could not in conscience give their stamp of approval for reception because not all witnesses could swear that she was without *una gota de otra sangre*—one drop of other blood.[27]

This emphasis on racial purity was necessary if the convent was to preserve its Indian character. The history of the convent registered a major challenge to its Indian nature. In 1742, just two years before the Indians were supposed to take over the government of the community, the Franciscan general commissary of New Spain, Fray Pedro Navarrete, and the white abbess and her council, in direct violation of the conditions under which Corpus Christi had been founded and also in defiance of two apostolic briefs that had confirmed the reasons for the foundation, purposely admitted three white novices in order to strengthen the community.[28] We do not know exactly what they meant by "strengthening" it, but some of the Indian nuns interpreted the action as part of a plan of the white nuns to continue in control. Indeed, there had already been a serious attempt to keep the Indians in an inferior position as subjects.

Table 5.1

Birthplaces of Nuns of the Convent of Corpus Christi

	Number of Nuns
DIOCESE OF MEXICO	
MEXICO CITY	
Parcialidades	
S. Juan Tenochtitlán	35
Santiago Tlaltelolco	14
Villas	
Coyoacán	2
N. Sra. de Guadalupe	2
Tacuba	3
Tacubaya	2
Tenayuca	1
Pueblos	
S. Antonio de las Huertas	6
S. Mateo Churubusco	1
CITY OF QUERÉTARO	2
CITY OF TOLUCA	1
PUEBLOS	
Alfajayucán	1
Amecameca	1
Atotonilco	1
Atzompán	1
Azcapatzalco	1
Calimaya	1
Campoala	1
Coyatepeo	1
Cuauhtlapa	1
Cuautitlán	3
Chalco	1
Guauchinango	1
Ozumba	1
Reyes	1
S. Agustín de las Cuevas	1
S. Bartolomé Capuluac	1
S. Cristóbal Ecatepec	3
S. Gerónimo	1
S. Juan Teotihuacán	1
S. Mateo Atenco	1
S. Mateo Xalpa	1
S. Pedro Tlahuac	1
S. Pedro Tlascoapán	1
Sichú de los Indios	1
Tecomatlán	1

Tepozotlán	1	
Tlalnepantla	1	
Tula	1	
Zacualpán	2	
Zapotitlán	1	
Zumpango de Lagos	2	
		106 (74.1%)

DIOCESE OF PUEBLA DE LOS ANGELES

CITIES		
Cholula	5	
Puebla de los Angeles	7	
Tlaxcala	2	
VILLA OF ATLIXCO	1	
PUEBLOS		
Acatzingo	1	
Sanctorum	2	
S. Agustín del Palmar	1	
S. Andrés	2	
S. Pedro Zacatlán	2	
Sta. Cruz Tlocotepec	1	
Sta. María Tonanzintla	1	
Tepejí de la Seda	1	
		26 (18.2%)

DIOCESE OF OAXACA

PUEBLOS		
S. Domingo Yanhuitlán	1	
S. Juan Huitache	1	
S. Mathías Xalatlaco	1	
Sta. Ana Amatlán	1	
Sta. María Ozolotepec	1	
Xtitlán	1	
		6 (4.2%)

DIOCESE OF GUADALAJARA

PUEBLOS		
Agualulco	1	
Cocula	1	
Tomatlán	1	
		3 (2.1%)

DIOCESE OF MICHOACÁN

CITIES		
Celaya	1	
Pátzcuaro	1	
		2 (1.4%)
TOTAL		143 (100.0%

Source: Informaciones.
Note: The table does not include the birthplaces of four Spanish novices who professed elsewhere.
    See note 33.

In 1728, claiming that they lacked the intellectual ability to assume any responsible position in administration, two Spanish nuns petitioned the same Navarrete to seek a brief that would limit the number of Indians to fourteen and allow nineteen Spanish nuns; that would require an eight-year novitiate for the Indians instead of the customary one year; and that would deprive the latter of voting in community affairs until professed for at least twenty years. [29] Although this request had not been pursued by Navarrete, the 1742 incident was viewed as a carry-over from that of earlier times. The Indians now had a champion in the person of a *cacique* and cleric, Diego Torres, who was disturbed enough over the whole issue to initiate proceedings directly in the Council of the Indies against Navarrete. [30] Meanwhile, in 1744, while the suit was still in process, the Indian nuns began to govern the community and continued to do so uninterruptedly for the rest of the colonial period. [31] The suit reached a climax in 1745 with a royal *cédula*, reconfirming the original intentions for the foundation and ordering the expulsion of the three white novices. [32]

In retrospect what can it be said that the study of the *informaciones* reveals about race and Corpus Christi? On the one hand, if we are to believe Borah and Cook's demographic reports that miscegenation had become so prevalent in Mexico that few individuals of pure race remained there by the end of the colonial era, then we can surely include Corpus Christi nuns and their families among that "few." [33] More important, this study shows that searching out proofs of pure Indian lineage had become an obsession with Corpus Christi. There is no single explanation for this attitude. It seems to have been rooted in a feeling of racial pride, racial prejudice, particularly against the white *criollas*, and a conviction that they, the Indians, could do well on their own. [34] It might also have stemmed from a strong desire to abide by the "letter of the law"—this is what their founder had wanted, what their constitutions had provided for, and what pontifical briefs and royal *cédulas* had confirmed.

However, while the order left no stone unturned in making sure that nuns fulfilled the requirement of *limpieza*, there was some leniency displayed when it came to exacting evidence of an equally important qualification—that of nobility. Eight (5.6 percent) of the 143 Indians received were *macehuales*, and one of these had been among the novices whose *limpieza* had been questioned. Little consideration was given to her being a commoner, and as long as supplementary investigations verified her pure Indian lineage, she was permitted to profess. [35] Documentation on the remaining seven commoners gives no clues at all to why they were allowed to enter and continue in the community.

Ninety-four percent of the nuns of Corpus Christi were classified as belonging to Indian nobility. A careful scrutiny of their *informaciones* showed them to be representative of the two levels of Indian nobility: *caciques* and *principales*. Nevertheless, it was impossible to determine with any degree of accuracy how many were *caciques*, of the upper nobility, and how many qualified as *principales*, the lower rank. In most cases witnesses used the terms interchangeably, an indication that in the eighteenth century the differences between the two classes was not so finely drawn as in earlier times.[36] But whether *cacique* or *principal*, all of them and their families had legitimate claims to nobility. Nobility implied various general privileges—exception from paying tribute or permission to carry arms, ride horses, dress in "Spanish style," and the like—conceded over the years by the Crown in respect for their social status (and also as a guarantee to Spain of their continued, needed cooperation).[37] A look into some examples will throw light on the specific qualities that granted nobility.

Three nuns were descendants of the Aztec Montezuma and one of these was his granddaughter to the seventh degree; five, of Tlaxcalan kings; one, of the prominent Tarascan family of the Nambo y Jiménez of Pátzcuaro; one, of the distinguished house of the Avalos y Bárcena of the pueblo of Alfajayucán in the present state of Hidalgo; and one, of the Almacens, who were all described as "very noble." Another was singled out as being of the "illustrious house" of Don Alejandro Zacarías Santiago Huitalahua of the province of Tlaxcala. Three nuns were descendants of the Chimalpopoca family, which had a major role in the conquest of Tacuba; one, of the Tlaxcalan Pedro de Torres, who accompanied Cortés on various campaigns; one, of Capitán Don Fernando Acamputize y Montezuma, well known for the important part that he played in the conquest and subsequent pacification of Tula; one, of the Tapia family, which had been so much involved in the conquest of the Otomíes and Chichimecas of the Querétaro-San Luís Potosí region; and one, of the Indians of Texcoco, who fought with Cortés and later adopted the surname of Palacios y Maldonado. The ancestors of three others either aided in the conquest of Tepeaca, accompanied Cortés to the Valley of Oaxaca, or supported the Indian Pedro Antonio Serrano in the conquest of Calimaya and other areas in the province of Metepeque.[38]

Numbered among the community members of Corpus Christi were also the progeny of founders and first families of Indian settlements.[39] Many of these families had received titles of nobility and coats of arms from the Crown. Witnesses were careful to point out that such honors were bestowed because of the loyalty displayed to Spain during the conquest and the period immediately following it. Such loyalty continued to be manifested through the years. The father of one nun was praised for being seriously wounded while supporting the royalist cause when rebel forces entered his pueblo of Cuatitlán during the initial phase of the War of Independence.[40] Most *informaciones* told of members of the nuns' families forming part of the Indian civic bureaucracy. Often these were only general references, but some were specific and can be cited: the father of one nun was a *regidor* (legislative councilor); the fathers of four others served as *alcaldes ordinarios* (judges) and of two others as *alcaldes mayores* (senior judges). Further, seventeen nuns were daughters of *gobernadores* (governors), who were held in high esteem.[41] Evidence was also given to show that family members inherited these and other offices. One nun's brother, for example, became governor after their father renounced the position. He later became general interpreter in the province of Michoacán due to his proficiency in various Indian languages as well as in Spanish. 42

But even though holding political offices signified high social status and though they were regarded by some families as their own possessions, there were Indians who had qualifications, but refused to aspire to them. Witnesses usually interpreted such rejections as signs of humility. However, they may better have been explained in terms of apathy or common sense, which took precedence over glorying in social prestige during a time when Indian civic officials were expected to meet many demands and to receive little or no remuneration in return. 43

Some other relatives of the nuns were directors in religious ceremonies and served as disciplinarians and teachers in their churches—offices that the nobility had been privileged to exercise 44 since the early phase of the "spiritual conquest." It is also worth noting that some of these people still showed traces of the kind of enthusiasm for church construction that had been so prevalent among the Indian nobility during the first several decades after the conquest.

For example, the attorney father of one nun was the founder of the "sumptuous church" in Mexico City's *barrio* of Necatitlán. 45 Another nun's father not only supplied materials at his own expense for the building of a church in San Mateo Xalpa (jurisdiction of Xochimilco), but as perpetual attorney he also supervised its construction and worked with the Indians whom he had conscripted for the project. 46

There were still other ties with the Church that gave support to claims of social superiority. One of them had to do with membership in the priesthood and religious life. Twenty-five (17 percent) of the 143 nuns had distant relatives who were secular priests. These included one who was an organist in the cathedral in Oaxaca and one who had traveled to Spain to represent his people in a land suit against the Spaniards before the Council of the Indies. 47 Ten (7 percent) other nuns had more immediate family members who were numbered among the secular clergy. For some of them no specific assignment was given; others were singled out as being very important because they had gained *curatos* (pastorships), positions for which the *criollos* were ordinarily given preference. Thus, one nun had two great-uncles who had been pastors; 48 five had uncles who were priests, but no office was named for them; 49 one had an uncle and a nephew who were priests, the latter being a pastor; 50 three had brothers who were priests, two of whom were pastors. 51 The number of female family members in religious orders was greater. Twenty (14 percent) of the Corpus Christi nuns were closely related, including two who were blood sisters. Also, two nuns had cousins in the Indian *monasterio* of Nuestra Señora de Cosamaloapan in Morelia; and one other had a cousin in Mexico City's Capuchin *monasterio* of Nuestra Señora de Guadalupe, which, incidentally, was for white nuns. [52]

In addition, all families could boast of being free of any involvement in idolatrous acts. While being commended for giving up practices that had been so much a part of the religion of their early ancestors, some families were likewise credited with having been prime figures in initiating and fostering popular religious devotions of the Church. One nun, for example, was the granddaughter to the fifth degree of Juan Diego, the Indian neophyte to whom the Virgin Mary is believed to have appeared shortly after the conquest of Mexico City and who, under the title of Nuestra Señora de Guadalupe, was later proclaimed the patroness not only of New Spain, but also of all Latin America. [53] Others were associated with the founding of local confraternities or even with miracles. [54]

But if so many proofs could be presented in support of high social rank, it is natural that we should seek evidence to throw light on the subject of economic status. On what did the livelihood of these people depend; what were their incomes; and did the social superiority that 94 percent of them claimed denote any degree of economic eliteness? To begin with, we have already seen that some of the nuns' fathers held civic and church offices; but for them we do not know what, if any, salaries were received. Table 5.2 gives us information on the occupations of sixty-nine (49 percent) of their fathers (including some who were among the holders of the civic and church offfices) and on the sources from which incomes were derived. Unfortunately, there is no way of knowing the true economic levels of the families, since a farmer might have been very well-off or he might have lived in misery. The pay of a smelter in the Real Caja de Moneda might have provided him and his family with many luxuries, but then, too, maybe it was insignificant when compared to that of a very successful gilder or sculptor.

Therefore, we must look for additional clues to this issue of economic position. In the *informaciones*, eight (5.6 percent) of the 143 families were said to be living in poor economic conditions; four nuns came from families of "poor Indians." [55] The mothers of four others were compelled to work either to support their families because they were widows or else to supplement their husbands' meager earnings. We might add that one of them was driven to selling *patitas de carneros* (lambs' feet), at the risk of being accused by her neighbors of having killed the animals, an act that would have been a "vile office" and hence a strike against her claims to nobility. [56]

Eleven (8 percent) families fall into the category of the better-off and possibly, in a few cases, the wealthy of Indian society. The *informaciones* of five nuns state that their families were living "in abundance," "comfortably," "with much comfort," "very comfortably," and "a comfortable life." [57] For six others the data are a little more informative. These include the two nuns

Table 5.2

Occupations or Professions of 69 Nuns' Fathers

Farmers	19	Embroiderer	1
Gilders	8	Employee in the	
Gardeners	4	Caja de Moneda	1
Painters	4	Flour merchant	1
Carpenters	3	Glove maker	1
Sculptors	3	Hat maker	1
Blacksmiths	2	Merchant	1
Button makers	2	Miller	1
Masons	2	Musician	1
Sail makers	2	Potter	1
Tailors	2	Shoemaker	1
Administrator of the buildings		Smelter in the	
of the Colegio de S. Andrés,		Caja de Moneda	1
Mexico City	1	Stonecutter	1
Binder	1	*Tilma* merchant	1
Bruñidor de ropa (?)	1	Weaver	1
Butcher a	1	Total	69 (49% of 143 nuns)

Source: Informaciones.
a A "vile office."

whose fathers were founders of churches.[58] In addition, one nun was of the Páez de Mendoza family, owner of a vast *cacicazgo* (estate) in Amecameca down to the end of the colonial era.[59] The parents of another were rich *caciques* of Santiago Tlaltelolco, who spent part of their fortune paying for the costs of their lavish wedding in Mexico City Church of Santo Domingo, before Spanish and Indian nobility alike.[60] The *cacique* father of another nun flaunted his wealth in the salaried Indian escort whom he hired to accompany her from Guadalajara to Mexico City for her reception of the habit.[61] Lastly, a *principal* of San Antonio de las Huertas (located on the outskirts of Mexico City) who was the father of one nun—and the only immediate family member for whom we have wealth spelled out in terms of money—valued his estate, including orchards, gardens, animals, houses, and furnishings, at 22,400 *pesos*.[62]

For the remaining 124 (87 percent) families, sources disclosed nothing on their economic life. Some of them were possibly of the small, affluent Indian society of the eighteenth century. It is more likely, however, that the greater number were part of the mass of Indians who had become so impoverished, especially in the late colonial period, that the traveler Alexander von Humboldt had to acknowledge his difficulty in distinguishing the nobles from the commoners in their economic circumstances. He also observed, however, that the former still took a great deal of pride in their social status and that the commoners continued to regard them with the greatest respect and as their superiors.[63] In summary, it can be said with nearly complete certainty that for most of the families whom we have been considering social eliteness by no means signified economic eliteness, and all that remained to them was their hereditary prestige. ·

Two other topics that pertain more directly to the nuns themselves merit study: their education and the reasons why they chose the religious life. In regard to the first, all had been educated at home by their parents, and in not a few cases this had been supplemented with tutoring by priests of neighboring churches. As far as any kind of formal schooling having been received, we know of eleven who were instructed in the cloisters of female religious establishments that existed primarily for the *criollas*. Seven had been entrusted to individual nun-teachers either in Mexico City's La Concepción, San Lorenzo, and Santa Isabel, in Puebla's La Concepción, or in Guadalajara's Santa María de Gracia. Two had been students in the Colegio de los Gozos in Puebla; one, in the Colegio de Jesús María in the *monasterio* of the same name in Mexico City; and one, in Querétaro's *beaterio* of Santa Rosa de Viterbo. Three others had been resident students in the Real Colegio de Nuestra Señora de Guadalupe de Indias in Mexico City. Thus fourteen (10 percent) of the 143 had benefited from a formal education—a number not so insignificant in view of the fact that there were so few opportunities for a formal education available to Indian women at this time. [64]

Concerning the extent to which they were educated either at home or in institutions, we know that all were instructed in Christian doctrine, all could read Latin for the Divine Office (with the possible exceptions of *legas*, or lay sisters, who would have been dispensed from this), and all had attained some proficiency in the domestic arts, such as sewing and cooking—qualifications that had to be met before being admitted into the community. There were also nuns who had been trained in music, with one singled out as an excellent singer and guitarist. That some knew how to write is evident in such sources as the petitions, licenses, and books of reception and profession that they left us. [65] Further, it is worth noting that before receiving the habit one nun had had enough education to assist her father in a school for Indian boys and girls that he had set up in their home. [66] Another, after leaving the community as a novice, felt sufficiently qualified to aspire to the position of a teacher in a school that she, with her father and sisters, hoped to establish in the sanctuary of Nuestra Señora de los Remedios near Tacuba. [67]

However, their education, like that of the Corpus Christi nuns in general, had been geared to what was practical and utilitarian for the community. For none of them is there an indication of anything remarkable in the line of academic achievement—a revelation that should not come as a surprise when we consider the curriculum of the Real Colegio de Nuestra Señora de Guadalupe de Indias, the model for female Indian education in Mexico. In 1781, the five-member teaching staff was responsible for training students in sewing, fluting (a type of sewing), washing clothes, and grinding chocolate. There is not a word

about teaching even the basics of the three R's, although the colegio's constitution did at least state that these should be taught to anyone showing "in-
clination" to learn them and that those aspiring to the religious life should be
tutored in saying the Divine Office. [68]

Perhaps the educational background of the nuns of Corpus Christi was best
summarized in 1814 by their chaplain. Before vacating that position which he
had occupied for many years, he wrote some words of wisdom for his successor,
cautioning him not to be carried away in deep theological exhortations when
giving spiritual direction to individuals or in conferences delivered to the total
community. His reason: "There never were nor are there now any intellectuals
in Corpus Christi; it is nothing more than a community of simple and holy Indian nuns." [69]

Why had these women left the world for the cloister? On this subject we have
the direct words of only two: one became a nun "for the honor and glory of
God" and because she was aware of the "evilness of the world"; another
wished "only to serve God." [70] On the other hand, the mother of a third could
write that her daughter wanted to be a religious "to serve God and give up the
world." [71] These three examples, plus statements in the published biographies
of seven, would lead us to conclude that spiritual motives were the principal
ones in the decisions of all ten to seek the religious life. [72] For the remaining
133, certain "signs" were interpreted to mean that their reasons were also of a
spiritual nature. Common phrases in their *informaciones* were that they
wanted to be nuns "always," "a long time," and "since very young." The spiritual director of one nun stated that the aspirant was so holy that Spanish girls
envied her. [73] In other instances, the aspirants had made private vows of
chastity or were renowned for their modesty and like virtues.

While some novices were much esteemed for preferring the religious to the
married life, there is nothing in the sources to denote that others might have
become nuns because they had no chance to marry in a society in which Indian
women outnumbered men or else were not attracted to the married state and
thus would have become social problems for the people—really the principal
factor behind Corpus Christi's Oaxaca foundation. [74] However, we do know of
circumstances in their lives that would have influenced them to choose the religious state. First of all, the fathers of thirty-five and the mothers of nineteen
aspirants to the habit were deceased, while the same was true of both parents of
thirteen others. Thus sixty-seven (47 percent) of them were orphans; and very
possibly for some of them at least, Corpus Christi was regarded as a place of
asylum as much as a *monasterio* in which a life under vows might be pursued.
Also, we have already seen that there were priests and religious in the nun's
families to encourage them in their vocations, and the students living
cloistered in religious institutions would have been exposed to situations and
people inducing them to become nuns. Not to be overlooked is the fact that
they all came from good Christian homes in which religious vocations would

have been fostered. Indeed, the home training of one was so exemplary that not even illegitimacy in birth disqualified her from receiving the habit, making her the only community member who failed to meet the requirement of legitimacy. [75] In addition, several who lived neither in religious institutions nor in their homes were afforded every opportunity for following virtuous lives in preparation for the religious state. Of these, one had been raised by a "very distinguished orphan" in Puebla and another by her Spanish *padrino* (godfather), a merchant in the Real de Minas de Zaculapán. Three others were employed as servants in the homes of prominent people in Mexico City: the Count of Santiago; Matías López Torrecilla, a secretary to the Holy Office of the Inquisition; and the renowned writer and once bishop-elect of Yucatán, Juan José de Eguiara y Eguren. [76]

Whatever their motives were, we know that 105 (74 percent) of them went on to profess; the remaining thirty-eight (26 percent) left the community as novices, either because they suffered broken health from the rigid life exacted of them or because, for various other reasons, they were judged to be without true religious vocations. Although documentation on all of their deaths is incomplete, it seems that a number of the nuns under consideration here would still have been living in 1841 when Frances Calderón de la Barca, wife of Spain's minister to Mexico, expressed regret over having to return to Europe without ever having paid a visit to "the convent of Indian nuns." [77] It is certain that at least two were living a decade later when an English traveler described his visit to Corpus Christi: "I saw nothing in Mexico which pleased me more." [78] What is more interesting is the fact not only that the same two were among the nuns expelled from the *monasterio* in 1863 when Benito Juárez closed all such religious institutions in the country, but also that they lived out their vows in the world until both died in 1878: one, at the age of 90, after seventy-two years of professed life, and the other, at the age of 115, ninety-two years after she had professed. [79] As far as is known, their deaths were the last ones of the 143 Indian women whose lives and family backgrounds we have been considering.

I could end this study here. However, it seems appropriate that a few words be directed to a related question: What services did these women render to the society of their day? They were committed to a life of prayer, which they offered for the population at large and also for the Crown and royal officials in particular. [80] In their church they participated in ceremonies of a social as well as of a religious nature (not the least of these were the festive ones for the reception of the habit), and at their *porterías* (doors in cloistered *monasterios* where large packages were exchanged between the nuns and outsiders) and in their *locutorios* (parlors) they distributed food to the needy and listened to and consoled numerous visitors. [81] By making two foundations—Nuestra Señora de Cosamaloapán, Morelia, in 1737, and Nuestra Señora de los Angeles, Oaxaca, in 1782—they proved opportunities for greater numbers of Indian women of the nobility to enter the religious state. [82] And, as members of a community that was regarded as among the most observant in Mexico, they were a source of edification to the general public.[83] Yet, in spite of these various contributions, perhaps they left no greater legacy to society than that of proving that the Indian woman, in the long run, was indeed capable of pursuing the religious life.

Notes

1. Published sources on Indian society considered appropriate for the essay will be cited throughout the notes. The topic of this study is dealt with more extensively in Sister Ann Miriam Gallagher, R.S.M., "The Family Background of the Nuns of Two *Monasterios* in Colonial Mexico: Santa Clara, Querétaro; and Corpus Christi, Mexico City (1724-1822) (Ph.D. diss., The Catholic University of America, 1972).

2. Mainly, these sources are the *Libros de informaciones* (three bound volumes as well as unbound manuscripts) located in the Archive of the Monastery of Corpus Christi in Mexico City (hereafter cited as ACC).

3. José Joaquín García Icazbalceta, *Obras*, 10 vols. (Mexico: Imprenta de V. Agüeros, 1896-1905), 2: 427.

4. José Joaquín García Icazbalceta, *Don Fray Juan de Zumárraga, primer obispo y arzobispo de Mexico* (Mexico: Antigua Librería de Andrade y Morales, 1881), pp. 17-18; Mariano Cuevas, S. J., ed., *Documentos del siglo XVI para la historia de Mexico* (Mexico: Talleres del Museo Nacional de Arqueología, Historia y Etnología, 1914), pp. 513-14; Fray Gerónimo de Mendieta, *Historia eclesiástica indiana*, 4 vols. (Mexico: Editorial Salvador Chávez Hayhoe, 1945), 3: 72-73; José María Kazuhiro Kobayashi, *La educación como conquista* (Mexico: El Colegio de Mexico, 1974), pp. 280-92.

5. See P. Angel Ortèga, O.F.M., "Las primeras maestras y sus colegios-escuelas de niñas en Méjico (1530-1535)," *Archivo Ibero-Americano* 31 (March-June 1929): 259-76, 365-87. As far as is known, these early *beatas* were women without formal religious vows.

6. It seems Zumárraga expected that the matrons and *beatas* would be so dedicated to the teaching apostolate that they would follow a kind of religious life. Instead, they disappointed him when they left the schools for teaching positions in private homes and, in some cases, also married. For information on the foundation of La Concepción and also for data clarifying 1540 as the disputed date of the foundation, see Archivo de S. José de Garcia, Mexico City, "Razón de la fundación . . . de este Real y más Antiguo Convento de la Purísima Concepción"; and Libro de profesiones (de la Concepción).

7. Juan de Torquemada, *Monarquía indiana*, 3 vols. (Mexico: Editorial Porrúa, 1969), 3: 109-12; Marilyn Ekdahl Ravicz, *Early Colonial Religious Drama in Mexico: From Tzompantli to Golgotha* (Washington, D.C.: The Catholic University of America, 1970), pp. 211-34.

8. Torquemada, *Monarquía indiana*, vol. 3; D. Juan de Palafox y Mendoza, *Virtudes de indios* (Madrid: Imprenta de Tomás Minuesa de los Ríos, 1893), p. 59; Alonso Franco, O.P., *Segunda parte de la provincia de Santiago de Mexico* (Mexico: Imprenta del Museo Nacional, 1900), pp. 494-95; Antonio de Paredes, S. J., *Carta edificante . . . de la hermana Salvadora de los Santos, donada del Beaterio de las Carmelitas de Querétaro* (Mexico: Imprenta del Real Colegio de San Ildefonso, 1763).

9. Luisa de Tapia (in religion, Sister Luisa del Espíritu Santo) was the daughter of the Otomí *cacique*, Captain General Don Diego de Tapia. He continued the work of his father, Captain General Don Fernando de Tapia, in the conquest and pacification of the Indians in the regions of Querétaro and San Luis Potosí. With her father, Luisa founded Santa Clara on 13 January 1607 and professed there on 22 April of the same year. She had been a novice since 1606 in Mexico City's San Juan de la Penitencia. From the beginning, Spanish residents in Querétaro and surrounding areas supported the foundation, in the belief that family members would one day profess there. See Archivo de la Provincia Franciscana de Michoacán, Celaya, Gto., "Escritura de la fundación de Santa Clara, Dic. de 1604"; "Petición de los vecinos españoles de Querétaro, 9 de enero de 1605"; "Mandamiento y licencia del Virrey, Año de 1606"; and Libro de profesiones . . . de Santa Clara. See also Fr. Alonso de la Rea, *Crónica de la orden de nuestro seráfico P. S. Francisco: Provincia de San Pedro y San Pablo de Michoacán de la Nueva España* (Mexico: Imprenta de J. R. Barbedillo, 1882), pp. 254-56, 262, 274-77; and Fray Isidro Felix de Espinosa, O.F.M., *Crónica de la provincia franciscana de los apostoles San Pedro y San Pablo de Michoacán* (Mexico: Editorial Santiago, 1945), pp. 356-60, 363.

10. Francisco Morales, O.F.M., *Ethnic and Social Background of the Franciscan Friars in Seventeenth Century Mexico* (Washington, D.C.: Academy of American Franciscan History, 1973), pp. 22-37.

11. Though Indians are credited with initiating San Juan de la Penitencia in the belief that Spanish nuns would be a source of edification to their people, it should be noted that the *monasterio* from the beginning was maintained principally by Spanish benefactors. See Archivo del Monasterio de Sta. Clara, Puebla, "Convento de San Juan de la Penitencia." See also note 9, above.

12. Palafox y Mendoza, *Virtudes de indios*, p. 58.

13. A dowry ranged from 1,000 to 4,000 *pesos* and was fixed by the Ordinary of the diocese in which a *monasterio* was located or else by a male religious order that had jurisdiction over it. The first *monasterio* for women to be founded in Mexico with a rule that did not require dowries from the professed was the Capuchin one of San Felipe de Jesús, founded in Mexico City in 1666.

14. The doctrine of *limpieza de sangre* is considered by Antonio Domínguez Ortiz, *La clase social de los conversos en Castilla en la edad moderna* (Madrid: Consejo Superior de Investigaciones Científicas, n.d.), pp. 191-209. For a study on the variations of the doctrine, see Albert A. Sicroff, *Les Controverses des statuts de "pureté de sang" en Espagne du XVᵉ au XVIIᵉ siècle* (Paris: Didier, 1960). See also Morales, *Ethnic and Social Background*, pp. 7-21.

15. Richard Konetzke, ed., *Colección de documentos para la historia de la formación social de Hispanoamérica, 1493-1810*, 3 vols. (Madrid: Consejo Superior de Investigaciones Científicas, 1953-62), 2: 62-63. There are indications that *mestiza* women sometimes escaped the *limpieza* requirement and became nuns in Mexico. For the most part, they were *legas* (lay sisters) who were employed in domestic work. For legislation relative to *mestiza* nuns, see *Concilio III provincial mexicano, celebrado en Mexico el año de 1585* (Mexico: Mariano Galván Rivera, 1859), p. 282; and Archivo General de la Nación, Mexico City, Reales Cédulas, vol. 89, exp. 42, fols. 87-90 (hereafter cited as AGN). For examples of *mestiza* nuns in Mexico, see Amada López Meneses, "Dos

nietas de Moctezuma, monjas de la Concepción de Mexico," *Revista de Indias* 12 (January-March 1952): 81-100.

16. ACC, "Escritura de la fundación de Corpus Christi."

17. AGN, Historia, vol. 109, exp. 2. In the same source we read of Jesuits who were willing to make a compromise as the construction work neared completion: the building could be used as a *beaterio* or retreat house for Indian women, and if in time they manifested sufficient virtue, then they might become nuns. However, they should not be given the habit until older than the regular requirement of fifteen years of age, and their novitiate should be much longer than the ordinary term of one year.

18. See same source as note 17 above for these and other "defenses" of Indian women.

19. ACC, "Real Cédula del 5 de marzo de 1724"; "Escritura de la fundación de Corpus Christi."

20. ACC, "Carta de la Abadesa y consejo . . . a Roma, 5 de Diciembre de 1753"; "Breve, Clemente XIII, 2 de Agosto de 1760."

21. This was to satisfy the Council of Trent's requirement that for profession (which ordinarily followed a one-year novitiate) the novice should be sixteen years old. It should be noted, however, that Corpus Christi had a *niñado* (aspirants' school) for girls desiring the habit, but not yet being fifteen years old.

22. The exclusion of women was practiced because their word under oath (which was required for the *información pública*) was regarded as valueless.

23. See *Primera Regla de la Fecunda Madre Santa Clara de Assís* (Mexico: Herederos de Doña María de Rivera, 1756), pp. 154-60.

24. Of the 147 women admitted into Corpus Christi, the *informaciones* of 143 have been located in ACC.

25. *Información*, Teresa Josepha Suarez y Mendoza (1724).

26. *Informaciones*, Juliana María Ramírez y Sánchez (1752) and María Gertrudis Pereda y Arieta (1816).

27. *Informaciones*, Mathiana de Mendoza y Mena (1724), María Barrera y Leonel (1763), and Simona María Corona y Torres (1782).

28. I have not been able to locate the first apostolic brief that was given probably around the time of the foundation. The second, which repeated the contents of the earlier one, is found in ACC, "Breve del Papa Benedicto XIII, 26 de Junio de 1727. Que no pudiesen admitirse, y recibirse en el Conservatorio y Monasterio de Corpus Christi sino, dichas Indias Nobles, ni jamás en algún tiempo pudiesen admitirse y recibirse de otra condición ó Nación, ó Niñas, o Mujeres estrangeras." See also ACC, "Informe del Comisario General Fr. Pedro de Navarrete al Rey sobre la fundación del monasterio de Corpus Christi, 1743."

29. ACC, "Carta de las Madres María del Sacramento y María de S. Crisóstomo al R.P. Fr. Máximo de Navarrete, 26 de agosto de 1728"; Biblioteca Nacional de Mexico, Archivo Franciscano, Caja 75, exps. 1263-64 (hereafter cited as BNAF); Archivo del Instituto Nacional de Antropología, Mexico City, Fondo Franciscano, vol. 93, fols. 111-25 (hereafter cited as AINAFF).

30. ACC, "Testimonio de los autos formados por [Diego Torres] y el Común de los Indios caciques de esta Corte y sus alrededores, con el Rvdo. Padre Comisario General del Orden de San Franciscano sobre que no admita españolas del hábito de Religiosas en el Convento de Corpus Christi."

31. Sor María Phelipa de Jesús Luna y Nota, who professed just five years before 1744, became the first Indian abbess. For this and information on subsequent elections, see ACC, Libro de elecciones, Toma de Hábito y Profesiones; Libro de Patentes I. AINAFF, "Libro . . . de tablas de oficios de elección de abadesas y discretas," vol. 93.

32. ACC, "Cédula, 12 de octubre de 1745"; also in Biblioteca Nacional, Mexico City, Cédulas Reales y Providencias, II, ms. 1374.

33. Woodrow W. Borah and Sherburne F. Cook, "Race and Class in Mexico," *Pacific Historical Review* 23 (November 1954): 341.

34. As illustrations of such attitudes in Mexican Indian society, see "Rivalidades entre indios y criollos, 1790," *Boletín del Archivo General de la Nación*, 1st ser. 6 (July-August 1935): 557-61; AGN, Temporalidades, vol. 173; Historia, vol. 98.

35. *Informaciones*, Francisca Thomasa Sandoval y Rosales (1742, 1744). Copies of these *informaciones* and other material relative to this case are also in AINAFF, vol. 93, fols. 78-106; vol. 100, fols. 1-5, 17-33.

36. In the biographies of seven of the nuns, written by an unnamed nun of the same community, the terms are used in such a way as to imply that there was no difference between the two by this time; e.g., the parents of the nuns are commonly referred to as "ambos caciques y principales" (both *caciques* and *principales*). Josefina Muriel, ed., *Las indias caciques de Corpus Christi* (Mexico: Universidad Nacional Autónoma de Mexico, 1963). See also Delfina Esmeralda López Sarrelangue, *La nobleza indígena de Pátzcuaro en la época virreinal* (Mexico: Universidad Nacional Autónoma de Mexico, 1965), p. 38.

37. López Sarrelangue, *La nobleza indígena*, pp. 109-48; Charles Gibson, *The Aztecs under Spanish Rule* (Stanford: Stanford University Press, 1964), pp. 164-65; and Richard Konetzke, "Estado y Sociedad en las Indias," *Estudios Americanos* 3 (January 1951): 54-55. Based on twenty-two *informaciones*.

38. Based on twenty-two *informaciones*.

39. *Informaciones*, Lorenza Juana (1729), Magdalena Rosales (1737), María Amador y Suárez (1781), María González (1782), and María Pérez y Jaramillo (1782).

40. Miguel Aparicio; *Información*, María Regina Aparicio y Sánchez (1812).

41. Based on *informaciones*. On Indian government, see Constantino Bayle, "Cabildos de indios en la América española," *Missionalia Hispánica* 8 (January-April 1951): 5-35.

42. Her father was Diego Nambo de la Serda of Pátzcuaro; her brother, Pedro. *Información*, Rosa María Nambo (1725). See also López Sarrelangue, *La nobleza indígena*, pp. 263-65.

43. For material on Indians who had to be compelled to accept political offices even at the end of the sixteenth century and on reasons for the decline in enthusiasm for political activity in Indian society, see Gibson, *Aztecs*, pp. 191-93.

44. See Robert Ricard, *La conquista espiritual de Mexico* (Mexico: Editorial Jus, 1947), pp. 205-9.

45. Nicolás Placer; *Información*, María Jiménez y Placer (1757).

46. Antonio Sebastián; *Información*, Rosa Gertrudis (1812).

47. Manuel Velasco and Cyrilo (?) of Tlaxcala; *Informaciones*, Aniceta María Velasco y Sánchez (1781) and María Nicolasa Ocatín y Zárate (1804).

48. Lorenzo de los Angeles Temalcanzingo and his brother, Miguel of Sichú de los Indios; *Información*, María Teresa Alvarado (1807).

49. Luís de Mendoza of Tlaxcala, Juan de Mendoza, Matías de Ortiz, José Joachin Roldán, and Felipe Suárez; *Informaciones*, María Josepha Villagrán (1724), Pascuala Mendoza (1724), María Avalos (1772), Sebastiana Roldán y Xicali (1781), and María Phelipa Suárez y Mendoza (1788).

50. José Escanilla and Miguel Escanilla, a pastor in Sichú de los Indios; *Información*, María Josepha Hernández y Gómez (1817).

51. Francisco de Castillo, pastor in Mexicaltzingo, an unnamed pastor in the diocese of Puebla de los Angeles, and an unnamed priest with an unknown residence; *Información*, Juliana Ramírez (1752), Ana Castillo (1782), and María Francisca Luna y Sánchez (1795).

52. *Informaciones*, María Leonor y Espinosa (1739) and Mariana Luna y Espinosa (1739); Inés Josepha Cavallero (1761) and Mariana Pérez y Mendoza (1770); and Angela Carranza y Sandoval (1805).

53. *Información*, María Micaela Escalona y Rojas (1739). She was declared patroness of New Spain by Benedict XIV in 1754 and of Latin America by Pius X in 1910. Angel María Garibay K., "Our Lady of Guadalupe," *New Catholic Encyclopedia*, 16 vols. (New York: McGraw Hill, 1967), 6: 822.

54. *Informaciones*, María Gertrudis Camacho (1725), Apolonia de Candía y Porras (1724), and Rosa María Nambo (1725).

55. *Informaciones*, Simona Montezuma (1724), María Martínez (1757), María Urban (1795), and María de Jesús Burgos y López y Pichí (1805).

56. *Informaciones*, María Ignacia (1752), María Eusebia Sandoval (1766), María Petra Luna (1805), and María Ramírez (1753).

57. *Informaciones*, Rosa María Nambo (1725), Bárbara Pérez (1782), María Coscatl (1788), Paula Gómez y Benítez (1733), and Gabriela Daniela y Tapia (1795).

58. Nicolás Placer and Antonio Sebastián; *Informaciones*, María Jiménez y Placer (1757) and Rosa Gertrudis (1812).

59. *Información*, María Francisca Zacatzín y Páez de Mendoza (1775). See also AGN, Tierras, vol. 1513, exp. 9; vol. 1518, exp. 5; vol. 1549, exp. 5; vol. 1595, exp. 2; vol. 1934, exp. 1. Also Gibson, *The Aztecs*, pp. 161, 266, 298. Guillermo S. Fernández de Recas, *Cacicazgos y nobiliario indígena de la Nueva España* (Mexico: Universidad Autónoma de Mexico, 1961), treats thirty-five *cacicazgos* in Mexico, including some which would have belonged to families remotely related to the nuns' families: e.g., those of the Cortés Montezuma Chimalpopoca family in Tacuba; the Tapia in Querétaro; and the Méndez y Luna in Tlaxcala.

60. *Información*, María Villagrán (1724).

61. *Información*, María Magdalena Jiménez (1724). See also Muriel, *Las indias caciques*, pp. 225-57.

62. Miguel Gerónimo Espinosa y Luna. His will is found in AGN, Historia, vol. 98, "Cuaderno de Autos sobre la fundación . . . de un Colegio, 1779."

63. Alejandro von Humboldt, *Ensayo político sobre el reino de la Nueva España* (Mexico: Editorial Porrúa, 1966), p. 67. We know the number of Indian nobles would have declined for the time that we are considering owing to deaths, miscegenation, the founding of new settlements and hence the uprooting of the nobility, etc. (See López Sarrelangue, *La nobleza indígena*, pp. 293-97.) I know of no studies that give statistics on this subject. .

64. In Mexico City there was the Real Colegio de Nuestra Señora de Guadalupe de

Indias. Other *monasterios* and *beaterios* were more concerned with the *criollas*. Some *colegios* for *criollas* admitted Indians, but only as day students. Elisa Luque Alcaide, *La educación en Nueva España* (Sevilla: Publicaciones de la Escuela de Estudios Hispano Americanos, 1970), pp. 290-96, considers *colegios* for Indian girls in Santiago Tlaltelolco and Toluca. These foundations received royal approval in the late colonial period, but the author fails to tell us when or if they ever opened.

65. E.g., the ACC.

66. *Información*, Rosa Gertrudis (1812). The school was in the home of her father, Antonio Sebastián, a *fiscal perpetuo* in San Mateo Xalpa.

67. Diega Martina Espinosa y Luna, who spent several months in the novitiate; see AGN, Historia, vol. 98, "Cuaderno de Autos sobre la fundación . . . de un Colegio, 1779."

68. Biblioteca Nacional, Madrid, Manuscritos de América, "Diligencias executadas . . . que acreditan el estado en que se hallara el Colegio de Indias de Nuestra Señora de Guadalupe, Año de 1781," ms. 3535, fols. 191-200; AGN, Historia, vol. 98, fols. 197-210, "Regla de el Colegio de Nuestra Señora la Virgen de Guadalupe. . . ."

69. ACC, Fray Jacinto López, an untitled collection of writings on various subjects.

70. Francisca Castrillo; for her will, made shortly before she professed (the common practice for religious), see Archivo de Notarías, Mexico City, "Testamento," José Anaya Bonilla (1780), fols. 550-52. María Amador, ACC, "Petición, 1780."

71. ACC, "Petición . . . Lorenza Juana, 1724."

72. María Antonia Pérez, Rosa Torres, Rosa Hernández, Apolonia Candía, Gertrudis Camacho, Magdalena Jiménez, and Phelipa Luna.

73. *Información*, Rosa Gertrudis (1812).

74. On population, see Delfina López Sarrelangue, "Población indígena de la Nueva España en el siglo XVIII," *Historia Mexicana* 12 (April-June 1963): 516-30, and Humboldt, *Ensayo político*, p. 575. As far as is known, no study has been published to throw light on the extent to which colonial Indian nobility utilized the system of marriage dowry common to the Spaniards. However, there are indications that it was employed by some of the Indian nobles. See AGN, Tierras, vol. 650, exp. 2, "Testamento otorgado por don Juan Miguel Roldán, 1743," (great grandfather of Margarita Roldán of Corpus Christi).

75. *Información*, Diega Martina Espinosa y Luna (1763). When sufficient proof could be given that aspirants had been raised well, thus compensating for the defect of illegitimacy of birth, they could be admitted into religious orders. See BNAF, Caja 143, exp. 1745, fols. 15-17, "Moderati Constitutionum, Sixti Quinti, felicis recordadionas, contra illegitimos regularum, Acta a S.D.N. Gregorio XIV, 1590."

76. In the homes of Josepha Valle and Sebastián de Torres de Cano; *Informaciones*, Barbara Pérez (1812) and Lorenza Juana (1729); also *Informaciones*, María Pérez (1782), María Aparicio (1817), and María Antonia (1763).

77. Frances Calderón de la Barca, *Life in Mexico* (Mexico: Ediciones Lara, n.d.), p. 458.

78. William Parish Robertson, *A Visit to Mexico*, 2 vols. (London: Simpkion, Marshal End, 1853), 2: 301.

79. Sor María Josefa de los Dolores González, who was born in 1788, received the habit in 1805, professed in 1806, and died in 1878; and Sor María Justa de Loreta Retama y Martínez, who was born in 1763, received the habit in 1785, professed in

1786, and died in 1879. These dates are taken from ACC, their baptismal certificates, and "Toma de Hábito y Profesiones" (the dates of their deaths are recorded in the last-mentioned source).

80. See ACC, "Patente del Ministro Provincial . . . 25 de Agosto de 1779, para co-operar a la prosperidad de las Armas Católicas," in which the community is urged to pray for the king and the royal army; "Despedida que hicieron a el Convento para irse a España los Excelentísimos Conde de Revilla Gigedo y su Consorte." The latter is actu-ally two letters which were written from Jalapa, Veracruz, 10 February 1756, when the Viceroy Revilla Gigedo and his wife were returning to Spain, and in which they ac-knowledged receipt of the nuns' earlier letters assuring them of prayers for a safe journey.

81. Calderón de la Barca, *Life in Mexico*, p. 458. An outgoing chaplain warned his successor to avoid the crowded *porterías* or else he would develop splitting headaches; ACC, Fray López, Untitled collection of writings.

82. There were also attempts as early as 1779 to found one in Puebla de los Angeles; it was still being considered in the early nineteenth century. See ACC, "Fundación . . . Puebla"; AGN, Bienes Nacionales, vol. 1376, exp. 2.

83. The nuns were, of course, not without faults. This is evident from ACC, Patentes, I and II, in which they are reprimanded occasionally for such failings as visiting too much at the *porterías* and *locutorios*, carrying on transactions with seculars, and allow-ing children into the cloisters for visits. Unlike many of the Mexican *monasterios*, Corpus Christi did not house secular women and students, nor were the nuns permitted private incomes, servants, or private cells. Hence, it was not among the ones in which major reforms were attempted in the eighteenth century. See Asunción Lavrin, "Eccle-siastical Reform of Nunneries in New Spain in the Eighteenth Century," *The Americas* 22 (October 1965): 182-203. The present study has not included the economic life of the community. That it continued as a strict mendicant one throughout its history can be seen in such sources as the following: University of Texas Library, Austin, Texas, Latin American Collection, "Revisión Auténtica de los legados y obras pías del Monasterio de Corpus Christi, Año 1757"; BNAF, "Expediente sobre la revisión de legados . . . de Corpus Christi . . . 1755-1757"; and AINAFF, "Libro de cuentas, de limosnas, gastos, obras pias y escrituras del Convento de Corpus Christi," vol. 72

6

Susan A. Soeiro

The feminine orders in colonial Bahia, Brazil: economic, social, and demographic implications, 1677-1800

The convents of Salvador, Bahia—the colonial capital of Portuguese America, Brazil—were in name and in practice houses of religion. In the first instance, they were temples of worship and sanctuaries for women dedicated to the service of God. But, in spite of their expressed spiritual commitment, religious communities were separated from lay society only by the bricks and mortar of their walls. Far from a state of contemplative and functional isolation, the female orders were bound by strong and intimate ties to the civil society of Salvador.

Conventual life answered both sacred and profane callings and served religious and secular needs. Convents could and did offer a foster family and an alternative life style to women seeking refuge from temporal society. They provided education and taught domestic skills. As forerunners of contemporary welfare agencies, nunneries gave shelter and support to destitute and single women. Religious houses served as convenient and respectable repositories for daughters of families whose high social standing and low finances precluded them from sufficiently endowing their female children for marriage. From a demographic perspective, convents relieved society of the burden of sustaining an excess of celibate women.

Nunneries, then, may be studied from a variety of perspectives with the intention of posing some very mundane, if not profane, questions. The bases of a social system can be analyzed by looking at its apparently atypical components. That is to say, it can be argued that nunneries reflected the fundamental workings of society, from the commonplace to the bizarre, despite their appearance as institutions distinct from the ordinary world. On the one hand, the founding of convents can be seen as the realization of universal Bahian values and aspirations. On the other, inhabitants of nunneries represented an unassimilable population, which required isolation. At one and the same time, nunneries were socially sanctioned approaches to accommodating socially anomalous persons. Studied as products of the temporal world, religious communities reveal considerable information about that secular society.

This paper seeks to explore the role of several nunneries within their demographic, social, and economic context. Attention is centered upon the four convents erected in colonial Salvador. A first section of the work, introduced by a comparison with Spanish America, explores the reasons for the belated founding and the paucity of nunneries in Brazil. Emphasis is placed upon economic and demographic factors. Following this, a second segment discusses the social composition and purpose of the nunnery. It is suggested that nunneries ultimately served as institutions buttressing an elitist system of values and stratification in Bahian society.

The Portuguese colonization of Brazil transmitted a dual heritage of a profound, pervasive Catholicism and an ideal of rigorous seclusion of women. In spite of these cultural legacies, the institution that clearly embodied the fusion of these values—the convent of nuns—was introduced at a remarkably late date and in extraordinarily small numbers in the colony. The first nunnery, Santa Clara do Destêrro, in the capital of Salvador, Bahia, was not founded until 1677—nearly two centuries after the region's discovery. More than another fifty years elapsed before the Crown authorized the construction of three additional nunneries in the city. For the entire eighteenth century, Brazil's capital city counted no more than four female orders.

By comparison, in Spanish America the erection of convents followed soon after the arrival of the male orders and was integrated with the developing colonial religious, social, and economic complex virtually from the conquest. The first house of female religious was founded in New Spain, in 1540 by the Conceptionist Order.[1] In the succeeding two centuries the proliferation of religious institutes extended even into the provincial towns of the viceroyalty. From 1540 to 1811 no less than fifty-seven nunneries were founded in New Spain. By 1800, Mexico City, the capital, had twenty-two feminine monastic centers.[2]

Even in relation to their respective urban populations, the number of nuns in Mexico City in the late eighteenth century was nearly twice that in Salvador. Around 1800, when the city of Salvador had approximately 60,000 residents, not more than 200 of the city's females were cloistered in nunneries. Mexico City at the same time had almost 900 nuns in a population of 137,000. Proportionately, for every nun in Salvador there were two in the Spanish American capital.[3]

The policies of the Iberian monarchs, ultimately responsible for the divergent patterns in the two colonies, were formulated in reaction to a complex interplay of social, economic, and demographic forces. After an initial period of neglect, the primary concern of the Portuguese sovereign became the settlement and population of the Brazil colony. For the first half-century after its discovery, when Portuguese attention was riveted upon the profitable Asian trade, Brazil was of only secondary interest to the metropolis. Organized efforts to settle the colony date from the arrival in 1549 of the first captain-general, Tomé de Sousa, whose company included a spectrum of settlers, among which were farmers, artisans, bureaucrats, churchmen, slaves, and some women.

White women were in critically short supply in the newly founded colony. Most immigrants were males from the north of Portugal and the region surrounding Lisbon. The exodus was so extreme as to depopulate many areas of the mother country. Nevertheless, married men rarely came to Brazil in the company of their families. Portuguese women were left behind. For the most part, sixteenth-century Brazil remained a haven for adventurers and a dumping ground for social deviants and undesirables of both sexes—prostitutes, secret Jews, and convicts. Although from time to time a few orphan women of good families were sent to the colony, they were too few in number to meet the demand.[4] The scarcity of peninsular women and the rigors of a frontier society made casual liaisons between Portuguese males and native and black slave women commonplace. Frequent concubinage, interracial unions, and passing sexual encounters shocked the clergy and vexed their efforts at conversion. How were they to teach the heathen Indians to follow the Church's precepts and to honor the sacrament of marriage when the Christians did not do so? Churchmen such as the Jesuit Manuel Nóbrega so despaired of founding a moral and viable European community in the tropical wilds of Brazil that he strongly pleaded for the importation of Portuguese prostitutes as a solution to the chronic absence of white women.[5]

The preoccupation with the population of the Brazil colony as a means to secure the territory within the imperial realm shaped royal policy regarding convents. By 1600, Salvador was a growing commercial center of some five thousand to ten thousand white inhabitants, in which the male orders were already numerous.[6] In spite of the early presence of clergymen, the king refused petitions for the erection of a convent of nuns on Brazilian soil. In 1603 he offered his concern with population growth as the pretext for his denial. He wanted to encourage "the growth of that State [to] become inhabited by worthy and noble persons. . . . It is therefore not regarded as convenient to erect in those regions convents of nuns—since they[the lands] are so vast that in order to populate them many more inhabitants are necessary than are there at present."[7]

Clearly, the needs of the empire superseded the urgings of the faith. In principle, the Crown's councillors agreed that women, like men, deserved the freedom to choose the religious life. But, in fact, they were not reluctant to deprive women of this perquisite. Women could be prevented from joining the orders, the august advisers reasoned, because "women [were] more essential to the propogation of the species than were men."[8] Marriages therefore had to be encouraged, even if it meant denying some women the option of conventual isolation. As an institution that removed potentially fertile members from society, the convent threatened royal objectives. The erection of a nunnery in Brazil was therefore consistently denied until later in the seventeenth century, when the Crown deemed the conditions appropriate.[9]

The permission granted to found Brazil's first nunnery in 1677—the Poor Clares in Salvador—did not signal a change in royal attitudes or a lesser concern with the population of the colony. Demographic considerations continued to overshadow the formulation of policy, even as other pressures forced its modification. In the absence of a colonial convent the daughters of prominent settlers persistently risked the dangers of the open sea and the threat of piracy to profess in the nunneries of the Atlantic islands or in Portugal itself. Under these circumstances the establishment of a convent on local ground eventually coincided with royal aims of preventing any further depopulation. In 1677 the Crown therefore allowed the foundation of a single house, the Destêrro, with a limited population of fifty professed nuns and fifty nuns of the lower category of the white veil.[10]

A secondary motive for the erection of the Destêrro at this time was political in nature. The foundation of a convent provided a means of rewarding the loyalty of the Crown's deserving vassals, particularly those who served in the Dutch wars. Several of the nunnery's advocates had emigrated to Brazil to defend its territory by taking part in the expulsion of the Dutch from Pernambuco. Others were prominent members of the royal bureaucracy.[11]

A concern with the expansion of the population and a desire to reward deserving subjects only partially explain the founding of the Destêrro at this particular juncture in the colony's development. Economic forces in the late seventeenth century also militated for the erection of a colonial convent. A glance at developments in Spanish America sheds significant light upon the timing of the founding of Brazil's first nunnery. The economy of New Spain, at one time centered exclusively on the extraction and export of silver, had by the mid-seventeenth century also evolved a substantial pastoral and agricultural base. Changes in society accompanied these shifts in the economic panorama. A native elite composed of rural patriarchs, commercial men, and miners dominated the social hierarchy of the later colony. Spanish American nunneries did not remain unaffected by the process of social and economic diversification. Asunción Lavrin has ably shown that "the growth in economic importance of nunneries corresponded to the establishment of a certain type of landed economy in the hands of a creole nobility, and a class of *hacendados*, miners and merchants."12 Earning social esteem by demonstrating their religiosity, such social groups became the patrons of nunneries. During the seventeenth and eighteenth centuries, largely owing to the bequests of this native elite, eleven nunneries were erected in the viceroyalty.13

A survey of convents in this Spanish dependence reveals the striking fact of the foundation of ten nunneries as early as the sixteenth century. The establishment of a nunnery was supported with the alms of the local community or the bequest of a patron. Sometimes gifts from prominent benefactors were supplemented by donations from the local populace.14 But, regardless of its source, a substantial initial outlay of capital was essential. The foundation of religious institutes was therefore logically contingent upon the prior existence of an economy and society that had sufficient resources to permit their allocation to such expressions of piety. The appearance of female religious so early in the history of New Spain might thus reflect the fortunes extracted from the mines or the existence of a privileged sector, such as the *encomenderos*, who became the patrons of such institutions.15

As in the case of New Spain, the foundation of the first Brazilian nunnery was related to certain minifestations of the economy. Indeed, the erection of the Destêrro in the late seventeenth century must be viewed in the context of the fluctuations of the Bahian economy, whose mainstay was the export of sugar. Unlike New Spain, throughout the sixteenth century Brazil lacked both the economic base and the social constituency that contributed to the need for a nunnery. Although by 1610 as many as fifty sugar mills (*engenhos*) studded the Bahian hinterland of the Recôncavo the export of the product still fell short of later levels.16 Moreover, many of the wealthy landed families—like the Silva Pimentels, Garcia D'Avilas, Rochca Pittas, and Vasconcellos e Albuquerques—who in the seventeenth and eighteenth centuries wielded immense power had just begun to amass vast territorial empires and significant fortunes. While the Bahian economy and elite were thus still nascent, the desire for a nunnery had virtually no expression. Aside from the legacy of Mem de Sá, governor-general of Brazil from 1557 to 1572, the creation of a local convent does not appear to have been much on the minds of the Bahian citizenry prior to the seventeenth century.17

Only with the economic and social transformations of the 1600s did both the need for a nunnery and the financial feasibility of its foundation emerge. The seventeenth century in Bahia was the century of sugar. With the monopoly of the European sugar trade lodged in the rich black soil of Salvador's surrounding countryside, the Bahian planter enjoyed an era of unsurpassed opulence. Yet the sugar plantation was more than just a source of profit for its owner; it symbolized a way of life. The mill owner, or *senhor do engenho*, was the "aristocrat" of colonial society, and his social position required that he maintain a life-style consistent with his privileged status. Luxury goods were imported from Europe and ostentatiously displayed. However, social position was re-flected not only in material goods such as clothing, jewelry, porcelain, and sil-ver, but also in the observance of certain behavioral conventions. Patronage was one such perquisite. Salvador's municipal council, a bastion of elite sugar mill owners and cattle ranchers, had persistently offered itself as the benefac-tor of a Bahian nunnery in return for the preferential admission of its daugh-ters. [18] In New Spain already in the sixteenth century, mining had prompted the rise of a society whose economic and social stratification was manifested in the endowment of convents. In Brazil it was only the export of sugar in the sev-enteenth century that permitted similar developments.

The final impetus for the royal concession to found the first nunnery in 1677 was the particularly critical economic situation of the late seventeenth century. The sugar region had plunged in the 1670s into a period of economic crisis, due to competition on the world market from the Dutch, French, and English Caribbean islands. According to local spokesmen, another reason for the financial distress of leading families was the burdensome services required by the Crown. Bahian citizens had fought in the wars to expel the Dutch from Brazil, and they were also encumbered—if loyally so—by the obligation to con-tribute to the dowry of the queen. [19] Specie, commonly scarce in the colony, be-came rarer. In the absence of a local nunnery, Bahians sent their daughters to convents overseas, which required a substantial outlay of capital. This meant that not only women, but large shipments of coin were leaving in the fleets for the mainland. [20] Thus convinced of the necessity of halting the depletion of women and capital at a time when the economic decline was particularly acute, the Crown decreed the foundation of the colony's first convent.

The creation of a single nunnery proved an inadequate palliative for prob-lems rooted in economic dislocation and demographic change. The fifty places of the Destêrro were filled by the 1680s, and the transatlantic exodus of women and specie continued unabated. Within the first twenty years following the founding of the convent, more than thirty women braved the voyage. In 1717 the municipal council reported that as many as eight to ten young women made the trip annually. The following year the governor-general wrote that in that fleet as many as twenty-three were destined for Lisbon and another four for the islands. Solutions for this dilemma involved two major proposals. First the city elders pleaded for the enlargement of the Convent of Poor Clares. When this was denied, the governor repeatedly suggested a ban on the traffic of women to the metropolis. However, none of these proposals spurred any im-mediate action, and the question was deferred until later Bahian developments made its resolution imperative. [21]

By the 1730s, economic and demographic factors forced royal policy to take new directions. Royal fears that past measures had failed to encourage both marriages and population expansion led the Crown to impose a ban on the traffic of women to the Continent in 1732. The king directly attributed "the lack of growth of that state [of Brazil to] the great excess of women coming to Portugal on the pretext of becoming religious."[22] Henceforth, no woman could leave Brazil without first obtaining royal permission. Those women who desired to enter convents in Portugal were required to prove to church authorities that their decision to take the veil had been sincere, "spontaneous [and] without pressure from any person."[23] Moreover, the punishment decreed for ships' captains caught smuggling women out of Brazil was a stiff fine and a jail sentence.[24]

Following the prohibition on departures of women, the Crown permitted the erection of three additional conventual centers in Salvador. The Lapa and the Mercês convents received the royal license for their foundations in 1733 and 1735, respectively. In 1741 the Retirement House of the Solitude and Heart of Jesus, which subsequently became a nunnery, was established. The creation of these communities meant that 110 additional places for aspiring religious were made available in Salvador.

Indeed, the royal allegation that the population stagnated was challenged by the demographic transformations actually taking place in the Bahian captaincy. The population of the region had, in fact, expanded considerably. The municipal council wrote to the king, claiming that Bahia and its Recôncavo had tripled in size since the founding of the original convent of the Destêrro.[25] In 1700 the city of Salvador had over twenty thousand inhabitants, compared with the five thousand to ten thousand a century earlier. By the mid-eighteenth century it was second only to Lisbon in the Portuguese empire and had nearly doubled its proportions. New parishes in the urban center as well as new municipalities in the surrounding suburbs and Recôncavo had sprung up. The Recôncavo itself grew from a population of approximately thirty-six thousand in 1724 to roughly eighty-five thousand in 1780 (see Table 6.1).[26]

The new convents of the mid-eighteenth century reflected the expansion of the rural areas in their composition. Dona Ursula Luisa da Monserrat, patroness of the Mercês, had petitioned originally to have a nunnery founded in the parish of Santo Amaro in the Recôncavo. Conventual admissions also indicate that professants in the Mercês and the Soledade stemmed mainly from the regions beyond the city. Seven of the nine initial entrants to the Mercês were residents of the Recôncavo.[27] The Destêrro, too, at mid-century had a preponderance of entrants from rural parishes.[28]

The general growth in the population had been accompanied by an alteration in its sexual composition. No longer was there any truth to the assertion that marriageable women were scarce. The municipal council vociferously argued quite to the contrary—the problem was now a superfluity of women: "That state [Bahia] is very fertile in feminine births; as can be seen, homes are full of up to four and five daughters, sometimes more in each family, without so much as a single son in many of them."[29] In the late seventeenth century the lure of the goldfields began to draw many men from Bahia to the mining re-

Table 6.1
Population Growth in Eighteenth-Century Bahia

	1600	1706	1718	1724	1755	1759	1768	1775	1780	1800
Salvador	5,000–10,000[a]	21,600[c]	39,209[d]		35,400[f]	40,263[i]	40,922[j]	33,635[k] 40,922[k]	39,200[l]	60,000[n]
Suburbs			6,676[d]				16,093[j]		26,076[m]	
Recôncavo				35,672[e]	37,500[g] 39,855[h]	62,833[i]	69,500[j]		93,386[m]	
Captaincy	21,000[b]					205,142[i]	179,061[j] 220,708[j]	220,665[k]	240,000[l] 287,850[m]	247,000[n] 347,000[n]

[a] Whites only; Stuart B. Schwartz, *Sovereignty and Society*, pp. 105–6 (see note 6).
[b] Stuart B. Schwartz, "Cities of Empire," p. 635 (see note 3).
[c] Archivo Histórico Ultramarino, Bahia, 1st ser. cat., no. 2010 (hereafter AHU).
[d] Thales de Azevedo, *Povoamento da cidade do Salvador*, p. 187 (see note 3).
[e] Ward J. Barrett and Stuart B. Schwartz, "Comparación entre dos economías azucareras coloniales," fig. 4 (see note 16).
[f] Inácio Accioli de Cerqueira e Silva, *Memórias historicas*, 5: 370–76 (see note 9).
[g] AHU, Bahia, 1st ser. cat., no. 2010.
[h] Accioli, *Memórias históricas*, 5: 396–436.
[i] José Antônio Caldas, *Noticia geral de tôda esta capitania da Bahia*, pp. 70–71 (see note 11).
[j] Barrett and Schwartz, "Comparación," fig. 4.
[k] AHU, Bahia, 1st ser. cat., no. 8813.
[l] José da Silva Lisboa, "Carta . . . [de] notícia desenvolvida sobre a Bahia . . .," *Anais da Biblioteca nacional do Rio de Janeiro* 32 (1914): 505 (hereafter cited as *ABNRJ*).
[m] Accioli, *Memórias históricas*, 3: 83–84.
[n] Luis dos Santos Vilhena, *A Bahia no século XVIII*, 1: 55–56 (see note 3).

gions of Minas Gerais. Moreover, the simultaneous decline of sugar agriculture undoubtedly prompted many males to seek their living elsewhere.[30] By 1724 census figures for the Recôncavo indicate that the imbalance in the sex ratio in favor of males had all but disappeared. In as many as seven of twelve Recôncavo parishes, women outnumbered men (see Table 6.2).[31]

In spite of the evidence of expansion, royal fears were not much allayed, primarily because they derived from a concern with the colonial elite. The Crown acted on the assumption that convents inhibited the reproductive vitality of the upper echelons. The establishment of the Destêrro did, in fact, contribute to the low incidence of marriage among the privileged sector. In a survey of fifty-three families over the period 1677 to 1800 it has been shown that 77 percent of the female offspring entered the nunnery, whereas only 14 percent married.[32] The infrequency of marriage among Bahia's leading families was also observed by one colonial governor-general, who in 1739 reported in dismay that among persons of repute not more than two marriages had taken place in the past four years.[33]

Economic conditions played an influential role in restricting marriages and swelling conventual admissions. The tendency among the elite to cloister women rather than marry them derived in part from the decline that Bahia had suffered since the late seventeenth century. Prominent families complained of their inability to marry off their daughters. The municipal council reminded the Crown that Portuguese inheritance law required that the estate of deceased parents be divided equally among the children. In times like these, when families were growing in size and fortunes diminishing, each child was allotted a lamentably miniscule share. Such a tiny portion was insufficient to furnish a dowry for a marriage appropriate to a family's social station. For inadequately dowered women of good families life in the cloister was deemed preferable to

Table 6.2
Sex Ratios in Bahia

1724—Selected Recôncavo Parishes	*Males*	*Females*
Itaparica	640	666
Sergipe do Conde	950	850
Paripe	187	118
Matoim	234	241
Socorro	289	315
Jaguaripe	720	626
1775—Salvador		
Caucasians		
Married	1,697	1,697
Widowed	184	702
Single	3,140	3,300
Total	5,021	5,699
Pardos		
Married	508	508
Widowed	39	231
Single	1,118	1,803
Total	1,665	2,542
Free Blacks		
Married	440	440
Widowed	37	156
Single	963	1,694
Total	1,440	2,290

Source: Barrett and Schwartz, "Comparacion," fig. 4; AHU, Bahia, 1st ser. cat., no. 9805.

lay celibacy.[34] Hence, during periods of economic stress, when large dowries were difficult to furnish, more women sought admission to a nunnery.[35] During the same period as the agricultural recession, the gold mines of Minas Gerais lured away young men with the promise of easy riches.[36] Eligible males were therefore in short supply. The infrequency of marriage among the elite was thus intimately related to the ongoing decline in plantation agriculture and the regional redistribution in population from the littoral to the interior of the colony.

Around the 1730s the Bahian economic crisis intensified. Poor harvests, droughts, and unfavorable weather conditions reduced the volume of sugar exported.[37] The difficulties in the sugar sector, moreover, followed closely on the heels of crop failures for Bahia's second major export, tobacco, in the 1720s.[38]

According to complaints of contemporaries, the critical situation was reflected in an excessive rise in prices. [39]

During this trying period economic factors led not only to a low incidence of marital unions, but also to an increase in conventual admissions. The heightened crisis following the 1730s was reflected, first, in the rise in the number of entrants to the Destêrro [40] and, second, in the creation of three additional convents in Salvador. The need for and the erection of convents must therefore be seen as a response to economic and demographic currents that affected the Bahian region.

The creation of the nunnery of Poor Clares in 1677 and the later establishment of additional female communities reveal how royal policy attempted to reconcile colonial interests with the intentions of the metropolis. The Crown consistently weighed its aims of encouraging the vitality of the elite against the demand of that group for local convents. The nunnery, as an institution that siphoned marriageable women from society, was viewed as a threat to royal objectives. In the end the privilege was conceded only when economic and demographic dislocations of considerable magnitude required royal action.

Just as economic and demographic circumstances influenced the creation of convents, social considerations also shaped their role in the Bahian setting. The Destêrro Convent, founded in 1677 as the first house in Brazil, was unique in the manner of its founding, its governing statutes, and its comportment. For more than fifty years it was the only convent in Portuguese America. The house of Poor Clares had been created at the behest of the municipal council, which pledged its patronage in return for royal preference in cloistering its daughters there. Daughters of *vereadores* (councilmen) therefore dominated the entrants into the convent in the late seventeenth century and comprised nearly 60 percent of the professing nuns in the period 1677 to 1700. [41] As the sole community of female religious in Brazil, intended to serve the entire colony, the Destêrro was in practice restricted to women of only the highest social caliber. Not only was a substantial dowry required for admission, but social pressures within the cloister also forced its inhabitants to maintain a costly and extravagant life-style. The Poor Clares of Salvador in the eighteenth century were renowned for their prominent families, their jewels and finery, their multitudinous personal servants, and their scandalous morality. [42]

Salvador's other convents differed from the Destêrro in the process of their foundations and in the character of their communities. Unlike the Destêrro, which because of its initial dependence on the municipal council was affected by the interests and oscillating financial support of that body, the other nunneries were founded by individual patrons. The house of N. S. da Conceição da Lapa was erected with a bequest from João de Miranda Ribeiro and Manuel Antunes Lima, two pious and wealthy men who sponsored the new convent with the intention of cloistering their daughters there. The royal license was issued in 1733 on the condition that the patrons assume the entire costs of building the nunnery and that the community be limited to twenty professants, or less than half the stipulated size of the Destêrro. [43] The Convent of N. S. da Mercês, founded two years later, was created at the instigation of Dona Ursula Luisa de Monserrat, sole heiress to the fabulous fortune of her father, the legendary Pedro Barbosa Leal. She became the abbess of the new community of fifty nuns. [44] Neither the Lapa nor the Mercês was ready for occupancy before the 1740s. The last nunnery, N. S. da Soledade e Coração de Jesús, was originally founded in 1741 by Padre Gabriel Malagrida, a Jesuit priest later burned at the stake for heresy, as a retirement house for impoverished women. Royal approval for its conversion to an institute of forty nuns was extended in 1751. [45]

The statutes and regulations of the eighteenth-century establishments were characterized by greater strictness than the Destêrro. None of the later convents required dowries. For admission these professants had merely to guarantee their future support with a regular income. Moreover, all three of the later communities were forbidden to inherit properties from their inhabitants—a privilege that had vastly swelled the Destêrro's patrimony. Lastly, the few slaves permitted were to be engaged exclusively in the service of the community; private servants were prohibited. Despite the failure to uphold this stricture rigorously, nowhere was it abused as extensively as in the Destêrro. In 1778 the archbishop reported to the Crown that the Destêrro housed over four hundred slaves. [46]

Although the royal limitations on servants, dowries, and inheritance appear to suggest the creation of communities that accommodated a broad spectrum of women, the nuns of all of Bahia's convents to a large extent derived from a privileged social sector of interrelated families. The Destêrro was the most desirable repository for daughters of the most prominent families of the region. Admission to its cloister was a virtual indicator of high social status. A close examination of the backgrounds of the fathers of the inhabitants has revealed the predominance of planters' daughters as nuns. As many as 30 percent of the women who entered during the period 1677 to 1800 were either children or close relations of sugar growers. Additionally, the daughters of especially prominent men engaged in commerce and those distinguished with honorific titles of the military orders and the Inquisition, with extreme affluence, or with high bureaucratic office were also admitted. [47] So concerned was the municipal council with the preservation of the social status of the institution that it petitioned the Crown for two categories of nuns, noble and plebeian. [48] Although this request was denied on the grounds that it stemmed from unwarranted pretensions, such a distinction within the Destêrro was in all likelihood unnecessary. The convent was actually founded with the capacity to house two classes of nuns—the superior grouping of the black veil and the lesser category of the white. The latter provided only half the dowry of the higher-status black veil. The fact that the white veil attracted few more than a handful of women throughout the eighteenth century underlines the uniformity of social background among the nuns of the Destêrro and suggests that women of humbler origins were rarely admitted. [49]

The Lapa Convent was founded almost as an extension—albeit more pious—of the Destêrro. One of its benefactors, Manuel Antunes Lima, "one of the wealthiest men in the city" [50] with a fortune invested in real estate and extended in personal loans, already had a daughter who was a professed nun in the Destêrro. As an engineer he had supervised much of the Destêrro's construction. [51] Moreover, the first two inhabitants, the abbess and her assistant, were both drawn from the Poor Clares. The new head, Maria Caetana da Assumção, was the daughter of João de Couros Carneiro, the scribe of the municipal council and a man with considerable property. The nun who accompanied her, Josefa Clara de Jesus, was likewise the child of a municipal councillor. [52]

A similar predominance of the propertied and well-to-do was also characteristic of the other convents. Certainly the affluence and lineage of Dona Ursula, the patroness and abbess of the Mercês, would have qualified her for admission to the Destêrro. Her father, Pedro Barbosa Leal, was an extraordinarily wealthy mill owner. Another nun in that convent, Joanna Francisca de São José, had prior to her profession maintained a hospital at her own cost. She was the daughter of a prominent sugar planter, Francisco de Sá Peixoto. [53]

The Convent of Soledade, presumably the most modest of institutions owing to its origins as a retirement house for the improvident, was virtually the only convent that could not emulate the Destêrro's exclusivity. Even so, at least one contemporary remarked that it was the affluence of the house that facilitated its conversion to an institute of nuns. [54] The Soledade did, in fact, have some women of means who enjoyed independent incomes. Five females of the Telles de Menezes sugar-growing clan were among the religious. The abbess, Beatriz Maria de Jesus, owned a *fazenda* (plantation) and seventeen slaves, which provided her livelihood in the convent. Another nun had a tobacco and manioc holding with slaves whose proceeds sustained her. [55]

The failure of the eighteenth-century feminine monastic centers to democratize significantly the religious population was due to several factors. In the first place, each convent was dominated by a few influential families who cloistered their female offspring there. In the case of the Destêrro, the Pires de Carvalho family complex, from the late seventeenth through the eighteenth centuries, housed nineteen of twenty-nine female descendants there. [56] When the Lapa was founded, five of the twenty professing religious were daughters of the patron, João de Miranda Ribeiro. [57] Cloistered in the Mercês were four children of Domingos Dias Lima. The Soledade Convent accommodated five sisters from the Telles de Menezes family, and the abbess had two sisters who had taken the veil as well. [58]

1. **Idealized Picture of the Incas of Peru.** Reprinted from Amédée François Frézier, *Reis . . . van Chili, Peru en Brazil . . . 1712, 1713, 1714* (Amsterdam: R. and G. Wetstein, 1718).

2. **Women in a Chilean Tertulia, ca. 1790.** Reprinted from Claudio Gay, *Historia física y política de Chile: Atlas* (Paris: E. Thunot y Cª, 1854).

3. **Bahian Lady.** Reprinted from Johan B. von Spix and Carl F. P. von Martius, *Atlas Zur Reise En Brasilien* (Munich: F. Fleischen, 1823–31).

4. **Colombian Woman in Riding Dress.** Reprinted from Isaac F. Holton, *Twenty Months in the Andes* (New York: Harper and Brothers, 1857).

5. **Tapada of Lima.** Reprinted from Comte De Gabriac, *Promenade à travers de l'Amérique du Sud* (Paris: Michel Levy Freres, 1868).

6. **Rabona (Camp Follower in Peru).** Reprinted from Laurent Saint-Cricq, *Voyage à travers l'Amérique du Sud, d l'Océan Pacifique à l'Océan Atlantique* (Paris: Librairie L. Hachette et Cie, 1891).

7. **Indian Vendors in Yucatan (Mexico).** Reprinted from Charles Wiener, *América Pintoresca* (Barcelona: Montaner y Simón, 1884).

8. **Ladies of Tarija, Argentina.** Reprinted from Arthur Thouar, *Explorations dans l'Amérique du Sud* (Paris: L. Hachette et Cie, 1891).

9. **Araucanian Woman Weaving a Poncho.** Reprinted from Marie R. Wright, *The Republic of Chile* (Philadelphia: G. Barrie and Sons, 1904).

10. **Chola Beauty of Potosí.** Reprinted from Marie R. Wright, Bolivia: *The Central Highway of South America* (Philadelphia: G. Barrie and Sons, 1907).

Moreover, if certain relatives failed to gain admission as religious, secular places were available to them. All the nunneries regularly acted as shelters for lay women who were able to supply their room and board. Salvador's prelate even alleged that a woman's choice of convent was determined by the number of relatives in each.[59] The Destêrro accommodated not only sisters, but aunts, cousins and nieces among its *recolhidas* (recluses) and *educandas* (wards). Similarly, the first *educanda* admitted to the Mercês was the daughter of the abbess's *compadre*.[60] The fact that in 1748 five nuns left the Destêrro to found the convent of N. S. da Conceição da Ajuda, the first feminine community in Rio de Janeiro, suggests that the network of conventual interrelationships extended even beyond the Bahian captaincy.[61]

Economic barriers were also a significant deterrent to broadening the spectrum of female religious. The Destêrro required a formidable dowry, whose level was raised several times during the course of the eighteenth century. Only rarely were women admitted without the requisite endowment. Over the years a few undowered women with exceptional musical talent were allowed to take the veil.[62] Although in the other nunneries the novice theoretically professed *titulo paupertitis*, or without a prescribed dowry, she had to guarantee an annual allowance (*vitalício*) with a written contract. If she failed to honor the agreement, two cosigners were liable for her support.[63]

The necessity of providing a yearly subsidy effectively eliminated all but propertied women from the Bahian cloisters, since the allowance was usually derived from the rental of a dwelling or a piece of land. Even in the Soledade, the most modest, only four of forty women lacked allowances to provide for their own sustenance. These women were, in fact, exceptions, as they had earlier been placed in the retirement house either by the Jesuit founder or by order of the governor-general. A number of recluses in the original retirement house were actually excluded at the time of its conversion to a nunnery because they were too poor and lacked relatives to support them.[64] Moreover, when provided as a lump sum, the stipulated allowance was virtually indistinguishable from a dowry. Because some families lived long distances from the city and wished to avoid an annual journey, they preferred a single contribution to a yearly obligation.[65]

The nunneries of Bahia were homogeneous racially as well as socially. Discrimination against New Christians and mixed-bloods was characteristic not only of nunneries, but also of brotherhoods, retirement houses, and monasteries. The Destêrro refused entry to such "contaminated" women even in the inferior positions of the white veil. In 1695 the illegitimate daughter of João Luis Ferreira was forced to demonstrate her racial purity. Her background was rigorously examined, and a number of witnesses were called to attest to her purity of blood (*limpieza de sangue*). Ironically, the fact of the woman's illegitimacy raised no objections other than those which stemmed from suspicions that her mother had been a mulatta.[66]

Like the Destêrro, the other convents also pursued policies of racial exclusivity. In 1754 an officer of the militia petitioned to have his three daughters admitted to nunneries in Portugal. He protested that they had been refused by the Bahian communities on the grounds of their color, in spite of their light skin and respectable upbringing.[67] Evidently, the exclusion of nonwhite women continued throughout the eighteenth century. In 1798 it was still so difficult for a woman of color to take the veil that one *parda* appealed to the Crown for a license to found a convent entirely for mixed-bloods. The supplicant argued that there were "innumerable women of color of reputable families, who were called by God" and who deserved the opportunity to profess.[68] The archbishop emphatically advised against her plea with the summary statement that mixed-bloods—albeit men more so than women—simply could not be trusted.[69]

In spite of their endeavors to maintain racial and social exclusivity, convents commonly housed illegitimate, unmarriageable, unprotected, disgraced, and even nonwhite women. This ironic situation is in part explained by the divisions within the convent. Each nunnery in Salvador accommodated women in two categories, religious and secular. The nuns of the black veil and white veil constituted the former grouping, and the *educandas* and *recolhidas* made up the latter. Purportedly, only reputable white women were admitted as religious. Those of more dubious circumstancces could be housed as seculars if an urgent need arose. For example, though women of mixed racial antecedents were barred from becoming nuns, they could by the late eighteenth century usually enter as seculars. A petition from one *educanda* in 1789 living in the Mercês revealed that she was the *parda* daughter of a wealthy businessman. Another pupil in the Destêrro was also a mulatta.[70] Apart from women with the taint of color, the secular inhabitants also included disgraced or adulterous women. In Bahian society the convent not infrequently sheltered women banished from their husbands' or fathers' households. Illegitimate daughters were also permitted admission as recluses. The Destêrro accommodated the two daughters of a priest among its inhabitants.[71]

The apparent paradox of the convent acting both as the exclusive preserve for the offspring of a local elite and as a refuge for disreputable women may be resolved only by regarding the nunnery as an institutional bulwark of the social order. In a variety of ways the convent contributed not only to the preservation of a social ideal for women, but also to the actual maintenance of the social hierarchy.

For the Bahian elite the convent served as a device that secured its social ascendancy. The upper sector of colonial society included probably not more than the 148 separate family lines listed by the eighteenth-century genealogical chronicler Jaboatão.[72] Since marriage was the primary means of cementing family alliances, several conventions surrounding the institution were observed by the elite. Unions were customarily arranged—generally with little regard to the ages of the prospective bride and groom. It was conceivable for a woman to be married to her father's brother, who might be more than thirty years her senior. [73] The effort to fortify the kin group by intermarriage among relatives further resulted in what Stuart Schwartz has aptly labeled the "thicket of constant cousin marriages." [74] Anyone who has consulted the genealogist Jaboatão can attest to the difficulty of untangling the twisted roots of prominent family trees. [75] Above all, ties based upon romantic love had little place in the value system of the elite, which emphasized the extended and devalued the nuclear family. Not only were marital bonds founded upon emotion anomalous, but they were also regarded as potentially threatening to the social hierarchy. Elopements could, for example, result in marriages across class lines. [76]

The seclusion of young women therefore conformed with the Lusitanian ideal of chastity and had the complementary utility of preventing opportunities for romantic encounters. The rigorous incarceration of the young maiden in the impenetrable chambers of the Big House graphically conjures up the essence of elite fears. [77] No Brazilian proverb better describes elite attitudes toward its female offspring than the following: "A black woman for work, a white woman for marriage, and a mulatta for sex." Although the cadence of the aphorism would surely have been ruined, it more correctly would have read, "a white woman for marriage or the convent." Given the desirability of the seclusion of women, it mattered little whether it took place in the house of the husband, the father, or the Lord. Since the service of God signified an honorable and socially acceptable rationale for cloistering young virgins, the convent provided the ideal means for preventing interclass marriages.

Despite the prevailing attitude that lauded the isolation of women, females frequently exercised independent and unprotected roles in colonial society. For example, women appear prominently as shopkeepers, vendors, and peddlers of all sorts. [78] Furthermore, some women were administrators of estates or acted as family heads. In one Bahian parish as many single women as men were listed as heads of households. Of a total of 522 families, 230, or 44 percent, were matrifocal. Living among these families were a number of unmarried women who supported themselves as seamstresses or laundresses. [79]

How may we reconcile the prominent appearance of females in positions traditionally assigned to males with a value system that conceived of women as abject dependents and sanctioned no female activity outside the home? The conflict between the ideal and the actual may be resolved by regarding the practice of secluding females as a social mechanism used to restrict marriages to a socially acceptable community of persons. For the elite, socially endogamous marriages served as a means of conserving the power or resources of an intragenerational and extended family. Among other sectors of the population the isolation of women served little practical purpose and was, in fact, counterproductive. The scattered available evidence suggests that the extended family was an uncommon type outside elite circles. Quite to the contrary, matrifocal or single-parent households were commonplace.[80] In most families, economic necessity forced all members, including women, to contribute to the household's survival. Thus, endogamous marriage for families without land, property, or assets had no meaning or usefulness. Beyond the bounds of a tiny elite, feminine isolation could remain a desirable, if unattainable, ideal.

The social endogamy typical of the Bahian elite was complemented by an infrequency of marriages. It appears that ordinarily not more than two of five children per nuclear family were wedded.[81] Because of its reluctance to marry off daughters to any but the most socially distinguished suitors, the elite stood accused of social pretension, snobbery, and conceit—"convinced that there are no marriages equal to their daughters."[82] One governor-general, who found the Bahians to be uncultured boors, mockingly described them as "hotentots" whose unwarranted airs led them to confine their daughters to a nunnery rather than give their hands in marriage.[83]

However, the pretensions of the elite were not the only considerations that made the convent an organ of indispensable utility for the upper sector. While often motivated by vanity and pretense, the removal of undowered elite women from society had very practical consequences. Since the social position of the elite was essentially based upon a monopoly of power and wealth, it was necessary to restrict marriages to prevent the dispersal of those resources.[84] For families in economic straits—a common characteristic of sugar growers in the eighteenth century—the convent offered the ideal solution. By siphoning off elite females into cloistered celibacy, the nunnery therefore allowed the concentration of wealth and assisted the domination of society by a restricted group of families.[85]

Perhaps the greatest contribution of the nunnery was to remove women of anomalous circumstances from the social order. The complex of values of Salvador's patriarchal society that defined the female role as subordinate to the unchallenged authority of the male made the "problem of the unassigned women"[86]—at least on the ideal plane—one of significance. The convent was the most suitable place for accommodating women either who were potentially disruptive to the social hierarchy or who represented misfits in the established patriarchal social order. As nuns, the convent sheltered undowered women of the elite and prevented possible encounters with males that could result in socially undesirable matches. As seculars, the nunnery housed women who no longer retained a secure niche in the outside world. In so doing, the convent signified the alternative to isolation or ostracism in secular society.[87]

In its secular places, the convent served as a refuge for a variety of women whose actual circumstances were not compatible with the patriarchal ideals guiding Bahian norms. Women alone or unprotected by a male guardian were the most common among Salvador's recluses. In such cases widowhood or even the temporary absence of a father or husband might prompt the woman's entrance. Frequently the daughters of wives of merchants, soldiers, or bureau-crats forced to travel assumed secular places in convents. For example, Bernardino de Senna Almeida, a merchant who intended to journey to Portugal on business, petitioned the Crown for a license to retire his wife and two daughters to the Convent of Soledade. He argued that the need for their seclusion arose from the fact that he lacked an elder son who might care for the women in his absence. [88] The Destêrro Convent housed a number of widows, many of whom had relatives among the nuns. Retiring to a nunnery thus signified an escape from solitude to the company of one's friends and family.

However, even for seculars the protective isolation of the convent was a privilege inaccessible to all but those of favorable financial circumstances. Economic barriers such as the necessity of sustaining oneself prevented many from entering. For example, Capitão Felipe Rodrigues de Sousa's wife and daughters remained in the custody of relatives because they lacked the funds for their conventual support. [89]

The nunnery also acted as a shelter for women who, because of their violation of patriarchal canons of behavior, were rejected by their society. Adulterous and deflowered women, misfits in a milieu that celebrated feminine chastity above all virtues, were frequently confined to convents. According to both law and custom, the male held absolute sway over his wife and daughters. Any offense against the sanctity of marriage or the family could warrant the justifiable murder of the wife or the expulsion of a daughter. One traveler claimed that as many as thirty women had been executed in a single year. [90] In lieu of such drastic measures as murder or disinheritance, the internment of the errant woman in a convent provided the wronged male with a milder, but still honorable, alternative. José Gomes Pereira, a merchant, pleading for the admission of his wife because of her adulterous relationship with a priest, claimed that his refusal to use violence made her commitment unavoidable. [91] A more notorious incident involved Dona Luisa Francisca do Nascimento, who had been admitted to the Lapa Convent in 1789, where she spent more than twenty years and much effort in petitioning before she gained her release as a repentant soul. [92] Unchaste daughters were similarly confined. One mother petitioned to have her deflowered child committed to a convent at the cost of the traitorous male offender. [93] For the disgraced woman, no longer suited for the sacred bond of marriage, the convent offered a convenient repository.

Sometimes the pressures of a male-centered society moved women to seek refuge from masculine domination in a convent. Marital problems provided the motive of some appeals. The wife of the prominent João de Couros Carneiro requested a place as a recluse on the grounds that her jusband beat her. [94] It was also customary, in the event of divorces—"which [were] frequent" [95]—for women to retire to conventual seclusion. Clara Maria do Sacramento, alleging that her husband abused her physically and attempted to cheat her of her rightful inheritance, abandoned him to become a *recolhida*. In spite of her identity as a member of the "miserable sex," she insisted upon her right to petition the Crown for justice. [96]

Apart from the divorced women who rejected their husband's authority, some women of independent spirit entered the convent as an escape from the restriction of a patriarchal society. Compared with their lives as captives in the home, the cloister offered liberty from the tyranny of men. [97] One novice claimed that she professed only at the instigation of a nun who revealed the promise of greater freedom within the convent. [98] Dona Ursula Luisa da Monserrat, the patroness and first abbess of the Mercês Convent, anxious to avoid the ties of marriage, believed she was "defended . . . from so many wolves and placed . . . in the cloister." [99] Whether it housed rebellious females, unprotected widows and children, or unchaste daughters and adulterous wives, the nunnery buttressed the established patriarchal social order by removing women whose circumstances diverged from the sanctioned models.

From the royal point of view the social contribution of the nunnery remained ambiguous. On the one hand, the convent received and sheltered women who might otherwise have remained marginal to their society. It performed a valuable service for the colonial elite by cloistering its undowered daughters. Spared the necessity of providing marriage portions for all of their female children, prominent Bahian families were able to prevent the dispersal of their wealth. Apart from reputable females who entered primarily for social or economic reasons, women of compromised circumstances were also admitted. Unprotected, violated, unchaste, and rebellious women were housed together as seculars in the nunnery. The isolation of such women was doubly beneficial, as it offered a sanctuary to the female and a means of protecting the society from her potentially pernicious influence.

On the negative side, by removing women of marriageable age from society, the nunnery circumscribed marriages. It particularly threatened the vitality of the colony's leading sector by permitting certain families to cloister a majority of their women. One contemporary even alleged that Bahia's convents were responsible for the extinction of some important clans. [100]

The economic and demographic circumstances of the colony had consistently shaped the contours of royal policy. By the 1750s the Crown seemed assured that Salvador's nunneries detracted little from the region's population growth. The city of Salvador now claimed more than 40,000 inhabitants, and the surrounding Recôncavo numbered roughly 69,500 persons in 1768. [101] In the estimation of one archbishop, the effects of cloistering two hundred nuns amounted to no more than five professions annually, a truly negligible figure. [102] Moreover, the original scarcity of females had been overcome. It now appeared that certain regions suffered from a superfluity of females and a dearth of marriageable men. In some cases women were forced to journey to Portugal to marry and settle there. [103]

While royal fears concerning the effects of nunneries on the colonial population had been assuaged, the economic circumstances of the orders became a problem of increasingly larger proportions. In the past the fortunes of the Bahian export economy had to some extent prompted the creation of nunneries and had similarly been responsible for increased pressure for conventual places. The expanded religious communities, filled to overflowing by the 1760s, were increasingly faced with financial problems stemming from their enlarged size. The cumulative effects of the declining agro-economy further threatened the welfare of the religious institutes. 104 In the face of these difficulties, royal actions, consistent with earlier policies, aimed to limit the size of the religious population. Crown policy was forged to maximize the role of active persons in society. The royal view held that the religious orders were a deterrent to colonial growth and expansion. They contributed neither to the population nor to the productivity of Brazil. After a period of inquiry into the status of the orders, the Crown in 1764 issued a ban on the admission of further novices into all religious bodies—male or female. Furthermore, an effort to diminish the secular populations within nunneries was also undertaken. The convents in Bahia remained limited to four, and to the end of the century petitions for additional monastic centers for women were emphatically denied. 105 In spite of its service to Bahian society, the nunnery was ultimately regarded as an institution that warranted strict controls.

Notes

ABBREVIATIONS

AHU   Arquivo Histórico Ultramarino
AN   Arquivo Nacional
APB   Arquivo Público do Estado da Bahia
ASCD   Arquivo do Convento de Santa Clara do Destêrro
BNRJ   Biblioteca Nacional do Rio de Janeiro

1. The investigation of the rôle of the convent in the economy and society of colonial Mexico has been admirably undertaken by Asunción Lavrin, "Women in Convents: Their Economic and Social Role in Colonial Mexico," in Berenice Carroll, ed., *Liberating Women's History: Theoretical and Critical Essays* (Urbana: University of Illinois Press, 1976), p. 255; Sister Ann Miriam Gallagher, "The Family Background of the Nuns of Two *Monasterios* in Colonial Mexico: Santa Clara, Querétaro; and Corpus Christi, Mexico City, (1724-1822)" (Ph.D. diss., The Catholic University of America, 1972), pp. 210-11. The first Franciscan nunnery of Poor Clares in the captaincy of Chile was established in Santiago in 1608. On the history of a convent comparable to the Destêrro, see P. Juan de Guernica, *Historia y evolución del monasterio de Clarisas de Ntra. Sra. de la Victoria en sus cuatro períodos* (Santiago: Sagrado Corazón de Jesús, 1944), pp. 13-28.

2. Gallagher, "Family Background," pp. 210-11.

3. Salvador da Bahia de Todos os Santos was the official capital de Brazil from 1549 to 1763, when the colonial seat was moved to Rio de Janeiro. Population estimates of Salvador vary considerably, and the figure of sixty thousand must be regarded as tentative. For a general discussion of Bahian demography, see Thales de Azevedo, *Povoamento da cidade do Salvador* (Salvador: Itapuã, 1969). An overview of nunneries in Salvador is given in Luís dos Santos Vilhena, *A Bahia no século XVIII*, 3 vols. (Salvador: Itapuã, 1969). 2: 449-51. For Mexican population figures, see Keith A. Davies, "Tendencias demográficas urbanas durante el siglo XIX en Mexico," *Historia Mexicana* 21 (January-March 1972): 501. The number of nuns is cited by Asunción Lavrin, "Values and Meaning of Monastic Life for Nuns in Colonial Mexico," *Catholic Historical Review* 58 (October 1972): 367. For a comparison of colonial Mexico and Salvador, see Stuart B. Schwartz, "Cities of Empire: Mexico and Bahia in the Sixteenth Century," *Journal of Inter-American Studies and World Affairs*, 11 (October 1969): 616-37.

4. Pedro Calmon, *História do Brasil, 1500-1800*, 7 vols. (Rio de Janeiro: José Olympio, 1959), 1: 233-34; José Justino Andrade e Silva, ed., *Collecção chronológica da legislação portugueza, 1603-1700*, 10 vols. (Lisbon: Imprensa de J. J. A. Silva, 1854-59), 1: 9 (23 March 1603); 1: 22 (2 September 1603).

5. Theodoro Sampaio, *História da fundação da cidade do Salvador* (Salvador: Beneditina, 1949), p. 182, quoting Padre Nóbrega's letter of 9 August 1549 to Padre Simão Rodrigues.

6. Stuart B. Schwartz, *Sovereignty and Society in Colonial Brazil: The High Court of Bahia and Its Judges, 1609-1751* (Berkeley and Los Angeles: University of California Press, 1973), pp. 105-6.

7. Andrade e Silva, *Collecção*, 1: 22 (2 September 1603).

8. *Documentos históricos da Bibliotheca Nacional do Rio de Janeiro*, 120 vols. (Rio de Janeiro, 1928-), 97 (1952): 193 (1 September 1719) (hereafter cited as *DHBNR*).

9. Andrade e Silva, *Collecção*, 1: 22 (2 September 1603); 2: 6 (11 March 1620): 4: 295 (3 February 1654); Inácio Accioli de Cerqueira e Silva, *Memórias históricas e políticas da província da Bahia*, ed. Braz do Amaral, 6 vols. (Salvador: Imprensa Oficial do Estado, 1919-40), 5: 216-17 (13 July 1646).

10. ASCD, "Livro da fundação," fols. 2-2v, 6-6v; Accioli, *Memórias*, 5: 217-18 (6 July 1665).

11. BNRJ, Manuscritos, II-33, 29, 113 (19 August 1718). Biographical information on 94 of 130 fathers of nuns was compiled from Frei Antonio de Santa Maria Jaboatão, "Catálogo genealógico das principaes familias . . . ," *Revista do Instituto Genealógico da Bahia*, nos. 1-4 (1945-48); *Documentos históricos do Arquivo Municipal da Bahia* (hereafter cited as *DHAMB*), *Atas da Camara, 1625-1700*, 6 vols. (Salvador: Prefeitura Municipal, 1949-55[?]); José Antônio Caldas, *Notícia geral de tôda esta capitania da Bahia . . .* , facsimile ed. (Salvador: Beneditina, 1951), pp. 429-42; *Anais do primeiro congresso da história da Bahia*, 5 vols. (Salvador, 1950-51), 2: 11-353; ASCD, "Livro das entradas e profissões . . ."; Affonso Ruy, *História da câmara municipal da cidade do Salvador* (Salvador: Camara Municipal, 1955), pp. 347-74.

12. A. Lavrin, "The Role of Nunneries in the Economy of New Spain in the Eighteenth Century," *Hispanic American Historical Review* 46 (November 1966): 372 (hereafter cited as *HAHR*).

13. Gallagher, "Family Background," pp. 210-11.

14. A. Lavrin, "Religious Life of Mexican Women in the XVIII Century" (Ph.D. diss., Harvard University, 1963), p. 13; Susan Soeiro, "A Baroque Nunnery: The Economic and Social Role of a Colonial Convent" (Ph.D. diss., New York University, 1974), pp. 30-35.

15. The *encomenderos* were those early settlers, participants in the conquest, who were rewarded for their services with allocations of Indians, from whom they received tribute either in labor or goods. In exchange, *encomenderos* were supposed to provide religious instruction to the Indians.

16. Frédéric Mauro, *Le Portugal et l'Atlantique au XVIIe siècle, 1570-1670* (Paris: Ecole Pratique des Hautes Etudes, S.E.V.P.E.N., 1960), pp. 193-94, 236-37; Ward J. Barrett and Stuart B. Schwartz, "Two Colonial Sugar Economies: Morelos, Mexico and Bahia, Brazil, A Comparison," Unpubl. manuscript, 1972, 9-10. In Spanish: "Comparación entre dos economías azucareras coloniales: Morelos, Mexico y Bahia, Brasil," in Enrique Florescano, ed., *Haciendas, latifundios y plantaciones en América Latina* (Mexico: Siglo XXI, 1975), pp. 532-72.

17. Accioli, *Memórias*, 5: 224. For a general statement on the formation of elites in colonial society, see Stephanie Blank, "Patrons, Clients and Kin in Seventeenth Century Caracas," *HAHR* 54 (May 1974): 264-65.

18. Accioli, *Memórias*, 5: 222 (16 November 1684).

19. AHU, Bahia, Papeis avulsos, 2d ser. (uncatalogued), case 303 (10), Municipal Council to Crown, 1662; *Procurador* of Bahia to Crown, 1663[?]; Consulta do Conselho Ultramarino, 14 August 1663.

20. *DHAMB, Cartas do Senado, 1638-1692*, 5 vols. (Salvador: Prefeitura Municipal, 1951[?]-53), 4: 54-55; APB, "Ordens regias," vol. 3, doc. 108 (19 November 1695).

21. Accioli, *Memórias*, 5: 222-23 (16 November 1684); APB, "Ordens regias," vol. 3, doc. 108 (19 November 1695); *DHAMB, Cartas*, 4: 54-55 (23 July 1695); *DHBNR*, 97: 189-94 (25 August 1717); BNRJ, Manuscritos, II-33, 29, 113 (11 February 1718); II-33, 29, 113 (19 August 1718); AN, codex 952, doc. 164 (22 September 1718).

22. AN, codex 952, vol. 26, fol. 398 (1 March 1732); fol. 318 (14 April 1732); APB, "Ordens regias," vol. 28, doc. 35, fol. 58 (14 April 1732).

23. AHU, Bahia, Papeis avulsos, 3d. ser. (uncatalogued), case 345 (23 April 1747); case 346 (17 December 1750); case 406 (11 June 1753).

24. AN, codex 952, vol. 26, fols. 398, 400-1.

25. *DHBNR*, 97: 189-94.

26. Barrett and Schwartz, "Two . . . Sugar Economies," Table 4.

27. Accioli, *Memórias*, 5: 506-7; BNRJ, Manuscritos, II-33, 26, 17, "Memórias da fundação do Convento de Ursulinas," fols. 195-98; AHU, Bahia, 1st ser., nos. 499-500 (23 March 1753).

28. ASCD, "Livro das entradas," nos. 134, 136, 139, 150, 153, 155, 158, 160, 161, 163, 164.

29. AHU, Bahia, Papeis avulsos, 2d ser. (uncatalogued), case 10 (303), *Procurador* of Bahia, 1663[?].

30. Thales de Azevedo, *Povoamento*, p. 195.

31. Barrett and Schwartz, "Two . . . Sugar Economies," Table 4.

32. Susan Soeiro, "The Social and Economic Role of the Convent: Women and Nuns in Colonial Bahia, 1677-1800," *HAHR* 54 (May 1974): 214-15.

33. Accioli, *Memórias*, 2: 176.

34. AHU, Bahia, Papeis avulsos, 2d ser. (uncatalogued), case 10 (303), Municipal Council to Crown, 1662; *Procurador* of Bahia to Crown, 1663[?].

35. Soeiro, "Role of the Convent," pp. 219-20.

36. Andre João Antonil, *Cultura e opulência do Brasil por suas drogas e minas*, ed. and annot. Andrée Mansuy (Paris: Institut des Hautes Etudes de l'Amérique Latine, 1968), pp. 368, 464; Stuart B. Schwartz, "Free Labor in a Slave Economy: The Lavradores de Cana of Colonial Bahia," in Dauril Alden, ed., *Colonial Roots of Modern Brazil* (Berkeley and Los Angeles: University of California Press, 1973), pp. 156, 181.

37. Wenceslau Pereira da Silva, "Parecer . . . em que se propoem os meios mais convenientes para suspender a ruina . . . Bahia 12 de fevereiro de 1738," *Anais da Biblioteca Nacional do Rio de Janeiro* 31 (1914): 27-31 (hereafter cited as *ABNRJ*); APB, "Ordens régias," vol. 39, docs. 7 (4 March 1743), 47 (30 September 1743); Pinto de Aguiar, ed. *Aspectos da economia colonial* (Salvador: Livraria Progresso, 195[?]), pp. 54-63.

38. APB, "Ordens régias," vol. 23, doc. 21 (19 March 1927); vol. 24, docs. 6 (29 April 1729), 6a (25 August 1729), 19-19a (9 May 1729).

39. Antonil, *Cultura e opulência*, pp. 378-87; *DHBNR*, 97: 272 (24 September 1721).

40. Soeiro, "Role of the Convent," pp. 220-21.

41. Ibid., p. 216.

42. AHU, Bahia, 1st ser. cat., nos. 6554-55 (25 March 1756). This episcopal *visita* describes the convent at the height of its decadence.

43. BNRJ, Manuscritos, II-33, 39, 110 (3 August 1733); AHU, Bahia, 1st ser. cat., nos. 382-83 (22 February 1753), 499-500 (23 March 1753), 6554-55 (25 March 1756).

44. BNRJ, Manuscritos, II-33, 26, 17, "Memórias"; II-33, 29, 112 (19 May 1742). AHU, Bahia, 1st ser. cat., nos. 6554-55; Accioli, *Memórias*, 5: 506-7.

45. AHU, Bahia, 1st ser. cat., nos. 382-83 (22 February 1753), 6554-55 (25 March 1756).

46. AHU, Bahia, 1st ser. cat., nos. 382-83, 6554-55, 9805 (1 December 1778).

47. Soeiro, "A Baroque Nunnery," pp. 42-45, 234-54.

48. *DHBNR*, 97: 190.

49. Soeiro, "A Baroque Nunnery," pp. 48-50.

50. AHU, Bahia, Papeis avulsos, 3d. ser. (uncatalogued), case 344 (61) (30 September 1749).

51. A. J. R. Russell-Wood, *Fidalgos and Philanthropists: The Santa Casa da Misericórdia of Bahia, 1550-1755* (Berkeley and Los Angeles: University of California Press, 1968), pp. 136, 157; APB, "Notas de escrituras," vol. 62, fols. 230-32; vol. 64, fols. 348-52.

52. Soeiro, "A Baroque Nunnery," pp. 243-49.

53. Antonil, *Cultura e opulência*, p. 269; BNRJ, Manuscritos, II-33, 26, 17, "Memórias," fols. 197-98.

54. Caldas, *Notícia geral*, p. 21.

55. AHU, Bahia, 1st ser. cat., nos. 499-500 (27 March 1753).

56. Soeiro, "A Baroque Nunnery," p. 228, Fig. 3.

57. Accioli, *Memórias*, 5: 228, 311.

58. BNRJ, Manuscritos, II-33, 26, 17, "Memórias," fols. 195-98; AHU, Bahia, 1st ser. cat., nos. 499-500 (27 March 1753).

59. AHU, Bahia, 1st ser. cat., no. 19537 (2 November 1799).

60. Soeiro, "Role of the Convent," p. 225; BNRJ, Manuscritos, II-33, 26, 17, Carta de Dona Ursula Luisa da Monserrat, n.d.

61. Frei Antonio de Santa Maria Jaboatão, *Novo orbe seráfico basilico*, 5 vols. (Rio de Janeiro: Instituto Histórico e Geográfico Brasileiro, 1859-62), pt. 2, vol. 3, pp. 749-50, 770; Accioli, *Memórias*, 5: 225.

62. *DHBNR*, 96 (1950): 9 (12 November 1710). AHU, Bahia, 1st ser. cat., nos. 10663 (25 October 1780), 10665-66 (30 October 1780), 10667-68 (28 October 1780).

63. APB, "Notas de escrituras," vol. 80, fols. 61-62 (20 December 1745); vol. 130, fols. 221-22v (16 December 1790); vol. 136, fols. 378v-82 (10 December 1796); vol. 136, fols. 405v-7 (27 January 1797); vol. 137, fols. 267-68v (14 December 1797); vol. 137, fols. 271-73 (16 December 1797); vol. 143, fols, 31v-35v (6 December 1800).

64. AHU, Bahia, 1st ser. cat., nos. 382-83 (22 February 1753), 499-500 (27 March 1753).

65. AHU, Bahia, 1st ser. cat., nos. 6554-55 (25 March 1756).

66. ASCD, case 1, portfolio 27 (12 October 1695); Mexican nunneries similarly discriminated—effectively excluding Indian women from their communities. See Lavrin, "Values and Meaning," pp. 368-72.

67. APB, "Ordens régias," vol. 53, fols. 167-72; A. J. R. Russell-Wood, "Colonial Brazil," in David W. Cohen and Jack P. Greene, eds., *Neither Slave Nor Free: The Freedmen of African Descent in Slave Societies of the New World* (Baltimore: Johns Hopkins University Press, 1972), p. 112.

68. APB, "Ordens régias," vol. 53, fol. 272v (26 October 1797).

69. AHU, Bahia, 1st ser. cat., no. 18422 (18 October 1798).

70. AHU, Bahia, 1st ser. cat., no. 13369 (28 December 1789); APB, "Ordens régias," vol. 83, fol. 272v (26 October 1797).

71. ASCD, "Livro das entradas," no. 122; ASCD, case 1, portfolios 13, 18(I).

72. Jaboatão, "Catálogo genealógico"; Schwartz, *Sovereignty and Society in Colonial Brazil*, pp. 338-39.

73. See, for example, Pedro Calmon, *História da Casa da Torre* (Rio de Janeiro: José Olympio, 1939), p. 91.

74. Schwartz, *Sovereignty*, p. 339.

75. On the marriages among the Pires de Carvalhos, see Soeiro, "A Baroque Nunnery," p. 228.

76. For an excellent study of this problem, see Verena Martínez-Alier, "Elopement and Seduction in Nineteenth-Century Cuba," *Past and Present* 55 (May 1972): 91-129. See also William J. Goode, "The Theoretical Importance of Love," *American Sociological Review* 24 (August 1959): 38-47, for a suggestive analysis.

77. Gilberto Freyre, *The Masters and the Slaves: A Study in the Development of Brazilian Civilization*, trans. Samuel Putnam, 2d ed. (New York: A. A. Knopf, 1966), pp. 352-54.

78. *DHAMB, Atas*, 2: 154-55, 390.

79. Avelino de Jesus da Costa, "População da cidade da Baía em 1775," in *Actas, V, Coloquio International de Estudos Luso-brasileiros*, (Coimbra, 1964), pp. 60, 8-53; *ABNRJ* 31 (1913): 211.

80. Donald Ramos, "Marriage and the Family in Colonial Vila Rica," *HAHR* 55 (May 1975): 200-225.

81. Soeiro, "Role of the Convent," pp. 214-15. Ramos suggests a lower frequency of

marriage for the general population: 16.6 percent of the population over the legal age was married. See Ramos, "Marriage and the Family," pp. 207, 209.

82. *DHBNR*, 97: 190 (1 September 1719); Caldas, *Notícia geral*, p. 19.

83. Quoted in Thales de Azevedo, *Povoamento*, p. 211.

84. Blank, "Patrons, Clients, and Kin," p. 266.

85. Soeiro, "Role of the Convent," pp. 219-21. See, for example, APB, "Ordens regias," vol. 7, docs. 731, 732 (15 June 1710).

86. Emily James Putnam, *The Lady: Studies of Certain Significant Phases of Her History* (Chicago: University of Chicago Press, 1970), p. 76.

87. In acting as a house of refuge, the nunnery resembled the secular institution, the retirement house. Much of what is said of the convent applied equally well to Bahia's retirement houses (*recolhimentos*). In the eighteenth century there were three retirement houses in Bahia: the house maintained by the Misericórdia, the Recolhimento dos Perdões, and the Recolhimento de S. Raimundo. On the Misericórdia's Retirement House of the Most Holy Name of Jesus, see Russell-Wood, *Fidalgos and Philanthropists*, pp. 320-36. For information on the histories of the remaining institutes, see Accioli, *Memórias*, 5: 229-31, 507-10.

88. APB, "Ordens régias," vol. 94, fol. 131 (1801). See also APB, "Ordens régias," vol. 86, fol. 201 (10 October 1798); vol. 95, fol. 109 (17 May 1802); vol. 99, doc. 27, fol. 97 (7 June 1804).

89. APB, "Ordens régias," vol. 17, doc. 14 (13 January 1723), 14A (19 October 1723).

90. Amédée François Frézier, *Relation du voyage de la mer du Sud aux côtes du Chily et du Perou, fait pendant les années 1712, 1713 & 1714* (Paris: Chez Nyon, 1732), p. 275.

91. BNRJ, Manuscritos, II-33, 29, 110; APB, "Ordens régias," vol. 95, fol. 239 (2 October 1802).

92. BNRJ, Manuscritos, II-33, 29, 110. APB, "Ordens régias," vol. 78, fols. 173-75 (31 March 1789); vol. 104, fol. 7 (12 January 1803). AHU, Bahia, 1st ser. cat., nos. 23657 (24 April 1802), 29811-12 (6 April 1807).

93. APB, "Ordens régias," vol. 97, fol. 9 (1803).

94. APB, "Ordens régias," vol. 23, doc. 109 (19 August 1728).

95. AHU, Bahia, 1st ser. cat., no. 11516 (16 April 1784).

96. APB, "Ordens régias," vol. 109, fols, 388, 389, 389v (16 July 1810).

97. Putnam, *The Lady*, p. 76.

98. Soeiro, "Role of the Convent," p. 226.

99. BNRJ, Manuscritos, II-33, 26, 17, Carta da Dona Ursula Luisa da Monserrat (23 September 1745).

100. Pinto de Aguiar, *Aspectos*, pp. 24-25.

101. Barrett and Schwartz, "Two . . . Sugar Economies," Table 4.

102. Accioli, *Memórias*, 5: 503-5.

103. APB, "Ordens régias," vol. 71, fols. 159 ff. (13 July 1771); Avelino da Costa, "População," pp. 62, 87.

104. AHU, Bahia, 1st ser. cat., nos. 6554-55 (25 March 1756), 9804, 9808 (22 November 1772).

105. AHU, Bahia, Papeis avulsos, 2d ser. (uncatalogued), case 334 (57); ASCD, "Livro das entradas," no. 193 (18 April 1764); APB, "Ordens régias," vol. 53, fol. 272v

(26 October 1797); AHU, Bahia, 1st ser. cat., nos. 18422 (18 October 1798), 19537 (2 November 1799); George C. A. Boehrer, "The Church in the Second Reign, 1840-1889," in Henry H. Keith and S. F. Edwards, eds., *Conflict and Continuity in Brazilian Society* (Columbia: University of South Carolina Press, 1969), pp. 113-16.

The feminine press: the view of women in the colonial journals of Spanish America, 1790-1810

Madre, ¿Qué cosa es casar?	Mother, what is marriage about? My child, it is spin-
Hija, hilar, parir, llorar.[1]	ning, bearing children, and crying.

For women of the age of discovery, as for women of our own times, marriage was thought to be the pivotal experience of feminine life. Be it marriage to man or God, this blessed sacrament and holy institution transferred a woman from the protection of her family to the security of wedded life. Ironically, the legal boundaries of the married state once again restricted her freedom. No doubt, the lines of this old Spanish refrain embodied the concept of women's fate that was carried to America with the conquest.

The arrival of women to the New World brought no change in their legal status.[2] However, legal theory diverged from practice. The actual conditions of feminine life were greatly affected by the social reality of Spanish conquest and settlement. Death of a spouse, father, or brother thrust women into new administrative positions; they became landowners,[3] benefactresses, and guardians of familial wealth. The traditional roles of motherhood and religious life, though basically unaltered in society's eyes, coexisted with the economic responsibilities of daily survival.[4]

The role of women in society was not often discussed in Spanish American intellectual circles during the seventeenth and early eighteenth centuries. However, as the ideas of the Enlightenment crossed the Atlantic, the condition of women emerged as an issue that received considerable attention. With the Age of Enlightenment began the process of rejecting classical Aristotelian authority and replacing this control with the need for experimental investigation. Beginning in England with Bacon and Newton and traveling across the channel to France and the north of Germany, the spread of new ideas had no geographical boundaries. The doctrines of the age aroused new interest in the status of women. By the late eighteenth century the discussion no longer centered on whether women were human beings, as the focus had shifted to more utilitarian purposes. The most obvious modification of feminism was the alliance of the movement with wider and contemporary social issues. One need only cite the works of Holbach, Alembert, Condorcet, and Diderot as examples of this association between the feminist movement and the reforms of the Enlightenment. These *philosophes* of *Encyclopedia* fame became the closest allies of women and their cause. The printed page became the battleground, as heated exchanges about the destiny of women were set down.[5]

In Spain the Age of Enlightenment was ushered in with the writings of the Benedictine monk, Benito Gerónimo Feijóo. More than any other Spaniard, Feijóo was responsible for an awareness of European learning. He appreciated the scientific method; he introduced Bacon to the Spaniards. Although Feijóo deplored the dearth of scientific works in comparison to the abundance of theological studies, it was this ability to combine new learning within the existing Catholic framework that gave the Enlightenment in Spain and its dominions a special character. The spread of this new and useful knowledge was epitomized with the publication of Feijóo's *Teatro crítico universal* in 1739.[6]

It is of particular note to this study that Feijóo also produced an important work on the position of women, *A Defense or Vindication of Women*, which questioned whether men were really the sole repositories of virtue. He cautioned readers about discourses written against women because they were usually authored by "superficial" men. Feijóo was among the first to credit the impetus for the age of discovery and exploration to the efforts of a woman, Queen Isabella.[7] Women's social role, as he perceived it, was different from men's since the female sex could excel in certain fields. Women showed a great proclivity for the arts and music. As long as women were kept ignorant, they could never assist their husbands in any decision-making process.

While he spoke out against female inferiority, this advocate of the experimental method had really argued the opposite. Feijóo, the anatomist, believed that the softness of the female brain decreased her ability to comprehend as much as men. Nevertheless, he acknowledged the place of the exceptional woman, such as Sor Juana Inés de la Cruz. The fight against injustice to women would have to be waged in the future. Feijóo's conclusion might be said to express vindication of their rights yet to come: "Let women then know that in point of understanding they are not inferior to men. They will then determine with confidence, on repelling and refuting those sophisms by which under color and pretense or reason and arguments, men attempt injustice and injuries."[8]

If Spain were to develop its resources, it would have to make an effort to learn about the latest discoveries. This utilitarian aspect of the Enlightenment represents the movement's clearest manifestations in Spain and its colonies. The pursuit of this knowledge was carried out with the formation of the economic societies. These organizations were yet another feature peculiar to the Spanish Enlightenment, for these groups were somewhat of a cross between royal academies and French salons. The creation of the Basque Society in 1763 marked the beginning of a movement that was to be carried in tone and spirit to America in the last decades of the century. Promoting the local economy, improving agriculture, increasing commerce, and developing industry were among the goals that these groups discussed. Although political economy lay at the heart of their interest, the economic societies' approach to the acquisition of "useful knowledge" was through education. Only by instruction could the ideas of the Enlightenment reign over the darkness of the past. This faith in learning, more than any other issue, was carried to the American colonies.[9] In the Indies three forces gave thrust to the spread of foreign ideas: the universities, the economic societies, and the development of the periodical press. The last form is of particular interest for this study.[10]

More than discussions in cafés, literary association, or borrowed books, these journals had a lasting impact on the colonial mind. By carrying local news, they evoked a spirit of incipient nationalism, a regard for being a part of a well-defined geographic unit. It was precisely through the daily curiosities that appeared in the various journals that colonist grew increasingly aware of their viceroyalties.[11] In many cases there existed an intimate affiliation between some of the economic societies in Spanish America and the development of journalism in a particular region. As an example of this interrelationship, there was the Economic Society of Quito, which published the *Primicias de la Cultura de Quito* in 1792. In the New Kingdom of Granada the foundation of an economic society was sponsored by two journals: the *Correo Curioso de Santa Fé de Bogotá* (1801) and, later, the *Semanario de Nuevo Reino de Granada* (1808). Of the four periodicals being discussed in this paper, two were outgrowths of these organizations, the *Mercurio Peruano* (Lima) and the *Telégrafo Mercantil* (Buenos Aires). Mexico had no economic society. In Lima and Buenos Aires the societies were established as organizations that would serve as a potential meeting place for the editors and collaborators of these new journals. The periodicals published became the official mouthpieces of these societies. Through the press the philosophies they professed and the purposes they claimed to pursue were circulated.

Contemporary ideas about the position of women in Spanish American society were best reflected in the periodical essays of the eighteenth century. In the many articles about women's place, these journals revealed a masculine point of view. Not one article was penned by a woman.[12] Nonetheless, the wide acceptance and popularity of the journals provided a vehicle for Creole opinion about the feminine sex as well as other topics of interest.[13] More than any other form of literature, they disseminated the ideas of the Enlightenment by discussing materials on a wide variety of themes. This process resulted in frequent exchanges about the quality of feminine life in Spanish America. This paper will examine the treatment of women in this form of popular culture. The evolution of their position and influence upon such views will be considered in a survey of four contemporary journals: the *Mercurio Peruano*, 1791-95; *Telégrafo Mercantil, rural político-económico, historiográfico, de Rio de la Plata*, 1801-2; *Diario de Mexico*, 1805-7; and the *Semanario Económico de Mexico, sobre noticias curiosas . . .* , 1810-11.[14]

Because of the extensive nature of this topic, discussion will focus on two areas: the contents of each journal in its articles about women and an assessment of how the material helps us to understand the problems of being upper-class and female in the colonial world. The first step toward understanding the condition of women on the eve of independence must lead us to the writing of men who paid lip service to women's enlightenment.

Articles about women filled the pages of these journals with many themes: health care, character, luxury and extravagance, and domestic problems. The nature of the material was instructive, rather than entertaining. Women, however, would have to be literate before they could be receptive to the ideas pronounced on their behalf. Therefore, the need for feminine education was a subject that recurred time and again.

In the lead article of the second volume of the *Semanario Económico* (Mexico) in January 1810, the reader was confronted with an important question being discussed in male circles: "Should women be enlightened? In what circumstances?" While the article states that women have the right to be educated, ironically it affirms that the enlightenment should be bestowed upon men, who by the magic of the new knowledge would better understand and interpret the role that women would play. Women would then be respected in the highest form as mothers and wives and "in all ways that they contribute to the happiness of the state," though this last role is never clearly defined. The article mentioned some of the contemporary arguments favoring the education of women, one of which was based on the ideas of an Englishman named Braceman. In a translation of his ideas, we are told that woman was not a slave to her husband's passions, but rather a companion to him. Her behavior was to be typified by a state of innocence when in her husband's company. Women were reproached for running out into the streets. They were warned to devote their attention to increasing the wisdom of their children and helping them to form good habits. This last statement on the mothers' influence in the education of their young was the primary concern in the articles written on the need for women's being educated: "Women have more right to be educated than men; women, not men, are the main influence on their young children." It was precisely this argument that was later used, after Rousseau, by antifeminists to justify the dictum that woman's place was at home, not in the classroom.[15]

Another article in dialogue form in this journal spoke of the future education of a daughter. A recalcitrant father argued that women were greatly drawn to lavish dresses and ornaments: "Those who try to overcome such passions should realize that they have lost before they start." Further, he felt that his daughter did not need a conventional school, as she could learn from her mother. Yet the mother had another view. She warned that results of such a process would only cause the child to grow up as "backward" and "ignorant" as she.[16]

Several years before (1805), the *Diario de Mexico* had offered an article that surely could have served as a defense of the wife's position. "Women are the most abandoned of creatures in the area of learning," said the editors. Their knowledge must be used for more than just household occupations, which keep their talents hidden. Since fathers generally did not watch over the domestic customs of their offspring, an intelligent wife was an asset; it was her example that her children followed. The fact that the *Diario* acknowledged the difficulty of women's civil state was an important step forward in understanding the problems that they faced.[17]

That the *Diario de Mexico*, an earlier publication, and the *Semanario Económico* expressed similar ideas about the education of women is understandable because of Juan Barquera's participation as an editor of both journals. It is important to point out that there was an evolution in Barquera's thinking on women. In the *Diario de Mexico* the neglect of women's enlightenment is evident, whereas the *Semanario Económico* actually brings up the issue of whether or not a woman should be entitled to an education.[18]

The concern about feminine education reflected in these articles reveals some of the changes that had taken place in New Spain during the eighteenth century. Nunneries had been in charge of a more traditional education for women throughout the seventeenth and eighteenth centuries, but owing to a drive for ecclesiastical reform, they had been ordered to stop admitting girls in 1774. The opening of the Colegio de San Ignacio de Loyola, popularly known as Las Vizcaínas, by the Basque brotherhood in 1767 and the establishment of the Convent of La Enseñanza in 1753 signaled the beginning of a period of great activity in school founding in New Spain. The opening of La Enseñanza was especially important, for it was the first religious order devoted exclusively to teaching. In spite of these improvements, the general state of feminine education in that viceroyalty did not improve in quality until well into the nineteenth century.[19]

The *Telégrafo Mercantil* of Buenos Aires contained articles that questioned why women were not educated if men were permitted this opportunity. In an

1802 article the ideas expressed are similar to those expounded before, in the *Semanario Económico,* about the education of women: they must be educated so that they can be useful marital partners. What is interesting about this article is that it was translated by a *porteña* from an original French source. The concept of domestic honor is discussed, since women in time of war serve as the guardians of a nation's heritage just as men serve to guard the security of the nation. Certain egalitarian doctrines are also enunciated: "No matter what the condition a woman comes from, she should be educated." Was this to say that education should have no class barriers? Since even a woman's meager education was determined by her social status and not by her inherent talent, such a statement was quite revolutionary. "Where women are left in ignorance there will be few enlightened and solid men." And we are informed that women do not hold public office not because they are incapable, but because they have so many domestic obligations.

Unlike the Mexican journals, education for women was not discussed in *The Telégrafo Mercantil* as a remedy for "erasing the superstitions that one's mother implanted on the child's mind." Rather, the editor of the *Telégrafo* felt that public education for the child would remedy the situation. No attempt was made to cure the disease at its source—the mothers. Contrary to the views expressed in the *Semanario Económico* and the *Diario de Mexico*, the *Telégrafo Mercantil* saw the father as the one responsible for the education of his family. This may have been true for financial reasons, but certainly Cabello y Mesa, the journal's editor, overlooked the role of a boy's mother in his development. One may understand why there existed the feeling that women could not be trusted to educate their young when the ignorance and superstition of women were issues of great concern. The idea was underscored when women in Buenos Aires refused to have their children inoculated against smallpox. Superstitious mothers were criticized for allowing their children to be exposed to such a dreadful illness. In a plea to these adamant women, the *Telégrafo Mercantil* appealed to their vanity, asking them if they would rather see their daughters pockmarked and crippled than submit them to vaccination.[20]

It is apparent that the *Diario de Mexico* and the *Telégrafo Mercantil* differed significantly in their view of whether the mother or the father had greater responsibility for the education of their children, though the latter journal is not really clear on the extent to which fathers should share in the teaching of their progeny. In this regard it is important to note that in another issue of the *Telégrafo Mercantil* there is information on the curriculum of a girl's school. Although limited to a privileged group, feminine education in Buenos Aires seemed to have become a dignified enterprise. The *colegio* established by Doña Josefa de Carballo for female "enlightenment" specialized in "decency." Doña Josefa's school for young girls planned to teach music, embroidery, and physical education. Literacy was required for entrance, and the starting age was eight years. This requirement would indicate that girls may have been taught to read at an earlier age and perhaps learned their first letters through a tutor or at home. 21

The small inroads made by the demand for feminine education marked the beginning of the battle. In spite of the importance of women, as indicated by the space devoted to this theme in the *Telégrafo Mercantil*, the quality of feminine education in Buenos Aires was deceptive. The notion that the women of that area were the most polished and refined of South America had been advanced at an earlier date in the well-known travelogue of Alonso Carrió (Concolocorvo), *El lazarillo de ciegos caminantes*. 22 Whether they were the most learned was another matter. Concern for the education of women was expressed by the Argentine patriot Manuel Belgrano in 1797. As a secretary of the *consulado* (merchant's association) of Buenos Aires, he spoke out for educating women in conventional subjects as well as in skills by which they could become economically useful members of society. Adversely impressed by the weak financial status of women, Belgrano voiced his opinion on the remedy for such a state by advocating schools for young women as well for young men. 23

Thus, the education of women, a task originally left to be carried out by the Church and convent, became an important subject of discussion in the enlightened journals, with the exception of the *Mercurio Peruano*. In none of the journals, however, is the tone of these articles strong enough to indicate a desire to effect the implementation of the ideas or to promote on other than intellectual grounds the cause of women's education. Rather, the remarks are generally of a laudatory nature, presenting women as sacred creatures about whom more must be learned before any action may be taken. 24

Another topic widely discussed in the journals was the role of women in colonial society. This subject was often discussed within the context of their need to be guided from the darkness of their ignorance. Nevertheless, in the journals in question, there are articles that can definitely be considered as being devoted purely to the role of woman, her rights and privileges in society, and the character traits that are recognized as "feminine." 25

The *Diario de Mexico* devoted substantial space to the plight of women and their role, past and present, in colonial society. One article launched an attack against people who looked at women "as creatures solely destined to be used for pleasure, servitude, and as incapable of contributing anything to the state." The only way for women to ascend in their role in society was through enlightenment. In applying reason to love, an article entitled "The Dangers of Love" stated that one could be elevated from the barbaric instincts that characterized the uneducated man or woman since "the corruption of customs, the lack of a good education, or too much liberty among both sexes are fatal." 26

One of the more significant articles on women that appeared in any of the journals was published in the *Telégrafo Mercantil* in 1805 and entitled "Portrait of a Respectable Lady." It was purportedly written by a woman in the form of a letter to the editor. It is doubtful, however, that such was the case. The letter was signed "La Amante del País," the subtitle used by the members of the economic societies in Spain and America. More likely it was the work of an irate male reader who saw a brighter future for the women of Buenos Aires. The ironic tone of this writing apparently came in response to an earlier article of Cabello y Mesa in praise of the women of Buenos Aires and in which sweetness, charm, happy disposition, and good looks were highlighted.[27] The writer inferred that his letter could serve to reveal the inequalities in the treatment of women in education, in public life, and in her role at home.[28]

The crux of this article hinged on the question of female happiness. Can women be happy solely at home as parasitic and pleasure-seeking individuals? Should they not seek a purpose in society beyond the gratification of their family? The author of this letter to the *Telégrafo Mercantil* suggested a new definition for women's happiness in contrast to the complacency and acceptance of her fate that Cabello y Mesa asserted to be a positive quality of the *porteña*. Challenging the traditional outlook that women were happiest in a subordinate position, the new definition encompassed the notion that only by serving a dual role could women truly achieve contentment. Being queen of her home would not suffice, unless women were allowed to partake in useful work. Social utility was not considered a source of feminine respect; it was also a doctrine that aroused fear in the male population. Taking a broader view of a women's role, the author placed women in competition with the *porteño* partriarchy.[29]

If woman were to achieve happiness in Buenos Aires, they would have to overcome such problems as susceptibility to disease, great sensitivity, and a lively passion. The *porteña*'s natural disposition for all kinds of knowledge needed guidance if she were to be a productive social participant: "The major problem women face is the ignorance of their own interests." Dilettantism could be directed toward specific goals. "Education of woman at an early age may prevent her from being overcome by the boredom of daily life . . . more dishonorable than passion itself. Woman does not have to choose men on the basis of her physical virtues if she is educated. . . . Woman, like all human beings, has the ability to learn." The article concludes: "Men will always be what women want them to be." Whether education was really a panacea for woman's inferior position is a question left for the reader to ponder. More likely, "for the clever and learned woman there was a place both intellectually and socially within narrowly circumscribed limits of feminine life."

Some sympathy for the position of woman may also be found in the *Diario de Mexico*, which expressed the opinion that it was almost barbaric to think that women must employ their talent in household chores. Yet the only compensation that the *Diario* could offer was to inform the husband of an intelligent wife that she was worth her weight in gold.[30]

While the *Telégrafo Mercantil* was willing to publish the letter of an angry *porteña* trying to asset her rights, it reprinted at the same time a section on feminine education in pre-Columbian times that was excerpted from the exiled Jesuit Francisco Clavigero's *Historia antigua de Mexico*.[31] The contradiction lies in Clavigero's remark that the Aztec women had similar roles to the women of the eighteenth century. Asserting that woman's place was in the home, he reminded the readers that she was also subject to her husband's dominance after marriage. There is a patent ambivalence in the printing of such contrary points of view in the *Telégrafo Mercantil*, suggesting that the ascription to women of a traditional role in society had not been obliterated in late eighteenth-century Spanish America.[32]

On the subject of selecting marriage partners several considerations came under scrutiny in the journals. In New Spain, the *Diario de Mexico* featured a series of articles on those factors that made for a good union. No longer could a happy marriage between social equals be firmly rooted on title alone. Financial equality now ranked high as a source of marital bliss. This paper suggested that to be equal unions would have to be both socially and financially secure. Cross-class marriage between the bourgeoisie and the aristocracy was being justified in the *Diario de Mexico*. The editors felt that only marriages between the upper and middle classes could achieve permanence since other groups lacked sufficient means for proper subsistence.[33]

Of interest to the student of social history is the *Diario*'s mention of the existence of a middle class (*estado medio*), which it considered to be of poor, but honorable, origins. This is important, since it serves as background to an article that appeared four years later in the *Semanario Económico* on the pitfalls of marriage. The discourse placed the blame for many a broken marriage on the woman who causes her husband to fear financial ruin. "Women indulge in so many luxuries that young men cannot possibly afford to maintain a household with all the expenses involved in its management. The squandering of money on pleasures is the first seed of corruption, especially among women in the middle and lower classes, which together form the majority of the population." The article implied that the reader knew who constituted the middle class: the wives and daughters of retail merchants, shopkeepers, more substantial artisans, and professionals, to mention a few. Those in the lower class probably included the wives of less affluent "shopkeepers, peddlers, artisans operating outside the guilds, servants and laborers."[34]

A young man who was considering marriage, advised the *Semanario*, should seek a woman whose fortune could provide for the future. The extravagant woman without a full purse was not a good prospect. It is obvious from this discussion that a woman who had some inheritance had greater social leverage. Her financial state was a decisive factor in her ability to seek and to make a good marriage of her own choice. James Lockhart believes that women could not independently enhance their position without great difficulty; even in the late eighteenth century "women took their original status from their families and it could be altered only through marriage." [35] The Cinderella story was the exception in colonial times. Thus, it well may be that the printed warnings against unequal marriages reinforced the already well-established class lines for matrimony.

In his *Historia de Mexico* Lucas Alamán refers to the alleged defect of *criolla* women that both the *Diario* and *Semanario* lamented. He praised the respectability of middle-class families just as the journals had done, but he, too, suggested a flaw inherent in the women—their weakness of character that led to the ill behavior of their children. Thus, another shortcoming was added to the list of imperfections already enumerated in the journals. Alamán, however, expressed such misgivings about the flabby character among *criolla* women that added to their penchant for the exotic. This leads one to conclude that some truth must be attributed to such observations. The Viceroyalty of Peru must have had spendthrifts among the upper classes, since the *Mercurio Peruano* printed a letter from a husband whose wife was ruining him with her extravagance. [36]

José María Ots Capdequí has also observed that American society in the colonies was distinguished by its proclivity toward extravagance and ostentation, in which women contributed no small role. However, could the problem of lavishness and luxury be solely attributable to the weakness of women's character? The issue had been frequently discussed by the *philosophes*, who were divided on the matter. One view of luxury decried its wastefulness. Those who took this position believed that the reason of the upper classes had been stunted by their wealth and irresponsibility. Another group believed that luxury could be productive if properly channeled, for it could stimulate the growth of native industry. This outlook was representative of the economic societies, which advocated the promotion of industry for the benefit of the country. It is therefore understandable that in Buenos Aires, the *Telégrafo*'s editor, Cabello y Mesa, did not consider spending to be wasteful. As a founder of the economic society in Buenos Aires, he could see no wrong in the maintenance of splendor and magnificence by the viceroy, bishop, or magistrate as long as they provided employment and economic gain for those of the viceroyalty. From his point of view, the financial benefits fostered by luxury industries outweighed the criticism displayed for the sin of prodigality of the middle class and its women. [37]

How women occupied their leisure is discussed in the *Mercurio*. These articles were geared less to the defense of their social status than to their interests and talents. The *Mercurio* noted that many establishments of *"buen gusto"* (good taste) had been organized in the last decade of the eighteenth century, especially for ladies "who were always looking for amusement." The list of establishments included an Italian school of dancing, in which classes were open to men and women, and a school of design for those ladies of superior taste. These schools were a source of pride to the editors since they were representative of the state of culture and comfort in the Peruvian capital. They encouraged women to cultivate these establishments because they lacked things to do. Other diversions for Lima's leisure class included café society and the theater. The theater, however, was frowned upon for women, since the *Mercurio* criticized their dress, their behavior, and their concern with securing good seats. In France, the *philosophes* also condemned the theater, but for altogether different reasons. They believed that plays too often depicted women in unflattering roles, thus reinforcing the negative image of the fairer sex to all those who attended such events. In Lima, unfortunately, the play was not the thing.[38]

It is significant that the *Mercurio* printed an article on "*maricones*" (homosexuals). Included in the article is a discussion of women, since the description of those "*raros fenómenos*" may be an accurate picture of feminine mannerisms. Although the review speaks of the way such men dressed, talked, and walked, one feels that it is women who are actually being satirized.

They appear in the streets dressed in extravagant outfits. Their hands on their hips, they disguise themselves in a cape. With a definite feminine air they proceed with their head erect and their shoulders swaying from side to side like windmills as they, in time to this movement, make a thousand ridiculous swaggers with their bodies, directing their stares in all directions.[39]

While homosexuality was not given a medical interpretation, there were numerous articles in the *Mercurio Peruano* that dealt specifically with feminine health and medicine. Emphasis on these subjects was due to the editor, Hipólito Unánue, who was one of the colony's finest physicians. His intense scientific curiosity undoubtedly led him to examine all aspects of human behavior and well-being. There are long discussions on the protection of pregnant women and on prenatal care. The paper felt that it was the duty of society to protect future mothers from harm. Barquera, in the *Diario de Mexico*, also devoted many articles to the discussion of pregnancy and childbirth, stating that women had the most serious task in our existence—the preservation of the species. Both the *Diario de Mexico* and the *Mercurio Peruano* warned against soliciting help or advice from *curanderas*, those witch-like, folk medicine ladies who were considered superstitious, barbarous, and dangerous to pregnant women. The tone and treatment of this delicate matter of pregnancy differ greatly in two journals. While the *Mercurio Peruano* strove for scientific accuracy in its descriptions and remedies, the *Diario de Mexico* used the topic in a more social vein to advocate general education for all women so that infant mortality would be reduced. In seeking to prevent infant deaths, the *Diario de Mexico* expressed the opinion that the main cause of death in the newborn was a sick mother or father. The adjective *sick* was used euphemistically to describe veneral disease, an illness that men "contracted through intemperance and [that] eventually could cause the birth of sick children."[40]

The *Diario de Mexico* inveighed against women who abandoned their children after birth; by abandonment the editors referred to entrusting the care of the young to wet nurses (*nodrizas*). The wet nurse was equated with the *curandera* in her ignorance. The discussion of wet nurses and the evils that they committed was not a new one. Rousseau had mentioned the subject in *Emile*, and the editors of the *Diario de Mexico* seemed to be fully cognizant of Rousseau's arguments in favor of mothers' breast-feeding their own progeny. Doña Josefa Amar y Borbón, a Spanish advocate of women's equality, had also criticized the use of wet nurses in a treatise on women's education. [41] Likewise, a treatise on the consequences of a mother's refusal to suckle her child appeared in Madrid in 1786. [42] The *Encyclopedia*, too, contained a long article on the pros and cons of the wet nurses that may have been the source for an article that appeared in the *Mercurio* and raised the question of whether children were harmed by being put in the charge of wet nurses. José J. Fernández de Lizardi, in his novel *La Quijotita y su prima*, spoke of the injurious effects of wet nurses on the young. [43] Whether the material in these journals pay tribute to colonial feminine culture may be debatable, but the discussions do emphasize concern for women's well-being and their role as mothers.

From the "new knowledge" these journals advanced, we may venture to speculate what it was like to be white and female in the Spanish Indies. First, let us examine how much attention each journal devoted to the subject of women. A purely quantitative breakdown is illustrated in Table 7.1. Included are essays that deal specifically with the theme of women as well as articles on related subjects. The latter encompass such topics as child rearing, fashion, cooking, beauty, and health care. From the percentages listed, the *Diario de Mexico* published the greatest number of articles on women and related themes. The *Telégrafo Mercantil* ran a close second in essays on women, with the *Mercurio* and *Semanario Económico* taking third and fourth place, respectively.

It is also significant that those journals which were published over a shorter time span—that is, the *Mercurio Peruano* of Lima, the *Telégrafo Mercantil* of

Table 7.1
Number and Percentage of Articles About or Related to Women Appearing in Four Journals

Journal	Number of Articles About Women	% of Total Articles	Number of Articles Related to Feminine Culture or About Women	% of Total Articles	Total Number of Articles in the Journal
Mercurio Peruano 1790–92	8	2.4	6	4.2	334
Telégrafo Mercantil 1801–2	8	3.6	3	4.9	224
Diario de Mexico 1806–12	64	3.4	30	5.0	1,875
Semanario Económico 1810–11	5	1.6	7	2.3	305

Buenos Aires, both biweeklies, and the *Semanario Económico* of Mexico City, a weekly—contain almost the same percentage of space devoted to the role of women as did the *Diario de Mexico*, a journal that appeared daily and ran a longer time. The *Diario*, which ran for six years, published approximately fifteen articles a year on or about women during its existence. The average does not really reflect the true focus of the journal. After 1810, political themes took precedence over the more popular topics such as education, health, women, and agriculture. In fact, a year-by-year breakdown of articles revealed that most essays about women appeared between 1806 and 1808. The switch is understandable in view of the growing revolutionary climate in New Spain after 1808.

What was the stated view of women that each paper adopted? Judging from the contents of the four journals, we find a marked similarity in the ideas concerning the role that women should play and the qualities that are associated with the feminine sex. The essays in the *Diario de Mexico* and the *Semanario* were far more sensitive to the condition of women. Both journals acknowledged the inferior status of women, and they advocated education as a way to improve their position in society. The *Telégrafo Mercantil*, though using extensive material about women, derived much of its matter from foreign sources that appeared in translation.

Articles published in the *Mercurio Peruano* were more critical of womanhood in their approach. They concerned themselves with the role that women played within their immediate family situation. The *Mercurio Peruano* demonstrated the least interest in any discussion of improving woman's downgraded position. Its concern for perpetuating the status quo is exemplified by the many articles discussing where the ladies of Lima society could while away the hours of ennui that overtook them. It should be noted that in the *Telégrafo Mercantil* as well as in the *Diario de Mexico* reference is made to the lethargy victimizing women. The former spoke of boredom as a fate more dishonorable than passion, and the latter bemoaned the fate of housewives trapped in their homes. It is probable that the attention devoted to amusements in the *Mercurio* was evidence of the awareness by these journalists of the quality of life that most women of society confronted. Boredom, as a complaint, also indicates that although women were destined to be housewives, their chores were not as arduous or time consuming as imagined. Ample opportunities for keeping servants existed, thereby lightening the household duties of the upper-class female. Acknowledging the existence of much leisure time may also have given the impetus to discussing alternatives for using these hours constructively. The *Diario de Mexico*, *Semanario Económico*, and *Telégrafo Mercantil* were more interested in devoting this time to women's enlightenment through conventional education; the *Mercurio Peruano* chose to relieve feminine inactivity by having women turn to an interest in the arts, a field that Feijóo had advocated as a possibility for women's self-expression.

While these journals represent a stated view of women as opposed to their real life situation, the value of these articles in establishing certain conclusions about the various aspects of feminine life is not nullified. Certainly, we may rightly assume that men who wrote about women borrowed as heavily from daily experience as from foreign ideas in setting down their opinions. It has been suggested that contemporary values toward women might represent male reactions to such an outstanding feminine colonial figure as Sor Juana Inés de la Cruz, the poetess-nun of Mexico. Scholars have expressed their doubts about this type of analysis. Guillermo Fúrlong has said that educated ladies of the colonies must be treated as anomalies, and historian Charles Gibson felt that extraordinary women, like most great figures in the colony, "were exceptional minds responding in unusual ways to an environment in which all of them felt ill at ease."44

The view of women expressed in these periodical essays may serve as a better source in attempting to establish a value system toward females. Given the limits of a stratified society that characterized the colonial situation, the articles demonstrate that the certain roles that women play are undoubtedly defined by class. Therefore, to be a woman not only implied a sexual designation, but carried with it a certain social rank as well. A female servant was considered not worthy of attention, and society rarely bothered itself with the task of improving the situation of these women. Not only were articles about women of lesser means infrequent in the journals examined, but also what was left unsaid was very revealing about colonial social attitudes.

What is apparent in these journals is that a role always existed for the aristocratic lady, sharply distinguished from that of the women of lesser station. Poor women had to accept whatever jobs they could find in order to subsist. In the essays discussed, mention of employment that carried a lower-class connotation included such occupations as *curanderas*, seamstresses, cooks, and wet nurses. These positions are contrasted with roles that demanded respect: motherhood, child rearing, and membership in a religious order. It becomes evident that women of rank had limited opportunities to display their creative talents since so many occupations were considered below their station.

One of the more important aspects of the essays is that in realizing the limited numbers of respectable roles that a lady could maintain, they envisioned expanded activities for women in elevated positions if they were to have the opportunity of being enlightened. The *Diario de Mexico* expressed the view that a woman could be more than housewife; if she were educated, she could be an assistant to her husband. José J. Fernández de Lizardi saw the need for women to participate in affairs outside the home, but he was against educating women of the lower classes, as he felt that vocational skills were more important to them than the cultivation of the mind. Neither Lizardi nor the *Diario de Mexico* suggested alternatives to the position of housewife, despite their hope that other roles would somehow develop. They acknowledged only that with an opportunity to be better informed, women could exert a more important force in the development of the nation. *The Telégrafo Mercantil* of Buenos Aires and the Mexican *Semanario* and *Diario* mentioned the role of women during wartime. All spoke of women as protectors and guardians of the cultural heritage of the land. More important, as the Wars of Independence were to prove, women—while tending to the home front—were to become a powerful economic force since they would be responsible for continuing the businesses that men had maintained, thus participating in activities vital to the life of the nation. [45]

We find evidence that women had assumed a ruling position as mistresses of their household not only during wartime, but also in daily life. Articles in the *Mercurio Peruano* about the plight of the father who had lost his leadership in family affairs are testimony to woman's strength, both economic and social. [46] Nevertheless, we must also be wary of social realities. The frequent absence of men from the household created opportunities for feminine domination on the home front.

All the journals, in one way or another, understood the pervasive influence that women had in the formation of ideas during the intellectual development of their children. This must certainly have served as a good reason for the journalists to advocate their education. It was agreed that only through education could the superstitions and ignorance with which mothers imbued their young be eliminated. It was not so much the education of women for their own self-improvement that captured the minds of the writers, but rather the education for the elimination of half-learning and for the sake of the children. With all the discussion on the need to educate women, the idea of public education was never broached. Ironically, after the Wars of Independence, the first public school for women was created in New Granada by the daughter of Antonio Nariño, intellectual leader of the independence. [47] Nonetheless, only in reference to men did public education become an issue. Furthermore, one of the institutions that had been responsible for what little learning enlightened women had received—namely, the convent school—never received any attention or any criticism in the essays devoted to the state of educational opportunities for women.

Of interest is the fact that the education of women was not totally equated with their ability to read or write. At least, literacy was not the goal of feminine education as much as concern for manners and standards of "decent" or "virtuous" behavior. Literacy was one barrier that they did not have to overcome in their quest for acceptance into society, whereas men who were illiterate were immediately lowered in status. As James Lockhart has pointed out, by proper manner and dress "she could make herself more nearly the equal of high society than could a man." [48]

One feature that is evident in all the journal articles is that race and class defined woman's role in colonial Spanish America. For example, articles that spoke about the attributes of women, referring to *criolla* and *peninsular*, used words to characterize ladies of colonial society such as *sophistication, decency, purity, virtue, sensitive,* and *goodhearted. Wisdom* was a term rarely ascribed to women. Words used to connote value in women of the lower classes were the antithesis of the qualities ascribed to highborn ladies. Words like *indecency* and *immorality* were frequently mentioned in describing their socially inferior employment. [49]

By making comparisons between women of different classes, these journalists honestly reflected an awareness of the social reality of their age—a society of exploiters and exploited—by which women's place was dependent on the economic conditions that modified the position they held and ultimately determined the role they could play. [50] That men were unwilling to put women on the same plane in their discussion of the feminine sex is also quite indicative of the fact that for many colonial gentlemen the concern for women was a scholarly and philosophical one. By paying lip service to what their role in society ought to be, men felt that they had contributed to their enlightenment. This is not to say that all men who wrote about women were not hoping to ameliorate their inferior status, but it would be naive to expect outright change in her status as a result of the greater amount of attention paid to her place in colonial society. Too many forces existed within Spanish America to prevent greater emancipation of women. Where the majority of women spent a significant part of their lives in church in prolonged prayers, the indoctrination of religious views that stressed the virtue of meekness and self-denial left women subject to even greater discrimination.

The use of these journals to express concern about the position of women was not a new phenomenon. An analogous situation existed in Great Britain and France, where, during the first half of the eighteenth century, the periodical essay played an important part in defining women's intellectual and social needs. [51] It is especially important to note, however, that in Spanish America, though essays on women appeared regularly in print, there was no real movement for women's rights. That these journals were sensitive to the role of woman is not purely the reiteration of foreign ideas on the subject. Rather, they represent a particularly Latin American view since they reflect Latin American situations. The themes touched upon in the essays were areas in which the journals believed that women's position could be improved. Improvement was not considered in terms of self, however. Editors looked to the advancement of women in ways that would benefit the colony.

At the time of the publication of these journals only a little more than a century had passed since the writings of Sor Juana Inés de la Cruz. However, a significant change in attitude toward women can be perceived. Even if the writing about women was done by the opposite sex, intellectual curiosity about women was undeniable. While restrictions on women's role in society were still maintained, the fact that women provided subject material for the leading journals was most revealing. It should not, however, be until women themselves demanded the right to be "liberated"—in the face of society's opposition and despite it—that any real change in their condition would ensue.

Notes

1. José Francos Rodríguez, *La mujer y la política española* (Madrid: Editorial Pueyo, 1920), p. 179.

2. Irving Leonard, *Baroque Times in Old Mexico* (Ann Arbor: University of Michigan Press, 1966), p. 179; Gustavo Otero Muñoz, "Figuras femeninas de la colonia," in *Academia colombiana de historia: Conferencias* (Bogotá: Editorial Selecta, 1936), p. 87.

3. An example of this comes from an official petition made by Doña María Menéndez Márquez, widow of the governor of Florida, to the Crown in September of 1631. Unable to support herself and her six children on her husband's pension, she requested that the surplus of the *situado* of the Florida garrison, which once was given to her mother, now deceased, be allocated to her five daughters and one son. Petitions such as this one are frequent in the Florida literature. Archivo General de Indias, Audiencia of Santo Domingo, 53-1-6, doc. 44, in the Mary L. Ross Collection, Georgia Department of Archives and History, Atlanta.

4. The transfer of *encomiendas* in the Sabana region around Bogotá serves as another example of the frequency with which women inherited this institution. Anthropologist Juan Villamarín demonstrated that between 1539 and 1599, 48.6 percent of all *encomiendas* in that region were transferred to women: 27.0 percent from father to daughter, and 21.6 percent from husband to wife; "Encomenderos and Indians in the Formation of Colonial Society in the Sabana of Bogotá, Colombia, 1537-1740" (Ph.D. diss., Brandeis University, 1972).

5. David Williams, "The Politics of Feminism in the French Enlightenment," in *The Varied Pattern: Studies in the 18th Century* (Toronto: A. M. Hakkerts, 1971), pp. 334, 337; and Jacob Bouten, *Mary Wollstonecraft and the Beginnings of Female Emancipation in France and England* (Amsterdam: H. J. Paris, 1922), p. 55. Williams states that it was the "scale and momentum" that gave to eighteenth-century feminism "and indeed to the whole superstructure of the Enlightenment much of its characteristic flavor. By the 1780's feminism had become well integrated into the broader movements of social change." Most ideas for this section have been based on the writings of Williams and of Leon Abensour, *La Femme et le feminisme avant la Revolution* (Paris: E. Leroux, 1923), chap. 1. See also Peter Gray, *The Enlightenment: An Interpretation*, 2 vols. (New York: A. A. Knopf, 1966).

6. Richard Herr, *The Eighteenth-Century Revolution in Spain* (Princeton: Princeton University Press, 1969), pp. 37-39.

7. Robert Shafer, *The Economic Societies in the Spanish World* (Syracuse, N.Y.: Syracuse University Press, 1958), p. 70. Shafer discusses the importance of Feijóo's ideas of Spanish America. The economic societies in Spain and the Indies were well acquainted with Feijóo's treatise, which fact may account for the great interest about women in the journals sponsored by these societies. Although Feijóo's work on women was translated into English in 1778, it is curious that it is not mentioned in recent

studies about the literature of feminism (e.g., Mary Benson). Regarding this ignorance of Feijóo's work, Mary Beard made the same point about Queen Isabella over 160 years later.

8. Benito Gerónimo Feijóo y Montenegro, *Three Essays or Discourses on the Following Subjects: A Defense or Vindication of Women* (London: T. Becket, 1778), p. 118.

9. R. A. Humphreys and John Lynch, eds., *The Origins of the Latin American Revolutions, 1808-1826* (New York: A. A. Knopf, 1965), p. 11. Shafer, *Economic Societies*, p. 304.

10. Arthur P. Whitaker, "Changing Interpretations of the Enlightenment in Spanish America," in A. Owen Aldridge, ed., *The Ibero-American Enlightenment* (Urbana: University of Illinois Press, 1971), p. 26; John Tate Lanning, "The Reception of the Enlightenment in Latin America" in Arthur P. Whitaker, ed., *Latin America and the Enlightenment* (Ithaca, N.Y.: Cornell University Press, 1965), p. 89.

11. Shafer, *Economic Societies*, pp. 345, 352.

12. Mary Beard has asserted that "the problem of woman who is known only through man is known wrong." *Women As a Force in History: A Study in Traditions and Realities* (New York: Collier, 1962), p. 213. Henry Adams, in his autobiography, *The Education of Henry Adams*, lamented woman's role in American history: "The American woman of the nineteenth century will live only as man saw her; probably, she will be less known than the woman of the eighteenth century . . . and all this pure loss to history"; as quoted in Beard, *Women in History*, p. 219. The same could have been said for the republics south of the Rio Grande.

13. Humphreys and Lynch, *Origins* p. 11.

14. The terms *journal* and *periodical essay* will be used interchangeably throughout this paper. I understand the prodigious task that an examination of the role of women in the colonies entails. Therefore, this paper is limited to a discussion of Spanish and *criolla* women since it is my opinion that Indian women deserve separate treatment. Their situation is far too complex to be cast aside in generalities. For a study of the contents of *Diario de Mexico*, see Ruth Wold, *El Diario de Mexico: Primer cotidiano de Nueva España* (Madrid: Editorial Gredos, 1970). The author emphasizes the literary contents of the newspaper, but there are chapters on the political writings of the *Diario* and on "popular types" of the city, as seen in its pages. There is some information on fashions and coquettish women.

15. *Semanario Económico*, vol. 2, no. 1 (4 January 1810): 4; vol. 1, no. 30 (22 June 1809): 230. See Victor G. Wexler, "Made for Man's Delight: Rousseau as Antifeminist," *American Historical Review* 81 (April 1976): 266-91.

16. *Semanario Económico*, vol. 2, no. 48 (29 November 1810): 391-93.

17. *Diario de Mexico*, vol. 1, no. 74 (13 December 1805): 325; vol. 5, no. 24 (1 January 1807): 2-3.

18. It is among the writings of Juan Barquera in the *Diario* that we find the first theories of education in Mexico and certainly the first systematic interest in the education of women. The influence of the *Semanario Económico* on the early nineteenth-century journalist José Joaquín Fernández de Lizardi is overwhelming. Literary critics believe that the article on the enlightenment of women cited in note 15 contains many parallels between the ideas of Lizardi and Barquera. See José Joaquín Fernández de

Lizardi, *La Quijotita y su prima* (Mexico: Editorial Porrúa, 1967), and *Diario de Mexico*, vol. 1, no. 50 (10 November 1805). In her introduction to Lizardi's *La Quijotita*, María del Carmen Ruiz states: "Many of the ideas of Lizardi on raising children, the role of superstition in primary election . . . are expressed extensively in the lectures of Barquera." Lizardi often quoted among his authoritative sources on women "*un sabio escritor de nuestro Mexico*," whom Dr. Ruiz claims to be Barquera.

19. Asunción Lavrin, "Religious Life of Mexican Women in XVIII Century Mexico" (Ph.D. diss., Harvard University, 1963). Regarding Las Vizcaínas, Lavrin states: "The school sustained the principle that women should be educated for family life; consequently, girls were taught those arts which would be useful for them in the management of their own home." The curriculum for the private school pupils included "elementary arithmetic, elements of natural sciences and some European history. . . . It is evident that one of the main gains of women in the eighteenth century was in the field of education." See also her "Women in Convents: Their Economic and Social Role in Colonial Mexico," in Berenice Carroll, ed., *Liberating Women's History: Theoretical and Critical Essays* (Urbana: University of Illinois Press, 1976), pp. 250-77.

20. *Telégrafo Mercantil*, vol. 3, no. 13 (28 March 1802): 189; vol. 1, no. 17 (27 May 1801): 159; vol. 1, no. 16 (23 May 1801): 121; vol. 1, no. 11 (16 May 1801): 83-88.

21. Ibid., vol. 5, no. 12 (10 September 1802): 19.

22. Alonso Carrió (a) Concolocorvo, *El lazarillo de ciegos caminantes*, Biblioteca de Autores Españoles, vol. 122 (Madrid: Ediciones Atlas, 1959), p. 292; Guillermo Fúrlong, *La cultura femenina en la época colonial* (Buenos Aires: Editorial Kapeluz, 1951), pp. 2, 242. Fúrlong devotes a section of this study to the significance of the *Telégrafo Mercantil*'s articles of women.

23. Juan Carlos Rébora, *La familia chilena y la familia argentina* (La Plata: Tomás Palumbo, 1938), p. 42.

24. Many arguments cited the works of Feijóo. Also influential to the journalists was Pedro Rodríguez, Conde de Campomanes, *Discurso sobre la educación popular de los artesanos y su fomento* (Madrid: Imprenta de B. Antonio de Sancha, 1775). Fénelon was frequently discussed, as was Jean Batiste Blanchard, *L'Ecoles de Moeurs*, which had a Spanish translation in 1786. Madame de Maintenon's *Letters on the Education of Girls* and *La Eufemia o la mujer instruída* were also quoted. For further details, see Dr. Ruiz's introduction to Lizardi, *La Quijotita*, cited in note 18, above.

25. See Louisa Hoberman, "Hispanic American Women as portrayed in the Historical Literature: Types and Archetypes," *Revista/Review Interamericana* 4 (Summer 1974): 136-47.

26. *Diario de Mexico*, vol. 5, no. 459 (2 January 1807): 5-7; no. 466 (9 January 1807): 34-35; no. 467 (10 January 1807): 37-39; no. 469 (12 January 1807): 41-42.

27. *Telégrafo Mercantil*, vol. 1, no. 20 (18 July 1801): 254-56; vol. 2, no. 37 (27 December 1805): 323.

28. Ibid., vol. 4, no. 7 (13 June 1802): 103; Mary Sumner Benson, *Women in Eighteenth-Century America* (New York: Columbia University Press, 1935), p. 99.

29. Jean Sarrailh, *La España ilustrada de la segunda mitad del siglo XVIII* (Mexico: Fondo de Cultura Económica, 1957), p. 515. Sarrailh states that the eighteenth century is "feminist" in the protests against the subjugation of women that appeard at that time.

30. *Didario de Mexico*, vol. 50, no. 74 (13 December 1805): 324.

31. This work was printed in Italian in 1781, but it did not appear in a Spanish edition until 1826. An English version was printed in 1787.

32. *Telégrafo Mercantil*, vol. 1, no. 32 (18 July 1801): 254-56.

33. *Diario de Mexico*, vol. 2, no. 149 (28 February 1806): 150; vol. 2, nos. 135-36 (12-13 February 1806): 171-71, 173.

34. Lyle McAlister, "Social Structure and Social Change in New Spain," *Hispanic American Historical Review* 43 (August 1963): 164.

35. *Semanario Económico*, vol. 3, no. 16 (19 April 1810): 123; James Lockhart, *Spanish Peru* (Madison: University of Wisconsin Press, 1968), p. 156.

36. Lucas Alamán, *Historia de Mexico*, 5 vols. (Mexico: Editorial Porrúa, 1968), 1: 10; *Mercurio Peruano*, vol. 3, no. 12 (10 February 1791): 119-22; vol. 4, no. 132 (8 April 1792): 231-38; Herr, *Eighteenth Century Revolution*, p. 52; Shafer, *Economic Societies*, p. 70. Although luxury and extravagance were characteristic of the elite in the colonies, conspicuous consumption had been condemned in the eighteenth century in Spain by economist Juan Sempere y Guarinos in his *Discourse on Luxury*. He spoke against any society that encouraged inequality "by permitting inheritance, and that admired a man more for his ostentation of wealth than for his virtue and moderation." The Spanish school of economists believed that if consumption was to continue at such a noticeably high level, at least the products consumed should be domestically manufactured. See Sempere y Guarinos, *Historia del lujo y de las leyes suntuarias de España*, 2 vols. (Madrid: Ediciones Atlas, 1973).

37. José María Ots Capdequí, "Bosquejo histórico de los derechos de la mujer en la legislación de Indias," *Revista general de legislación y jurisprudencia* 132 (March-April 1918): 161-82; *Telégrafo Mercantil*, vol. 3, no. 14 (4 March 1802): 204.

38. *Mercurio Peruano*, vol. 3, no. 42 (26 May 1791), p. 64; vol. 3, no. 3 (13 January 1791), p. 29.

39. *Mercurio Peruano*, vol. 3, no. 94 (27 November 1791), p. 230. The description of homosexuals appears to be derived from the *Encyclopedia*'s article on hermaphrodites. While no credit is given to sources, such deviances from normal behavior aroused "scientific" interest.

40. *Mercurio Peruano*, vol. 3, no. 45 (5 June 1791), pp. 81-94; *Diario de Mexico*, vol. 3, nos. 264-65 (21, 22 June 1806): 213-15; nos. 276, 278 (3, 5 July 1806): 257-59, 269-71; vol. 2, nos. 125, 126 (2, 3 February 1806): 130-31, 133-34.

41. Josefa Amar y Borbón, *Discurso sobre la educación física y moral de las mujeres* (Madrid: Imprenta de D. Benito Cano, 1790): 23.

42. *Diario de Mexico*, vol. 2, no. 173 (22 March 1806): 323; no. 120 (28 January 1806): 110-12; Jefferson R. Spell, *The Life and Works of José Joaquín Fernández de Lizardi* (Philadelphia: University of Pennsylvania Press, 1931), is a useful source for the entire period with regard to the development of the periodical press in Mexico; Anastasio Chinchilla, *Anales históricos de la medicina*, 4 vols. (New York and London: Johnson Reprint, 1967), 4: 143-49.

43. Fernández de Lizardi, *La Quijotita*, pp. 5-6.

44. Fúrlong, *La cultura femenina*, p. 8; Gibson, *Spain in America* (New York: Harper & Row, 1966), p. 133.

45. One of the most striking testimonies to the role of women played during the Wars of Independence appeared in a journal entitled *Las ilustres americanas; de las influencias de las mujeres en la sociedad; y acciones ilustres de varias americanas*

(Caracas, 1826). See also Evelyn Cherpak's article (chap. 8) in this volume. Tulio Halperin-Donghi also speaks of the role of women as entrepreneurs in regions of the Viceroyalty of Rio de la Plata: "Perhaps because of the Indian heritage, perpetuated owing to the participation of women in economically important activities, in agriculture and above all in domestic crafts, the life of the Interior had a more marked feminine character"; *Politics, Economics and Society in Argentina in the Revolutionary Period* (Cambridge: Cambridge University Press, 1975), p. 57.

46. *Mercurio Peruano*, no. 5 (16 January 1791), p. 59; no. 8 (27 January 1791), p. 59.

47. Guillermo Hernández de Alba, *Aspectos de la cultura en Colombia* (Bogotá: Biblioteca Popular de la Cultura Colombiana, 1974), p. 245.

48. Lockhart, *Spanish Peru*, p. 153.

49. Vicente Gregorio Quesada, *Escenas de la vida colonial en el siglo XVIII: Crónica de la Villa Imperial de Potosí* (Buenos Aires: Editorial Huarpes, 1945), p. 202. Quesada narrates the tale of a noble lady of Potosí who was considered to be "of perfect virtue," of wealth, discretion, and beauty. She is contrasted with a lady of lesser station, whose description is the antithesis of those qualities of the noble woman. Such contrasts frequently appeared in the journals' discussion of women.

50. Lucila Rodas de Villagrán, *Desarrollo histórico de la educación de la mujer y su situación actual* (Guatemala: Universidad de San Carlos de Guatemala, 1965), pp. 5, 17.

51. Bouten, *Mary Wollstonecraft*, p. 54. For the English journals, see Peter J. Miller, "Eighteenth-Century Periodicals for Women," *History of Education Quarterly* 9 (Fall 1971): 279-85. Two other examples of feminist journals were Madame Le Prince Beaumont's *Noveau Magasin Français* and the *Bibliothèque des Femmes*. See Evelin Sullerot, *Histoire de la presse feminine des origines à 1848* (Paris: A. Colin, 1966); Jane Herrick, "Perodicals for Women in Mexico During the Nineteenth Century," *The Americas* 14 (October 1957): 135-44. June Hahner's essay, chap. 10 in this volume, deals with the Brazilian feminist press of the nineteenth century. In Spanish America no feminist periodicals emerged until after the Wars of Independence. In Mexico there was the *Semanario de las Señoritas Mexicanas* (Mexico City, 1836), and in Bogotá there was *El Rocío* (1872).

8

The participation of women in the independence movement in Gran Colombia, 1780–1830

The struggle for independence in the area known as Gran Colombia during the years 1780 to 1822 has long received the attention of scholars.[1] Historians have studied the origins, the leaders, and the aftermath of the Wars for Independence. Yet, little notice has been paid to the women who participated in them. This neglect of half of the population is no longer acceptable. Women were not passive bystanders in this conflict. They participated in it and were affected by it, as individuals, as mothers, and as wives. Therefore, it is necessary to reassess the nature of their contribution and the effects of the wars on their role and status in society. This approach will lead to a fuller understanding of the revolutionary era.

The proper role for the Ibero-American woman of the colonial era was that of wife and mother. Girls were directed toward marriage from childhood for a variety of reasons. The Catholic Church, a traditional and conservative institution of great influence, encouraged matrimony and the continuance of family life. There were few other acceptable economic opportunities by which women could sustain and support themselves independently. Although the upper-class widows often carried on their husbands' businesses and had more legal freedom than single or married women, the incidence of remarriage among them was high, for many still felt in need of a male protector. Men themselves recognized the importance of a legal wife in Latin America, so they, too, responded to social pressure to marry. Although women married early and were encouraged to produce large families, they did make contributions to certain areas of life both in and outside the home. Women engaged in trade and commerce; held large amounts of money and property; collected debts; controlled the female religious orders; sponsored, organized, and financed *colegios* for girls; sustained charitable activities; contributed to the religious literature of the day; managed and organized their homes; supervised the servants; gave the rudiments of education to their progeny; and moved to exert control over their husbands.[2] The Latin American woman, although homebound much of the time, was not a docile, passive type invested with little responsibility, for she took on much and exerted herself on behalf of her family and society in general.

Given the participation of women in various spheres of life, it is not altogether surprising to find them active in and supportive of the struggle for independence in Gran Colombia. Women contributed to the independence movement in numerous ways. First, and perhaps most dramatic, was their personal participation in combat, accessory actions, and espionage. Second, women lent their support in their traditional helping roles as hostesses of political *tertulias* and as nurses. Third, they made significant economic contribution by donating moneys and supplies to the insurgents. Finally, personal sacrifices— such as loss of loved ones, confiscation of properties and personal wealth, and poverty and exile—were endured by many.

In the decades before 1810 various socially prominent women throughout the Viceroyalty of New Granada held and attended *tertulias* where ideas of independence and revolution were discussed. Manuela Sanz de Santamaría de González Manrique of Bogotá periodically held meetings of her literary circle, El Buen Gusto, where *políticos* like Camilo Torres met to discuss radical ideas.[3] In 1808 in Caracas, Josefa Palacios and her husband, José Félix Rivas, sponsored a gathering at their home at which they hoped to convert supporters of the Spanish system to the side of independence. In Quito, another colonial hotbed of discontent, Manuela Cañizares held a *tertulia* where the 10 August 1809 movement for independence was hatched. Deeply implicated in the plot, Manuela's name was put on a wanted list and a reward offered for her capture. In order to escape arrest, she entered a convent in Quito, where she remained until her death in 1813.[4]

While a select group of well-educated white women were exposed to ideas of revolution at social gatherings, others became directly involved in the preindependence *tumultos* that occurred in the area prior to 1810. The Comunero revolts of 1781 in Socorro, Antioquia, Neiva, and Maracaibo saw women in leadership, participatory, and supportive roles.[5] The Coro slave revolt of 1795, which had republican government in Venezuela as one of its goals, numbered women among its participants,[6] as did the Gual-España episode of 1797. In the latter affair, Joaquina, the wife of José María España, the prime suspect, hid her husband from the authorities, encouraged a revolt of their slaves, and along with Isabel Gómez, a *parda* midwife, distributed revolutionary literature throughout Caracas. These two women were imprisoned and then exiled, while the female relatives of the other men involved in the scheme were deported to Spain.[7]

The revolts that occurred in Gran Colombia prior to 1810 served as a prelude to the Wars for Independence that were fought in the area until 1822. Just as women were active in the preindependence conflicts, so were they present during the revolutionary wars. Feminine participation in the events of the day was an individual matter, dictated solely by choice. Although the patriots of Gran Colombia were well aware of the activities of women in the preindependence period, nothing was done directly by them to enlist their aid in the war effort. Nevertheless, participation was broadly based; lower-class females and those of mixed blood were as active and effective as women of the upper classes.

The women who became involved did so for a number of reasons. The ties of kinship, no doubt, influenced some to declare themselves for independence. Those who belonged to families with male members deeply involved tended to commit themselves more readily than their less politicized sisters. The economic and financial aspects of the Bourbon Reforms—namely, increased taxes and imposts, which directly affected the prosperity of many households in Gran Colombia of which women were a part—served as motivating factors. Patriotic feeling was not alien to women and could have stimulated some of them to action. Certain individuals may have had specific personal reasons for wanting to work for independence. Some may have hoped to profit from the properties and goods that their male relatives might obtain at some later date as a reward for service. Added wealth and the perquisites of political power might filter down and be enjoyed by them, too, albeit indirectly. Others may have found in the politically turbulent times a perfect channel for expressing their personal rebellion against society, which, at the moment, took a political form.

While some individuals may have hoped to benefit personally in the aftermath of independence, most did not expect their sex to profit collectively from whatever freedom might bring. The involvement of women was tangential to any improvement in their own legal, political, and economic position, and they neither championed, hoped for, nor expected any improvement in their status. Most women still did not aspire to any role other than the traditional one of wife and mother. Developments in the sphere of women's rights, then, would await a later date.

Whatever their reasons for involvement in the independence movement, the presence of women was apparent during the years 1810 to 1822. Although women were not expected to fight and conscription was unheard of in Gran Colombia, some individual women joined the independence armies. Females who traveled with the troops did so intermittently, most of the time in disguise. Records attest to the fact that women fought at the battle of Boyacá in 1819, the turning point of the war in New Granada. Evangelista Tamayo, a native of

Tunja, fought there under Simón Bolívar and continued to serve until she died at San Luis de Coro in 1821, with the rank of captain.8 Teresa Corneja and Manuela Tinoco, both from San Carlos, Venezuela, and Rosa Canelonés of Arauca dressed up as men and took part in the battles of Gameza, Pantano de Vargas, and Boyacá.9 Women were also present at the battle of Pichincha, which liberated the Audiencia of Quito in 1822.10

While some women joined the troops to fight far afield, others remained home to defend their cities. Juana Ramírez was one who helped to organize a battery of women called Las Mujeres that fought in the defense of Maturin, Venezuela.11 Women also figured in the defense of the Venezuelan cities of Barinas, Valencia, and Ospino.12 A foreign traveler to Venezuela reported that the women of the island of Margarita were especially brave and capable in battle. When General Pablo Morillo first attempted to invade the island, he found that "these gallant amazons constantly worked the guns in the battalion under General Gómez; and the havoc which they made among the enemy, sufficiently proved the skill and dexterity they had acquired in the management of their artillery."13 The participation of women was instrumental in forcing Morillo's retreat.

Simón Bolívar speedily acknowledged the contributions, deeds, and achievements of female combatants. In a proclamation to the army that liberated Trujillo province, Venezuela, he praised not only the male soldiers, but also the women who fought there. Moreover, he cited their example to inspire men. According to Bolívar:

... even the fair sex, the delights of humankind, our amazons have fought against the tyrants of San Carlos with a valor divine, although without success. The monsters and tigers of Spain have shown the full extent of the cowardice of their nation. They have used their infamous arms against the innocent feminine breasts of our beauties; they have shed their blood. They have killed many of them and they loaded them with chains, because they conceived the sublime plan of liberating their beloved country!14

In addition, Bolívar expressed gratitude to the women who defended the city of Socorro, New Granada. When the Liberator visited the area in 1820, he composed a tribute to the women and had it entered into the *cabildo* books. In their response the women assured him of their continued support.15

However, not all women who wanted to fight on the side of the insurgents were able to do so. The principal society women of the province of Barinas, Venezuela, who had embraced the republican cause from the beginning, wrote a letter to the governor dated 18 October 1811, in which they offered their services as soldiers. Apparently a garrison stationed in the capital had left to repel a royalist attack, and the ladies wanted to defend their area. In the letter that the women composed they discounted feminine weakness as a factor meriting special consideration, and they showed their zeal for battle. They wrote: "We are not unaware that you, attentive to the weakness of our sex, perhaps have tried to excuse us from military hardships; but you know very well that love of country animates crueler beings than us and there are no obstacles so insurmountable that cannot conquer it."[16] Nicolás Pumar, secretary of the Provincial Government, answered the petition and thanked the ladies for their generous offer of support, but he refused to use them in the defense of the province. However, the editors of the *Gaceta de Caracas* were so impressed by this sanguine display of patriotism that they reprinted the letter in their 5 November 1811 edition.[17]

While some women engaged in combat, others lent services of a different, but equally valuable, kind to the military struggle for independence in Gran Colombia. Since women were less suspect, many were used in espionage work as spies, couriers, and informers. Perhaps the most notorious female spy of the period was Policarpa Salavarrieta of New Granada. Pola, as she was called, used her talents as a seamstress to gain access to the homes of royalist women in Bogotá where she uncovered valuable information and delivered it to the insurgents. Her success in espionage spurred the Spanish authorities' interest in her capture.[18] In 1817 she was arrested by the royalists as one of the principal republican agents and sentenced to death. On 14 November 1817 she was shot in Bogotá's main square.[19] Her death occasioned great public notice and consternation, and over the years she became somewhat of a national heroine, a symbol of patriotism and resistance.[20]

Policarpa Salavarrieta was only one of many New Granadan women who were arrested, tried, and then executed for aiding and abetting guerrillas during the 1816-19 resistance movement. General Pablo Morillo, whose forces occupied the territory during these years, gave his military commanders orders to proceed swiftly against all traitors, regardless of sex. Shortly thereafter, the executions began.[21]

Other women who were suspected of working for the insurgents faced prison terms or were forced into exile. The usual procedure was temporary incarceration in a Bogotá jail and then removal to a distant town. In a circular directed to the judges and priests of the towns where exiled women lived, General Antonio Casano, the military governor of Bogotá, gave explicit instructions on how to deal with the offenders. The women were forbidden to attend social functions, ordered to wear simple clothing, and made to receive religious instruction, since it was assumed that only the godless supported independence.[22]

Those who were not exiled were often forced to perform works of charity. Certain women were ordered to quarter royalist soldiers in their homes and to cook and sew for them. Some women were even made to clean streets. In order to facilitate these so-called charitable acts the Society of Beneficence was created by Governor Casano. Although this society was modeled on one that existed in Spain during the wars with the French, vast differences separated the two. While the women of Spain gave of their services freely, the women of Bogotá were forced to contribute. 23

According to Elvia Gutiérrez Isaza, a Colombian historian, 44 women were executed during the resistance, 119 were arrested and then exiled, and 15 were sentenced to hard labor. It is practically impossible to unearth accurate statistics regarding the number of women persecuted, but these figures serve as a rough, albeit conservative, estimate. 24

Women also made useful contributions to the independence effort in their role as noncombatants; they guided the patriot armies along their way, carried water to soldiers in battle, and helped to bury the dead. 25 Women played an important role as nurses in field hospitals where the services that they rendered were vital. Trinidad Morán noted: "The military hospital in Caracas was the meeting place for the most beautiful and pleasant ladies in the world: . . . Each one of us believed to have in these ladies a mother or a sister interested in our health and I am not mistaken in saying that many escaped and owe their salvation to such merciful offices." 26

Although many women lent their services to the troops while maintaining their permanent residences, others left home and hearth to follow the soldiers throughout their campaigns. These so-called *juanas* or *cholas* (camp followers) were usually women of the people, half-castes, who went along as wives, mistresses, or companions of the common soldiers. Since it was difficult for an army to provide all the services that it needed in those days, the tasks performed by these women were invaluable. Their help was essential, and without it the armies could not have functioned effectively. The camp followers traveled tens of thousands of kilometers on foot, prepared food, nursed the sick, and even bore arms when need be. 27 No doubt, their presence boosted the morale of the troops and discouraged desertions.

Despite their good deeds, the camp followers were not welcomed by the leaders of either the independence or the Spanish armies. Apparently they feared that women might slow up their movements, drain rations, and, in general, prove a nuisance. Both Generals Pablo Morillo and Francisco Santander issued orders in 1817 and 1819, respectively, that forbade women from traveling with the troops. 28 These orders, however, did not hold, for women continued to march with their menfolk, tend to their needs, and, in this way, maintain a semblance of family life in a period of change and disorder. The presence of camp followers was a time-honored custom that could not be abolished by military proscriptions.

The economic support that women gave to the independence armies in gifts of money, food, and matériel was vitally important to the insurgents' success. Throughout the span of the wars women figured as generous contributors, and as early as 1811 they began to donate both cash and goods. The *Gaceta de Caracas* reprinted lists of the names of contributors that same year and periodically thereafter. Although some of the donations made by women were as small as one-half *peso*, others like Juana López, a widow from Calabozo, gave as much as 100 *pesos*. [29] The vast majority of women who contributed money and wartime supplies did so on an individual basis and without any outside pressure. However, María Antonia Bolívar, whose sympathies lay with the royalists, was forced by her brother to hand over 300 slaves from her estate at San Mateo to the republican army. [30] There is no indication that women formed societies dedicated to supporting independence, materially or otherwise, like the Daughters of Liberty of the American Revolution. When women banded together, they did so informally, intermittently, and briefly, usually to meet an immediate crisis. For example, in 1820 the women of Socorro offered to house and clothe, at their own expense, a hundred men who were scheduled to receive military training, and in that same year almost all the women of Tunja joined together to sew three thousand jackets urgently needed by the army. [31]

The economic contributions that women made to the war effort were indispensable in sustaining the insurgents, yet some also made contributions of a personal nature that were, perhaps, even more of a sacrifice. One of the most celebrated females of this stripe was a widow, Simona Duque, of Antioquia province. Despite the fact that she was poverty-stricken, she encouraged her five sons to join the independence army. She even presented them herself to General José María Córdova when he came through her area. Córdova reportedly was reluctant to induct all five, but Simona insisted. Impressed by her patriotic spirit, he wrote to Vice-President Santander, urging him to give her a pension. Santander assigned her the sum of sixteen *pesos* a month and ordered her story published in a Bogotá newspaper. [32]

Besides being active participants in the independence conflict, the women of Gran Colombia were also its victims and martyrs. The immediate effects of the revolution on the women caught up in it were traumatic. The women who took part in the struggle and those who remained aloof from it alike faced rape, capture, and death as insurgent and royalist armies swept across their lands. The Black Legend of Spanish cruelty had a measure of truth to it, given some of the atrocities committed by the royalists. For example, in San Mateo, Venezuela, in March 1814, Pedro Armas reported to a priest that the royalists had killed his eighty-year-old mother and three of his children, raped his daughter, and kidnapped his wife. [33]

Many of the women who were lucky enough to escape with their lives faced an uncertain future. During the War to the Death in 1813-14 in Venezuela, the Spanish armies used women and children to carry baggage and foodstuffs. [34] In some instances women were forced into prostitution and made to follow the troops. Others had their properties destroyed, as royalist soldiers usually burned and pillaged the areas that they marched through. Moreover, they stole women's jewels and even their very clothing. [35] Occasionally royalist generals forced women to emigrate to other areas in lieu of killing them. In October 1814, José Tomás Boves, a *llanero* in the employ of the Spanish army, ordered numerous women to leave Cumaná province; and more than eight thousand people perished en route to their destination.[36]

The conclusion of the Wars to the Death in 1814 did not better the situation of Venezuelan women, for as long as the Spaniards held Venezuelan territory, women were persecuted. In 1816 four women in the province of La Paz were punished for their disloyalty to the king: Vicenta Eguina was fined 6,000 *pesos* and exiled in perpetuity from the area; Ramona Sinosan y Palisa was sent to a convent; and Simona Manzaneda and Ursula Goiziuta were admonished in public.[37] When the royalists occupied Maracaibo in 1823, they arrested Ana María Campos and then whipped her as she was ridden nude through the city streets.[38]

The conditions brought about by continuous war in Venezuela impelled women to take action to save themselves and their families. Some entered convents where they hoped to sequester themselves from the upheavals that surrounded them, but many others chose to emigrate. In some cases the migrations were of short duration, as women fled to neighboring towns to escape the enemy, only to return home when the danger had passed. In other instances women left their countries altogether and made their homes in foreign lands until the fighting was over. In either case, numerous women were compelled to emigrate from Venezuela for reasons of political affiliation and personal safety. The most extensive migration of Venezuelan women took place in July 1814, when twenty thousand individuals of both sexes left Caracas to march east to safety. Many of the women drowned, starved, or died of exhaustion on their way.[39] The casualties of the Caracas emigration of 1814 were matched only by those of the 1815 Cartagena evacuation.[40]

Despite the latter two unfortunate migrations, many other women made it safely to foreign shores. Those who left, either by choice or by force, took their children with them, while their husbands remained behind. As the emigrés expected to return home shortly, most of them chose to live out their exile in the nearby Caribbean islands. The lot of the displaced female was not a happy or prosperous one. Several island governors, namely those of Trinidad and Curaçao, were overtly hostile to the republican sympathizers. The governor of Trinidad refused to accept the emigrants from Caracas in 1814,[41] on grounds that the scanty resources of the island could not sustain them. Poverty and misery seemed to be the fate of the wealthy women from Caracas and Cumaná who lived in exile in Saint Thomas. Many of them, now heads of households, took menial jobs to support themselves and their families during these years. Several members of the Sojo y Herrera family, accustomed to the aristocratic life of Caracas, were forced to play the harp and guitar at local dances in order to earn a living. Others, like Melchora Palacios, shipped back small amounts of goods to Caracas and received payment in cacao.[42] In spite of the hardships and poverty experienced by women in exile, the added responsibilities that they assumed during these years helped to prepare them for the task of rebuilding plantations and *haciendas* in the postwar era.

Throughout the war years women in both royalist and insurgent camps were victims of property confiscations. Whether the sequestration of landed property or personal wealth was undertaken by the republicans or the royalists, its purpose was the same—to attract recruits from the lower classes by promising them booty and to supply the armies with the moneys that they constantly needed.[43] The royalists were the first to initiate a policy of confiscation with the formation of the Junta de Secuestros in 1812. Individuals who were in any way involved in the revolution against the king lost their property, women being no exception. The cacao *hacienda* of Jerónima de Tovar y Ponte in the Cuyagua Valley of Venezuela, along with the properties and wealth of María del Carmen Peláez, Sebastiana Rodríguez del Toro, the Countess of Tovar, Francisca Antonia Sandoval, and María de los Angeles Zandaeta of Venezuela, were seized by the royalists in this early period. Although many of the estates were rented out and worked for the benefit of the government, a great number of those not seized were destroyed and ruined. Thus agriculture, which had been the mainstay of the Venezuelan economy for centuries, suffered a drastic decline.[44]

While the royalists hoped to profit by the use of republican wealth during the time period in which they controlled Venezuela, the insurgents attempted to do likewise when they came into power. In order to support the independence movement, the republican government first imposed taxes and fines upon the enemy, based on their possessions and the degree of enmity shown to the insurgents. María del Carmen Machillanda, a rich proprietress from Ocumare, Venezuela, was accused of agitating on the king's behalf in the Valley of Tuy and was fined 10,000 *pesos*, payable in six months.[45] Since the instances of fines imposed on female enemies of the revolution were so few, it is apparent that the patriots were rather inefficient in carrying out their own premises of taxation. Their efforts in this regard were more a matter of policy than of action, for the government still remained bankrupt.

It seems that the attitude of the insurgents toward royalist women was marked more by mercy than by vindictiveness. Hispanic gallantry was evident in Bolívar's decrees of the confiscation of wealth. According to a proclamation of 18 October 1817, women were allowed to keep both inherited wealth and that of their dowry, despite the fact that their husbands' properties might be subject to seizure.[46] According to a law of confiscation enacted on 16 June 1819, the wealth of women and children who remained in free territory was not to be taken, while those females who had shown themselves hostile to the government and had emigrated were free to return within a year's time to claim their properties. If they did not return, whatever they possessed could be confiscated. Hence, even women who were violently opposed to independence and had actively worked against it received lenient treatment. [47] Laws pertaining to the confiscation of property remained in force until 1830, but at the Constitutional Convention in Valencia in August of that year, a strong current of public opinion arose against the continuation of the laws of seizure, and they were abrogated. [48]

Poverty and widowhood, twin consequences of the Wars for Independence, were conditions experienced by a great many women in Gran Colombia during the years of fighting there. Many widows and wives of men in army service were destitute and relied on government charity to survive. Both patriot and royalist officials supplied indigent women with daily rations of meat and bread; [49] however, these women did not depend solely on the goodwill of the government, for they themselves set out to recoup what was stolen or taken from them during the wars. The nature of most of their petitions, put forth between the years 1816 and 1825, involved questions of property, chattel or landed, or matters of family. In many cases women addressed petitions to the government requesting that their sons be returned from the army to support them [50] or that they be indemnified for slaves who had left their households to join the troops. [51] Some solicited the government for the payment of rent on homes occupied by soldiers, [52] while others demanded reimbursement for the damage that these occupants had done to their property. [53] The protection of their property and its upkeep proved to be a continuing interest of women not only in war, but also in peacetime.

It is impossible to estimate the number of women who were widowed during the Wars for Independence, but it certainly must have been great, given the continual stream of petitions for pensions that the government received between the years 1811 and 1821. In the late eighteenth century, the Spanish government had established pension funds (*montepíos*) for both civil servants and military personnel. The patriot governments followed suit by establishing similar pension funds with the express purpose of providing for the descendants of government servants and soldiers.

In 1815 the Congress of the United Provinces of Cundinamarca began to formulate policy regarding widows and orphans of deceased soldiers. On 3 March 1815, the congress decreed that widows of veteran soldiers, sergeants, or corporals were to receive one *real* daily; if they had children, they were entitled to receive one and one-half *reales* per day. In order to obtain these payments the widow had to produce the death certificate of her husband. [54] Both the Congress of Angostura in 1819 and the Congress of Cúcuta in 1821 passed resolutions on the rights of widows. The Congress of Angostura decided that widows were entitled to one-half of their husbands' assets, while his other heirs had the right to the remainder. [55] The Congress of Cúcuta allowed widows and orphans to tap the military pension fund, provided that the individual on whom they laid claim had qualified for the fund. Those widows and orphans whose husbands or fathers did not belong to the pension system would be provided for by the government once the war was over and national rents increased. 56 Since financial insolvency and debt plagued the insurgent governments both during and after the revolutionary period, the pension schemes that were formulated by the various congresses were never fully realized. Again, the government was simply too bankrupt to carry out its provisions regarding widows and dependent children. 57

Despite the facts that the women of Gran Colombia were involved in the pre-1810 conspiracies and revolts and that they participated in the Wars for Independence, their role and status in society remained much unchanged in the aftermath. The failure of women to move to expand their privileges or to raise any challenges to their traditional roles arose from their own lack of consciousness, which led them to accept their status, the negative attitudes of men toward female role change and, thus, reciprocal role change, and the politically conservative atmosphere of the postindependence period.

One activity that still remained beyond the scope of women in peacetime was politics. In postwar Gran Colombia, women theoretically had political rights before the law, but were insulated from direct political action, denied participation in the formal institutions of power, and excluded from decision making. According to the provisions of the Angostura Constitution of 1819, the Cúcuta Constitution of 1821, and the Colombian Constitution of 1830, some women most certainly met the requirements for citizenship and suffrage since, according to the letter of the law, sex was not a deterrent. 58 Few women, however, were educated or had any notion of their own political rights or any idea of what the political implications of independence might mean for them as a group. Society regarded women primarily as wives and mothers; for this they were rewarded, as they still are today in many areas of Latin America, as well as the rest of the world. The notion of accepting women as equal to men in the political arena would have been just as alien and absurd a notion to women as to men in those days.

Even if we consider the more educated persons who participated in the wars—not only in Gran Colombia, but in other areas as well—there existed little possibility of real change. Even if they were conscious of the new political rights that men were accruing, what could a handful of women do to influence the politicians? These women were just too few and had too little bargaining power.

The important male leaders involved in decision making in the new nations did not favor female participation in the body politic. In a letter of 10 August 1826 to his favorite sister, María Antonia, Simón Bolívar sternly warned against the dangers of partisanship. He urged her to devote her energies to the care of her home and family (the proper business of women) and to leave politics to men. No doubt, he expressed the sentiments of countless other males when he wrote:

I warn you not to mix in political business nor adhere to or oppose any party. Let opinion and things go along although you believe them contrary to your way of thinking. A woman ought to be neutral in public business. Her family and her domestic duties are her first obligations. A sister of mine ought to observe a perfect indifference in a country which is in a state of dangerous crisis and in which I am viewed as the point at which opinions meet.[59]

Hence, the involvement of women in politics was abhorrent and totally unacceptable to Bolívar, as well as to leaders elsewhere. Women were not denied new responsibilities in extraordinary times like the independence period, but they were to return to their proper spheres once the crisis had passed.

In addition, the conservative political mood after independence was inimical to any real change, political or otherwise, for women. A strong desire for a stable social order was apparent, and any changes in the nature of the family and women as the pillar of the family were not even considered, much less encouraged. Women were at the heart of family life and were the last segment of society to be seen as candidates for radical role change.

Just as women gained little in the political area, so they gained little in the sphere of legal rights as well. They still retained the rights that they possessed in the colonial period: namely, to hold, buy, and sell property; to inherit and bequeath wealth; to petition the government; to sue and be sued; and to initiate legal action in a variety of circumstances. However, civil codes formulated by men in the postindependence era tended to curtail, not expand, the rights of women in many areas of South America.

One area in which women seemingly made progress, though not by dint of their own efforts, was education. Opportunities for women to gain a limited education were encouraged in the aftermath of independence. By an act of the Congress of Cúcuta, effective 6 August 1821, the government assumed full responsibility for the education of women. Since the national government did not have funds to erect schools at its own expense due to wartime outlays, plans were made to establish *colegios* for girls in convents.[60] Despite government support, the goals of education were still the same preparation for marriage and motherhood. The curriculum stressed domestic skills and social graces; in no way were girls prepared to be active social participants. Furthermore, the education offered to women was of an elementary character and was valued as a passport to a better marriage or merely as a charming and attractive asset. Thus, education proved to be one aspect of modernization that was more apparent than real. It barely survived during the first decades after independence, and it was not until the latter part of the nineteenth century that any real progress was made and then only in those countries where the *ambiente* was right.

In sum, the participation of women in the Wars of Independence did not lead to any major changes in their role or position in society. Traditional attitudes toward women's place (that of a subordinate) were held by both men and women; women had little notion of their rights, political or otherwise; and indices of modernization with regard to women—fashion, consumption of luxury items, and education—proved to be more symbolic than real. It was only through education, and much later in the nineteenth century, that women became aware of their plight and feminism was born. In the meantime, women followed the paths that were open to them: marriage, motherhood, the nunnery, beneficence, or other nurturing roles that were acceptable to society at large.

Notes

1. The political entity known as Gran Colombia was created by Simón Bolívar at the 1819 Congress of Angostura. This union of present-day Venezuela, Colombia, and Ecuador lasted a mere eleven years. Regional distinctions and civilian and military rivalries for political office, along with the death of Bolívar, its president, led to the dissolution of the short-lived state in 1830.

2. For the varied activities of women in the colonial period, see Petition of Francisca María Urbina al Intendente, 19 October 1786, briefed in *Boletín del Archivo General de la Nación* 39 (October-December 1951): 47 (hereafter cited as *BAGN*); Livia Stella Melo Lancheros, *Valores femeninos de Colombia* (Bogotá, 1966), pp. 1123-24; Bernard Moses, *Spanish Colonial Literature in South America* (London: Hispanic Society of America, 1922), pp. 382-83; Gustavo Adolfo Otero, *La vida social en el coloniaje*, 2d ed. (La Paz: Editorial Juventud, 1958), pp. 66-67, 215; Francois Depons, *Travels in South America During the Years 1801, 1802, 1803, and 1804 . . .* , 2 vols. (London: Longman, 1807), 1: 130-32. See essays by Lavrin (chap. 1), Russell-Wood (chap. 2), and Couturier (chap. 4) in this volume.

3. José María Vergara y Vergara, *Historia de la literatura en Nueva Granada desde la conquista hasta la independencia (1538-1820)*, 2 vols. (Bogotá: Editorial ABC, 1958), 2: 102, 104, 106, 112.

4. José Dolores Monsalve, *Mujeres de independencia* (Bogotá: Imprenta Nacional 1926), pp. 23, 43-44.

5. Monsalve, *Mujeres*, pp. 12-13; Vincente Dávila, *Investigaciones históricas*, 2 vols. (Caracas: Imprenta Bolívar, 1923), 1: 330; Roberto María Tisnés J., *Movimientos pre-independientes grancolombianos* (Bogotá: Editorial e Imprenta Salesiana, 1962), pp. 61-68; Carlos E. Muñoz Oráa, *Los communeros de Venezuela: Una rebelión popular de pre-independencia* (Mérida: Universidad de Los Andes, 1971), p. 187.

6. Luis Arturo Domínguez, "Sublevación de negros y zambos en la sierra de Coro en 1795 . . .," *Boletín de la Academia Nacional de Historia* 41 (April-June 1958): 143-44 (hereafter cited as *BANH*).

7. For the best accounts of the Gual-España plot and the role of women in it, see Hector García Chuecos, ed., *Documentos relativos a la revolución de Gual y España* (Caracas: Pan American Institute of Geography and History, 1949), pp. 251-52, 267; Carmen Clemente Travieso, *Mujeres de la independencia: Seis biografías de mujeres venezolanas* (Mexico: Talleres Gráficos de Mexico, 1964), pp. 21, 32, 38, 42-44; Carlos Fulgencio López, *Juan Picornell y la conspiración de Gual y España: Narración documentada de la pre-revolución de independencia venezolana* (Caracas: Ediciones Nueva Cádiz, 1955), p. 296.

8. Ramón C. Correa, *Diccionario de boyacenses ilustres* (Tunja: Imprenta Departamental, 1955), p. 323.

9. *Corona fúnebre, homenaje a la memoria de los héroes y mártires de la independencia de la Gran Colombia en los centenarios de su emancipación* (Bogotá: Imprenta de Medina e Hijo, 1910), pp. 53-58, 94.

10. Roberto María Tisnés J., *Los mártires de la patria, 1810-1819* (Bogotá, 1966), pp. 69, 93.

11. *Heroínas venezolanas* (Caracas: Imprenta Nacional, 1961), pp. 16, 35.

12. Monsalve, *Mujeres*, pp. 55, 58; José Félix Blanco, *Bosquejo histórico de la revolución de Venezuela* (Caracas: Academia Nacional de la Historia, 1960), p. 206.

13. *Recollections of a Service of Three Years During the War-of-Extermination in the Republics of Venezuela and Colombia by an Officer of the Colombian Navy*, 2 vols. (London: Hunt and Clarke, 1828), 1: 31.

14. ". . . hasta el bello sexo, las delicias del género humano, nuestras amazonas han combatido contra los tiranos de San Carlos, con un valor divino, aunque sin suceso. Los monstruos y tigres de España han colmado la medida de la cobardía de su nación, han dirigido las infames armas contra los cándidos y femeninos pechos de nuestras beldades; han derramado su sangre; han hecho expirar a muchas de ellas, y las han cargado de cadenas, porque concibieron el sublime designio de libertar a su adorada patria!" *Las fuerzas armadas de Venezuela en el siglo XIX: Textos para su estudio*, 12 vols. (Caracas, 1963-), 1: 242.

15. Horacio Rodríguez Plata, *La antigua provincia del Socorro y la independencia* (Bogotá: Publicaciones Editoriales, 1963), p. 532.

16. "No ignoramos que V.E., atendida la debilidad de nuestro sexo, acaso ha procurado eximirnos de las fatigas militares; pero sabe muy bien V.E. que el amor á la patria vivifica a entes más desnaturalizados y no hay obstáculos por insuperables que no venza." Virgilio Tosta, *Sucedió en Barinas: Episodios de historia menuda* (Caracas: Editorial Sucre, 1964), pp. 134-35.

17. Ibid., p. 135.

18. Oswaldo Díaz Díaz, *Historia extensa de Colombia*, vol. 6, *La reconquista española* (Caracas: Ediciones Lerner, 1964), pp. 400, 251; Pedro M. Ibáñez, *Crónicas de Bogotá*, 3 vols. (Bogotá: Imprenta Nacional, 1913), 3: 371.

19. José Hilario López, *Memorias*, 2 vols. (Bogotá: Editorial ABC, 1942), 1: 140-42. Another martyr of national renown was Antonia Santos, whose story is narrated by Horacio Rodríguez Plata, *Antonia Santos Plata* (Bogotá: Editorial Kelly, 1969).

20. Newspapers carried accounts of Pola's death, and fellow patriots, in their private correspondence, assessed the impact of her execution on the populace. A spate of poems, plays, and even novels rapidly appeared, telling her story and contributing to her fame as a Colombian martyr. *Correo del Orinoco*, 1 January 1820, p. 4; Oswaldo Díaz Díaz, *Los Almeydas: Episodios de la resistencia patriota contra el ejército pacificador de Tierra Firme* (Bogotá: Editorial ABC, 1962), p. 289; Díaz Díaz, *La reconquista*, p. 379.

21. Tisnés J., *Los mártires*, p. 27.

22. José Manuel Restrepo, *Historia de la revolución de la república de Colombia en la América meridional*, 4 vols. (Paris: Besanzon, 1858), 1: 431.

23. Ibáñez, *Crónicas*, 3: 223.

24. *Historia heroica de las mujeres próceres de Colombia* (Medellín: Imprenta Municipal, 1972), pp. 79-80, 111-12, 122-24, 155-61, 202-14, 221-30.

25. Correa, *Diccionario*, p. 357; Tisnés J., *Los mártires*, p. 24; Melo Lancheros, *Valores femeninos*, p. 1142.

26. "El hospital militar de Caracas era el punto de reunión de las más bellas y afables señoras del mundo: . . . Cada uno de nosotros creía tener en estas señoras una madre o una hermana vivamente interesada en nuestra salud y no me equivoco en decir que muchos escaparon y deben su salvación a tan piadosos oficios"; Vicente Lecuna, "Documentos: La guerra a muerte," *BANH* 18 (January-March 1935): 176.

27. Carlos Arturo Díaz, Las mujeres en la independencia," *Boletín de Historia y Antigüedades* 55 (July-September 1968): 370 (hereafter cited as *BHA*).

28. Pablo Morillo y Morillo, *Mémoires du Général Morillo* . . . (Paris: Chez P. Dufart, Libraire, 1826), p. 268; Enrique Otero D'Costa, "Libro de órdenes militares del General Santander en la campaña de 1819," *BHA* 28 (November 1942): 1129.

29. *Gaceta de Caracas*, 22 November 1811, p. 4; 21 May 1811, p. 4.

30. Pinzón Uzcátegui, "La hermana de Bolívar donó a la patria 300 esclavos," *Boletín Histórico: Academia de Historia de Cartagena de Indias* 6 (February 1930): 68.

31. Rodríguez Plata, *La antigua provincia*, p. 726; Diego María Gómez Tamayo, *Anotaciones históricas* (Medellín: Academia Antioqueña de Historia, 1969), p. 116.

32. Manuel Ezequiel Corrales, ed., *Documentos para la historia de la provincia de Cartagena de Indias*, 2 vols. (Bogotá: Imprenta de M. Rivas, 1883), 2: 389-90.

33. Lecuna, "Documentos: La guerra a muerte," p. 169.

34. Vicente Lecuna, "La guerra a muerte, San Mateo, Bocachia, y Valencia," *BANH* 28 (April-June 1945): 198.

35. Juan Manuel de Cajigal, *Memorias del Mariscal de campo sobre la Revolución de Venezuela* (Caracas: Junta Superior de Archivos, Ministerio de Justicia, 1960), pp. 128, 133.

36. Francisco Javier Yanes, *Historia de la provincia de Cumaná en la transformación política de Venezuela, desde el día 27 de abril de 1810 hasta el presente año de 1821* (Caracas: Ediciones del Ministerio de Educación Nacional y Dirección de Cultura y Bellas Artes, 1949), p. 148.

37. *Gaceta de Caracas*, 14 May 1817, p. 1022.

38. Yanes, *Historia*, p. 167.

39. Narciso Coll y Prat, *Memoriales sobre la independencia de Venezuela* (Caracas: Academia Nacional de la Historia, 1960), p. 297.

40. Monsalve, *Mujeres*, pp. 123-26.

41. *150 años de vida republicana (1811-1961)*, 2 vols. (Caracas: Ediciones de la Presidencia de la República, 1963), 2: 80.

42. Vicente Lecuna, *Crónica razonada de las guerras de Bolívar*, 3 vols. (New York: Colonial Press, 1950), 1: 432.

43. *150 años*, 2: 82.

44. Blas Bruni Celli, *Los secuestros en la guerra de independencia* (Caracas: Imprenta Nacional, 1965), pp. 23-29, 34.

45. Vicente Lecuna, "La guerra a muerte," *BANH* 27 (July-September 1944): 282.

46. Bruni Celli, *Los secuestros*, pp. 89-90.

47. Roberto Cortázar and Luis Agusto Cuervo, eds., *Congreso de Angostura: Libro de Actas* (Bogotá: Imprenta Nacional, 1921), p. 93.

48. Bruni Celli, *Los secuestros*, pp. 89-90.

49. Communiqué to Chief of the General Staff, 27 October 1818, *BAGN* 17 (July-August 1934): 103.

50. Petition of Juana Tomasa Martínez, Maracay, Venezuela, 27 March 1816, *BAGN* 45 (April-June 1958): 568.

51. Petition of Rosa Ramona Pérez, Caracas, Venezuela, 22 December 1825, *BAGN* 4 (December 1925): 49.

52. Petition of Simona Nadal, San Carlos, Venezuela, 29 December 1816, *BAGN* 45 (July-September 1958): 778.

53. Judicial Petition of Cipriana Pezón, Maracay, Venezuela, 7 August 1819, *BAGN* 45 (July-September 1958): 778.

54. Eduardo Posada, comp., *Congreso de las provincias unidas* (Bogotá: Imprenta Nacional, 1924), p. 104.

55. Cortázar and Cuervo, *Congreso de Angostura*, p. 292.

56. Roberto Cortázar and Luis Augusto Cuervo, eds., *Congreso de Cúcuta: Libro de Actas* (Bogotá: Imprenta Nacional, 1923), pp. 756-57.

57. Given the data available, it is difficult to construct a group profile of those widows who were eligible for pensions or those who actually received government moneys. Records attest to the fact that the government was barraged with petitions and solicitations from widows seeking compensation, but statistics regarding those remunerated have not been found. Archival records of the Ministry of Defense relating to pension schemes (which might or might not exist) could possibly contain information of this kind.

58. Cortázar and Cuervo, *Congreso de Angostura*, pp. 129-30; Great Britain, Foreign Office, *British and Foreign State Papers, vol. 9, 1821-1822*, "Constitution of the Republic of Colombia," Rosario de Cúcuta, 30 August 1826, pp. 699-701; Great Britain, Foreign Office, *British and Foreign State Papers, vol. 17, 1829-1830*, "Constitution of the Republic of Colombia," 29 April 1830, pp. 1199-1201.

59. "Te aconsejo que no te mezcles en los negocios políticos, ni te adhieras ni opongas a ningún partido. Deja marchar la opinión y las cosas aunque las creas contrarias a tu modo de pensar. Una mujer debe ser neutral en los negocios públicos. Su familia y sus deberes domésticos son sus primeras obligaciones. Una hermana mía debe observar una perfecta indiferencia en un país que está en estado de crisis peligrosa, y donde se me vé como punto de reunión de las opiniones"; Vicente Lecuna, *Cartas del Libertador corregidas conforme a los originales*, 11 vols. (Caracas: Litografía y Tipografía del Comercio, 1929-48), 6: 53.

60. Cortázar and Cuervo, *Congreso de Cúcuta*, p. 374.

9

Education, philanthropy, and feminism: components of Argentine womanhood, 1860-1926

Histories of Argentina have, for the most part, narrated and interpreted the history of that country's men and the institutions that they created. Except for casual passing remarks most texts overlook the role of women in the nation's development. Women may not have been viceroys, generals, or presidents, but they did contribute in other ways to Argentina's growth. They organized a complex social welfare system in Buenos Aires, educated thousands of students in the public school system, and provided a cheap source of labor. During the period 1860 to 1926, rapid urbanization, high foreign immigration, and thoroughgoing economic changes combined to alter many aspects of Argentine life. [1] Even the role of women, long considered a constant, began to change due to these pressures. This essay will explore the ways in which education, philanthropy, and feminism allowed some groups of Argentine women to break away from the Spanish tradition of sheltered womanhood and to emerge as participants, albeit second-class, in the nation's growth.

During the latter part of the eighteenth century the ideas of the European Enlightenment filtered into Latin America, where they formed the philosophical undergirdings for the soon-to-emerge new republics. [2] In Buenos Aires the liberalizing effects of the Bourbon reforms stimulated economic growth, added to the city's political importance, and afforded the elite increased contact with new ideas. [3] The intellectual's exposure to a philosophical outlook favorable to improving the status of women in society did not seem to foster any action specifically directed toward women's issues.

During the early national period only the liberal reformer Bernardino

Rivadavia articulated his concern about women's status and the institutions serving their welfare. As minister of government in 1823, Rivadavia transformed his words into action by establishing the Society of Beneficence of Buenos Aires. He charged the Society with the establishment and administration of a public elementary school system for girls and the reorganization of the San Miguel school and orphanage for girls. The charter stipulated that as the Society grew in experience and competence, its responsibilities would expand to include other social welfare services. The funding for these projects came primarily from the national budget, but individuals' donations of cash and goods also were accepted. Rivadavia entrusted the administration of the organization to thirteen prominent women who represented a cross section of the *porteño* elite. Subsequently, members elected all future members of the Society. Throughout the Society's long history, 1823 to 1948, the organization expanded its institutions and services to encompass the entire spectrum of social services for women and children.

During the 1850s the Society took over the administration of Buenos Aires's only charity hospital for women, reorganized and expanded the city's foundling home, established the country's first insane asylum for women, and organized a poor fund to provide monthly stipends to selected indigent women. This decade also witnessed the reestablishment of many schools closed during the Rosas era and the establishment of many new ones.

The devastating 1871 yellow fever epidemic prompted the establishment of emerging shelters, dismantled once the epidemic ended. The same year the Society opened the Orphans' Asylum, for both sexes, in an attempt to provide care for children whose parents had died of yellow fever. In 1903 the girls were placed in a separate institution. During the 1860s and 1870s the police continually asked the Society to establish a women's prison. This became a reality in 1873 with the opening of the Good Shepherd Asylum; insufficient funding forced it to close in 1888. In October 1878 the Society prevented the city's only public eye clinic from closing by incorporating it into the Women's Hospital.

The turn of the century found the Society expanding and modernizing its existing facilities to meet increasing demands for social services. The Society continued its tradition of giving emergency aid to victims of natural disasters and civil disorders in both Buenos Aires and other parts of Argentina. Moreover, it carried on its custom of awarding annual Virtue Prizes to selected poor women whose lives exemplified the virtues of hard work, self-sacrifice, and morality. [4]

The Society of Beneficence provided the model for numerous other female charity groups that emerged in Buenos Aires during the last half of the nineteenth century. These groups were a response, in part, to the social dislocations endemic in a growing urban center with a large immigrant population. They also provided a socially approved outlet for the energies and talents of nonworking educated women. The activities of the Society of Beneficence and its imitators foreshadowed the direction of many projects that twentieth-century Argentine feminists advocated. In order to understand this link, one must delve into the history of Argentine education.

Argentina's famous Generation of 1837, which comprised reformers like Juan Bautista Alberdi and Domingo Faustino Sarmiento, spent many years in exile because of their opposition to Juan Manuel de Rosas's government. Their travels in Europe and the United States brought Alberdi and Sarmiento into contact with the most advanced ideas on education and women's role in society. The impressive pace of economic progress and industrialization in these areas convinced them of the need to apply such principles in Argentina. The fall of Rosas after the 1852 battle of Caseros cleared the way for them to return from exile.[5]

Alberdi, who coined the motto "to govern is to populate," believed that Argentina would not advance until its women no longer lived under the yoke of Spanish law and customs that subjugated them first to their fathers' and then to their husbands' control. He maintained that with scant opportunities to develop identities beyond wife and mother, most women were no more than mere children. Alberdi advocated that Argentine women should be educated to assume the full duties of citizenship and to contribute to the country's economic growth.[6]

Nineteenth-century Argentina's most outstanding educational reformer, Domingo F. Sarmiento, traveled extensively during his exile. In North America he established a close relationship with Horace and Mary Mann, the parents of American public education.[7] From his contact with the Manns and their colleagues, Sarmiento became convinced that govermentally supported, free public schools would transform Argentina into a prosperous, civilized nation.[8] This school system ideally would encompass kindergarten through secondary instruction and be staffed only by teachers with normal school training. The curriculum in the school system would emphasize physical fitness, responsible citizenship, vocational instruction, and the standard skills such as reading, writing, and arithmetic.[9] Sarmiento was adamant in his insistence that public education be secular; this created discord in many circles.

Once Sarmiento returned to Argentina and became president (1868-74), he set out to convert his ideas into practice. As a basis for his projected public school system, he founded a normal school at Paraná in 1870, choosing a famous New England educator, Dr. George Stearns, to serve as the school's director. This coeducational institution provided the training ground for Argentina's first generation of normal school teachers.[10] These men and women made a substantial contribution toward lowering Argentina's illiteracy rate from more than two-thirds in 1869 to less than one-third in 1914.[11]

Sarmiento's observation of North American women teachers convinced him that an intelligent woman had a natural ability to educate young minds.[12] Consequently, he decided to encourage Argentine women to become schoolteachers. As an enticement his administration established a number of schools, coeducational ones for the more progressive recruits and all-female ones for the more traditional students.[13] Many young women took advantage of these educational opportunities because they were practically the only institutions offering secondary training to their sex in the nineteenth century.

Hiring North American women teachers was another method that Sarmiento used to encourage Argentine parents to send their daughters to normal school. Because Sarmiento wanted to attract young women from good Argentine families, he insisted that foreign recruits be attractive, come from respectable families, have irreproachable morals and manners, and possess a normal school education. With the cooperation of Mary Mann, Kate Newell Dogett, and others involved in the North American normal school movement, sixty-five women signed contracts to teach in Argentina between 1869 and 1898. This remarkable group of women, twenty of whom lived out their lives in Argentina and thirty-six of whom stayed beyond the three-year contract, brought North American school plans and methods to Argentina. They made an invaluable contribution toward expanding the horizons of their students, particularly the women. Frances Allyn, one of the twenty-two teachers from Minnesota, stated that "their schools created for the Argentine girl new aims, ambitions, and many have become teachers and are not only self-supporting, but support entire families."[14]

The normal schools established by Sarmiento offered interested students the opportunity to learn the latest North American pedagogical philosophies and methods. Unlike traditional educational practices, which stressed the rote memorization of a set body of facts, the new approach encouraged questioning and reasoning. Moreover, the normal schools emphasized the importance of self-discipline, physical fitness, and manual labor. Sarmiento hoped that teachers trained along these lines would raise the level of Argentine culture and increase the country's productivity.[15]

Sarmiento attached great importance to women's education because he realized their influence over young children. He believed that all the progressive ideas that youngsters acquired in the classroom easily could be undone in a backward home environment.[16] Therefore, he insisted that female students be well instructed in physical fitness and a housewife's duties. Domestic economy courses became standard in the public schools and attempted to elevate homemaking to a quasi-science. Rather than taking the traditional passive female role in the home, female students were encouraged to exert greater influence over the management of their homes and families. They were taught how to distribute work among various family members, to manage income and expenses, and to save funds and borrow for special needs. Students also learned methods for economizing on clothing and furniture purchases, preserving foods, and cultivating small gardens.[17] Courses in scientific child rearing and personal hygiene filled out many schedules.[18] Sarmiento believed that knowledge on such topics would enable students (presumably all future mothers) to raise healthy, hard-working Argentine citizens. Moreover, he hoped that such instruction would convince mothers not to relegate their children to the care of ignorant and superstitious maids.[19] The housewife role, at least in the curriculum, had become to move toward scientific home management and guardianship of the nation's young.

Adhering to the Greek philosophy that a healthy body made for a healthy mind, Sarmiento required all normal and public schools to offer regular physical education classes for both sexes. For women, he viewed outdoor exercise as conducive to improving their general health and to giving them a feeling of control over their bodies. His arguments in favor of physical training for women also implied its benefits for the nation, because Sarmiento believed healthy women would be better workers and bear stronger children than would weak ones who led sheltered and sedentary lives.[20]

Until 1876, when the provincial government of Buenos Aires put all state-funded schools under its control, the Society of Beneficence continued to administer most public female education in Buenos Aires. For some years Sarmiento and reformers had tried to convince the Society to bring its girls' schools more in line with modern pedagogical ideas. Even though Sarmiento referred to the Society's members as "ignorant old women" and considered them to be a reactionary force in *porteño* life, he recognized their power and tried to work with them. Therefore, he helped them to find two Catholic teachers qualified to reorganize the Society's normal school. However, no sooner had one of the teachers, Emma Caprile, set up a model school than the provincial government, impressed by her skills, persuaded her to work for it. In 1874 she organized Normal School No. 1 in Buenos Aires, which became an important watershed in women's education. The other teacher, Agnus Trégent, directed one of the Society's schools for orphans and later replaced Caprile in the Society's normal school. After 1876 the Society no longer administered public schools, but it did continue to supervise other schools under its direction.[21]

After 1870, Argentina's growing commercial and agricultural sector demanded an ever increasing supply of skilled workers of both sexes. In response to the country's needs many vocational schools sprang up: industrial and trade schools, commercial schools, and agricultural schools. Many of these institutions had special training programs for women. The government lagged behind private efforts in this area and did not approve a manual education program for the public schools until April 1896.[22] Three years later the government opened its first Crafts and Services Institute in Buenos Aires; many others followed in the early 1900s.[23] They were established for students in their middle teens who had completed elementary school, but did not have the ability, desire, or resources to attend the more prestigious normal and secondary school. The vocational institutes for male students concentrated their courses on industrial skills such as mechanics, metal work, and engineering.

All such skills were in demand and held out the possibility of steady employment and good pay. In marked contrast, comparable schools for female students stressed training in the traditional skills such as needlework and domestic services. [24]

Although the combination of skills taught to women varied from one institute to another, the majority offered a selection encompassing the following courses: corsetry, millinery, lace making, hem stitching, embroidering, linen making, dress design, and glove making. By encouraging fine handwork, the government hoped to encourage the production of domestic items competitive with similar foreign goods. The directors of such schools viewed needlework as a means to offer women the opportunity to work at home as independent craftspeople rather than as servile factory workers. They also maintained that piecework performed at home enabled mothers to spend more time with their children and to improve the home environment. [25] Supporters of this concept did not confront the fact that many women who had done such piecework received very low wage rates for long hours of work. Working in the home offered no automatic guarantee that a woman would have time to improve her family's life or that she would be anything more than a servile worker.

The art departments in the crafts and services institutes taught applied design for decorating pottery, lamp shades, boxes, paper products, and fabrics. Students also could learn jewelry making, for example, carving saints' medallions out of mother-of-pearl. The art of fine hand bookbinding fascinated many students, but, unfortunately, its demand decreased with the advent of cheaper machine-made books. [26]

Although the majority of students enrolled in the needlework and applied design classes, a few took the ironing and laundering classes. These skills did not hold much appeal for students because of the hot, damp, unhealthy environment in most laundries. In addition, workers tended to earn low wages for long hours of back-breaking work. It is curious that the crafts and services institutes bothered to offer such training because neither laundering or ironing could be considered particularly creative jobs. They were, in fact, jobs that most women tried to avoid.

In keeping with the government's desire to raise the general level of culture and to foster patriotism, crafts and services institutes set aside time each day for instruction in domestic economy, literacy, physical fitness, and Argentine history. These institutions endeavored to make future Argentine mothers into intelligent, industrious, skilled people conscious of their part in building the nation. [27]

From the viewpoint of economic self-sufficiency, the usefulness of many skills taught by crafts and services institutes seems dubious. The luxury nature of a large percentage of the items limited their marketability. Most lace workers and embroiderers never would receive a substantial wage if they had to depend on sales, nor would they be compensated for their years of training unless the government subsidized them to save such arts. Women could offer such products for sale at places like the Women's Exchange or the institutes' annual sales and exhibits. They also could work on a commission basis for a large department store such as Harrods or Gath and Cháves. Women fortunate enough to have some financial backing could open small shops to sell their work. In 1919 Katherine Dreier, a North American woman familiar with trade schools for women in New York, commented after visiting a crafts and services institute in Buenos Aires that the students did not receive training in skills conducive to their becoming self-supporting above the most basic level. Dreier thought the idea of preserving artistic handwork to be admirable, but unrealistic, given most working women's economic needs. [28]

Buenos Aires's emergence as a major trade and commercial center in the 1880s stimulated an increased demand for clerical workers, sales personnel, and other white-collar employees. Professional schools for women gradually responded to these realities by adding classes in typing, telegraphy, accounting, stenography, sales techniques, and modern languages. [29] Like their counterparts in the United States, Argentine women inundated the lower echelons of office workers and sales clerks, laboring long hours and receiving minimal pay and few benefits. [30]

Not until 1912, when it established the Commercial High School No. 1 in Buenos Aires, did the Argentine government recognize the need to offer qualified young women a substantial commercial education. The five-year program included standard courses in typing, shorthand, composition, business, arithmetic, and economics. In the fifth year students also took courses in geography, civic laws, and history to round out their education. [31] Despite their sound preparation for a business career, few graduates could expect to do more than secretarial work, because customarily men would receive the in-office training enabling them to move up into better-paying, more challenging positions. [32] Furthermore, the restrictive nature of the Argentine Civil Code as it related to women hindered them from competing as equals in business. For example, a married woman had to receive her husband's permission before engaging in any profession, and she could not sign a contract. [33] The long struggle to reform the Civil Code culminated in 1926 with the passage of some important modifications allowing women to participate in economic life on a more equitable basis. [34]

Young women with aspirations for a university education, if qualified, could attend one of the selective national girls' high schools. The first school of this kind, National Girls' High School No. 1 in Buenos Aires, opened its doors in 1907 with an enrollment of 261 students in all five grades. [35] The students followed a university preparatory program, encompassing subjects such as chemistry, natural history, anatomy, psychology, and geography. They also were required to take nonacademic courses in domestic science, needlework, music, and physical education. In her report on this high school for 1911

Ernestina P. Lopez, a professor and well-known women's rights advocate, lamented most students' poor preparation, most clearly demonstrated by their inability to think rationally. [36] The following year the school's director, Luis Herrera, blamed students' poor grades on bad-quality elementary education and health problems rather than on any innate inability to do academic work. [37] The slowly, but steadily, increasing enrollment of women in Argentine universities after this high school graduated its first class in 1911 suggested that it had begun to achieve its goal. [38]

The student body at National Girls' High School No. 1 was almost half foreign. This reflected the immigrant drive for upward mobility and the willingness of these parents to deviate from traditional aspirations for their daughters. Herrera noted that "foreign women study those subjects that would open the road to higher culture." Concomitantly, he remarked on the Argentine upper classes' preference to confine their daughters to the state of *sancta simplicitas* in the fashionable confessional schools. Consequently, the benefits of academic secondary education went, for the most part, to girls from middle-income groups rather than the elite. [39] The national girls' high schools, with their emphasis on high educational standards, career goals, and social involvement, were instrumental in creating a small, but influential, group of professional women in Argentina.

Many of the attitudes propelling Argentine women into the vanguard of the Latin American feminist movement resulted from their experiences in the public school system. The national girls' high schools, particularly No. 1 in Buenos Aires, developed a variety of activities to make students aware of current ideas and to heighten their sense of community responsibility. For example, National Girls' High School No. 1 brought in María de Maetzu to speak about her experiences as director of Madrid's only residence for young, single women. The famous Italian educator María Montessori lectured the same students about her theories on early childhood education. [40] Members from the local Temperance League came to warn students about the dangers of alcoholism. [41] In order to increase students' patriotism, the school administration organized a program to raise money for national monuments and to teach Argentine music. One group of teachers organized a three-part publication series that focused on topics like morality, patriotism, and possibilities for individual growth at a girls' high school. Traditional philanthropic activities for students included raising money for the Childrens' Home and sending clothing for the baskets distributed to indigent mothers. Former students organized alumni associations that sponsored numerous social and cultural events for alumni, students, and faculty. [42]

Faculty members at the national girls' high schools urged their students to achieve as individuals as well as to pursue altruistic social goals. These outlooks reflected the life-style and attitudes of many teachers. For example, the careers of notable Argentine socialist feminists such as Elvira López,

Ernestina López de Nelson, and Elvira Rawson de Dellepiane included some time teaching in one of these schools. Their orientation undoubtedly influenced students and helped to enlarge the ranks of both feminism and socialism.

From its inception in 1896, the Argentine Socialist party was an outspoken supporter of feminism.[43] Its platform always included demands for universal suffrage and equality of the sexes in the Civil Code. The Socialists also supported the right to absolute divorce, paternity investigations, and legal equality of legitimate and illegitimate children.[44] Alfredo Palacios, Argentina's first Socialist deputy, frequently spoke out on behalf of women's rights during the two terms he served in the Chamber of Deputies (1904-8 and 1912-15). Particularly, he articulated the ideas of the Feminist Center, an organization founded in 1905 to press for women's equality and rights.[45] In June 1906, Palacios presented the chamber with statistical evidence demonstrating the miserable working conditions of large numbers of women and children, which contributed to the country's high infant mortality rate. In order to ameliorate this situation the Feminist Center, through Palacios, demanded legislation regulating working conditions for women and children, day care facilities in factories, shorter working hours, and safer equipment in factories. The passage of protective legislation in 1907, even though ultimately ineffective, encouraged members of the Feminist Center and other socialists to persevere in their struggle.[46]

Until the 1926 reform of the Civil Code, the improvement of women's civil status constituted a major feature of Argentine feminism. The 1870 Vélez-Sarsfield version of the Civil Code denied Argentine women, unless widowed, a separate legal identity from their husbands, fathers, or other male guardians. This meant that women could not enter into professions or contracts without permission, had no right to their earnings, could not own a bankbook, lost all right to their own property at marriage, and could not serve as a legal witness to public documents and wills.[47] Women affiliated with socialist feminism, such as Alicia Moreau de Justo, Cecilia Grierson, Julieta Lanteri-Renshaw, and Elvira Rawson de Dellepiane, pioneered this long, frustrating struggle,[48] Their opposition most frequently declared that civil rights for women would destroy the fabric of the home because no one person would have the final word on important decisions.[49] Others believed that giving women civil rights would damage their maternal instinct by emphasizing female aggressiveness over passivity.[50] In 1907, Palacios asked the Chamber of Deputies to consider the following changes in the Civil Code:

... the right of the natural mother to the administration of the income and property of her children; the right of married women to be members of mutual aid and cooperative societies ... the right of aunts and sisters of minors to become guardians and the right of a married woman to administer and dispose of her own property. . . .[51]

The Chamber of Deputies soundly rejected Palacios's proposals, but neither he, the members of the Feminist Center, nor other interested persons allowed the need for these reforms to sink into oblivion.

The 1910 centenary celebration of Argentine independence afforded women's groups an excellent opportunity to publicize women's contributions to the country's development. The centennial also presented an opportune time to stress the necessity of expanding educational and job opportunities for women and of reforming the Civil Code. [52]

The tenor of the May 1910 National Council of Women's Conference was reflected in the theme for its literary contest: "that the culture for women which our institution pursues is not in any manner what is commonly understood as feminism." [53] Throughout the week-long conference, delegates discussed a variety of topics that they considered exemplified their definition of feminism. Some speakers extolled the normal school for women's contributions to national progress and advocated more cooperation between school and the home. Others discoursed on women's important contributions during the independence period, the Society of Beneficence's projects on behalf of indigent women and children, and the National Council of Women's role in national progress. [54] The Catholic liberal Celia La Palma de Emery urged the National Council of Women to support groups and individuals endeavoring to pass protective legislation for working women and to help establish leagues dedicated to protect the moral development of young working women—that is, to safeguard them from socialism and anarchism. Following the latter line of thinking, Emery asked the National Council of Women to pressure newspaper owners not to publish articles prejudicial to the social order, such as those advocating revolution, socialism, or anti-Catholicism. [55] In closing the conference, Elsa M. Martínez assured the audience that women would exert the most influence on the world by educating future generations to civic-mindedness, rather than by voting in elections or holding public office. [56] This contrasted markedly with the conclusions about women's influence and status that the First International Feminist Congress of Buenos Aires produced the same month.

The Argentine Association of University Women sponsored the First International Feminist Congress to discuss what its members viewed as the most pressing issues confronting Argentine women. Unlike the generally self-satisfied tone about women's role and status, excepting La Palma de Emery's opinions, this congress's delegates expressed anxiety. These women identified themselves as feminists and believed in feminism, which in the words of Cecilia Grierson was "the evolution of the woman toward superior ideals and her participation in the progress of humanity." This definition also included a belief in socialism, which Grierson asserted could not be separated from feminism because the socialists had been such traditional supporters of women's emancipation. [57] The First International Feminist Congress met for five stimulating sessions between 18 and 23 May. Several foreign delegates attended, representing Peru, Chile, Uruguay, Italy, and the United States. Most participants, however, came from women's groups in Buenos Aires. [58] A sampling of the most important themes discussed included education, child abandonment and infanticide, society in general, women's legal position, and suffrage.

The sessions on education ranged over a wide variety of topics. Generally, delegates advocated free, coeducational, lay schools with similar standards for both sexes. Because of the immigrant background of many participants, the congress passed a resolution insisting that standard patriotic teachings not foster national sentiments for Argentina to the extent that students had no positive feelings for their country of origin. On the other hand, as a way to preserve Argentina's native crafts of the interior provinces, the delegates voted to encourage more schools to teach such skills.

Concern about increasing absenteeism among students in the public schools prompted delegates to advocate fining parents for not complying with the compulsory education laws. Some teachers who worried about many students' poor health suggested that many should attend school only half-days. Another demonstration of concern about health came out in a proposal to provide free milk to needy students between classes. Recognizing that many parents forced their children to do heavy work at home, delegates voted to admonish parents not to overburden their offspring with excessive responsibilities. This did not take into consideration, however, the economic realities forcing many children to work in order to contribute their fair share to the family unit.

Focusing specifically on the educational needs of young women, the delegates demanded more technical and scientific education, which, they asserted, would allow women greater participation in the economy. Not forgetting the home, delegates supported establishing special schools to train home management teachers. They also believed that female students at all levels should take domestic science courses. Following Sarmiento's lead in the field of physical fitness for women, the delegates demanded more gyms, playgrounds, and girls sport clubs. General health education also should include classes informing students about venereal diseases, prostitution and white slavery, and means of avoiding pregnancy out of wedlock. [59]

The sessions exploring society in general produced a wide assortment of resolutions. For example, one delegate called on women to work for peace and the principle of arbitration in international disputes. Another woman urged society to allow women to develop their full potential by allowing them access to higher education, which would bring them economic independence. She continued by asserting that feminists did not want to create a battle between the sexes; rather they desired that women's rights be respected. Ultimately, she hoped, the struggle would cease, and collective harmony between the sexes would emerge. Other speakers emphasized the theme of feminist as moral arbitrator and reaffirmed their support for one moral standard for both sexes.

Continuing this line of thinking, the delegates reaffirmed their stand against prostitution, white slavery, and legalized brothels. 60 In order to disseminate these and other feminist ideas, the delegates encouraged interested women to become journalists for the cause. 61

The problems of abandonment and infanticide occupied much of the delegates' attention. Traditionally, women forced to abandon an infant left it in the turnstile of the Society of Beneficence's Foundling Home. From there the infant was farmed out to a wet nurse and later placed in an orphanage. Feminists opposed this system, which, they maintained, harmed both the mother and the child. Instead, they supported institutions like the Juana Manuela Gorriti Center, which was trying to establish a mothers' home for women and their children. Delegates believed that the government should give financial assistance to any woman wanting to keep her child. This, they maintained, would lower the infanticide rate and decrease the orphanage's population. 62

The sessions of the congress devoted to exploring women's legal status focused on the Argentine Civil Code. Carolina Muzzilli saluted the liberalized divorce laws in Uruguay and strongly recommended that the Argentines follow this lead. Muzzilli maintained that under the present Code, a married woman had no means to protect herself from an unscrupulous husband's whims or habits. If she ran away from the situation, the law gave the husband the right to force her return, like a runaway slave. 63 In another appeal to honor the basic human rights of both sexes, Elvira Rawson de Dellepiane stressed the need for a complete overhaul of the Civil Code. She demanded that women be granted full adult status, including the same control over earnings, property, professional life, and children as men had. 64 The passage of these types of reform became the central focus of Argentine feminism until 1926, when a major reform of the Civil Code gave women more control over their lives.

Universal suffrage long had been a part of the Socialist program in Argentine. Raquel Messina, representing the Feminist Socialist Center, read a paper advocating women's suffrage. She based her argument on the French Revolution's supporters, who proposed that every citizen—including women—had the right to representation in government. Demonstrating the salutary effect of women's suffrage on public life, Messina cited the experience of Wyoming. In this first North American state to grant women suffrage, election day was more orderly and less drunken than the time when voting had been exclusively a male activity. 65 These arguments and others did not sway conservative male legislators who believed that women's suffrage would destroy the home. Liberal male legislators often opposed women's suffrage because they feared women would support reactionary Catholic candidates. In 1912, Argentina passed a law granting universal male suffrage; women had to wait until 1947 for the same right.

The First International Feminist Congress of Buenos Aires concluded on a note of enthusiasm, but with a realization of the long struggle ahead. Delegates pledged to work for the betterment of women's and children's legal status and living conditions. They also decided to meet three years later in Chile to evaluate their progress. [66] The ideas expressed during this congress reflected the eclectic nature of Argentine feminist thought, which drew on the European Enlightenment, the Generation of 1837, nineteenth-century liberalism, and European socialism. Feminists also based their actions on a belief in women's moral superiority that would enable them to cleanse the world or war, poverty, and prostitution.

The years immediately following the centennial did not live up to the delegates' high expectations for legislative and moral victories. A number of groups dedicated to suffrage and civil rights for women started up, only to dissolve within a year or two because of discouragement from lack of widespread support. [67] During World War I feminist activity waned in Argentina, as all eyes focused on the fighting in Europe. In the United States and Europe feminist leaders, for the most part, also let women's rights take second place to the war effort. For the first time in history large numbers of women poured into the factory labor force while the men fought. Countless other women worked for the International Red Cross as nurses and volunteers at home or at the front. This massive demonstration of women's patriotism and ability to perform men's work helped women throughout the world to gain leverage for their struggle for basic rights. In Europe and the United States feminists immediately pointed out that now there were no excuses for delaying women's suffrage and other essential civil rights. [68]

Argentine feminists renewed their struggle for civil equality in November 1918, when Dr. Julieta Lanteri-Renshaw founded the National Feminist Union, an organization dedicated to women's political and civil emancipation. This group launched an active program of speeches, lectures, and publications to advertise their causes. The following year Dr. Lanteri ran as an unofficial candidate for the National Congress. Although she had no real chance of gaining a seat, her campaign brought many women's issues into the public arena again. In 1920, Lanteri's group sponsored a mock general and municipal election in Buenos Aires. Approximately three thousand women registered, with the majority declaring party affiliations with leftist leanings. For some observers, the small turnout indicated that women did not really want suffrage, and for others the leftist preferences proved that women based their decisions on emotion rather than reason. [69]

The indefatigable feminist Elvira Rawson de Dellepiane spearheaded the formation of the Women's Rights Association, which welcomed all women regardless of their religious or political affiliations or class background. The main prerequisite for membership was a desire to fight for women's rights, particularly civil rights. This group claimed a membership of eleven thousand. [70] Both the National Feminist Union and the Women's Rights Association were able to benefit from a frequently supportive press and a lecture series on women's rights held at the respectable Peoples' Institute of Lectures. In addition, the administration of Hipólito Irigoyen gave at least lip service to the improvement of women's civil status. Moreover, the Argentine desire to appear progressive by imitating the United States and Europe also must have influenced many politicians to view with favor certain major reforms in the Civil Code.

Even though several legislators had presented proposals to reform the Civil Code between 1918 and 1926, these were sidetracked into committees for further consideration. [71] By 1926, finding legitimate excuses not to grant women civil rights became increasingly more difficult to justify, because large numbers of women worked outside the home and more than ever were receiving secondary and higher education. [72] Stalwarts who refused to recognize the expanded roles of women in Argentine life, which were best demonstrated in the 1914 census and interim reports on the nation's vital statistics, remained adamant in their convictions that women belonged in the home with no legal rights and under male tutelage. [73] In August 1926, after much stalling, the joint Senate and Chamber of Deputies' Committee studying the proposed revisions to the Civil Code issued a favorable report. [74] When the historic bill became law on 22 September, Argentina took its first significant step toward emancipating its married women from the legal status of minors.

The major provisions of this bill gave women the right to their own earnings; the ability to inherit in any amount; the option, if married, to form any part of a civil, commercial, or cooperative association; and the nonresponsibility for their husband's debts, and vice versa. The revised Civil Code did not include all the provisions that feminists would have liked, but it was an improvement over the past. The law still considered the husband as the administrator of the conjugal property. If a woman wanted to share in this authority, she had to apply for it through a legal procedure; by 1929 only 522 women had done so. [75] This lack of interest could be attributed to a combination of factors, such as the relatively small numbers of women with enough education to know their legal rights and, perhaps even more important, most women's psychological dependency on their mates to manage important family matters such as finances. Nevertheless, the press and other vocal groups declared the new civil code to be an indication of Argentina's progressiveness. The long, frustrating battle for suffrage and other basic rights that Argentine women would wage, with little success, in the following years demonstrated the tenacity of traditional ideas about women's proper sphere.

During the period 1860 to 1926 philanthropy, education, and feminism each offered Argentine women opportunities for individual growth and participation in the country's social and economic life. The philanthropic tradition, as established by the Society of Beneficence, provided a basis for women's involvement in essential social services. The Argentine public school system, even with its many flaws, offered most young women their best opportunity to improve their minds and to acquire skills allowing them to become at least partially self-supporting. The country's early commitment to female education produced groups of women anxious to achieve political, legal, and economic parity with men. Many of these educated women also utilized their abilities and zeal to work toward the eradication of social ills, particularly those affecting women and children. Feminism, both socialist and bourgeois, offered these women a framework in which to place their activities.

Argentine feminists failed to create a solid front by not integrating women from all classes into their movement. They put too much faith in the power of law and reforms to change age-old customs and deep-seated psychological attitudes toward women. Their tendency to accentuate the moral and cleansing characteristics of women served to limit women to their traditional spheres and allowed men not to deal with them as equals in life's battles. The women's proclivity to act with moderation and in a ladylike manner in order to prove that feminists retained their womanly qualities reduced their effectiveness when the issue called for a show of force to emphasize their seriousness.

But hindsight, which always offers the best vantage point for critical appraisal, often has a tendency to ignore the positive. The Argentine feminist movement did not claim sufficient membership or power to sway the mainstream of life, but it did contribute to making the nation aware of the debasing legal and political status of women and the ghastly conditions in which many lived and labored. The movement's most significant victory was the passage of the 1926 reforms to the Civil Code, but lesser-known pieces of legislation regulating working hours and conditions for women and children reflected feminist influence. The demands of the early Argentine feminist movement anticipated some of the accomplishments of the Peronist feminist movement in the 1940s, such as suffrage and better pay. For the individual woman who chose to dedicate herself to this cause and even for the woman who only flirted with it temporarily, the feminist movement offered a sense of self-pride and a feeling of commitment to the betterment of society.

Notes

1. James R. Scobie, *Argentina: A City and a Nation*, 2d ed. (New York: Oxford University Press, 1971), 112-216, passim.

2. Arthur P. Whitaker, *Latin America and the Enlightenment* (New York: D. Appleton-Century, 1942).

3. José Luis Romero, *A History of Argentine Political Thought*, trans. Thomas F. McGann (Stanford: Stanford University Press, 1963), pp. 36-58. For ideas on women in a Buenos Aires newspaper during the late eighteenth century, see Mendelson's essay (chap. 7) in this volume.

4. S. Madrid Páez, *Sociedad de Beneficencia de la Capital: Su misión y sus obras* (Buenos Aires: Talleres Gráficos del Asilo de Huérfanos, 1923). The Society of Beneficence had a continuous history until 1948 except during the years 1838 to 1852, when

Juan Manuel de Rosas halted the organization's activities by withholding funding as part of an austerity program. When the Society of Beneficence resumed its activities in 1852, it entered into an era of rapid expansion of its social welfare services. In 1948, Juan Domingo Perón ordered the Society of Beneficence to place its institutions and funds under complete governmental control and to cease all other activities.

5. Romero, *History of Political Thought*, pp. 126-64.

6. Juan B. Alberdi, *Obras completas de Juan Bautista Alberdi*, 8 vols. (Buenos Aires: La Tribuna Nacional, 1886-87), 8: 396-97.

7. Mary Mann translated many of Sarmiento's works into English, interviewed applicants for teaching positions in Argentina, and sustained a long correspondence with him about new educational ideas and practices. Sarmiento also admired Elizabeth Peabody, a sister of Mary Mann, who trained kindergarten teachers in Cambridge, Massachusetts. Some of the women whom she taught helped to establish public kindergartens in Argentina.

8. Domingo Faustino Sarmiento, *Obras completas de Domingo Faustino Sarmiento*, 53 vols. (Buenos Aires: Editorial Luz del Día, 1948-56), 12: 139-60.

9. Argentine Republic, Consejo Nacional de Educación, *Programas y horarios para las escuelas comunes de la capital federal sancionadas por el Consejo Nacional de Educación* (Buenos Aires: Martín Biedma & Hijo, 1901).

10. Charles Henry Schutter, "The Development of Education in Argentina, Chile and Uruguay" (Ph.D. diss., University of Chicago, 1943), p. 65. See also Alice Houston Luiggi, *Sixty-five Valiants* (Gainesville: University of Florida Press, 1965), p. 28.

11. Scobie, *Argentina*, p. 154.

12. Domingo F. Sarmiento, *Ideas pedagógicas de Domingo Faustino Sarmiento* (Buenos Aires: Talleres Gráficos Consejo Nacional de Educación, 1938), p. 22.

13. Luiggi, *Sixty-five Valiants*, pp. 17-18.

14. Ibid., pp. 50-67, passim.

15. Juan Manuel Chavarría, *La escuela normal y la cultura argentina* (Buenos Aires: El Ateneo, 1947), p. 362.

16. Sarmiento, *Ideas*, p. 39, See Sarmiento, *Obras completas*, 47: 124-26. At the First Pedagogical Congress in Argentina held in 1878, Clementina C. de Alio, one of the only two women to speak from the podium, reinforced Sarmiento's ideas in this statement: "... que la naturaleza le ha dado a la mujer una función docente desde que la ha hecho mujer; y, por consiguiente, que se debe educar a la madre, para que, a su vez, pueda educar a sus hijos" ("nature has given woman a natural ability to teach, which is why she was made a woman; and consequently, one must educate the mother in order for her to educate her children").

17. Argentine Republic, *Estudios generales secundarios y normales: Programas de pedogogía, ejercicios físicos, trabajo manual, labores de mano, economía doméstica y música* (Buenos Aires: Publicación Oficial, 1901), p. 19.

18. These types of courses were seen as necessary to make female students better wives and mothers. Schools encouraged their students to participate in the activities of the Mother's Club and its annual event, Children's Week, as a means to reinforce the importance of good child care. Since 1917 the Mother's Club had been dedicated to the struggle against infant mortality and had tried to encourage more modern and hygienic child care practices. The club operated a clinic to which mothers could bring their infants for advice and care. Club volunteers made home visits to see if clients followed the

doctors' advice. See Club de Madres, *Memoria y balance 1923-1925: Lista de socios y adherentes* (Buenos Aires: Vda. de Molinari e Hijos, 1926), pp. 3-5.

19. Sarmiento, *Ideas*, p. 5.

20. D. F. Sarmiento, *Páginas confidenciales: Sus luchas, sus pasiones, sus triunfos, las mujeres en su vida* (Buenos Aires: Editorial Elevación, 1944), p. 328.

21. Luiggi, *Sixty-five Valiants*, pp. 28, 114-22, passim.

22. Shutter, "Development of Education," pp. 59, 80-83. Publicly supported schools in Buenos Aires were nationalized in 1880. In 1881 the national government established the National Council of Education, which administered and directed all primary schools.

23. Argentine Republic, *Censo general de educación levantado el 23 de mayo de 1909*, 3 vols. (Buenos Aires: Oficina Meteorológica Argentina, 1910), 3: 29.

24. Shutter, "Development of Education," p. 100.

25. Argentine Republic, Ministerio de Justicia e Instrucción Pública, *Memoria presentada al Honorable congreso nacional correspondiente al año de 1911; Anexos de Instrucción Pública* (Buenos Aires: Talleres Gráficos de la Penitenciaria Nacional, 1912), 2: 477.

26. Katherine Dreier, *Five Months in the Argentine from a Woman's Point of View, 1918-1919* (New York: Frederic Fairchild Sherman, 1920), pp. 118-20. This fascinating book described the visit of a North American feminist to Buenos Aires.

27. Argentine Republic, *Memoria 1912*, 3: 541.

28. Dreier, *Five Months*, p. 120. The Women's Exchange in Buenos Aires was founded in the 1880s by a group of North American women interested in affording women a place where they could find part-time work. One of the founding members, Clara Armstrong, was a well-known educator and headed a variety of schools in Argentina.

29. Argentine Republic, *Memoria 1912*, 3: 402-7, 534-36.

30. Manuel Gálvez, *Nacha Regules*, trans. Leo Ongley (London: J. M. Dent & Sons, 1923), pp. 137-58. In this classic urban novel about the demimonde in Buenos Aires, Manuel Gálvez had the madam of a top house of prostitution describe the bad working conditions and long hours for sales clerks that forced many into prostitution. United States Department of Commerce, Bureau of Foreign and Domestic Commerce, Misc. Series no. 68, *Wearing Apparel in Argentina* (Washington, D.C.: Government Printing Office, 1918), pp. 38-44.

31. Dreier, *Five Months*, p. 122.

32. Tomás Roberto Fillol, *Social Factors in Economic Development: The Argentine Case* (Cambridge: M.I.T. Press, 1961), pp. 8-20.

33. *La Prensa*, 21 June 1910, p. 9. In an article entitled "El caso de la doctora Barreda," one could clearly see the problems that would arise as more women became professionals. Dr. Barreda's law diploma had been approved by the Supreme Court; but because she was a woman, she could never become a magistrate or, if she married, she would have to receive her husband's permission to practice under the current civil code.

34. Alfredo Colmo, *Derechos civiles de la mujer ante la experiencia* (Buenos Aires: Talleres Gráficos Tudor, 1929).

35. Luis Herrera, "Liceo nacional de señoritas de la capital," *Boletín de la Instrucción Pública* 12 (May 1913): 367.

36. Argentine Republic, *Memoria 1911*, 2: 108-9.

37. Herrera, "Liceo nacional," p. 365.

38. Argentine Republic, Ministerio del Trabajo, Oficina Nacional de la Mujer, Dirección Nacional de Recursos Humanos, *Evolución de la mujer en las profesiones liberales en Argentina, años 1900-1965*, 2d ed. (Buenos Aires: 1970), p. 82. This survey showed that in 1900 only one woman had matriculated at the university level. Between 1901 and 1910 this situation changed very slightly, with numbers of two or three in medicine and no more than seven in architecture. Other academic disciplines claimed fewer women recruits. Only after 1916 was there any clear increase in the number of women in Argentine universities, with thirty-eight women in medicine and more women entering fields such as law, pharmacy, and education.

39. Herrera, "Liceo nacional," p. 365.

40. Argentine Republic, *Memoria 1926*, 2: 195.

41. Angel Giménez, *Antología antialcohólica* (Buenos Aires: La Vanguardia, 1933), pp. 78-79.

42. Argentine Republic, *Memoria 1926*, 2: 194-200.

43. Enrique Dickmann, *Recuerdos de un militante socialista* (Buenos Aires: La Vanguardia, 1949), p. 102.

44. Hobart Spalding, *La clase trabajadora argentina: Documentos para su historia, 1890-1912* (Buenos Aires: Ed. Galerna, 1970), pp. 268-75.

45. Lucila Lavie, *Trayectoria de la condición social de las mujeres argentinas* (Santa Fe, Argentina: Extensión Universitaria, 1947), p. 8. Elvira Rawson de Dellepiane was one of Argentina's first female doctors. Her varied and long career, which she devoted to the lives of women and children, included serving as professor in hygiene and child care at the National Home for Military Orphans, annexed to National Girls' High School No. 4 (1920-22); organizer and director of the first vacation home for chronically ill women teachers and students (1916); medical inspector for the National Department of Hygiene (1907-18) and for the National Council of Education (1919-34); and representative for Argentina at a number of congresses on children's health. For further details on her career, see *Quién es quién en la Argentina*, 2d ed. (Buenos Aires: Guillermo Kraft, 1941), p. 203.

46. Alfredo Palacios, *Por las mujeres y los niños que trabajan* (Valencia: F. Sempere, 1910), pp. 6-12, 59.

47. Juan Carlos Rébora, *La familia chilena y la familia argentina* (Buenos Aires: Tomás Palumbo, 1938), pp. 50-80.

48. Alicia Moreau de Justo was a writer, professor, and physician who utilized her talents on the behalf of women, children, and socialism. Her name was always prominent in any organization working for the rights of women, such as the Feminist Center and the National Feminist Union. Cecilia Grierson was Argentina's first woman doctor, having graduated in 1889, and the founder of the National Women's Council, of which she was vice-president for many years. Julieta Lanteri-Renshaw was Argentina's third woman doctor.

49. Clodomiro Cordero, *La sociedad argentina y la mujer* (Buenos Aires: Alfa y Omega, 1916), p. 38. See also *La Prensa*, 5 September 1926, p. 12.

50. *La Prensa*, 12 August 1926, p. 14.

51. Dreier, *Five Months*, p. 251.

52. *Cargos a la Comisión Directiva del Consejo Nacional de Mujeres* (Buenos Aires: Talleres Gráficos Mentruyt, 1908). This pamphlet-like publication recorded the corre-

spondence dealing with the split between the National Council of Women and the Argentine Association of University Women that led to each group's holding its own congress on women's issues rather than participating in a joint session, as originally planned.

53. *La Prensa*, 20 April 1910, p. 5.

54. *La Prensa*, 10 May 1910, p. 11.

55. Celia La Palma de Emery, *Discursos y conferencias: Acción pública y privada en favor de la mujer y del niño* (Buenos Aires: Alfa y Omega, 1910), pp. 203-4.

56. *La Prensa*, 13 May 1910, p. 11.

57. *Cargos a la Comisión directiva*, p. 12.

58. *Primer Congreso Femenino Internacional de la República Argentina* (Buenos Aires: Fallica y Escoffier, 1910), pp. 23-29.

59. Ibid., pp. 5-12.

60. Ibid., pp. 13-17.

61. Ibid., pp. 305-6.

62. Ibid., pp. 9-10, 301-3.

63. *La Prensa*, 22 May 1910, p. 8.

64. *Primer Congreso*, pp. 428-29.

65. Ibid., pp. 404-9.

66. *La Prensa*, 24 May 1910, p. 9.

67. Dreier, *Five Months*, p. 237.

68. Eleanor Flexner, *Century of Struggle: The Woman's Rights Movement in the United States* (New York: Atheneum, 1971), 276-324, passim.

69. Alicia Moreau de Justo, *La mujer y la democracia* (Buenos Aires: El Ateneo, 1945), pp. 7-13. See also Ernesto Quesada, *El feminismo argentino: Tendencias y orientaciones* (Buenos Aires: L. J. Rosso, 1920), pp. 7-8.

70. Lily Sosa de Newton, *Las argentinas de ayer a hoy* (Buenos Aires: Librería y Edit. L. V. Zanetti, 1967), p. 149.

71. *La Prensa*, 22 May 1918, p. 6. *La Prensa* gave reports on the actions of the Chamber of Deputies and the Senate, when in session. When the issue of increased civil rights for women came up, there always seemed to be more important topics to debate or there were not enough legislators for a quorum.

72. *La Prensa*, 13 August 1926, p. 11.

73. *La Prensa*, 14 August 1926, p. 11.

74. *La Prensa*, 11 August 1926, p. 13.

75. Colmo, *Derechos civiles*.

10

June E. Hahner

The nineteenth-century feminist press and women's rights in Brazil

The existence of a women's rights movement in nineteenth-century Brazil may surprise readers who are familiar with the traditional view that women in Brazil, to an even greater extent than their sisters in Spanish America, still suffered from centuries of Moorish seclusion and obscurity. As this essay will disclose, during the last half of that century some Brazilian women advanced arguments and undertook feminist activities similar to those of better-known feminists in the United States. During those decades a number of newspapers edited by women appeared in the cities of south central Brazil. Unlike fashion journals or major Brazilian newspapers, those now-forgotten periodicals preached women's rights.[1] Starting with calls for improved education and additional respect for women, some then supported changes in women's legal position and careers outside the home. Several finally advocated the right to vote.[2] These feminist newspapers both fostered and reflected changes in the status and aspirations of Brazilian women and represented a growing degree of consciousness among some of them. The twentieth-century women's suffrage movement and the emergence of the middle- and upper-class urban woman into the job market were not phenomena arising out of a historical vacuum. Nor did they represent an abrupt break with the past. Part of the lost nineteenth-century female past in Brazil can be reconstructed through the feminist press.

According to the common stereotype of the Brazilian patriarchal family, the authoritarian husband, surrounded by slave concubines, dominated his children and submissive wife. She developed into an indolent, passive creature, kept at home, who bore numerous children and abused the Negro slaves. Various foreign travelers' accounts support this image. For example, John Luccock, a British merchant, caustically commented in 1808 on the premature aging and increasing bad temper and fatness of Rio de Janeiro's upper-class women, which he attributed to habits of reclusion and indolence.[3] Nevertheless, the stereotype of the guarded, pure female was not universally valid. Actual behavior varied according to class. Lower-class women knew greater personal freedom as well as harsh physical labor. Even among the elite, not all women were confined to the private sphere of the home and excluded from the public sphere assigned to men, as in the case of the active widows running *fazendas*.[4] In the cities, elite women who remained largely secluded in their homes often managed sizable establishments, full of relatives, retainers, and slaves. Such women could exercise influence indirectly, behind the scenes, on men occupying formal positions in the public sphere. However, the authority of the husband and father remained paramount, and the wife was subject to him.[5]

Nineteenth-century foreign visitors reported changes slowly occurring in the lives of women of the urban elite. After the arrival of the Portuguese court in Rio de Janeiro in 1808, Brazilian upper-class women began to follow more European modes of behavior. According to two Bavarian scientists, Johann B. von Spix and Karl F. P. von Martius, women participated "in the change which the removal of the court hither has occasioned and are now more frequently seen in the theatre, and in the open air."[6] By mid-century, Daniel Paris Kidder and James C. Fletcher, two American Protestant missionaries, noted an increased tendency of upper-class women in Rio de Janeiro to venture out to parties, church, and the theater. But like John Luccock, decades earlier, they contended that these women quickly grew stout from a lack of outdoor exercise and were constantly surrounded by slaves.[7] An American naturalist traveling in the Amazon, Herbert H. Smith, reported the decreasing seclusion of upper-class women in the city of Belém, but not in the smaller towns of the area.[8]

In the mid-nineteenth century, Brazil was still a highly stratified society, with an economy dependent on a slave labor system. The seven million inhabitants of this sparsely settled country of three million square miles were concentrated on the coast. Most of the population lived on the land, farming with crude techniques. Through the first half of the nineteenth century, most of the towns remained small, sleepy places, with muddy streets frequented by pack mules, pigs, and chickens, although they also served as social, religious, and market centers for nearby areas. Methods of transportation were rudimentary and manufacturing industries practically nonexistent.[9]

Changes of all kinds, including those which would affect the lives of upper-class urban women, came more quickly in the second half of the nineteenth century. European technological advances were exported to Brazil, as to many other countries. The advent of the railroad, the steamboat, and the telegraph stimulated the rapid growth of many urban centers, both in physical area and in population. By the end of the century Rio de Janeiro was no longer principally a commercial and political-social center, but an industrial center as well, as befitted the nation's major consumer market and financial center. Regional imbalances within Brazil increased. The south became dominant, São Paulo in particular becoming prosperous and influential. Social organization in the south underwent rapid changes, with increasing numbers of wage-earning laborers both on the coffee plantations and in the cities, growing European immigration, and agriculture based on small farms in the southernmost states. [10]

While educational opportunities for girls generally remained limited even in the cities, some improvements occurred during the second half of the nineteenth century. [11] But only a small proportion of Brazil's population ever became literate. Education was largely the prerogative of those entitled to its benefits by birth or position. According to the Brazilian census of 1872, Brazil had a total population of 10,112,061. Only 1,012,097 free men, 550,981 free women, 958 slave men, and 445 slave women were able to read and write. [12] In 1873 the empire contained merely 5,077 primary schools, public and private, having a total of 114,014 male and 46,246 female pupils. [13] In wealthier families children were often educated at home rather than in the frequently poorly run schools.

Girls' education remained backward compared to boys'. Even women's reading, according to Luccock, "was not to extend beyond the prayerbooks, because it would be useless to a woman, nor were they to write lest, as was sagely remarked, they should make a bad use of the art." [14] But slowly the idea of schooling for girls was added to the older idea of domestic education, although not an education identical to that given boys. With time, rich girls not only learned to prepare cakes and sweets and to sew and embroider, but they also could study French and piano, so as to provide more charming and agreeable company on social occasions. While Kidder and Fletcher in the mid-nineteenth century believed the number of schools for girls was increasing, they held that "in eight cases out of ten, the Brazilian father thinks that he has done his duty when he has sent his daughter for a few years to a fashionable school kept by some foreigner: at thirteen or fourteen he withdraws her, believing that her education is finished." [15] As Elizabeth Agassiz, wife of the American naturalist, observed with dismay, "the next step in [the Brazilian girls'] life is marriage." [16]

The first legislation concerning women's education came in 1827, but the law admitted girls only to elementary schools, not to institutes of advanced learning. The stress remained on the needle, not the pen. Relatively few public shcools for girls were ever set up, and the low salaries offered teachers proved generally unattractive. An 1834 amendment led to far lower-paid and less trained women to teach girls. The inadequacies of both public and private shcoolteachers prompted the creation of normal schools to train primary schoolteachers. Although the first school appeared in Niterói in 1835, followed by Bahia in 1836, normal schools remained few in number, small in enrollment, and precarious in position until the last years of the empire. For example, the São Paulo normal school, established for boys in 1846, added a section for girls thirty years later. By the end of the nineteenth century, these few available urban professional schools were generally coeducational and not only prepared girls for teaching careers, but also provided one of the few available opportunities for them to continue their education.[17] However, many girls still received their scanty education at home or in private schools, some religiously oriented and some run by foreign women.

The slow growth in education provided a larger audience for newspapers and magazines during the second half of the nineteenth century, including a few daring periodicals edited by women, beginning with *O Journal das Senhoras*.[18] On 1 January 1852, the first issue of *O Jornal das Senhoras* appeared in Rio de Janeiro, edited by Joana Paula Manso de Noronha, an Argentine living apart from her husband (a Portuguese violinist and composer) and teaching school in Rio, where she collaborated on Brazilian newspapers and published several literary works. In the introductory editorial she stated her intentions to work for "social betterment and the moral emancipation of women." She recognized what a novelty it was for a woman to edit a newspaper in Brazil. People would inquire as to "what kind of a Hydra-headed monster it would be." She knew that to "speak of the rights, the mission of women," and their education would cause others to say that "this is not the kind of reading matter that should be permitted inside a family's home." But God gave woman a soul and made her "equal to man" and "his companion." Women were not inferior to men in intelligence. Moreover, the nineteenth century was the "century of knowledge," and South America should not remain apart and stationary. Like later feminist newspaper editors in Brazil, Joana Paulo Manso de Noronha believed strongly in progress and looked to the examples set by European nations and by the United States, which she had visited in 1846. Since many members of the Brazilian elite favored progress in theory and responded to foreign leadership in other matters, she argued that Brazil must not remain apart "when the entire world marches toward progress and moves toward the moral and material improvement of society."[19]

While Dona Joana denied raising a standard of rebellion or being utopian and instead wished to use persuasion as her weapon, she felt obliged to blame men and male egoism for the unfortunate condition in which women found themselves. For her, the moral emancipation of women must include "the just enjoyment of their rights, of which they have been robbed and disinherited by *brutal male egoism*, because men have physical force and because they are still not convinced that an angel will be more useful to them than a doll." Women's education must be improved, and men must cease considering women "as their property."[20]

The picture that emerges from Dona Joana's articles of the way in which Brazilian men regarded women is not dissimilar to that painted by foreign travelers. Decades earlier, John Luccock had also perceived Brazilian women as "regarded by the men as dolls, or spoiled children."[21] Like women in other countries during the nineteenth century, including the United States and Great Britain, Brazilian women might well complain that they were not taken seriously. A women was considered modest and proper only when "always looking at the ground and responding in monosyllables." But the problem went deeper. According to Dona Joana, some Brazilian men would even deny a woman a soul. Many Brazilian men thought women came into the world "only to serve as a *propagation machine*." And they commonly blamed women for "all human distresses and imperfections."[22]

Men and women viewed marriage very differently. According to *O Jornal das Senhoras*, for a woman marriage was "the goal, the purpose of her life," since love was the only hope for her existence. But love, the greatest thing in the world, could not exist between master and slave. In marriage women always found deception, unbearable tyranny, or abandonment. In contrast, for most men marriage was just a "means for satisfying a desire, a whim, or simply a way to alter their civil status. Or to assure their fortune." Hence, a man would say "my wife—with the same vocal intonation that he uses to say—*my horse, my boots*, etc.," for all were "household instruments he used," unworthy of his attention. *O Jornal das Senhoras* held that until men ceased to "consider women as their property, we will not have accomplished anything."[23] The problem then, according to Joana Paula Manso de Noronha, was to convince men, not women, of "the injustice with which [women] are treated," since women "were perfectly well aware of male tyranny." Through its entreaties and arguments, *O Jornal das Senhoras* attempted to persuade Brazilian men of the mid-nineteenth century to elevate their women to that position which later writers often stated they had actually occupied. The image of the secluded, passive female has often been accompanied by that of the glorification of the woman as the mother of Brazil's sons; and it has been argued that even though she was denied economic and political influence outside the home, she was very influential within the confines of the family circle. The fervent pleas of the outspoken, determined editor of *O Jornal das Senhoras*—that men see their wives as the focal personality around whom all the members of the family should group themselves spiritually, bound by sentiment—are evidence that their "unknown mission" often went unrecognized.[24] Again, image did not match reality.

While some later women would find a position on a pedestal uncomfortable, it evidently would have been a marked improvement for many women of the mid-nineteenty-century Brazilian elite. If they could mount the pedestal, they would elevate their position and would no longer be treated brutally or as possessions, be just ignored or be relegated to the kitchen.

The pathway up to the pedestal, to becoming an angel rather than a doll, led through the family, with an assist from Jesus of Nazareth. He "was the first who raised you from your ignominy! He was the first who revealed your mission to the world." While some later women might thing that the Virgin Mary cast too deep a shadow across their lives, *O Jornal das Senhoras* attempted to enlist her assistance and that of her son in its efforts to improve women's lot. But perhaps of more immediate importance was the continued appeal to male self-interest as a means of ameliorating the position of women. After all, men were concerned for the future of their sons, and that must include their education. The way in which women could "have any influence other than that over pots" or "a mission beyond needlework" was through "the education of their children," for the children learned their first lessons and their morality from their mothers. This noble task of educating children gave women value. Moreover, one way to change men's minds was by molding those of boys. Mothers could help women by "eradicating this fatal prejudice in their son's souls, this idea of an unwarranted superiority." To fulfill their duties, women had to be educated and treated with respect. As Dona Joana retorted to a male critic of her journal, "the more learned a woman is, the more amply she will fulfill her sacred mission as wife and mother."[25]

In addition to facing male hostility, which did not deter Joana Paula Manso de Noronha from her "perilous course," an early feminist periodical like *O Jornal das Senhoras* also had to confront the timidity of its readers and would-be supporters. It encountered both to a greater degree than would its successors. In its first issue Dona Joana called for collaborators, urging them not to "fear giving vent" to their thoughts, for she promised to be the "discrete confidante" of their "literary products," publishing their contributions anonymously, and she strongly reassured them that they "should not fear to entrust these to her." Some of her readers, women well enough educated to translate works from foreign languages, reacted to her novel invitation to put their words into print with enthusiasm, though others showed hesitation and trepidation. One reader, who had learned of the journal through an announcement in a major Rio newspaper and who had to ask her father to order the paper, expressed her "gratitude" to the editor. It was as if "I were very thirsty and hot, and you offered me ice cream." She complained that women in Brazil were "almost passive," but *O Jornal das Senhoras* "came to open a field of activity" in which they could exercise their talents and "escape [their] state of vegetation." However, like other readers who offered to contribute to the journal, she wished to remain anonymous. Even the author of the section on fashions showed herself to be very much afraid of possible ridicule and, admitting that she lacked the editor's courage, requested that her anonymity be maintained. [26] Within four years some change came, and a few women signed their initials to their writings. Some male contributors also appeared, giving their full names.

Despite the editor's efforts and those of her collaborators, *O Jornal das Senhoras* could not survive on exhortations or feminine literary attempts alone. Fashion prints from Paris and embroidery designs served as key means of attracting subscribers. In fact, the subtitle of the periodical read: "Fashions, literature, fine arts, theater and criticism." Before the newspaper ceased publication on 30 December 1855, four years after its inception, stories, poetry, fashion, and social news would take increasing precedence over the preaching of women's rights, especially since "compelling reasons" obliged Joana Paula Manso de Noronha to leave the editorship six months after she began in order "to attend to other duties." [27]

Dona Joana lacked private fortune and, no doubt, had found it financially impossible to continue as editor of *O Jornal das Senhoras*. In order to save the newspaper, she turned it over to Vilante Atabalipa Ximenes de Bivar e Vellasco, the widow of João Antonio Boaventura Vellasco and the well-educated daughter of Diogo Soares de Silva de Bivar, member of the Imperial Council and founder and director of the Brazilian Dramatic Conservatory in Rio de Janeiro. Before collaborating on *O Jornal das Senhoras*, Dona Violante had translated French and Italian comedies, only one of which appeared in print, and had reviewed some plays for the Dramatic Conservatory, which had the power to license and censure them. Moreover, she probably was the hesitant author of the section on fashions in *O Jornal das Senhoras* who learned to be more resolute and courageous. [28] During her year as editor, the newspaper continued to defend women, much more so than it would under her successor, Gervasia Nunezia Pires dos Santos, a contributor who had been signing herself just Gervasia P. and whose husband was able to aid the journal. [29]

As editor, Violante Atabalipa Ximenes de Bivar e Vellasco stressed the emotional superiority of women and their numerous spiritual qualities, for which they should be venerated. Using arguments similar to those employed by her predecessor, she contended "that which can be venerated can very rightly and reasonably be FREE." Just like men, women were "capable of intellectual labors." Nor did Dona Violante neglect calls to progress nor the examples set by more advanced countries. She also appealed to man's self-interest as well as to his need to do his moral duty, arguing that when men deny women education, they are endangering society and their own existence. If men entrusted their children to their wives, they should educate and free the women also. *O Jornal das Senhoras* attempted to utilize woman's role as mother in order to raise her position. A "well-educated woman replete with the religiosity that is always natural to her" would better exercise "her sacred functions as wife and mother." [30]

While Dona Violante had stated her intention to "follow the path that

[Dona Joana] had traced in editing this newspaper," her enthusiasm and priorities differed. Dona Violante employed the figure of the Virgin Mary more than Dona Joana had in her efforts to help the Brazilian woman mount the pedestal and become a venerated symbol of love. Despite the Brazilian woman's aptitude for education and her right to freedom, *O Jornal das Senhoras* projected an image of her as a gentle, passive figure, for she was "this saintly companion, this sister of Mary, simple and humble." Christ, who deeply loved his mother, had held her up as an archetypal woman, and he "intended woman to be held and valued by humanity as a privileged being." And Mary remained woman's advocate.[31] Perhaps only after women had mounted the pedestal and were accepted as symbols of Christianity and love, made in Mary's image, could they progress to becoming equal human beings absolved from the need for all to marry and be viewed only as wives and mothers.

As ideas such as those advocated by *O Jornal das Senhoras* gained wider acceptance, they could be used to help improve the position of women. Later editors of feminist newspapers did not call so insistently for a place on the pedestal. They assumed that womanhood, especially motherhood, was respected and enjoyed a somewhat elevated position. They employed such esteem in their efforts to help women move beyond a restricted family circle and to improve their position in the outer world. Perhaps it would be easier for an angel than for a doll to become an active, equal human being. But the pathway remained a difficult one for either to tread.

While the contributors to *O Jornal das Senhoras* had demonstrated great timidity, they had taken a small step along the road toward overcoming their fears and had become more conscious of the problems they faced. A further awakening, and a different method for facilitating it, became evident with the publication of *O Bello Sexo* in Rio de Janeiro in 1862, less than a decade after the demise of *O Jornal das Senhoras*.[32] No longer would contributors feel the need for complete anonymity, although they seemed reluctant to sign their full names to their writings despite the editor's insistence that no unsigned articles would be published. Nor, perhaps more important, did they wish to remain unknown to one another. In fact. a group of women met once a week to discuss items to print in *O Bello Sexo*. Their number increased steadily, from ten at the first session to thirty-seven by the fifth. Through their discussions, new viewpoints and ideas could emerge, and women who had acquired a secondary education—like the editor, Julia de Albuquerque Sandy Aguiar, and those she called upon to aid her—could express themselves more freely.[33]

By present-day standards or those of *O Jornal das Senhoras* in its early months, neither the language employed by the editor and contributors to *O Bello Sexo* nor their aim of aiding "social progress" and helping to develop women's intelligence and capacities was radical. Even the journal's masthead proclaimed its moderate intentions, as a "Religious Newspaper, of Instruction and Diversion, News and Moderate Criticism." But its mild attitudes and the deference displayed toward both readers and other organs of the press did not suffice for everyone. One man, expounding on his refusal to subscribe to *O Bello Sexo*, claimed that not only had he no time to read it, but the newspaper also lacked sufficient "discretion" and insulted "those whom it aspired to convince." A female reader contended that some women feared that an increase in knowledge and intelligence would damage their rights. [34]

Other women wished change. As one contributor to this short-lived newspaper stated, they wanted to become useful members of society. They opposed a world that kept them busy inventing new fashions, that provided them "with so many gatherings to tire us out gossiping instead of working for others," or that expelled them from secondary schools when they had "barely begun to read, scribble, add, subtract, and multiply" in order to attend parties and look out windows and "sleep until ten or eleven o'clock in the morning." Such women did not want to let society "always distract us from what is more useful, though more difficult." While they still wished to marry well and be happy, they also saw the need to "regenerate" their sex and to assure all its members "moral and physical liberty." Then they could help remedy society's imperfections, a slow, difficult task necessitating patience and goodness, not excesses. [35] For such women, charity work outside the home would constitute a step forward. Choosing a motto of "Religion, Work, Literature and Charity," they assigned the hoped-for profits from *O Bello Sexo* to be given in the name of their sex to the Imperial Sociedade Amante da Instrucção, a charity for orphans. [36] But their newspaper died quickly, leaving no immediate successors.

New journals founded by women appeared in the 1870s. In 1873 a forthright and outspoken school teacher, Francisca Senhorinha da Motta Diniz, published her first newspaper, *O Sexo Feminino*, in Campanha, Minas Gerais. [37] The next year both *O Domingo*, [38] edited and owned by Violante Atabalipa Ximenes de Bivar e Vellasco, and *Jornal das Damas* [39] appeared in Rio de Janeiro, followed by Maria Heraclia's *Myosotis* [40] in Recife in 1875, and Amélia Carolina de Silva Couto's incisive *Echo das Damas* [41] in Rio de Janeiro in 1879. Although several women were now publishing feminist journals, an increase over the previous decade, they remained isolated. Only toward the end of the nineteenth century would the number of women editing or writing for such newspapers be sufficiently large for mutual support and intellectual interchange. In the 1870s these women often lacked not only personal contact with one another, but also knowledge of their predecessors and contemporaries. [42]

From the beginning, feminist newspaper publishers like Francisca Senhorinha da Motta Diniz stressed the importance of education for women, both to benefit them and to improve the world. Dona Francisca dedicated *O Sexo Feminino* to "the education, instruction, and emancipation of women"; in it she would "continually fight for the rights of our sex, which up to now have been trampled underfoot by the opposite sex." Instead of directing herself to men, pleading with them to change their attitudes and behavior toward women in their own interests, or repeatedly appealing to the image of the Virgin Mary, as had *O Jornal das Senhoras* two decades earlier, she strove to awaken women to their conditions, needs, and potential. Dona Francisca saw the enemy they were fighting as hiding in the "ignorance of women," which "is determined by the body of knowledge of men." She could not forget the evils promoted by men who considered their wives just "a household utensil," depriving them of education and knowledge of the outside world. But she preferred to attack women's lack of knowledge and awareness. Most lived in ignorance of their rights, even those due them by law. They did not even realize how their husbands might waste their money, leaving them with debts, or abandon them and their children. Now these "meek lambs" must "cease being subjugated" and "always manacled, oppressed, and dominated" by men. They must open their eyes "to the injustices, the control, and the neglect of their rights" of which they were "victims." With education they could recuperate lost rights, raise their children properly, understand their families' business and finances, and be their husbands' companions, not slaves. "With instruction we will attain everything, and we will also break the chains that have choked us since the remote centuries of obscurantism." [43]

Francisca S. da M. Diniz had no doubts as to the abilities and potential achievements of women. They were "endowed with the same mental powers as men, with intellects and minds apt for the cultivation of the arts and sciences, so that they could be useful to the nation and fulfill their mission in society." Not only did Dona Francisca argue that women have "the necessary capacity to learn all sciences," but she also contended that they would surpass men in this area, as they had more of "the needed patience for such disciplines as physics, pharmacy, and medicine." [44]

Just as Francisca S. da M. Diniz inverted traditional beliefs about the differences between men and women in order to assert female superiority in new areas like the sciences, she also utilized the old notion of separate spheres of activities for men and women, long employed to keep women in the home, to carve out additional realms for them. The nurturing and maternal functions could easily be extended beyond the home into the classroom. Dona Francisca declared not only that women made superior primary schoolteachers, but also that this field should be exclusively theirs, thus opening the door to more jobs for women. In turn, some fields, especially those involving brute force or violence, like soldiering, would be left exclusively to men. But Dona Francisca insisted that all other careers be open to women, since they were not inferior to men. Through work and the right education, girls could "acquire the ways and the means of obtaining what was necessary for their subsistence and even for their fortune" and could be "independent of men."[45] Dona Francisca had grasped the essential idea that economic dependence promoted female subjugation and that improved education could help raise women's status.

Society as a whole would also benefit from these changes. Dona Francisca was convinced that Brazilian society would not be "regenerated" until all women had a "complete education." She contended that over "half the evils that oppress" men were due to this neglect of women's education and to "the false supposition that women were no more than old household implements."[46]

Francisca Diniz's faith in the power of education was closely related to her belief in progress. Continually affirming her century to be that of "knowledge," as had Joana Paula Manso de Noronha, she noted "gigantic steps of progress." Those opposed to the "rational emancipation of women" would find themselves "isolated before the progress of the present time." Seeing "a new era of prosperity and justice for our humiliated sex" dawning in different countries Dona Francisca eagerly reported specific examples of female achievements. Like later feminists, she argued that if women in other countries could attend institutions of higher education, they should be permitted to do the same in Brazil. She rhetorically questioned "why our Brazilian empire, which prides itself in being the submissive imitator of Europe and the United States in every advancement, does not pass legislation permitting women to graduate in the fields of knowledge most indispensable in life." "Can it be," she sarcastically inquired, "that the government fears some revolution resulting from feminine knowledge?" Dona Francisca stressed the economic and moral benefits accruing to a country whose women became active participants in national life, an argument that might interest those Brazilians hoping to modernize and develop their homeland. In the United States, her preferred country, which had "sounded the cry of the independence of women," females are "free from the ridiculous prejudices that vex them in older societies, and they are an active element of progress, zealous coparticipants in social improvement and prosperity."[47] While Brazil's women faced a more difficult struggle for their freedom, Dona Francisca remained confident of eventual success.

Other feminist journals, like Violante Atabalipa de Bivar e Vellasco's *O Domingo* and Amelia Carolina da Silva Couto's *Echo das Damas*, defended Brazilian women and their rights with many of the same arguments employed by Francisca Senhorinha da Motta Diniz in *O Sexo Feminino*, although somewhat less forcefully. Dona Violante and Dona Amélia also drew inspiration and evidence of women's capacities from female accomplishments in other countries, including famous women in history. The *Echo das Damas* asserted the United States that provided "examples of the moral and material improvements" reaped by a nation that not only progressed in technology and industry, but also cultivated women's intelligence. Like Dona Francisca and Dona

Amélia, Dona Violante held that a country's progress depended on its women; those peoples not according women their rightful place "would always deserve the epithet of barbarians."[48] With education, Brazilian women could assume their rightful place in the world.

A firm believer in the equality of women and in the benefits and revolutionary changes that education would bring them, Dona Violante protested the barring of women form Brazilian institutions of higher education, as did Dona Francisca and Dona Amélia.[49] When a group of young Brazilians studying at Cornell University took the same position in their student newspaper,[50] Dona Violante hastened to reprint their article in *O Domingo*.[51] These engineering students had observed that the people of the United States "advance with giant strides toward their perfectibility, as they have an inexhaustible treasure of benefits in their women." They opposed the ignorance, pride, and egoism that led men to consider women "inferior in intelligence and discernment."[52] Such male support for the "intellectual emancipation of women" might well please and encourage Dona Violante and other feminists, especially those stressing the need to persuade men as well as to awaken women, and might give them more hope for the future when such young men would play leading roles in Brazil.

Despite her strong defense of women's right to higher education and her own love of the intellectual life, Dona Violante demonstrated greater ambivalence than did Dona Francisca regarding the role of women and the goals of their education. Dona Violante strongly emphasized maternal love and the importance of motherhood and religion. For her, the value of women's education lay in the realm of morality and duty. She did not think in terms of economic survival or of self-realization, although she felt that "the pleasures of study are, perhaps, the only ones that completely fill the soul."[53] Women needed an education equal to that given men in order to educate their children properly and to be good wives.

Perhaps because she was older than Dona Francisca and possessed an independent income, Dona Violante did not connect education and work as strongly. Despite her belief in the equality of women, she envisioned fewer career opportunities for women than did Dona Francisca. Dona Violante envied foreign women, who, unlike Brazilians, could enter medicine, law, journalism, and business, but she still endorsed the field of letters and literature as that in which women could best distinguish themselves without losing their femininity. While she wished women to walk through the gates of universities, she also wanted them to receive the respect that might be theirs on a pedestal. For Dona Violante, woman's chief profession was still to "love and please men," to be wife and mother, although this was not her only profession. Like many other Brazilian feminists, she placed family concerns above all others. She described the well-educated woman as "the terrestial *goddess*, who spreads a sweet perfume of purity and goodness, who reigns over everything through love, affection, and affability."[54] Remaining faithful to the old image of the Brazilian woman as tender mother and devoted wife, Dona Violante attempted to use these roles to elevate the actual position of women.

Feminist newspapers like *O Domingo* or *O Sexo Feminino* could not rely solely on defenses of motherhood or of women's rights and abilities to maintain their readers' attention and loyalty. Those women wanted practical knowledge in such areas as health and homemaking and enjoyed news of fashions and the theater. While their scientific horizons could be expanded by articles on locomotives of the world and agriculture in other countries, they were also given instruction on how to kill mosquitoes or make essence of roses.[55] The feminist journals felt obliged to amuse as well as to instruct, presenting puzzles in *O Sexo Feminino* and theater news in *Echo das Damas* as well as the serialized novels found in all types of newspapers, including the major circulation dailies. In its efforts to gain a wider audience, "with free admission into the bosom of families," a periodical like *O Sexo Feminino* stressed "the special care with which it is written" and published articles on morality and religion.[56] The feminist journals also served as outlets for female literary energies, filling many pages with their compatriots' poetry, short stories, and essays. However, they stressed fashion less than had *O Jornal das Senhoras*, leaving expensive fashion plates and embroidery patterns to their nonfeminist competitors.

During these same years a variety of periodicals published by men were also directed toward Brazil's women.[57] Some emphasized fashions and others, literature. While several endured for decades, others lasted only a few weeks. Most relied upon male contributors, although some published female literary efforts. Few attempted to provide more than entertainment, let alone to question the established order. One newspaper even sought to explain how "the emancipation of women should not be, as some insist, the same as the emancipation of men, because for women religion is everything and women's influence is manifested in all their deeds and acts." Other journals compared women to flowers or lauded them as "the smile of the world."[58] But most preferred to limit their opinions to matters of fashion, balls, and the theater. Many literate Brazilian women no doubt found such journals less challenging or upsetting and more enjoyable than the feminist newspapers. But the defenders of women's rights continued to fight on, pressing in new directions, and by the late 1880s some even added national and world news and political commentary.[59]

Judging the nature of the response to the feminist newspapers and their message is no easier than measuring the direct influence of other new ideas. Some readers wrote in to express their agreement with the mind-expanding notions presented in a periodical like *O Sexo Feminino*, as they had to *O Jornal das Senhoras* two decades earlier, and to urge others to publish their thoughts, for it was time that Brazilian women "imitate, if not exceed [their] contemporaries" in other countries. Francisca S. da M. Diniz expressed satisfaction and pride when important personages like Emperor Dom Pedro II and his daughter Princess Isabel subscribed to *O Sexo Feminino*. Perhaps some members of the elite who wished to keep abreast of the latest intellectual developments— such as the emperor, with his cherished reputation as a scholar—felt obliged to purchase and possibly to read *O Sexo Feminino* and other feminist newspapers. At other times, however, Dona Francisca felt discouraged, for most women in Rio de Janeiro seemed never to have heard of her journal.[60]

She had moved *O Sexo Feminino* from Campanha, Minas Gerais, where it had proved successful, to the nation's capital in 1875, with high hopes of extending her work among the people of Rio, "always enthusiastic for ideas of progress." During its year in Campanha, *O Sexo Feminino* had attained a circulation of 800, with some subscriptions from various parts of the Brazilian empire.[61] Since only 1,458 women out of a total population of 20,771 in Campanha could read and write in 1872, *O Sex Feminino* probably reached a sizable percentage of the local literate female population, as well as an audience beyond the town's limits.[62] In fact, reader response led Dona Francisca to reprint 4,000 copies of the first ten issues to satisfy new subscribers and to sell in Rio de Janeiro. But publishing in Rio proved more costly and difficult than in Campanha. Lacking a private fortune, Dona Francisca could not subsidize her feminist newspapers as had Violante A. Ximenes de Bivar e Vellasco. Only by increasing the number of subscriptions could her journal survive, for Dona Francisca refused to go to the "extreme of depriving my family of bread" in order to propagate her ideas and aid women. Indifference, as she no doubt realized, can be more deadly than hostility. Not all women responded to ideas of "liberty" or "emancipation"; many preferred to spend their time on their physical appearance rather than cultivate their minds.[63]

For almost three years *O Sexo Feminino* survived without diluting its message or compromising its standards in a Brazil replete with ephemeral newspapers that often endured only one or two issues. Then a yellow fever epidemic forced Francisca S. da M. Diniz to leave Rio de Janeiro and to suspend *O Sexo Feminino* in 1876. While she hoped for a speedy return, she found herself compelled to remain in the provinces "to restore the health of persons dear to us."[64] But she would not abandon the struggle, although it proved longer and more difficult than she had once believed. Four years passed before she could begin another journal in Rio de Janeiro. *Primaveira*[65] appeared in 1880, but did not survive the year, to be followed by the short-lived *Voz da Verdade*[66] in 1885. In 1889, *O Sexo Feminino* reappeared and encountered more success than before, achieving a circulation of 2,400.[67]

By 1890, the number of literate women in major cities had increased, providing a larger potential audience for this and other feminist journals, but an audience still limited to upper- and middle-class women. The proportion of literates among the total female population in Rio de Janeiro, for example, rose from 29.3 percent in 1872 to 43.8 percent in 1890.[68] In the 1880s and 1890s more feminist newspapers, both new and old, appeared. *O Domingo* had ceased publication in 1875 with Violante A. Ximenes de Bivar e Vellasco's death at the age of fifty-seven. The number of subscriptions had not been sufficient to cover expenses.[69] But Amélia Carolina da Silva Couto's *Echo das Damas*, suspended in 1880, returned in 1885, defending women's equality and right to education more strongly than before. New feminist journals appeared: Idalina d'Alcantara Costa's *O Direito das Damas*,[70] in Rio de Janeiro in 1882; Josephina Alvares de Azevedo's *A Familia*,[71] also in Rio in 1888, and moved; and *A Mensageira*,[72] directed by Presciliana Duarte de Almeida, in São Paulo in 1897. Rio, the nation's largest city and its political and intellectual center, continued to provide the most fertile ground for feminist newspapers; very few appeared elsewhere.

Of all the new feminist voices appearing in the 1880s and 1890s, Josephina Alvares de Azevedo's *A Familia* proved to be one of the most forceful. Like her predecessors, she stressed the need to educate women well, both for their own benefit and for "the aggrandizement of Brazil," because "the principal basis of true progress is education." Appealing to male self-interest and patriotism, as did other feminists, Dona Josephina queried men: "Do you wish to see Brazil placed alongside the most civilized nations in the world within a short time? Educate women. Do you wish to live a life of pleasure and enchantment? Educate women, and you will see your home transformed into a veritable Eden."[73]

Josephina Alvares de Azevedo bitterly opposed "the ancient, stupid prejudices" that ruled Brazilian society and kept women "always in such an atrophied state that we were not even permitted to have aspirations." Brazilian women should profit from the examples of history and of other nations, especially the United States, where women had proven that they could ably compete "in whatever field" previously reserved to men. In *A Familia*, Dona Josephina urged her compatriots to escape "the restricted sphere in which they were maintained" and to act "as complete human beings, intellectually, morally, and materially." Beyond "the domestic hearth," they would find "a vast field of opportunities that has been forbidden them up to now," including those in the political arena.[74]

Compared to *A Familia*, *A Mensageira* appeared less radical and more literary. A collection of writings by various women authors favoring different degrees of change in women's status, rather than the work of one strong individual, *A Mensageira* resembled both the feminist newspapers and the literary magazines edited by women, which by the late nineteenth century had provided an outlet for some of the prose and poetry created by well-educated Brazilian women. Some contributors, like Júlia Lopes de Almeida, one of the best known feminine authors in Brazil, tended to stress the need for women to be good housewives in addition to being well educated. By the late nineteenth century, a number of women from prominent families—like Júlia Lopes, Inéz Sabino, Maria Vaz de Carvalho, and Maria Clara Vilhena da Cunha—contributed to various feminist and nonfeminist periodicals.[75] Unlike Francisca S. da M. Diniz, they were not obliged to support themselves and their families, which no doubt influenced their views on women's rightful place and activities. Nor did they suffer the isolation endured by earlier women writers in Brazil, for the ranks of both feminists and literary ladies had grown, and some women could be numbered among both.

Brazilian feminists demonstrated concern with a number of major issues, including the legal status of women, family relationships, access to higher education and careers, the abolition of slavery, and, finally, the vote for women. In *O Sexo Feminino*, Francisca S. da M. Diniz urged wives to become aware of their property and other rights, although she knew these to be insufficient; women suffered from their position of perpetual minors under the law. Unlike women in advanced countries like the United States, who enjoyed "greater privileges," Brazilian women endured "the yoke despotically exercised through the husband's authority." Although she felt obliged to speak indirectly about certain matters occurring within some families, she strongly advocated legal changes making penalties for these misdeeds equal for both sexes. [76]

Women had made small gains. Single women could administer their own property. The commercial code of 1850 permitted women owning businesses to marry without disturbing their commercial rights and obligations. In addition, married women could engage in commerce with their husband's permission. These rights, according to Dona Francisca, marked "a beginning of practical emancipation." [77]

In matters of family relationships, Josephina Alvares de Azevedo favored more changes than had her predecessors, including Francisca S. da M. Diniz. In the 1850s Joana Paula Manso de Noronha had contended that "every family needs a head [*chefe*], and that the head of the family is the man." [78] Dona Josephina thought otherwise, even envisioning, in some cases, the dominance of the woman within a family. She found man "always a despot," attempting to exercise whatever dominion over "the other individuals of the species" he could. When forced by circumstances to yield power to other men, he increased his preponderance within the home in proportion to his losses outside. Against this Dona Josephina rebelled, opposing "every idea of the preeminence of the masculine sex." She found absurd the idea that the "principle of authority" within the family should "always reside in the man," as under the "current organization of society." If a woman were superior to a man in intelligence, education, or other ways, "if the superiority of the couple resides in the woman, why should a simple question of sex give him the attributes of authority?" [79]

Unlike most Brazilians, feminists or not, Dona Josephina favored divorce laws permitting, by mutual consent, the dissolution of marriage ties already broken. Otherwise, she said, the law was tyrannical. If a woman "could repudiate the husband whom her parents chose without consulting her desires," she would control "her destiny" more than the women who "sacrifices her entire existence so as not to disobey parental authority."[80] But even Francisca S. da M. Diniz considered the marriage contract indissoluble.[81] Some changes outside the home would come more quickly than others within the family or the legal structure.

In the early 1850s, Joana Paula Manso de Noronha lamented in *O Jornal das Senhoras* that in Europe and the United States women "exercise almost all the professions that among us are prohibited by prejudice." In Brazil, men thought the only occupations for women were those of being "seamstresses, or doing ironing or other minor labors."[82] The feminist newspaper editors advocated higher-status occupations for women, but limited their demands for increased opportunities to women of their own class. They demonstrated little concern for the larger numbers of women already employed outside their homes in poorly paid and regarded positions. The slow spread of education and male-female salary differentials helped to open a new field to some women, schoolteaching, which long remained one of the few respectable ways for non-lower-class women to earn a living. In various parts of Brazil women— including Francisca S. da M. Diniz—not only taught, but also directed, schools. While Dona Francisca emphasized schoolteaching as a career for women and as a secure source of income, she foresaw many other possibilities. Properly educated women could "occupy the position of doctor, chemist, naturalist, pharmacist, painter, telegraph operator, typist, botanist, post office agent," among others.[83] Of these, medicine, like teaching, might be seen as an extension of the traditional female nurturing role. But, as she and other feminist editors lamented, until the 1880s any Brazilian girl wishing medical training had to go abroad to pursue her studies. And several did.

In 1874, a fourteen-year-old Brazilian girl, Maria Augusta Generosa Estrella, left Rio de Janeiro to study medicine in the United States. Three years later, following some preparatory work, she secured special permission (necessary because she was underage) to enter the New York Medical College and Hospital for Women. Before she obtained her degree in 1881 and became the first Brazilian woman doctor, she was joined by a second young Brazilian girl, Josefa Agueda Felisbella Mercedes de Oliveira. The saw themselves as "two Brazilians who abandoned our homeland and left the bosom of our dear families to make the great sacrifice of coming to study medicine in order to be useful to our country and to serve suffering humanity." Two "great ideas" burned in their hearts—"love of country and defense of our sex, so attacked as incapable of receiving higher education."[84]

These two medical students, "fervent partisans of human progress," published a newspaper, *A. Mulher*,[85] designed to convince Brazilian women of their latent abilities and to show that "women like men can dedicate themselves to the study of the sciences." They cited evidence from history and science and the "evolution of modern civilization" to prove that "women are intelligent and capable of great undertakings." But for them, as for other Brazilian feminists, the United States, the "country favored by God to be the cradle of female emancipation," provided the best examples. Through *A Mulher* they attempted to inform their compatriots of American women's achievements and activities in fields ranging from law to medicine to philanthropy to the temperance movement. 86

Like older Brazilian feminists, such as Francisca S. da M. Diniz and Violante A. Ximenes de Bivar e Vellasco, these two medical students believed in the work ethic and the necessity of preparing women to be self-supporting. They were "convinced that without working one does not achieve a more or less independent life." Any "women who believes that because she is a woman she has no need to study, learn, and work commits an irreparable error." Through "work, the perennial source of human well-being," women could support themselves and "live free and independently." They hoped other Brazilian women would follow their example, "demanding higher education," and they expected to be followed by a "phalanx" of women doctors in Brazil. 87

Even before Maria A. G. Estrella obtained her degree in 1881, the *Echo das Damas* lauded her courage and pioneering efforts. The journal's editor agreed that women doctors were urgently needed in Brazil, since many sick women would rather die than "reveal a part of their bodies to a man." 88

Once the Brazilian government opened the nation's institutions of higher learning to them in 1879, other Brazilian women followed Maria A. G. Estrella's lead. In 1887, Rita Lobato Velho Lopes became the first women to receive a medical degree in Brazil. The *Echo das Damas* jubilantly proclaimed her an "example for young Brazilian girls, who only through education can hope to aspire to independence and personal dignity." 89 In 1888, Ermelinda Lopes de Vasconcelos earned her degree, and others followed shortly afterwards. 90 Just as *Echo das Damas* praised Maria A. G Estrella's and Rita Lobato's accomplishments as living proof of Brazilian women's capabilities, so did *A Familia* claim Antonieta Dias's graduation from the Rio de Janeiro medical school in 1889 as "one more victory for the sex she represents over the brutal prejudices of a limited education, still unfortunately in effect." Her accomplishment reinforced "the most vehement protests against opinions contrary to our emancipation." 91 But such opinions persisted, as did overt male hostility to women's practicing medicine.

Another step beyond the home taken by some Brazilian women in the 1880s involved the abolition movement. By this time, abolition had become a praiseworthy goal, the object of a broad-based movement in various urban circles. 92 Like charity work, this noble cause could safely evoke certain female efforts, seen as an extension of traditional female benevolence.

Though their assistance has since been largely forgotten, some Brazilian women contributed to the abolition movement, but not in policy-making positions. Women's roles and activities in the abolition campaign reflected their subordinate situation in society. They helped to raise funds to free slaves rather than participate in public debate over emancipation. Since elite women had long entertained at private social gatherings by piano and voice performance, few Brazilians could think it improper for Luiza Regadas of Rio de Janeiro to lend her lovely voice to abolitionist fund-raising meetings. Like other abolitionist women she also sold flowers and dainty handmade objects for the cause. Some women were sent by male members of abolitionist clubs to collect funds at the entrances to cemeteries and churches. [93] While these activities necessitated a certain resolve and a determination to undergo physical discomfort, such as standing in the rain all day, they could also reinforce the noble, self-sacrificing female image.

Some women established their own abolitionist societies, often sponsored or suggested by male abolitionists. The female organizations founded in different Brazilian cities included the Sociedade da Libertação, installed in Rio de Janeiro on 27 March 1870; the Sociedade Redemptora in São Paulo, on 10 July 1870; Avé Libertas in Recife, on 20 April 1884; and the short-lived club José do Patrocínio in Rio. The experience that these women gained might have increased their ability to deal with the outside world and improve their organizational skills. But few Brazilian women ever spoke out publicly on the issues involved in abolition, although the president of Avé Libertas, Leonor Porto, published newspaper articles and pamphlets. [94] Only a rare woman like Maria Amélia de Queiroz of Pernambuco gave public lectures on abolition. Later she became a leading collaborator on the outspoken feminist newspaper *A Familia*, as well as continuing to travel and lecture. [95] However, she did not present as startling a sight to her contemporaries as had a group of American women advocates of dress reform who had traveled to Brazil over thirty years earlier to promote the use of bloomers. [96] But those women, active in the abolition movement in the United States, had experience in public speaking and debating issues, which Brazilian women were much slower to acquire. Perhaps only in the classroom did many Brazilian women have an opportunity to address an audience, albeit a less demanding or voluntary one.

Unlike the women's rights movement in the United States, born in the abolition movement, the nineteenth-century Brazilian pioneers had not received their earliest training and stimulation from the struggle to free the slaves. [97] They began their work long before the abolition movement gathered strength, but they remained in subordinate positions and their contributions proved far less significant than those of women in the United States.

A few editors of feminist newspapers favored abolition, as did Amélia Carolina da Silva Couto in *Echo das Damas* in the mid-1880s. [98] Before the movement became widespread, Francisca S. da M. Diniz published a pro-emancipation poem in *O Sexo Feminino* in 1875, the same poem being reprinted in her abolitionist *Voz da Verdade* a decade later. By then she was devoting more attention in *Voz da Verdade* to abolition than to women's rights. Dona Francisca combatted slavery in the name of "the great principle of equality" and fought for the "holy cause of abolition as the solemn execution of the revindication of the rights of humanity."[99] But she never drew definite parallels between the cause of the slaves and that of women.

Women's contribution to the abolition movement had not posed a threat to men. But the further women moved from their traditional domestic, nonassertive roles, stepping out of the home in ways not easily viewed as extensions of their maternal functions, the more male opposition they encountered. If some men objected to female schoolteachers and doctors, they would find the thought of female lawyers and politicians much more upsetting. Women performing charity-like tasks outside the home were more easily accepted than women breaching the male preserve of public affairs.

In Brazil, law had long served men as a path to political success. The first women law graduates in the late 1880s encountered difficulties in practicing law, to the chagrin of *O Sexo Feminino* and *A Família*. However, by the end of the century, a woman gained admittance to the bar, to the applause and rejoicing of even a less fervently feminist newspaper, *A Mensageira*. This São Paulo-based journal followed the events in Rio de Janeiro with great interest. Following consideration of the question by various legal bodies and decisive action by one judge, Myrthes de Campos was permitted to defend a client in court in 1899. For *A Mensageira*, "Brazilian women had obtained a great triumph in the struggle for their undeniable and just demands."[100]

In the late 1880s some feminists carried their desire for equal rights to the point of demanding the vote, horrifying many other Brazilians, male and female. Suffrage did not lay within women's world of sentiments and the home, but marked a definite breach of the active male sphere. Many feared that if the purer and nobler of the sexes stepped down from the pedestal and out of the isolation of the home, she might be soiled or corrupted and society disrupted.

The early feminists had not advocated the vote for women. In the mid-1870s, Violante A. Ximenes de Bivar e Vellasco opposed women's admittance to either government or the army.[101] Like *O Domingo*, *Echo das Damas* denied wishing to provoke "pernicious aspirations to triumphs in politics" in women through education.[102] Even *O Sexo Feminino* did not demand the vote in the mid-1870s. However, unlike the other two journals, *O Sexo Feminino* demonstrated sympathy for this proposal and expressed hope for its eventual achievement in Brazil.

At first, *O Sexo Feminino* saw little benefit to women's suffrage and less possibility of achieving it. Few could vote in Brazil, and an expanded suffrage was not a major issue. Changes in forms of government scarcely affected women. To opponents of the Brazilian monarchy Francisca S. da M. Diniz retorted that in no "great republic or so-called republic did women cease being slaves and enjoy *political rights*." But even before she moved from Campanha to the nation's capital, she responded favorably to the idea of women voting in municipal elections, for which foreign precedents could be cited. [103] In Brazil, as elsewhere, municipal concerns might be viewed as an extension of the domestic sphere. Dona Francisca had seen the connection between complete equal rights and the vote. Although she did not stress suffrage as an immediate goal, she viewed it as a logical extension of women's rights.

The ferment of the republican agitation of the late 1880s not only strengthened feminist desires for political rights, but also furnished women with additional prosuffrage arguments and with opportunities to seek the vote. The declaration of the republic on 15 November 1889, provided the possibility of a slightly more open, fluid political structure. Various groups, such as the skilled urban workers whose self-confidence and assertiveness had been stimulated by the abolition campaign, attempted to mobilize and to unify themselves and entered the political arena. The establishment of a republic might open a new world of possibilities for women, also. Dona Francisca immediately changed the title of *O Sexo Feminino* to *O Quinze de Novembro do Sexo Feminino* (The Fifteenth of November of the Female Sex), symbolizing her determination to gain full political rights and freedom for women, as well as her hope for success.

Now the newly entitled *O Quinze de Novembro do Sexo Feminino* devoted its columns to the women's suffrage issue above all others. No longer would a limited vote, as advocated by many in England or as once envisioned by Dona Francisca herself, be sufficient. Women had the right to a voice on the national scene, including election to congress, although nowhere in the world had they yet achieved this. [104] Dona Francisca surpassed many of her feminist colleagues in her advocacy of effective suffrage. While *Echo das Damas* proved more sympathetic toward the vote in the 1880s than previously, its editor, Amélia Carolina da Silva Couto, still believed it to be "very soon in our country for women to vote in political elections." All she wanted them to do was study public affairs. [105]

Francisca S. da M. Diniz no longer placed the same stress on educating and freeing women so that they could serve their families or even society. Now self-fulfillment was important. Women could not continue being "mutilated in our personalities." When men treated them as queens, it was only to give them "the scepter of the kitchen, or the procreation machine." [106] Now they must have full freedom and equality of rights. And the right to vote formed an intrinsic part of their rights: without suffrage women could not be truly equal.

Dona Francisca was not the only feminist newspaper publisher strongly advocating women's suffrage in Brazil. Both in print and in public discourse, in Rio de Janeiro and on an 1889 speaking tour of northern Brazil, Josephina Alvares de Azevedo employed similar arguments, stressing women's equality, abilities, and accomplishments. She blamed the "natural egoism of the so-called stronger sex" for preventing women from "entering directly into our titanic political battles." Women "also have rights to defend," and with the vote they could improve their position within and beyond the home. Aware that she could not cite foreign precedents for full women's suffrage, she appealed to Brazilian patriotism, contending that "some nation will have to be the first to initiate this great improvement; why not Brazil?"[107]

Not only Josephina Alvares de Azevedo and Francisca S. da M. Diniz sought the vote. Hoping to take advantage of the vagueness of various electoral regulations, some Brazilian women strove to enter their names on voter's lists. Under the empire, Isabel de Matos Dilon, a law graduate, attempted to vote. Later she collaborated on Josephina Alvares de Azevedo's *A Familia*. When the republic was declared, five women in the far western state of Goiás requested inclusion on the electoral lists, but were refused. In Minas Gerais two other women attempted to register and vote.[108] Dona Josephina saw their actions as a sign that women now intended to "affect social destinies, to escape from the complete nothingness in which we hitherto have lived." Despite setbacks, she affirmed that "with resolution and constancy we will obtain everything that society owes us and the law does not approve."[109]

Both Josephina Alvares de Azevedo and Francisca S. da M. Diniz directed many of their arguments to the nation's male leaders. Since the new Brazilian republic was attempting to reconstruct government and society on a basis of "full liberty and fraternal equality," men should not work against the emancipation of women. Dona Francisca charged "men who proclaim equality" to "put it into practice."[110] As Dona Josephina reminded men, since women have to obey the law, they should have a voice in making it. No longer should men "with impunity deny women one of the most sacred individual rights." Dona Josephina considered the vote crucial for women; on it depended their "elevation in society." She even published a comedy entitled *O voto feminino*, which she presented at the Recreio Dramatico theater in Rio de Janeiro to help persuade the nation's leaders to act.[111]

Male resistance to women's suffrage proved difficult to counter. Much of the opposition centered on men's conception of the family and female duties. As recognized by one of Dona Josephina's collaborators on *A Familia*, Maria Clara Vilhena de Cunha, many men believed that a woman should not deal with public affairs or even show interest in them because "she has the domestic hearth, where she is queen, able to exercise her domain there." But, as Maria Clara retorted, not only was this "such a limited domain," but men also ruled there, making all the basic decisions.[112] Dona Josephina, in response to male arguments that women should dedicate themselves to motherhood alone, contended that "a woman who is a mother does not forfeit anything in being a citizen"; she can both educate her children and fulfill civil duties, just as a man assumes family duties and those of a citizen.[113]

In the Constituent Congress, which met in 1891 to frame a republican constitution for Brazil, men debated women's suffrage as well as other political issues that most thought far more important. Few congressmen believed, as did Lacerda Coutinho, that women were physically and mentally incapable of withstanding the excitement of struggles in the outside world.[114] Rather, they admitted women's intellectual capacities, but opposed suffrage in the name of the conservation of the family, fearing the consequences of any female departure from the home. For Moniz Freire, women's suffrage was "immoral and anarchic." He held that "the day Congress passes such a law we will have decreed the dissolution of the Brazilian family."[115]

This opposition to women's suffrage, based on the supposed nobility and purity of women, was carried to its extreme by the positivists, both within and outside Congress. They had elevated the old belief in separate spheres of male and female activities to the level of religious dogma. For them, the woman formed the moral part of society, the basis of the family, which in turn was the cornerstone of the nation. Womankind as a whole was to be worshipped and set apart from an evil world.[116] In Congress, Lauro Sodré, proclaiming his adherence to positivist doctrine, denounced women's suffrage as an "anarchic, disastrous, fatal" idea. While Sodré advocated giving women "complete, solid, encyclopedic, and integral education" for the sake of increased morality,[117] another positivist and member of the provisional republican government, Benjamin Constant Botelho de Magalhães, closed Brazil's institutions of higher education to women. In her angry and scornful denunciation of this temporary restriction on women, Josephina Alvares de Azevedo attacked the "wild and tormented positivist philosophy" for viewing women as "brainless beings, underdeveloped animals."[118]

Foreign examples, which served many purposes among the elite—as feminist newspaper publishers had long recognized—could also be employed to limit women to a subservient position in Brazil. Congressmen like Lacerda Coutinho cited the lack of foreign precedents for suffrage. Without regard to complete accuracy, he proclaimed that "in no part of the world does one find women enjoying voting rights."[119] But César Zama, who chastised his colleagues for not always taking the subject seriously, knew "it will be sufficient that any important European country confer political rights on [women] and we will imitate this," without weakening the family.[120]

Despite support from some radical Republicans in Congress—such as Lopes Trovão, who favored divorce as well as women's suffrage—the advocates of the vote for women remained a decided minority.[121] Even a proposal in favor of limited suffrage, for highly qualified women with university or teaching degrees or property who were not under a husband's or parent's authority, failed. Congress also refused to enfranchise illiterate men, a proposal favored by positivists, but opposed by most of the political elite.[122] The constitutional article on voter eligibility stood as originally drafted. Electors were "citizens over twenty-one years of age," properly registered, except for paupers, illiterates, soldiers, and members of religious orders.[123] For decades to come this article would be interpreted as excluding women, since they were not specifically included.

Despite the defeat of women's suffrage in the Constituent Congress, the issue could no longer be ignored. Now more men and women viewed it as part of women's rights. By 1920 the advocacy of female suffrage became almost fashionable in some elite circles. The achievement of the vote by women in several major European countries following the conclusion of World War I aided the cause in Brazil.

The twentieth-century women's suffrage movement in Brazil utilized these precedents, together with a variety of arguments and tactics in its struggle for the vote, achieving final victory in 1932.[124] Brazil became the third country in the Western Hemisphere to grant women the vote, following the United States, the nation so often admired by the Brazilian feminist press, and Ecuador, a country far removed from Brazilian concerns.

During the second half of the nineteenth century, Brazilian feminists voiced their dissatisfaction with the traditional male-determined roles assigned women. Through their newspapers théy endeavored to awaken other women to their potential for self-advancement and to raise their level of aspirations. The feminist press attempted to spur changes in the economic, social, and legal status of women in Brazil. Believers in progress, feminist newspaper editors drew inspiration and promises of future successes from women's achievements in other countries. Well aware of male opposition, female indifference, and the limited acceptance of their own ideas, they remained convinced of the importance of their cause and its eventual success. Unlike many of their male detractors, who assumed women to be easily corruptible should they step outside the home and the family to be weak and in need of defense, these editors displayed their confidence in women and their abilities. Through the persistence and bravery of this small band of pioneers, part of the groundwork was laid for future changes in the status of women in Brazil.

Feminist newspapers reflected the felt needs of many urban upper- and middle-class Brazilian women for education as well as for respect. As the nineteenth century progressed, some of their readers demonstrated less timidity and hesitancy. More Brazilian women entered the public sphere traditionally assigned men, as the feminist press urged. Increasing numbers of women received education, and the doors of Brazil's institutions of higher learning were finally opened to them. More women found employment outside the home, especially in the classrooms, government offices, and commercial establishments. As in other countries, such an increase in middle-level jobs helped lay the basis for future political and social changes. Some Brazilian women eventually sought the vote as well.

Despite the changes reflected in the feminist press, many Brazilian women still suffered from the semislavery and treatment as mere sexual beings or adornments that had been denounced by the early feminists. The majority of women, like that of men, remained uneducated. Among more comfortably situated Brazilians, most women still occupied a subordinate position, with their horizons limited to the home. Hesitant or indifferent, many did not attempt to traverse the long, painful road to equality and independence.

To move from family-centered matters to issues of the outside world proved a slow and difficult process for women. Even some feminist editors demonstrated ambivalence about the role of women beyond the family that limited their activities and weakened their arguments. They wanted both equality and motherhood, but were unsure how all potential conflicts might be resolved. They had long struggled to mount the pedestal, to improve their position within the family, and to gain approval for what they knew to be worthy tasks. But while some women hesitated, others were ready to plunge into a turbulent outer world. In this way they could defend and expand their rights, gain true equality, and act as complete human beings, while still not renouncing motherhood. Like Josephina Alvares de Azevedo, they envisioned women working on an equal footing with men in all spheres, occupying "all positions, performing all functions; in everything we should compete with men—in governing the family as in directing the nation."[125] The "emancipation of women," advocated for decades by the editors of feminist newspapers in Brazil, had acquired an ever broader significance. By the end of the nineteenth century, some women no longer wanted merely respect and favorable treatment within the family or the right to education, even university education, but the full development of all women's abilities, both within and outside the home.
home.

Notes

1. Just as standard histories of Brazil basically ignore women, so do books on the Brazilian press overlook the nineteenth-century feminist press. Nelson Werneck Sodré, *A história da imprensa da Brasil* (Rio de Janeiro: Civilização Brasileira, 1966), the most complete study of the Brazilian press, mentions more than one thousand journals, but ignores all of the feminist periodicals that will be considered in this paper. Fanny Tabak, "O status da mulher no brasil: Victorias e preconceitos," *Cadernos da PUC*, no. 7 (August 1971), pp. 165-201, mistakenly claims as the "first feminist periodical" *Nosso Jornal*, founded in 1919 (p. 180). Nor does Heleieth I. B. Saffioti, *A mulher na sociedade de classes: Mito e realidade* (São Paulo: Livraria Quatro Artes Editôra, 1969), perhaps the best study of women in Brazilian society, refer to any of the feminist newspapers or cite any nineteenth-century feminists other than Nísia Floresta Brasileira Augusta, who is confined to a footnote. Saffioti holds that "feminist manifestations had their beginning in Brazil" with Bertha Lutz in the second decade of the twentieth century (p. 270).

2. Newspapers devoted to women were not unique to Brazil in the nineteenth century. But such periodicals tended to be edited by men, not women, and were designed to provide entertainment or moral uplift, not to change women's lives. Although Latin

American journals intended for women have received virtually no attention, Jane Herrick has described several "Periodicals for Women in Mexico During the Nineteenth Century" in *The Americas* 14 (October 1957): 135-44. However, with one exception, *El Album de la Mujer* (1883-93), they were edited by men. Herrick does not indicate that this one periodical differed in any major respect from the general run of those concerned with home medicine, cooking, poetry, and pictures. Nor does she consider the fact that a woman owned and edited a journal to be a matter of interest.

3. John Luccock, *Notes on Rio de Janeiro and the Southern Parts of Brazil taken during a residence of ten years . . . 1808-1818* (London: S. Leigh, 1821), p. 111.

4. Traveling through Minas Gerais in the late 1820s, Reverend Robert Walsh, chaplain to the British ambassador, observed that "the wives of fazendeiros are frequently left widows, manage by themselves, afterwards, the farms and slaves, and in all respects assume the part and bearing of their husbands"; Robert Walsh, *Notices of Brazil in 1828 and 1829*, 2 vols. (London: Frederick Westley and A. H. Davis, 1830), 2: 28. See also essays by A. J. R. Russell-Wood (chap. 2) and Susan Soeiro (chap. 6) in this volume.

5. For a concise study of the family in Brazil, see Antônio Cândido, "The Brazilian Family," in T. Lynn Smith and Alexander Marchant, eds., *Brazil: Portrait of Half a Continent* (New York: Dryden Press, 1951), pp. 291-311. Under the existing civil law structure, an extension of the Philippine Code of 1603, which basically remained in effect in Brazil until the promulgation of the Civil Code of 1916, women were perpetual minors under the law. See Tristão de Alencar Araipe, *Código Civil Brazilerio, ou leis civis do Brazil dispostas por ordem de materias em seu estado actual* (Rio de Janeiro: H. Laemmert, 1885). Moreover, the new Civil Code of 1916 did not really change matters.

6. Johann B. von Spix and Karl F. P. von Martius, *Travels in Brazil in the Years 1817-1820*, 2 vols. trans. H. E. Lloyd (London: Longman, 1824), 1: 159.

7. James C. Fletcher and Daniel Paris Kidder, *Brazil and the Brazilians Portrayed in Historical and Descriptive Sketches*, 7th ed. (Boston: Little, Brown, 1867), pp. 163-70.

8. Herbert H. Smith, *Brazil: The Amazons and the Coast* (New York: Charles Scribner's Sons, 1879), pp. 50, 122-23.

9. For general studies of the empire, see Clarence H. Haring, *Empire in Brazil: A New World Experiment with Monarchy* (Cambridge: Harvard University Press, 1958); Manoel de Oliveira Lima, *O Império Brasileiro, 1821-1889*, 4th ed. (São Paulo: Edicões Melhoramientos, 1962); João Camilo de Oliveira Torres, *A democracia coronada: Teoria política do império do Brasil*, 2d ed. (Petrópolis: Editôra Vozes, 1964). For urban developments, see Pedro Pinchas Geiger, *Evolucão da rede urbana brasileira* (Rio de Janeiro: Instituto Nacional de Estudos Pedagógicos, Ministério da Educação e Cultura, 1963); Paul Singer, *Desenvolvimento econômico e evolucão urbana: Analise da evolução econômica de São Paulo, Blumenau, Pôrto Alegre, Belo Horizonte e Recife* (São Paulo: Companhia Editôra Nacional, 1968); Michael L. Conniff, Melvln K. Hendrix, and Stephen Nohlgren, "Brazil," in Richard M. Morse, ed., *The Urban Development of Latin America, 1750-1920* (Stanford: Stanford University Press, 1971), pp. 36-52; Fernando de Azevedo, *Brazilian Culture: An Introduction to the Study of Culture in Brazil*, trans. William Rex Crawford (New York: Macmillan, 1950), pp. 68-87.

10. For discussions of social and economic changes during the last decades of the

empire, see Richard Graham, *Britain and the Onset of Modernization in Brazil, 1850-1914* (Cambridge: Cambridge University Press, 1968), pp. 23-50; Octavio Ianni, *Industrialização e desenvolvimento social no Brasil* (Rio de Janeiro: Civilizacão Brasileira, 1963), pp. 75-114; Emilia Viotti da Costa, *Da senzala à côlonia* (São Paulo: Difusão Européia do Livro, 1966), pp. 428-41.

11. For education under the empire, see the multivolumed studies by Primitivo Moacyr, *A instrução e as provincias*, 3 vols. (São Paulo: Companhia Editôra Nacional, 1938). The best and only extensive study of women's education, but just for São Paulo, is Leda Maria Pereira Rodrigues, *A instrucão feminina em São Paulo: Subsídios para sua história até a proclamação da repúbliça* (São Paulo: Faculdade de Filosofia "Sedes Sapientiae," 1962).

12. Brazil, Directoria Geral de Estatistica, *Recenseamento da população do Império do Brazil a que se procedeu no dia 1º de agosto de 1872*, 22 vols. (Rio de Janeiro: Typ. Leuzinger, 1873-76), 21 (Quadros gerais): 1-2, 61.

13. Rui Barbosa, *Obras completas de Rui Barbosa*, vol. 10, bk. 1, *Reforma do ensino primario e varias instituições complementares da instrução pública* (Rio de Janeiro: Ministério da Educação e Saúde, 1947), pp. 9-11.

14. Luccock, *Notes on Rio de Janeiro*, p. 111.

15. Fletcher and Kidder, *Brazil and the Brazilians*, p. 164.

16. Louis Agassiz and Elizabeth C. Agassiz, *A Journey in Brazil* (Boston: Ticknor and Fields, 1868), p. 479.

17. Saffioti, *A mulher na sociedade de classes*, pp. 202-10; Reynaldo Kuntz Busch, *O ensino normal em São Paulo* (São Paulo: Livraria Record, 1935), pp. 41-43; L. M. P. Rodrigues, *A instrucão feminina*, pp. 151-62.

18. *O Jornal das Senhoras*, "Modas, Litteratura, Bella-Artes, Theatros e Critica." Rio de Janeiro, 1 January 1852 to 30 December 1855, weekly, 8 pp., 8" x 11-1/4".

19. *O Jornal das Senhoras*, 1 January 1852, p. 1; 11 January 1852, pp. 12, 14; 8 February 1852, p. 42. César H. Guerrero, *Mujeres de Sarmiento* (Buenos Aires: Artes Gráficas Bartolomé U. Chiesino, 1960), pp. 77-80. Innôcencio J. Francisco da Silva, *Diccionário bibliographico portuguez*, 27 vols. (Lisbon: Imprensa Nacional, 1858-1923), 10:144; 11:275.

20. *O Jornal das Senhoras*, 1 January 1852, p. 6; 11 January 1852, pp. 12-13.

21. Luccock, *Notes on Rio de Janeiro*, p. 114.

22. *O Jornal das Senhoras*, 1 January 1852, p. 5; 11 January 1852, p. 12.

23. Ibid., 11 January 1852, pp. 12-13.

24. Ibid., 11 January 1852, pp. 12, 14.

25. Ibid., 1 January 1852, p. 6; 11 January 1852, pp. 13-14; 8 February 1852, p. 43.

26. Ibid., 1 January 1852, pp. 1, 2; 11 January 1852, p. 14; 8 February 1852, pp. 42, 44.

27. Ibid., 4 July 1852, p. 1.

28. I. F. da Silva, *Diccionário bibliographico portuguêz*, 7: 450. Augusto Victorino Alves Sacramento Blake, *Diccionario bibliographico brazileiro*, 7 vols. (Rio de Janeiro: Imprensa Nacional, 1883-1902), 2: 182-86; 7: 386-87. First Secretary of Conservatório Dramático Brasileiro to Violante Atabalipa de Bivar e Vellasco, Rio de Janeiro, 3 July 1850, Biblioteca Nacional, Manuscript Section, I, 2, 725. Olímio Barros Vidal, *Precursoras brasileiras* (Rio de Janeiro: Editôra a Noite, [1955]), pp. 121-31.

Following the fall of the Argentine dictator Juan Manuel Rosas in 1853, Dona Joana and her two daughters returned to Argentina, where she achieved a distinguished, though difficult, career as an educator and follower of the educational principles of Domingo Faustino Sarmiento. She also edited a periodical for women, *Album de Señoritas*. See Guerrero, *Mujeres de Sarmiento*, pp. 81-101, and Jim Levy, "Juana Manso: Argentine Feminist," *Occasional Paper No. 1* (Bundoora: La Trobe University, Institute of Latin American Studies, 1977).

29. *O Jornal das Senhoras*, 5 June 1853, p. 177; Barros Vidal, *Precursoras brasileiras*, p. 131.

30. *O Jornal das Senhoras*, 25 July 1852, p. 82; 19 September 1852, pp. 89-90; 3 October 1852, pp. 106-7.

31. Ibid., 4 July 1852, p. 1; 3 October 1852, p. 106; 10 October 1852, pp. 113-14.

32. *Bello Sexo*, "Periodico Religioso, de Instrucção e Recreio, Noticioso e Critico moderado." Editor-in-chief Julia de Albuquerque Sandy Aguiar. Rio de Janeiro, 21 August 1862 to 28 September 1862, weekly, 4 pp., 7" x 10 1/2".

33. *Bello Sexo*, 21 August 1862, pp. 1-2; 12 September 1862, p. 1.

34. Ibid., 21 August 1862, p. 1; 31 August 1862, p. 1; 28 September 1862, p. 1.

35. Ibid., 7 September 1862, pp. 2-4.

36. Ibid., 21 August 1862, p. 2; 7 September 1862, p. 2. See Cynthia Little's work (chap. 9) in this volume.

37. *O Sexo Feminino*, "Semanário dedicado aos interesses da mulher." Principal Editor Francisca S. da M. Diniz. Campanha, Minas Gerais, 7 September 1873 to 7 September 1874, weekly, 4 pp., 6 3/4" x 9 1/4". Rio de Janeiro, 22 July 1875 to 2 April 1876, generally semimonthly, 4 pp., 8 3/4" x 12 1/4". Second phase: Rio de Janeiro: 2 June 1889 to probably 1896; title changed to *O Quinze de Novembro do Sexo Feminino* after November 1889; weekly, then generally semimonthly; 4 pp.; from 8 3/4" x 12 1/4" to 12" x 17".

38. *O Domingo*, "Jornal litterario e recreativo." Editor and Owner Violante A. Ximenes de Bivar e Vellasco. Rio de Janeiro, 23 November 1873 to 9 May 1875, weekly, 4 pp., 8 3/4" x 12 1/4".

39. Described in *O Sexo Feminino*, 25 April 1874, pp. 1-2.

40. Cited in *O Sexo Feminino*, 29 August 1875, p. 3.

41. *Echo das Damas*. Owned by Amélia Carolina da Silva & Comp., Rio de Janeiro; 8 April 1879 to 1880, then 1885 to 26 August 1888; generally semimonthly or monthly; 4-8 pp.; from 10 1/4" x 13 3/4" to 14 1/2" x 21 3/4".

42. *O Sexo Feminino*, 28 January 1874, p. 4; 27 December 1873, p. 4; 25 April 1874, p. 2. *O Domingo*, 18 January 1874, p. 2; 19 April 1874, p. 2.

43. *O Sexo Feminino*, 7 September 1873, p. 1; 14 September 1873, p. 2; 20 September 1873, p. 1; 25 October 1873, pp. 1-2; 15 November 1873, p. 1; 23 March 1874, p. 1.

44. Ibid., 14 September 1873, p. 2; 14 January 1874, p. 2.

45. Ibid., 8 November 1873, p. 2; 29 November 1873, p. 1; 14 January 1874, p. 2; 22 July 1875, p. 2; 29 July 1875, p. 2; 5 September 1875, pp. 1-2; 10 October 1875, p. 3; 31 October 1875, pp. 1-2; 12 December 1875, p. 1.

46. Ibid., 7 September 1873, p. 1; 18 April 1874, p. 1.

47. Ibid., 7 September 1873, p. 1; 20 September 1873, p. 1; 18 October 1873, p. 2; 8 November 1873, p. 4; 28 January 1874, pp. 3-4; 7 April 1874, p. 1; 2 May 1874, p. 2; 18 July 1874, p. 4; 22 July 1875, p. 2; 29 August 1875, p. 3.

48. *O Domingo*, 30 November 1873, p. 1; 14 December 1873, p. 3; 21 December

1873, p. 3; 28 December 1873, p. 3; 18 January 1874, p. 3. *Echo das Damas*, 18 April 1879, p. 1.

49. *O Domingo*, 30 November 1873, p. 1; 14 December 1873, p. 1.

50. *Aurora Brasileira*, "Periódico litterario e noticioso." Editor H. de Aguino. Ithaca, New York; 22 October 1873 to 20 May 1875; generally monthly; 8 pp.; 8" x 12".

51. *O Domingo*, 1 March 1874, pp. 1-2.

52. *Aurora Brasileira*, 20 January 1874, p. 28.

53. *O Domingo*, 7 December 1873, p. 1.

54. Ibid., 14 December 1873, p. 1; 18 January 1874, p. 1.

55. *Primaveira* (see note 65, below), 16 September 1880, pp. 2-3; 17 October 1880, p. 2. *O Sexo Feminino*, 22 July 1875, p. 3; 14 August 1875, p. 3.

56. *O Sexo Feminino*, 8 August 1875, p. 1.

57. These include:

Correio das Modas, "Jornal critico e litterario das modas, bailes, theatros, etc." Rio de Janeiro, 5 January 1839 to 31 December 1840.

Novo Correio de Modas, "Novellas, poesias, viagens, recordações, historicas, anecdotas e charadas." Rio de Janeiro, 1852 to 1854.

Recreio do Bello Sexo, "Modas, litteratura, bellas artes e theatro." Rio de janeiro, 1852 to 1856.

Jornal das Familias. Rio de Janeiro and Paris, 1863 to 1878.

A Estação, "Jornal illustrado para a familia" (Brazilian edition of a Portuguese journal). Oporto, 15 January 1879 to 15 February 1904.

Leque. "Orgam litterario, dedicado ao bello sexo." São Paulo, 1886-87.

A Violeta, "Folha litteraria dedicada ao bello sexo." São Paulo, 1887.

Various similar Portuguese journals also circulated in Brazil, including:

O Correio das Damas, "Jornal de litteratura e de modas." Lisben, 1836 to at least 1849.

O Panorama, "Jornal litterario e instructivo." Lisbon, 1850s.

Jornal das Damas, "Revista de litteratura e de modas." Lisbon, 1867 to at least 1870.

58. *Leque*, 16 January 1887, p. 1; *A Violeta*, 17 June 1887, p. 1.

59. *Voz da Verdade* (see note 66, below), 28 May 1885, pp. 1, 3; *Echo das Damas*, 7 August 1886, p. 2; *O Quinze de Novembro do Sexo Feminino*, 15 December 1889, pp. 1, 4.

60. *O Sexo Feminino*, 15 November 1873, pp. 2-3; 29 July 1875, p. 3; 14 August 1875, p. 2; 29 August 1875, p. 3.

61. Ibid., 7 September 1874, p. 1; 22 July 1875, p. 1.

62. Brazil, *Recenseamento da população 1872*, 9 (Minas Gerais): 1070.

63. *O Sexo Feminino*, 15 November 1873, p. 4; 8 August 1875, p. 1; 21 November 1875, p. 2.

64. Ibid., 2 April 1876, p. 1; *Primaveira*, 29 August 1880, p. 1.

65. *Primaveira*, "Revista semanal instructiva noticiosa." Under the direction of Francisco Senhorinha da Motta Diniz. Rio de Janeiro, 29 August 1880 to 31 October 1880, weekly, 4 pp., 9 1/4" x 12 3/4".

66. *Voz da Verdade*. Editor and Owner Francisca Senhorinha da Motta Diniz. Rio de Janeiro, 12 May 1885 to 25 June 1885, semimonthly, 4 pp., 10" x 13".

67. *O Quinze de Novembro do Sexo Feminino*, 15 December 1889, pp. 3-4.

68. Brazil, Directoria Geral de Estatistica, *Recenseamento do Brazil realizado em 1*

de setembro de 1920, 5 vols. (Rio de Janeiro: Typ. da Estatistica, 1929), vol. 4, pt. 4, p. xiii.

69. *O Domingo*, 22 March 1874, p. 1; Barros Vidal, *Precursoras brasileiras*, p. 138.

70. *O Direito das Damas*. Owned by Idalina d'Alcantara Costa & Comp. Rio de Janeiro, January 1882, 4 pp., 9" x 12".

71. *A Familia*, "Jornal litterario dedicado á educação da mãe de familia." Edited by Josephina Alvares de Azevedo. São Paulo 1888 to 1889; Rio de Janeiro, 1889 to perhaps 1897; generally weekly; 4 or 8 pp.; 9" x 13".

72. *A Mensageira*, "Revista literaria dedicada á mulher brasileira." Director Presciliana Duarte de Almeida. São Paulo, 15 October 1897 to 15 January 1900, semi-monthly, 16 pp., 10" x 13".

73. *A Familia*, special number, 1889, p. 2; Josephina Alvares de Azevedo, *A mulher moderna: Trabalhos de propaganda* (Rio de Janeiro: Typ. Montenegro, 1891), pp. 92-93. Many of her newspaper articles and speeches and her prosuffrage play were reprinted in this volume.

74. *A Familia*, 6 July 1889, p. 2; 30 November 1889, p. 1; 31 December 1889, p. 1. J. A. de Azevedo, *A mulher moderna*, p. 124.

75. *A Familia*, 2 February 1889, p. 4; 25 May 1889, p. 5; 6 July 1889, p. 4; 14 November 1889, pp. 4, 6. *Echo das Damas*, 31 January 1888, pp. 1-2; 26 August 1888, p. 2. *O Quinze de Novembro do Sexo Feminino*, 6 December 1890, p. 2. *A Mensageira*, 15 October 1897, p. 3. Sacramento Blake, *Diccionário bibliographico brazileiro*, 3: 279-80; 5: 241-42; 6: 231. I. F. da Silva, *Diccionário bibliographico portuguez*, 16: 358. José Brito Broca, *A vida literaria no Brasil, 1900*, 2d ed. (Rio de Janeiro: José Olympio, 1960), p. 252.

76. *O Sexo Feminino*, 9 June 1889, p. 1; *O Quinze de Novembro do Sexo Feminino*, 30 September 1890, p. 2; 6 December 1890, p. 1.

77. Ibid., 6 December 1890, p. 1.

78. *O Jornal das Senhoras*, 11 January 1852, p. 14. The man would remain the head [chefe] of the family according to Brazilian law until the 1962 modification of the Civil Code. See Ruth Bueno [Ruth Maria Barbosa Goulart], *Regime jurídico da mulher casada*, 2d ed. (Rio de Janeiro and São Paulo: Forense, 1970).

79. *A Familia*, 14 November 1889, p. 4.

80. J. A. de Azevedo, *A mulher moderna*, pp. 116-17.

81. *O Sexo Feminino*, 16 June 1889, p. 1.

82. *O Jornal das Senhoras*, 11 January 1852, pp. 12-13; 8 February 1852, p. 42. For the changing structure of employment of Brazilian women and their working conditions and wages, see June E. Hahner, "Women and Work in Brazil, 1850-1920: A Preliminary Investigation," in Dauril Alden and Warren Dean, eds., *Essays Concerning the Socioeconomic History of Brazil and Portuguese India* (Gainesville: University of Florida Press, 1977), pp. 87-117.

83. *O Sexo Feminino*, 29 July 1875, pp. 1-2.

84. *A Mulher* (see note 85, below), April 1881, p. 26.

85. *A Mulher*, "Periodico illustrado de litterature e Bellas Artes consagrada aos interesses e direitos da Mulher Brazileira." Editors Josepha A. F. M. de Oliveira and Maria A. G. Estrella. New York, January 1881 to June 1881, monthly, 8 pp. plus cover, 8 1/2" x 11 3/4".

86. *A Mulher*, January 1881, pp. 2, 6; February 1881, p. 16; March 1881, pp. 18, 22;

284   *Latin American Women*

April 1881, pp. 26-30.

87. Ibid., April 1881, p. 29; June 1881, pp. 43-46.

88. *Echo das Damas*, 18 April 1879, p. 1. Maria A. G. Estrella's biography in both chronological and novelistic forms appeared in *Echo das Damas*, 26 May 1879, p. 1; 20 July 1879, pp. 1-2.

89. Ibid., 4 January 1888, p. 1.

90. Alberto Silva, *A primeira médica do Brasil* (Rio de Janeiro: Irmãos Pongetti, 1954), pp. 12, 51-52; Francisco Bruno Lobo, "Rita Lobato: A primeira médica formada no Brasil," *Revista de História* 42 (April-June 1971): 483-85.

91. *A Familia*, 30 November 1889, p. 6.

92. For the abolition movement, see Robert Conrad, *The Destruction of Brazilian Slavery, 1850-1888* (Berkeley and Los Angeles: University of California Press, 1972), and Robert Brent Toplin, *The Abolition of Slavery in Brazil* (New York: Atheneum, 1972).

93. Ignez Sabino, *Mulheres illustres do Brazil* (Rio de Janeiro and Paris: H. Garnier, [1892]), pp. 251-57; *Journal do Comércio*, 5 October 1880, p. 2; *Gazeta da Tarde*, 3 November 1880, p. 2; Evaristo de Moraes, *A campanha abolicionista, 1879-1888* (Rio de Janeiro: Livraria Editôra Leite Ribeiro, 1924), p. 24; Conrad, *Destruction of Brazilian Slavery*, p. 149.

94. José Jacintho Ribeiro, *Chronologia paulistana: Ou, Relação histórica dos factos mais importantes ocorridos em S. Paulo desde a chegada de Martim Affonso de Souza em S. Vicente até 1898* (São Paulo, 1899-1901), vol. 2, pt. 1, p. 59; *Jornal do Brasil*, ed. *Galeria Nacional: Vultos proeminentes da história brasileira 6° Fascículo* (Rio de Janeiro: Officinas Graphicas do Jornal do Brasil, 1933), pp. 562-63; *Gazeta da Tarde*, 5 October 1885, p. 1; Mello Barreto Filho and Hermeto Lima, *Histórica da policía do Rio de Janeiro: Aspectos da cidade e da vida carioca, 1870-1889*, 3 vols. (Rio de Janeiro: Editôra A Noite, 1944), 3: 148; Moraes, *A campanha abolicionista*, p. 41; Richard M. Morse, *From Community to Metropolis: A Biography of São Paulo, Brazil* (Gainesville: University of Florida Press, 1958), p. 147.

95. Sacramento Blake, *Diccionário bibliographico brazileiro*, 6: 224; *A Familia*, Special number, 1889, p. 3; 31 December 1889, p. 7.

96. *Novo Correio de Modas*, vol. 1, no. 3 (1852), p. 37.

97. For the suffrage movement in the United States, see Eleanor Flexner, *Century of Struggle: The Woman's Rights Movement in the United States* (Cambridge: Harvard University Press, Belknap Press, 1959); William L. O'Neill, *Everyone Was Brave: A History of Feminism in America* (Chicago: Quadrangle Books, 1971); Aileen S. Kraditor, *The Ideas of the Woman Suffrage Movement, 1890-1920* (New York: Columbia University Press, 1965).

98. *Echo das Damas*, 6 February 1886, p. 3.

99. *O Sexo Feminino*, 7 November 1875, pp. 2-3. *Voz da Verdade*, 12 May 1885, p. 1; 28 May 1885, p. 4.

100. *A Mensageira*, 15 October 1899, pp. 169, 174; 15 December 1899, pp. 201-4; 15 January 1900, pp. 217-21. *O Sexo Feminino*, 16 June 1889, p. 2. *A Familia*, 30 November 1889, p. 6.

101. *O Domingo*, 14 December 1873, p. 1.

102. *Echo das Damas*, 18 April 1879, p. 1.

103. *O Sexo Feminino*, 20 December 1873, p. 3; 14 January 1874, p. 2; 7 March

1874, p. 4; 11 April 1874, pp. 3-4.

104. *O Quinze de Novembro do Sexo Feminino*, 6 April 1890, p. 2.

105. *Echo das Damas*, 7 August 1886, p. 2.

106. *O Quinze de Novembro do Sexo Feminino*, 6 April 1890, p. 1.

107. *A Familia*, 6 July 1889, pp. 1, 8; 3 October 1889, pp. 1, 3-4.

108. Barros Vidal, *Precursoras brasileiras*, p. 165. *A Familia*, 6 July 1889, p. 8; 23 November 1889, p. 3; 31 December 1889, p. 2; J. A. de Azevedo, *A mulher moderna*, p. 14.

109. *A Familia*, 23 November 1889, p. 3.

110. *O Quinze de Novembro do Sexo Feminino*, 6 April 1890, p. 2.

111. J. A. de Azevedo, *A mulher moderna*, pp. 23, 25, 30-73.

112. *A Familia*, 19 October 1889, p. 1.

113. J. A. de Azevedo, *A mulher moderna*, p. 20.

114. Brazil, Câmara dos Deputados, *Annaes do Congresso Constituinte da República*, 3 vols., 2d ed. (Rio de Janeiro: Imprensa Nacional, 1924-26), 2: 544, session of 14 January 1891.

115. Brazil, *Annaes do Congresso Constituinte*, 2: 456, session of 12 January 1891.

116. See Raimundo Teixeira Mendes, *A mulher: Sua preeminência social e moral, segundo os ensinos da verdadeira siencia pozitiva*, 4th ed. (Rio de Janeiro: Igreja Pozitivista do Brazil, 1958).

117. Brazil, *Annaes do Congresso Constituinte*, 2: 478, session of 13 January 1891.

118. J. A. de Azevedo, *A mulher moderna*, p. 109.

119. Brazil, *Annaes do Congresso Constituinte*, 2: 543, session of 14 January 1891.

120. Ibid., 3: 356-57, session of 29 January 1891.

121. Ibid., 1: 276.

122. Ibid., 1: 439.

123. Ibid., 1: 438.

124. For the twentieth-century suffrage movement in Brazil, see João Batista Cascudo Rodrigues, *A mulher brasileira: Direitos políticos e civis* (Fortaleza: Imprensa Universitária do Ceará, 1962). A brief summary of the movement is found in Saffioti, *A mulher na sociedade de classes*, pp. 267-77.

125. J. A. de Azevedo, *A mulher moderna*, p. 28.

11

Anna Macías

Felipe Carrillo Puerto and women's liberation in Mexico

The late Frank Tannenbaum, in his *Peace by Revolution*, published in 1933, believed that the upheaval that began in Mexico in 1910 "was essentially an agrarian movement. The other aspects of the Revolution have been incidental by-products and trimmings."[1] This attitude may explain why Felipe Carrillo Puerto (1874-1924), the Socialist governor of the state of Yucatán from February 1922 until his execution by political enemies in January 1924, is remembered almost exclusively as a modern, and martyred, apostle of the oppressed male peasantry of Yucatán. Very little attention has been paid to Carrillo Puerto's program for Yucatecan women, whom he regarded as a group oppressed by most men, rich or poor, strong or weak.[2]

How does one account for Carrillo Puerto's interest in women's liberation? Why did Yucatán become the center for such a movement? What influence did Carrillo's predecessor, the profeminist Governor Salvador Alvarado (1915-18), have on Carrillo's ideas about the emancipation of women? What did Carrillo seek to do for women in Yucatán and elsewhere? Lastly, how did Mexican women respond to his ideas on their future liberation? The purpose of this essay is to provide some answers to these previously unraised questions and to try to shed some light on a largely ignored and almost totally forgotten aspect of twentieth-century history.

In *Peace by Revolution* Tannenbaum remarked that the 1910-20 upheaval "has not been a national revolution in the sense that all of the country participated in the same movement and at the same time. It has been local, regional, sometimes by counties."[3] This is the case with respect to women's liberation in

Mexico, for Yucatán became its capital under the leadership of Salvador Alvarado and Felipe Carrillo Puerto, just as the state of Morelos became the center of the agrarian revolution under the leadership of Emiliano Zapata.

There are a number of reasons why Yucatán became the center for a women's liberation movement in Mexico. In contrast to many of the land-locked, mountainous states of Mexico's interior, Yucatán faced the sea and exported most of her henequen abroad. For at least fifty years before the Revolution, that region had regular steamship service with Havana, New Orleans, New York, and European ports. As a result, Yucatán was in closer contact with, and subject to greater influence by, the United States and Western Europe than were most Mexican states. Mérida, the capital, was only twenty-two miles from Yucatán's chief port, Progreso, and at Mérida an incipient feminist movement began in 1870. In that year a number of primary school-teachers, led by the gifted poet and dedicated teacher Rita Cetina Gutiérrez, founded one of the country's earliest feminist societies, *La Siempreviva*. The group published a newspaper and founded a secondary school, which eventually merged with the government Instituto Literario de Niñas. The dynamic Profesora Cetina directed that institute from 1886 to 1902 and educated a generation of female teachers who taught in the capital, in the major towns, and on the few *haciendas* that provided primary schools for the children of peons.[4] At Mérida there were also a few distinguished teachers in the School of Jurisprudence and later at the School of Medicine who favored the cause of feminism in Yucatán. Between 1910 and 1915 eight students at the School of Law prepared theses on the subject of divorce and the legal rights or women, an extraordinarily large number, considering the school's small size.[5] And later, in the early 1920s, Dr. Eduardo Ursáiz, rector of the University of Yucatán and author of a profeminist novel, *Eugenia*, was to give the first lectures on birth control to medical students in Mérida.[6]

Encouraged by the progressive ambience he found in Yucatán, General Salvador Alvarado, appointed governor of that state in early 1915 by the leader of the triumphant Constitutionalist Forces, Venustiano Carranza, developed more radical programs in every area of life in Yucatán than Carranza did in Mexico City. Tannenbaum observed that Alvarado's "coming to Yucatán was like a cyclone that destroyed a feudalism rooted deep in the soil. . . . He, perhaps more than any other Mexican who took an active part in the Revolution, attempted to formulate its program."[7]

In his advocacy of feminism Alvarado was probably influenced by the writings of socialists on the subject, for in the nineteenth century, as Simone de Beauvoir observes in *The Second Sex*, Proudhon was the only important socialist thinker to hold traditionalist views about women.[8] Alvarado was also influenced, no doubt, by what he saw in the United States during his trips there as a merchant before the Revolution. In any case, between 1915 and 1918 Alvarado implemented a number of demands first voiced by feminists who published the periodical *La Mujer Mexicana* in Mexico City from 1904 to 1908. In Yucatán, Alvarado opened up jobs in public administration to women, ameliorated the working conditions of female domestic servants, allocated large sums of money to female vocational education, and reformed the civil code to give single women the same right as men to leave the parental home at age twenty-one if they so desired. [9] He encouraged women to take an active part in public affairs by calling the first two feminist congresses in Mexican history at Mérida in January and November 1916. [10] At these two congresses, attended primarily by Yucatán's female teachers, the majority approved resolutions in favor of laical schools and progressive education. The delegates also favored an end to religious superstition, bigotry, and intolerance, thus challenging the conventional view that women were conservative in religious matters. [11] Other resolutions favored greater educational and vocational opportunities for women, and the majority voted that in the future females should be encouraged to participate in politics, first on the municipal and eventually on the state and national levels. [12] The participants at the January congress also demanded that the Civil Code of 1884 be reformed to remove the legal discriminations against women. The April 1917 Law of Domestic Relations, issued by President Carranza, corrected some of the more glaring injustices in that code, endowing a married woman with a legal personality to draw up contracts, take part in legal suits, and administer her personal property. It also equalized her authority in the home with that of the husband.[13]

Once Mexico's new constitution of early 1917 ended the preconstitutional or military phase of Carranza's revolutionary government, Alvarado sought to consolidate his reforms and launch his candidacy as constitutional governor of Yucatán by founding, by June 1917, the Socialist party of Yucatán. [14] However, when it became clear that legal obstacles against Alvarado's candidacy could not be overcome (he was not a native Yucatecan, nor had he resided in the state a minimum of five years), the political ambitions of Alvarado's protégés in the newly formed Socialist party were kindled. It was at this point that Felipe Carrillo Puerto emerged as one of the key leaders of the radical left in Yucatán.

Felipe Carrillo Puerto was born in Motul, Yucatán, in 1874, of a large, but not impoverished, white, middle-class family.[15] His friend and biographer Edmundo Bolío Ontiveros states that since childhood Carrillo Puerto had felt great sympathy and affection for the oppressed masses of Indians and peasants of Motul. Like most whites, however, Carrillo never worked in the henequen fields. Instead he tried his hand at various occupations and business ventures, all of which failed. His attempt to run a newspaper, *El Heraldo de Motul*, also ended in failure, not necessarily because Carrillo lacked business sense, but more probably because his muckraking irritated powerful landlords. At the start of the Revolution he was business agent and correspondent in Motul for the prestigious *Revista de Mérida*, and his friendships with its owner, Delio Moreno Cantón, and its ablest reporter, Carlos R. Menéndez, helped launch Carrillo Puerto's political career.[16]

A lifelong enemy of the *"casta divina,"* as the *hacendados* of Yucatán were called, Carrillo Puerto also seems to have had differences with whatever government was in power in Mexico, whether Porfirian, Maderista, or Carrancista.[17] Nor did he become a close associate or member of Alvarado's inner circle, although later as governor, Carrillo was to carry on many policies and programs first initiated or proposed by Alvarado in 1915 through 1918. In 1916, Carrillo Puerto was president of the Agrarian Committee of Motul, organizing peasants into "leagues of resistance" against the landowners. His political influence grew, and in late 1916 and early 1917 he served as alternate delegate to the Querétaro constitutional convention. In 1918, when Alvarado had to step down as governor, Carrillo Puerto became the head of the Socialist party. Working from the offices of the Central League of Resistance in Mérida from 1918 to 1921, Carrillo became the most powerful political figure in Yucatán (while also serving in the national Chamber of Deputies), supported by some seventy thousand peasants and workers whom he had organized into militant resistance leagues. In addition to providing muscle against the Yucatecan upper classes, the workers each paid monthly dues of at least one and one-half *pesos*, thus providing Carrillo Puerto with campaign funds. On 1 February 1922, at the age of forty-eight, Felipe Carrillo Puerto became governor of Yucatán, a post that he was to hold until his execution on 3 January 1924 by enemies who took advantage of the De la Huerta uprising to stage a counterrevolutionary military coup in Yucatán.[18]

Despite the fact that Alvarado and Carrillo Puerto had never been close personal friends, as Socialists they shared similar ideas on social and economic issues, and this was especially true of their ideas on women. In some cases Carrillo continued programs and policies first initiated by Alvarado, while in others he implemented ideas first suggested, though never realized, by his predecessor. However, Carrillo did not merely plagiarize Alvarado, as his conservative enemies charged,[19] but took some radical initiatives, especially with respect to "free love," easy divorce, and birth control, which owed little to Alvarado and even less to Mexican feminists.

Both Alvarado and Carrillo Puerto viewed religion as an archenemy of progress, and both sought to free women from Church control and to convert them into active agents of "defanaticization," as they both characterized their campaign against Catholicism in Yucatán. In his campaign against the Church, Alvarado won the support of the more radical teachers at the feminist congresses of 1916, who advocated a "rationalistic" approach to religion. Carrillo Puerto went further, trying to enlist women of all classes, not just secular schoolteachers, in his effort to rid Yucatán of religion altogether. However, he seems to have underestimated the depth of religious sentiment among the ordinary people of Yucatán, and his campaign against religion alienated many women as well as men who otherwise agreed with his policies. [20]

Alvarado and Carrillo Puerto deplored the influence of the Church over women and sought to diminish its power by interesting women in political affairs. In *La reconstrucción de México* (1919), Alvarado advocated that women should first vote in municipal and later in state and national elections. Once their civic education had progressed, Alvarado urged that women be permitted to run for office. Carrillo Puerto, who had built up what amounted to a one-party regime in Yucatán and thus controlled elections, accelerated the process. Early in 1922 he proposed a law to the state legislature giving women the right to vote. Then he urged women who agreed with his principles to run for office. That same year, schoolteacher Rosa Torres, who participated in the First Feminist Congress of Yucatán in January 1916, became the first woman in Mexican history to hold an elective office and served as president of the Municipal Council of Mérida. [21]

In elections for the state legislature in 1923, Carrillo's Socialist party picked three women as deputies and one as an alternate, out of a total of eighteen deputies and eighteen alternates. His younger sister, Elvia Carrillo Puerto, a close collaborator in all his initiatives on behalf of women, ran in the fifth district and won by an overwhelming majority of 5,115 votes. [22] Beatriz Peniche, a librarian who had also participated in the First Feminist Congress called by Alvarado, won in the second district, while Raquel Dzib and Guadalupe Lara were successful as candidate and alternate in the third and fourth legislative districts, respectively. [23]

Their victory was short-lived, however, and the November 1923 elections were set aside when Carrillo Puerto's enemies gained control in Yucatán in December. When Socialists regained power in Yucatán by April 1924, they did not reinstate the women candidates. Furthermore, there was no further reference to women in politics in Socialist party platforms for the rest of the decade. [24]

Alvarado and Carrillo Puerto believed that women's liberation meant primarily the liberation of women from exclusive concern with domestic life. They advocated that women join the work force, but the economic opportunities available to women in a one-crop, agricultural economy were severely limited, even when the price of henequen was high, as was the case during World War I. By 1922, however, the price of henequen had plummeted, and, worse, Yucatán's chief customer, the United States, was turning to other producers of sisal to satisfy its needs for binder twine. Without economic diversification, growth, and development, none of which occurred under Alvarado or Carrillo Puerto, women could not possibly join the work force without competing with men for the few available jobs in public administration, commercial houses, banks, and the like. Women dominated in primary school education simply because the pay was so wretched, usually less than two *pesos* a day, and the need for dedication so total that few men sought these positions. [25]

Given this situation, one can understand why Alvarado and then Carrillo Puerto urged women to devote some of their time to unremunerated educational, charitable, and welfare activities. In his essay, *Mi sueño*, in which Alvarado described his hopes for Yucatán's future, he envisioned the day when Yucatecan women would form organizations to combat alcohol, drugs, and prostitution and would establish the Republic of Virtue that is the dream of modern revolutionaries. [26] He wanted to see educated women help unemployed females, care for abandoned children, and redeem fallen women. [27] No doubt influenced by the important role that women played in charitable activities in the United States, he urged Yucatecan women to hold charity bazaars, care for and console the sick, set up *cocinas económicas* for working women, administer a free milk program for poor children, organize literacy campaigns for adults, establish children's libraries, and give talks on home economics and hygiene to poor women. These many goals were to be carried out by women themselves, organized into *ligas femeniles*, with financial and moral support from the state. [28]

Carrillo Puerto agreed with Alvarado that women should organize into associations and take active part in the transformation of Yucatecan society. Helped by his sister Elvia, who shared Carrillo's radical sentiments, *ligas feministas* were established throughout Yucatán, beginning in Mérida with the Rita Cetina Gutiérrez Feminist League. Elvia Carrillo became president of the Mérida league and dominated it and the provincial feminist leagues, as Felipe Carrillo dominated the male resistance leagues through his control of the Central League in Mérida. The *ligas feministas* of 1922-23 addressed themselves to the problems that Alvarado mentioned in his writings, and Elvia Carrillo and her associates conducted a moralizing campaign designed to rid Yucatán of drugs, alcohol, and prostitution. In addition, they stimulated the literacy campaign, awarding prizes to those who taught the most women to read and write in a given period of time. And, as urged by Alvarado in *Mi sueño*, members of the Rita Cetina Gutiérrez League also gave talks on home economics, child care, and hygiene to poor women. However, it was precisely in this area that the *ligas* soon scandalized "*la gente decente*" by advocating birth control in their talks to "*la gente humilde*" of Yucatán. [29]

While governor, Alvarado sought to introduce some modern ideas on sex in Yucatán, but he met such a wall of resistance that he was forced to retract his suggestions for sex education in the schools and even had to abandon his program of coeducational classes beyond the first three grades. [30] Carrillo Puerto ignored this resistance, and at the beginning of his administration in February 1922, he had a thirteen-page pamphlet by Margaret Sanger, entitled *La regu-*

lación de la natalidad, o la brújula del hogar, published in Mérida for wide distribution.[31] It was precisely this pamphlet "on safe and scientific measures for avoiding conception" that Mrs. Sanger could not distribute in the United States at the time because, as she stated in 1920 in *Woman and the New Race*, "a law dating back to 1873 . . . prohibits by criminal statute the distribution and regulation of contraceptive measures."[32] In mid-1923, Carrillo Puerto, through his friend Dr. Ernest Grüening, a member of the National Council of the American Birth Control League, Inc., invited Mrs. Sanger to come to Yucatan to set up birth control clinics. On 3 July 1923, Mrs. Anne Kennedy, executive secretary of the league, wrote Carrillo Puerto that Mrs. Sanger could not come herself, but had instructed Mrs. Kennedy to go in her place and report to the governor on the league's clinical work in New York. As a result of Mrs. Kennedy's visit to Yucatán in August 1923, plans were made to establish two birth control clinics in Mérida.[33] Ernest Grüening wrote that the clinics were set up to provide recently married couples with information on contraception.[34] However, *Tierra*, the mouthpiece of Carrillo's Socialist party, specified that one of the clinics was being established at the Women's and Children's Hospital in Mérida, while the other "would be established in the segregated district for prostitutes," thus contradicting Grüening's assertion that the birth control clinics were solely for young proletarian couples seeking to rear only as many children as they could support. In retrospect, it appears that in providing prostitutes with contraceptive information, Carrillo Puerto was trying to reduce the high rate of venereal disease in Yucatán (he even decreed a law requiring men to present the prostitutes whom they solicited with a certificate of health), but few of his contemporaries saw matters with such scientific detachment; most people were outraged at his actions. Carrillo Puerto's measures with respect to prostitutes called into question his claim of moralizing society, and his efforts to help them were viewed as evidence that Carrillo Puerto and his friends were receiving payoffs from prostitutes.[35]

Even if one sympathizes with Carrillo Puerto's desire to help women to avoid having unwanted children, it is questionable if his methods were of any real help to most women in that society at that particular time. What good were Mrs. Sanger's methods to women who could not read and write, who lacked a supply of uncontaminated running water, and who could not afford to pay for the syringes, douche bags, douche solutions, suppositories, or pessaries recommended in her pamphlet? Also, Mrs. Sanger's assertion that the methods she advised were safe, sure, and harmless was misleading and, in fact, untrue. After considerable experimentation—and then in 1923, a year after the Sanger pamphlet was published in Yucatán—Dr. Dorothy Bocker, head of the Clinical Research Bureau in New York, found that the most successful contraceptive techniques required the use of a spermicidal jelly in combination with a Mensinga-type diaphragm that was produced only in Germany.[36] That may have been great news for middle- and upper-class women in New York, but it could hardly help the impoverished women of the world who lacked the means of purchasing such sophisticated items. Lastly, Mrs. Sanger's advice that women take a good laxative four days before the menstrual cycle began was downright dangerous in a region where diarrhea, dysentery, and gastroenteritis were (and still are) endemic. In 1924, Sofía Villa de Buentello summed up the views of moderate feminists on the subject of birth control by stating that "we are not yet ready to advocate it."[37]

Carrillo Puerto's radical views on marriage and divorce also aroused considerable controversy in Yucatán. He supported the idea of "free love," which to radical socialists meant that a man and a woman, moved by instinct to preserve the species, united their hearts, minds, and bodies without the sanction of Church or state.[38]

As a result, Carrillo believed that marriage was neither a religious rite nor a civil contract, thus departing from both age-old tradition as well as from more recent secular liberal legislation. This legislation and Carranza's divorce law of 1914 and the Law of Domestic Relations of 1917 defined marriage as a civil contract that could be dissolved only by mutual consent or at the request of the guiltless spouse.[39] Carrillo Puerto's March 1923 divorce law, on the other hand, defined marriage as "a voluntary union based on love, for the purpose of founding a home, and dissoluble at the wish of either party," guilty or innocent, we might add.[40]

Socialists insisted that Carrillo Puerto's ideas on free love and divorce would have a moralizing effect.[41] However, on 5 March 1923, Carrillo Puerto's old and once intimate friend, Carlos R. Menéndez, published an article in his *Revista de Yucatán*, the most widely read newspaper in the peninsula, that did not support the Socialist thesis that Carrillo Puerto's divorce law was intended as a moralizing factor. The article revealed that Carrillo had sent a note to all Mexican consuls in the United States, informing them that Americans could get a divorce with ease after thirty days' residence in Yucatán. Divorces by mutual consent would cost $15, while those at the request of only one of the spouses would cost $125. All divorce cases were to be handled exclusively by lawyers who were members of Carrillo's leagues of resistance, which was another way of saying that Carrillo Puerto would personally profit from each divorce case, as every member of the resistance leagues paid dues commensurate with his income.[42]

Carrillo Puerto's image was further tarnished when he took advantage of the very divorce law that he promulgated and left his wife of thirty years, Isabel Palma, to court a much younger woman, the American writer Alma Reed.[43] His behavior gave credence to the charge that in Mexico, where male supremacy was the rule, divorce would be an advantage only to "the blackguards who, avid for pleasure, will increase the number of repudiated women."[44]

For all its radical features, Carrillo Puerto's divorce law kept intact the sexual double standard so conspicuous in Mexican legislation and so galling to feminists. Under the new law, adultery by men was viewed with indulgence, and any divorced man could remarry immediately. A divorced woman, on the other hand, had to wait 300 days before she could remarry, which was obviously intended to assure the second husband that she was not pregnant by the first.

The reaction of most legally married Yucatecans to Carrillo Puerto's divorce law was to ignore it. From March 1923 until Carrillo Puerto's death ten months later, many Americans sought a divorce in Yucatán, but fewer than a dozen Yucatecan couples resorted to the new law. [45] Until very recent times, divorce has been fairly uncommon in Mexico. The 1930 census noted that only 40,534 persons, or slightly more than 1 percent of the legally married population, were divorced. [46] This confirms American lawyer R. B. Gaither's observation in 1923 that laws like the recent Yucatecan divorce decree are "not really the basic laws of the people of Mexico. They were merely the nightmare of the respectable element." [47]

Carrillo Puerto had an opportunity to publicize his ideas on women's liberation, and feminists to react to them, when the Mexican branch of the Pan American League for the Elevation of Women decided to hold its first congress in Mexico City on 20-30 May 1923. The congress was the brainchild of Profesora Elena Torres, a remarkable woman who, possibly because of her radical ideas, has received very little attention from the more conventional feminists who have compiled the few books available on notable Mexican women. [48] Profesora Torres was a pioneer in progressive education in Mexico and a close collaborator of both Salvador Alvarado and Felipe Carrillo Puerto. She was also a friend of Hermila Galindo, Mexico's most radical feminist, from 1915 to 1920 and went to Yucatán to represent her at the Second Feminist Congress of Mérida, convoked by Alvarado in November 1916. [49] Impressed with her abilities and her advanced views on education, Alvarado asked Profesora Torres to establish a Montessori school in Mérida, the first in the republic. After Alvarado left Yucatán, Profesora Torres remained, and in 1918 she and Felipe Carrillo Puerto were among the original organizers of the Latin American Bureau of the Third International, a socialist organization that sought to create solidarity between the Mexican and Russian working classes. [50]

In April 1922, at the first Pan American Conference of Women, held in Baltimore, Maryland, Profesora Torres was elected vice-president for North America (comprising the United States, Mexico, and the Caribbean) of the newly formed Pan American League for the Elevation of Women. [51] In this capacity she issued invitations to all state governors of Mexico and to feminist organizations in the United States, Cuba, and Mexico to send representatives to a Congress on Women to be held in Mexico on 20-30 May 1923. The congress was attended by delegates from at least twenty Mexican states, some appointed by the governors and others representing the various feminist organizations that were springing up in Mexico City and the larger provincial cities. [52] Most of the delegates were professional women, and among the distinguished representatives were Matilda P. Montoya and Columba Rivera, Mexico's first women doctors, and Julia Nava de Ruisánchez, one of the founders in 1904 of La Sociedad Protectora de la Mujer, the oldest feminist society in Mexico City. In addition, the National League of Women Voters, the Women's International League for Peace and Freedom, the Parent Teachers Association, the YWCA, the Los Angeles Council of Catholic Women, and the American Birth Control League, also sent one or more delegates from the United States.[53] With each divergent organizations represented, the historic congress promised to be most interesting.

It was, not because the American delegates ever had a chance to air their differences, but because the three delegates from Yucatán, led by Elvia Carrillo Puerto, had the congress in an uproar from the beginning. Undaunted by their total lack of experience as delegates to an international congress, the Yucatecan delegation sought to impose their views and dominate the meetings, much to the distress of President Elena Torres, who privately shared many of their radical ideas. However, Profesora Torres was an experienced parliamentarian who had worked long and hard to bring the congress to fruition; and although decidedly anticapitalist and anti-imperialist in her views, she found herself in the ironic position of conspiring with the American delegates to keep such controversial issues as female sexuality, birth control, free love, and sex education in the schools from dominating, and possibly wrecking, the congress.[54]

On the second day of the congress, President Torres had a secret meeting with the American delegates. Backed by the majority of the feminists of the congress, who feared that the Yucatecan delegates would discredit the women's movement in Mexico, they passed a resolution limiting debate on each matter under discussion. However, the Yucatecans countered by boycotting the sessions and threatened to leave the congress altogether. The Yucatecan delegation won out, and articles in the leading newspapers of Mexico City revealed that the debate on birth control and sexual problems, for example, dominated two of the six days of meetings.[55] In addition, the Yucatecan delegates presented a number of other papers on controversial issues. They denounced conventional marriage as "legal slavery," offered remedies for the white slave traffic, advocated coeducation and sex education in the schools, and said that easy divorce would force women to seek work outside the home. They also propagandized in favor of socialist leagues of resistance as the only means of bringing social reform to Mexico.[56] By the end of the conference, the delegates had been fully apprised of Felipe Carrillo Puerto's ideas on women's liberation in Yucatán.

The Yucatecan delegation stole most of the headlines and monopolized most of the sessions, but the published resolutions of the congress reveal that their more controversial suggestions were either rejected or considerably watered down. For example, their proposal for birth control was rejected overwhelmingly in favor of a resolution calling on the Superior Council of Health to establish prenatal and postnatal clinics throughout Mexico to combat the very high infant mortality rate in the country.[57] The Mexican delegates reasoned that birth control was not the answer for a country which had experienced severe population decline during the Revolution, which every day continued to lose workers to the United States, and in which as many as 80 percent of all infants born died within weeks. One delegate noted that "first it is necessary to teach people to read before you can teach them not to have children," an observation that experience has confirmed.[58] In an article published in 1973, Nora Scott Kinzer observed that in Latin America "birth rates are low where there is a high literacy rate . . . and lowered drastically where literacy campaigns are combined with governmental birth control efforts."[59]

The delegates also rejected the Yucatecan proposal that the congress endorse the idea of "free love" on the grounds that such a doctrine only encouraged licentiousness. Instead they passed a resolution calling on feminist organizations to use their influence to change the marriage ceremony from an expensive, theatrical display to a simple one that emphasized the nobility of the act.[60] Another resolution asked that the law providing that no fees be charged for the civil marriage ceremony be strictly enforced.[61]

The delegates rejected the use of the term *sex education*, but did recommend that biology, hygiene, prenatal and infant care, eugenics, and euthenics be part of the school curriculum, without further elaboration. The Yucatecan recommendation for coeducational schools was not mentioned in the resolutions. Lastly, the Yucatecan recommendation that militant leagues of resistance be established in Mexico was diluted into a resolution calling for the formation of women's associations to be active in social reform.[62]

Susana Betancourt of Yucatán made one recommendation that was heartily endorsed by the congress, as it had been a persistent demand of feminists for some time. The Mexican branch of the Pan American League of Women went on record "emphatically in favor of a single sexual standard for men and women." In this connection, the president of the congress, Elena Torres, presented a paper at the last working session of the meetings, calling on the Mexican Congress to remove the inequitable features in the Law of Family Relations of 1917. Specifically, Ms. Torres wanted Articles 77, 93, 97, and 101 to apply the same criterion to men and women, and she recommended that two other articles be suppressed, one which did not permit an innocent wife to remarry for 300 days or a guilty one for two years.[63] Articles 77 and 93 severely punished a wife's infraction of the moral code, both before and after a divorce, and article 97 specified that a guiltless wife could lose custody of her children if she did not live "honestly." At the same time, article 101 made it possible for the ex-spouse to pay an amount equivalent to five years of support and be free of any further obligation.[64] In a country where honest labor by unskilled women is paid a pittance and where divorced women, like unwed mothers, are considered "unowned goods of easy access" (as María Elvira Bermudez observed in 1955 in *La vida familiar del mexicano*), it is easy to see why Ms. Torres and other feminists objected to the stern dictates of the Law of Family Relations insofar as women were concerned. [65]

At the Thursday, 24 May 1923, meetings when the assembly voted down birth control, Elvia Carrillo Puerto accused the majority of being "bourgeoise," reactionary, and ignorant of the misery in which the masses lived. [66] The charge was inaccurate, for while most Mexican feminists rejected the very ideas that had gained Carrillo Puerto notoriety in the country, they supported other proposals that reveal their acquaintance with Mexico's most pressing social problems and their desire to participate in their solution. For example, the delegates petitioned the Mexican Congress to pass the labor legislation provided for an Article 123 of the 1917 Constitution, a reform not enacted until 1931. They asked that domestic servants be protected by that same legislation; today they are still virtually unprotected. Only in 1975 did domestic servants become eligible for national health services, *but* at the discretion of their employers. The delegates also urged that juvenile courts be established in Mexico, an urgent need that began to be attended to only in 1929, when the first juvenile court was established in Mexico City. [67]

Unlike their more timid predecessors at the Feminist Congress of Yucatán of 1916, who asked for political rights at some future time, the majority of the delegates at the First Feminist Congress of the Pan American League agreed that the only way women would see enactment of the laws that they proposed was to vote and run for office. They therefore resolved to petition the Mexican Congress to establish the equality of political rights for men and women. No doubt, the extension of the vote to women in England and the United States a few years earlier accelerated the demand for political rights in Mexico, but it took the feminists another thirty years to convince the men in power to end the political inferiority of women. [68]

The 1923 Pan American Women's Congress provides the historian with evidence that Carrillo Puerto's espousal of women's liberation during 1922-23 did not win the endorsement of the country's leading feminists. They rejected his ideas on free love and birth control, not because these women were religious bigots, as was suggested, but because they saw social problems in another light. To the moderate feminists, Mexico's big problem was "paid love," not free love; and prostitution was as much in evidence in Yucatán, despite all the revolutionary rhetoric, as anywhere else. [69] Also, advocating free love in a country in which at least 700,000 couples lived in free union and an unspecified number of mothers had no mate at all must have struck these feminists as superfluous, if not perverse. [70] As for birth control, the majority of the feminists attending the 1923 congress rejected it as inapplicable and premature. Only when Mexico's population growth, which was -0.5 percent in 1921, rose dramatically would birth control begin to get serious attention. [71]

What feminists had most consistently demanded since 1904, a single sexual standard, was not found in Carrillo Puerto's divorce law, nor was it conspicuous in his own behavior. On close scrutiny, the claim by his North American admirers that Carrillo Puerto was a champion of women's rights in Mexico needs to be qualified. [72] On the one hand, Carrillo Puerto did further the right of women to participate in activities outside the home, but, on the other, his controversial ideas merely convinced conservatives that feminism was dangerous. [73]

In 1923, Mexican feminists had their work cut out for them. In their efforts to end their exclusion from the world, to terminate their legal, social, and political inferiority, and to achieve greater personal freedom, they had to contend with powerful conservative enemies while at the same time dissociating themselves from male champions like Felipe Carrillo Puerto whose radical ideas had discredited their cause.

Notes

1. Frank Tannenbaum, *Peace by Revolution: An Interpretation of Mexico* (New York: Columbia University Press, 1933), p. 127.

2. Of all the writers who praised or damned Carrillo Puerto in the 1920s only one, the North American Ernest Grüening, noticed that Mayan Indian women were sexually exploited by the henequen plantation owners. See Ernest H. Grüening, *Un viaje al estado de Yucatán* (Guanajuato: Talleres Gráficos de *Los Sucesos*, 1924), p. 8.

3. Tannenbaum, *Peace by Revolution*, p. 121.

4. Rodolfo Menéndez, *Rita Cetina Gutiérrez* (Mérida: Imprenta Gamboa Guzmán, 1909), pp. 15-39; Efrem Leonzo Donde, "Páginas históricas: La educación pública en Yucatán. El Instituto Literario de Niñas (1877-1912)," in *La Revista de Yucatán* (Mérida), 13 May 1923, p. 12.

5. A list of these works is found in the section on social structure in volume 1 of Luis Gonzáles, *Fuentes de la historia contemporánea de Mexico*, 3 vols. (Mexico: El Colegio de Mexico, 1961-62).

6. Antonio Bustillos Carrillo, *Yucatán al servicio de la patria y de la revolución* (Mexico: Casa Ramírez Editores, 1959), p. 182.

7. Tannenbaum, *Peace by Revolution*, p. 117.

8. Simone de Beauvoir, *The Second Sex*, trans. H. M. Parshley (New York: Modern Library, 1968), pp. 112-13.

9. For more details on Alvarado's revolutionary program for women, see Anna Macías, "The Mexican Revolution Was No Revolution for Women," in Lewis Hanke, ed., *History of Latin American Civilization: Sources and Interpretations*, 2 vols., 2d ed. (Boston: Little, Brown, 1973), 2: 463-65.

10. Congreso Feminista de Yucatán, *Anales de esa memorable asamblea* (Mérida: Talleres Tipográficos del "Ateneo Peninsular," 1916), and articles in *La Voz de la Revolución* (Mérida) 9-17 January 1916 and 23 November-3 December 1916.

11. Congreso Feminista, *Anales*, p. 111. Some 620 women, most of them urban primary school teachers and, hence, not representative of the overwhelmingly rural and in-

digenous population of Yucatán, attended the January 1916 Feminist Congress. The second congress was even less representative, with only 234 women in attendance, the majority of whom lived and taught in Mérida.

12. *La Voz de la Revolución*, 28 November 1916, pp. 1-2.

13. Venustiano Carranza, *Ley sobre relaciones familiares*, official edition (Mexico: Imprenta del Gobierno, 1917).

14. Luis Rosado Vega, *El desastre: Asuntos yucatecos. La obra revolucionaria del General Alvarado* (Havana: Imprenta El Siglo XX, 1919), p. 202.

15. Edmundo Bolío Ontiveros, *De la cuna al paredón: Anecdotario histórico de la vida, muerte y gloria de Felipe Carrillo Puerto* (Mérida: Talleres de La Compañia Periodista del Sureste, n.d.), pp. 14-17.

16. Ibid.

17. Ibid., p. 55.

18. See the chapter on Carrillo Puerto and the *Ligas de Resistencia* in John W. F. Dulles, *Yesterday in Mexico: A Chronicle of the Revolution, 1919-1936* (Austin: University of Texas Press, 1961), pp. 136-44.

19. Bernardino Mena Brito, *Bolshevismo y democracia en Mexico*, 2d ed. (Mexico, 1933), p. xxv.

20. By his own account, Carrillo Puerto was meeting considerable resistance in his antireligious campaign. See *Tierra*, "Organo de la Liga Central de Resistencia" (Mérida), 8 July 1923, p. 9.

21. Bustillos Carrillo, *Yucatán al servicio de la patria*, pp. 180, 273.

22. *Tierra*, 2 December 1923, p. 7.

23. Ibid., 18 November 1923, p. 27.

24. Bartolomé García Correa, *Cómo se hizo su campaña política* (Mérida: Imprenta y Litografía Gamboa Guzmán, 1930), pp. 46-48.

25. Ernest H. Grüening, *Mexico and Its Heritage* (New York: Century Co., 1928), p. 630n.

26. *La Voz de la Revolución*, 7 January 1917, p. 4.

27. The 1921 census reported that 102,969 women were unemployed, as opposed to 55,471 men out of work; *Resumen del censo general de habitantes de 30 de noviembre de 1921* (Mexico: Talleres Gráficos de la Nación, 1928), p. 99.

28. *La Voz de la Revolución*, 7 January 1917, p. 4.

29. "Propaganda feminista," in *Tierra*, 19 August 1923, pp. 4-13.

30. [Salvador Alvarado], *Informe que el Gral. Salvador Alvarado . . . rinde al primer jefe del Ejército Constitucionalista . . . C. Venustiano Carranza: Comprende su gestión administrativa desde el 19 de marzo de 1915 al 28 de febrero de 1917* (Mérida: Imprenta del Gobierno Constitucionalista, 1917), p. 38.

31. A copy of this now rare pamphlet is found in the Basave Collection of the Biblioteca de Mexico in Mexico City. According to Adolfo Ferrer, *El archivo de Felipe Carrillo: El callismo. La corrupción del régimen obregonista* (New York: Carlos López Press, 1924), p. 55, "pamphlets on birth control were distributed even to minors in the schools."

32. Margaret Sanger, *Woman and the New Race* (New York: Brentano's Publishers, 1920), p. 130.

33. The letter of Mrs. Kennedy to Governor Carrillo was stolen by the latter's executioners and reproduced in Ferrer, *El archivo de Felipe Carrillo*, p. 57, to discredit the

memory of the assassinated leader. Evidence of Mrs. Kennedy's visit is found in *Tierra*, 30 September 1923, p. 9.

34. Ernest H. Grüening, "Felipe Carrillo Puerto," in *La Reforma Social* (Havana), February 1924, p. 222. The English version of this article appeared in *The Nation* on 16 January 1924.

35. Gardner Hunting in an article highly critical of Carrillo Puerto in *Collier's Weekly*, 26 April 1924, as quoted by Ferrer, *El archivo de Felipe Carrillo*, p. 58.

36. David M. Kennedy, *Birth Control in America: The Career of Margaret Sanger* (New Haven: Yale University Press, 1970), p. 183.

37. Sofía Villa de Buentello in an interview published in the *New York Times*, 2 March 1924, sec. 9, p. 13.

38. Rosendo Salazar and José G. Escobedo, *Las pugnas de la gleba, 1907-1922*, 2 vols. (Mexico: Editorial Avante, 1923), 1: 259.

39. Carranza, *Ley sobre relaciones familiares*, arts. 13, 17.

40. Ernest H. Grüening, "The Assassination of Mexico's Ablest Statesman," *Current History* 19 (October 1923-March 1924): 738.

41. *Tierra*, 15 July 1923, p. 20.

42. Ferrer, *El archivo de Felipe Carrillo*, p. 13.

43. For details of the Reed-Carrillo relationship, see Erna Fergusson, *Mexico Revisited* (New York: A. Knopf, 1955), pp. 116-17.

44. Quoted in Moisés González Navarro, *El porfiriato: La vida social*, vol. 5 of *Historia moderna de Mexico*, ed. Daniel Cosio Villegas, 8 vols. (Mexico: Editorial Hermes, 1955-65), p. 411.

45. Grüening, "Felipe Carrillo," p. 222.

46. Estados Unidos Mexicanos, Secretaría de la Económia Nacional, Dirección General de Estadística. *Quinto censo de población: 15 de mayo de 1930. Resumen general* (Mexico, 1930), p. 51.

47. R. B. Gaither, "The Marriage and Divorce Laws of Mexico," *American Law Review* 57 (May-June 1923): 412.

48. See, for example, Consuelo Colón R., *Mujeres de Mexico* (Mexico: Imprenta Gallarda, 1944); Artemisa Sáenz Royo, *Historia política-social-cultural del movimiento femenino en Mexico, 1914-1950* (Mexico: M. León Sánchez, 1954); and Rosalía d'Chumacero, *Perfil y pensamiento de la mujer mexicana*, 2 vols. (Mexico, 1961).

49. Hermila Galindo, *Estudio de la Srta. Hermila Galindo con motivo de los temas que han de absolverse en el segundo congreso feminista de Yucatán* (Mérida: Imprenta del Gobierno Constitucionalista, 1916), p. 4.

50. Salazar and Escobedo, *Las pugnas de la gleba*, 2: 64.

51. *Sección Mexicana de la Liga Pan-Americana para la elevación de la mujer* (Mexico: Talleres Linotipográficos "El Modelo," 1923), p. 7.

52. *El Universal* (Mexico), 17 May 1923, p. 1.

53. Ibid.

54. Ibid., 23 May 1923, p. 1.

55. Ibid., 17-30 May 1923, and *El Demócrata*, 21-30 May 1923. *Excelsior* refused to cover the congress in its news columns and published two long editorials on 24 and 28 May 1923 denouncing the congress as "scandalous."

56. *La Revista de Yucatán*, 23 May 1923, p. 1.

57. *Primer Congreso Feminista de la Liga Pan-Americana de Mujeres* (Mexico: Talleres Linotipográficos "El Modelo," 1923), p. 5.

58. *El Demócrata*, 25 May, 1923, p. 1.

59. Nora Scott Kinzer, "Priests, Machos and Babies: Or, Latin American Women and the Manichean Heresy," *Journal of Marriage and the Family* 35 (May 1973): 306.

60. *Primer Congreso Feminista*, p. 4.

61. Ibid., p. 5.

62. Ibid., p. 6.

63. *El Universal*, 27 May 1923, p. 8, and *El Demócrata*, 30 May 1923, p. 8.

64. Carranza, *Ley sobre relaciones familiares*, pp. 31-32.

65. María Elvira Bermúdez, *La vida familiar del mexicano* (Mexico: Antigua Librería Robredo, 1955), p. 77.

66. *El Universal*, 25 May 1923, pt. 2, 8.

67. Salvador M. Luna, *Los niños moralmente abandonados y la función social del tribunal para menores de la ciudad de Mexico* (Mexico: Herrero Hermanos Sucesores, 1929), p. 33.

68. Ward M. Morton, *Woman Suffrage in Mexico* (Gainesville: University of Florida Press, 1962), p. 84.

69. Anastasio Manzanilla, *El bolchevismo criminal de Yucatán* (Mexico: Ediciones de "El Hombre Libre," 1921), p. 188.

70. The 1921 census did not provide figures on free unions, but by 1930, when the number of free unions had declined, the census still reported 695,619 women as living in free union; Estados Unidos Mexicanos, *Quinto censo de 1930*, p. 51.

71. *Resumen del censo general de 1921*, p. 59.

72. Ernest H. Grüening and Erna Fergusson are unqualified in their praise of Carrillo Puerto as a champion of feminism.

73. See especially the editorials in *Excelsior*, 24 May 1923, p. 3, and 28 May 1923, p. 3.

12

Some final considerations on trends and issues in Latin American women's history

The preceding eleven essays have tried to open new windows into the history of Latin American women by asking new questions and using new and old sources in a different manner. However, because the historical literature on Latin women is rather limited and the field of women's history is rapidly expanding, a final appraisal of the trends in research, issues under discussion, and potential topics of study for the future seemed necessary at this point. This will, hopefully, enhance the purpose of this book: to serve the present needs of all students and scholars on Latin America and others who may wish to use that cultural and geographical area for comparative studies.

A survey of the available recent literature in English on Latin American women shows that little of it follows the historical method or deals with issues in a historical fashion, having been written mostly by social scientists. Lacking a fuller bibliography in their own field, historians may use these works profitably to remedy their own scarcities and, at the same time, to adapt some of the techniques of research of the social scientist to their investigations. In turn, the historian may provide answers to some of the social scientists' questions and give support—or disproof—to some of their theories. This essay does not pretend to provide a full bibliographical coverage of the topics discussed. The previous bibliographical surveys by Ann Pescatello, Meri Knaster, and June Hahner and the recently published annotated bibliography on Spanish American women by Meri Knaster would make of such an attempt an exercise in futile repetition.[1] It is not possible to discuss the wide range of historical issues, either. I attempt what is called in Spanish a *planteamiento*: the tracing of a plan for future construction, the asking of some questions in order to elicit answers. I will try to define some topics of interest in the history of women in Latin America as potential research topics for historians. Some examples and sources will be quoted when they raise important issues or serve to illustrate a point.

In the past there have been two main approaches to the history of Latin women. One seeks to define women using sources that reflect cultural norms rather than typical behavior. Among those, educational or legal material are the most common.[2] The other approach concentrates on the deeds of a number of women from the sixteenth century onwards, individuals who are assumed to be representative models of what women have been, but who, for the most part, are exceptional cases rather than true representatives of the majority of their sex.[3] By themselves neither of these two approaches is satisfactory any longer, insofar as they present only partial views of women's activities and values. Legal and prescriptive sources need to be implemented by others that add more elements to the complex picture of women's past. In the second instance, the biography of the great woman has been overworked without any significant improvement in quality or additional interpretive nuances. Therefore, it needs to be superseded by a type of work that would allow us to sample the lives of a larger number of women, closer to being more representative of their times and classes. What must remain is a concern for the definition of ideals that served as guidelines of women's behavior and for the study of the actual behavior of women in their historical reality.

The examples of prescriptive literature quoted by Russell-Wood, Mendelson, and myself in this volume, reflect aspirations to perfection seldom achieved, but retained as models for emulation. They are useful points of reference against which one may gauge the harmonious or discordant chords of real life. Both Spanish and Portuguese sources offered very similar approaches and changed little throughout time, attesting to the stability achieved prior to the conquest and throughout the centuries of colonial life.[4] New editions of these centuries-old prescriptive books were reissued—and still are—but after the late eighteenth century, new writings of this genre became rarer. This was partially the result of the weakening of the role of the Church as the arbiter of women's behavior. After the first half of the nineteenth century this role was taken over by the State and its educational institutions, although the religious influence of the Church was by no means obliterated. In order to find normative material resembling that of early centuries, although with a different emphasis, one must look for educational works written for women by essayists and educators. Examples of prescriptive literature written in the nineteenth century by lay writers are mostly conservative in character and do not depart from canons established in earlier centuries.[5]

Conservatism seems to have been well entrenched in the educational goals set for Latin women by educators. However, there were reformists and liberals as well. Cynthia Little's essay illustrates some of the main currents of thought on women's education in Argentina. Similar studies should be undertaken for other countries. The major impulse for feminine education was shared by both male and female educators, although it is important to point out that the ministries of education, from which all policies emanated, were controlled by men, not women.

Such noted educators as Domingo F. Sarmiento or Juana Manso are well represented in the literature on education in Spanish. Although all of the reformers shared a belief in the elevation of women's status through education, they had not abandoned the main assumption underlying all education for women: their preparation was to serve better their ultimate destiny as wives and mothers. Reformism did not amount to radicalism.

If one accepts the premise that prescriptive literature was replaced by educational literature in the mid-nineteenth century, the possibilities of researching the values upheld by Latin societies for the socialization of women are greatly broadened. The writings of male and female educators would serve as an index to the behavioral norms sought for women. There is a broad spectrum of ideas: the initial hopeful statements and plans of the beginning of the nineteenth century; the more activist educators of the second half of the century, ardently defending women's right to education, but still feeling ambivalent about how to utilize it when confronted with the choice of work versus marriage and children; and the more openly profeminist position of the authors of the twentieth century.[6] None of these currents substituted for the other; they all eventually coexisted side by side, some being more influential than others in their respective countries. While it is likely that such champions of reform as Sarmiento or Cecilia Grierson will continue to be the favorite topics of future studies, there were other lesser known educators just as influential in their own milieu. Conservative ideology was the guiding principle of two Central American educators, David Joaquín Guzmán and José V. Vázquez, who wrote books endorsed by the Ministries of Education of Nicaragua and Guatemala, respectively.[7] A short-lived publication for teachers in late nineteenth-century Venezuela similarly endorsed education for *madres de familia* (motherhood), underscoring the emotional, not the rational, potential of women.[8] Well into the twentieth century one finds examples of strict conservatism. Although these are in a minority, it is worthwhile to consider the milder, but pervasive, conservative character of the education for women still prevailing in most of Latin America. This topic deserves coverage as good as that devoted to more popular reformers.

Women educators have left a varied catalog of opinions and attitudes. The lion's share in the bibliographical output belongs to the Chilean Nobel laureate Gabriela Mistral, who was a teacher throughout most of her life. Her educational objectives for women underscored a spiritual preparation for what she regarded as their most noble roles in life: wives and, above all, mothers.[9]

Beauty and morality buttressed what she regarded as the "highest form of patriotism" in women: "perfect maternity." Another remarkable educator, also Chilean, was Amanda Labarca, who was deeply committed to the elevation of women's status in society through education. Like Mistral, she did not wish that women lose their femininity or their commitment to spiritual values. However, she is far bolder than Mistral in her advocacy of women's participation in social activities outside of the home.[10] The works of other women educators in Spanish and Portuguese America could be explored as research topics. Their ideas are the best indices to women's own conception of themselves and their aspirations. Indicative of the realities in which they moved, their educational concepts and projects mirror their societies and times.[11]

One step beyond the works of individual educators are the educational programs for women devised by the State. By defining educational objectives, the State had a great degree of control, then as well as now, over the quality of life, the work opportunities of men and women, and the ultimate question of how to utilize its human resources. The State may contribute to stereotyping certain occupations and roles for women by providing certain specific forms of education to them. Since the inception of the first schools for women, all school systems, private or public, expressed the social consensus on the role of women. Women were taught what they were expected to need for functioning in society. The first schools for women founded in the eighteenth century put emphasis on "feminine" education, which was confined to occupations suitable to complement their role as mothers and wives. Even when such a restricted view was overcome with the admittance of women to the universities, women sought out professions that would allow them to combine their roles in the home with their careers.[12] The study of educational systems should help understand the availability of options open to women and the way that such conditions—which were beyond personal choice—molded the destiny of most of them.[13]

Legislation is another important social norm, despite the *caveats* expressed at the beginning of this review. Laws determine the boundaries of women's actions and their status in society. Iberian legal traditions molded women's lives in Latin America for three centuries, and some vestiges are still visible in the twentieth century.[14] A number of studies deal with the bare bones of civil codes and legislation as applicable to women.[15] However, beyond the legal documentation lies the inquiry into the application of the law, which remains to be undertaken in full. It was already suggested in the Introduction that there are significant gaps between written law and actual practice in Latin America. Thus, it is necessary to measure the manner in which the law affected women's lives. Legal case histories and criminal or police records will furnish the evidence necessary to interpret the real nuances of male-female relationships and the implication of such aspects of the law as divorce laws, reform legislation for deviant women, and the like. There are few studies along such lines for the colonial period. Inquisitorial and ecclesiastical records, as well as civilian criminal records, would provide excellent material for social history.[16] Most of the works available for the twentieth century on female delinquency focus on the problems of prostitution, and most are male-authored. Some contain statistical data that should be very useful. These works could also be used to analyze the intellectual man's attitude toward prostitution and female criminality. It is significant that prostitution is mostly conceived as a crime, with no consideration of the fact that it is a means of subsistence to those women who engage in it.[17] The main agenda for the future of historicolegal studies is to inject empirical data into the basic legal framework. The social historian, in this instance, should examine the anthropologist's or sociologist's *métier* for the most interesting results.

It is obvious that in all subjects of study there will be a dividing line between what is normative and what is actual behavior. The latter is a complex response to laws, moral codes, economic incentives, and educational opportunities. Studies focusing on real situations stress reactions and choices, as opposed to or as a consequence of directives or norms. Both normative and actual can be intermingled to a point that makes clear-cut distinctions difficult. This is the case in many historical situations involving women in the two spheres in which they moved: the family and public sphere.

As a theme, the family has been studied mostly by anthropologists and sociologists rather than by historians.[18] Only recently have historians of Latin America begun to examine the historical roots of the family.[19] As a result, many of the techniques and concepts utilized by historians have been borrowed from the social scientist, a trend that will probably continue. For example, the concept of kinship and its meaning in establishing political, economic, and social ties has been used to analyze the links within colonial and modern families.[20] The structure of the family is less well known, but a growing interest in historical demography promises to yield important results in the future. Marriage patterns, the size of the family, and infant and female mortality are under scrutiny. Parochial records and censuses—taken from the end of the eighteenth century onwards—are very useful tools, although they require either team work or a lot of patience. The techniques of family reconstruction are not, as yet, widely used in Latin American family research, and most of the works produced have concentrated on patterns of family structure.[21] These investigations have so far demonstrated the existence of significant numbers of matrifocal families among colonial lower classes. This phenomenon was probably quite widespread all over Latin America, given the similar circumstances of poverty, consensual unions, and migrant men.

Thus, the historical demographer and the ethnohistorian have an almost unexplored territory at their disposal. Some key issues have not as yet been resolved: Was the Latin family extended or nuclear during the period prior to the twentieth century? There might be vast differences in widely separated geographical areas with very different cultural attitudes and economic bases.

Structural changes must have occurred in response to pressures such as de-population due to disease, as in the late sixteenth century, rural and urban migration, and immigration waves, as in nineteenth-century Argentina and Brazil. Rural and urban families, Indians and whites—each must have devel-oped different family patterns, but we still do not know much about either. The increasing interest in tracing the relationship nets among elite families will hopefully also spur interest in other social classes. Perhaps one of the most neglected areas of family history in Latin America is that dealing with indige-nous, *casta*, and black families. Recent studies in United States history, such as that of Herbert Gutman, might serve as a model for similar studies in Latin America. [22]

The new society, produced by the confluence of three races in a new environ-ment, led to the development of a different set of values and expectations and introduced important variants in such institutions as the family. It is necessary to elucidate to what extent the European, Indian, and African models changed as a result of the formation of a new society and what basic characteristics they retained. For example, the scarcity of white women and the availability of sub-jugated races led to the well-known phenomenon of *mestizaje*. In heavily Indian regions and in plantation societies the numbers of illegitimate offspring were extremely large, and the phenomenon of illegitimacy became not only an everyday occurrence in many areas, but a cultural trait as well. This situation was different from that of the mother countries, where illegitimacy was not as widespread, although it did exist. Even the very concept of illegitimacy was new for some of the peoples involved, and within some groups it was deter-mined by class. The isolation of certain areas either stressed some cultural values or created new ones. In such remote areas as the northern provinces of Mexico there was a high incidence of endogamy among the whites due to the scarcity of the population and its slow growth, and the degree of *mestizaje* was lessened by the nomadic character of the indigenous groups. Spanish traits survived longer and, thus, the Iberian character of institutions involving women and the home. Further research of such idiosyncrasies would help characterize the many patterns in family formation in Latin America and could lead to studies in related topics, such as illegitimacy patterns.

Some of the themes suggested by contemporary studies on the family, which so far lack a historical counterpart, are patterns of matrilocality and patrilo-cality and role assumptions leading to contemporary *machismo*, *hembrismo*, and *marianismo*. Also of interest are courtship, child rearing and early child-hood socialization, interclass and interracial marriage, influence of wider choices in employment and education, and availability of broader civil rights in the family role of women. Sources for these topics, which are partially cul-tural, can be found in magazines, educational tracts, governmental statistics (for interracial marriage, for example), or, for the colonial period, sources al-ready mentioned, such as divorce suits or ecclesiastical trials. There are also some topics of study, as yet unresearched, that could lead to a fuller re-creation of the world in which women moved, especially of the more difficult-to-research colonial period. Examples of these would include such topics as patterns of consumption of homeware and personal products, or home and folk medicine, which was largely women's responsibility. The skillful assemblage of such data may lead to a lively reconstruction of what constituted a substantial part of women's lives. Since most women were trained to be housewives, the home and its immediate concerns and surroundings should be the object of historical research. These topics reflect larger social and economic issues. Patterns of consumption of daily needs, such as food or clothes, are indices of market demands and trade, be it regional, viceregal, or national. Local industries or businesses—textile sweatshops, butcher shops, or candlemakers—developed as demands required. Thus, it might not be as banal as it might first appear to trace down the origin of the fabrics used for women's clothes, the consumption of silver for jewels or silverware, or the people's preference for mutton or beef.

Mendelson has pointed out some sources of information on medical practices and beliefs in the late eighteenth century. There are some other sources for earlier periods and certainly many more for the nineteenth and early twentieth centuries. These can provide a great deal of information and insight into women's and children's diseases, practices of hygiene, and the concern for health and welfare that led to the creation of special institutions for the care of women and children. Other social values may be derived from such sources. For example, the habit of wet-nursing among the upper-middle and upper classes—was this a cultural pattern brought from Europe and enhanced in Latin America? Vives and other educators and writers of the eighteenth and even late nineteenth centuries condemn it, attesting to its survival. This is an upper-class social phenomenon, as is the reliance on servants for household work. The availability of servants not only indicates the existence of leisure for some women, but explains the greater opportunity of modern women to engage in professional activities outside the home. [23] The possession of a slave or the services of a servant was not confined to the upper classes. Many women who had little else owned a slave, and in more recent times the low wages of servants have made them available to the middle class. The slave or servant availability also contributed to the enhancement of class lines, which are particularly significant in the determination of social interrelations among women. [24]

Before I pass to activities of women in the public sphere, it is worthwhile to add some comments on yet two other approaches to the history of women that cast light on them as individuals. The life-cycle approach, used successfully in the history of U.S. women, has not been developed properly for Latin American women. [25] Women's experience and the roles that they assumed in life depended greatly on their age and marital status. For example, the productivity of women is affected by their life cycles. Married women drop out of work and

never seem to recover the same independence that they had as single women. 26
It has been seen that in both Spanish and Portuguese America marriage conferred a new status to woman, and widowhood gave her yet a different role.
Such changes or roles merit separate analysis. While we are now aware of the
significance of widowhood for women during the colonial period, there are no
historical studies of widows for other periods. Did widows in the nineteenth
century lose some of the vigorous roles that they had assumed during the colonial period? Is the situation of the twentieth-century widow better or worse
than before, especially since the adoption of social security systems in some
countries? The single woman, whose status in colonial times was ambiguous,
emerges with greater strength in the twentieth century due to greater economic
opportunities and an assumed lessening of prejudices about the unmarried
status, especially in the cities. However, the ideal of most Latin women is still to
be married, and changes with regard to single women may have taken place
more in the area of work and education than in the area of social values. 27

Historical group profiles of women would be very useful in order to determine the general characteristics of women united by specific sets of circumstances, such as profession in religious orders, participation in feminist movements charity activities, or membership in labor unions. Such group profiles
have been recently used by Cohen and Kinzer for twentieth-century women,
but have not been used much for women of previous historical periods, where
they would be extremely helpful. Group profiles may be used to give greater
accuracy to generalizations on women for whom specific personal data are
missing. Equally useful is the collective biography approach, whereby the historian attempts to reconstruct the life experience of women who left few historical records. By drawing a composite picture of the group derived from
partial information on each of the members, one is able to recapture circumstances and nuances that otherwise would be lost. These methods should be of
great help for the reconstruction of the lives of women in the colonial period
and of women of the lower classes.

The public sphere of women's activities encompasses such a broad spectrum
of topics that it cannot all be covered in this survey. Thus, I will concentrate on
women in politics, women's work, feminist activities, and women's participation in some female or women-controlled institutions. The participation of
women in the political movements of Latin America has been one of the major
topics of interest of those political scientists writing on both women and Latin
America. 28 The theme is intriguing. Latin American women have been regarded for so long as home-bound and uninterested in politics that their
gradual emergence into the political arena and the manner of such incorporation cannot but attract the scholar. Analyses of the political activities of women
concentrate on the last thirty years of history. This is largely explained by the
fact that the majority of Latin American women received and started to exercise the right to vote in national elections just around that time, and politicians

had to start taking into consideration their participation in the broader picture of national politics more seriously than before. However, in Latin America affiliation to a party or participation in a political movement does not constitute the totality of political activism. At present, as in the past, periods of dictatorship precluded the vote and open discussion of political issues by both men and women. In most areas only a small male elite was able to exercise the vote, and, more importantly, politics was regarded as a masculine bastion, either because women were assumed to be unable to understand its intricate manipulations or because they were said to be too good and too pure to stain themselves with the political mud. Thus, the historian interested in gauging the political awareness of women in periods when they were barred from organized politics faces no easy task.

The key to solving this situation is a broader concept of what constitutes political participation. The political activities of women are directly correlated to the options open to them at a given time. If the options are limited, the activities are also limited, and one may not expect much. Also, the definition of what is political needs to be flexible to adapt itself to different times and circumstances. Political activity during the colonial period, the nineteenth century, and even the twentieth century extends to participation in street demonstrations, manipulation of regional political kinship, or the search for popular support for a husband or relative in power.[29] Much of the available literature in print is based on a straightforward masculine interpretation of politics and concerns itself with voting patterns, female attitudes toward politics, or exceptional women leaders. Almost all countries in Latin America can boast of a constellation of heroines for the period of independence or of several *mujeres fuertes* during the nineteenth and twentieth centuries.[30] There is, however, a need for a definition of who were the women participants in those riots or wars or protests by using group profile techniques.

While the limelight shines on the few women politicians of certain countries, the subtle manipulations and personal expertise of some women have gone largely unnoticed. For example, the letters of the early nineteenth-century Argentinian socialite Mariquita Sánchez are full of perceptive remarks on the political events of the period.[31] How many like her have been overlooked? Morris Blachman makes a good case for what he calls "selective omission" in the writing of history in Brazil, where most historians have neglected women completely in their writings.[32] The situation is similar for other Latin American nations. What is needed in the future is an attempt to explain the motivations for political participation among women (as individuals or as groups), their response to political situations, their objectives and the techniques they used to obtain them, their effectiveness as a pressure group, and their degree of communal consciousness in the pursuit of political goals. Such studies need not focus on a particular issue—such as the right to vote—but could cover several issues in a wider span of time in order to elucidate general patterns of behavior and response. Another potential approach is that of investigating the attitudes of male politicians of political parties toward women. During certain historical periods radical, or populist, parties and their leaders have sought women's support. Their writings, speeches, and publications are excellent sources for the study of the issues that appeal to women and the way in which politicians handle them. 33 The literature produced by integralism, by Peronism, or by the Bolivian, Cuban, and Mexican revolutions—and in the latter case by the ruling party, PRI—could sustain such studies. 34 Conservative ideology and leaders have also successfully mobilized women in politics, as events in Brazil and Chile attest. 35 The factors that elicit women's response to conservative or radical ideologies have not been determined for many historical situations. Social scientists are aware of the need to understand the roots of female political attitudes, but historians have failed to provide them by their neglect of women in political activities. In a recent study of the political attitudes of Colombian women, Steffen W. Schmidt added a valuable dimension to his work with a discussion of how the historical conditions under which Colombian women entered into politics—at their lowest ebb in the late 1940s—conspired against their interest in participating in politics. 36

Cuban women under the Castro regime are perhaps the most dramatic example of female political mobilization on a large scale in recent years, comparable to that taking place under Perón's Argentina, but deeper and longer-lasting. Perhaps the key to Castro's success has been his rejection of arguments previously used by other male politicians. He appealed to women as actors in the revolution, considering them as people, not roles. The appeal that he exerted was directly correlated to the situation of women in Cuban society prior to the revolution and the way in which they saw a release of their potential or a solution to their grievances in the new political situation. Yet, as some observers have pointed out, traditional attitudes still persist in Cuba in the privacy of the home and even at some governmental levels. 37 The success or failure of the revolution, with regard to women, may lie in its ability to change traditional role concepts in Cuban society. A comparative study of the Cuban revolution to other revolutions or populist regimes might be useful to establish patterns of attitudes and behavior among the female population and the political leaders.

The topics of women's work and their participation in economic activities and economic development have been among the favorite themes of historians of U.S. and European women. They are broad and complex subjects with manifold ramifications, especially since industrialization multiplied the involvement of women in the economy and in the labor force. The output of historical studies on Latin American women's incorporation into the labor force is as meager as others under survey, but due to the increasing interest of economists, sociologists, and political scientists, production is likely to expand in the future.

It has been difficult to convince some historians that women's work or their activities as economic agents were significant and continuous—not just sporadic—during the colonial period. The difficulty in perceiving the role of women as part of the economy and the labor force is due to the lack of consideration of the labor of Indian and black women. Few remarks have been written on their share of the burden of work throughout several centuries. The persistence of the stereotype of the white women shut in their homes also contributed to a lack of interest in gauging the activities of this social group. The third reason for the neglect of this area of research has been the difficulties posed by locating its sources. Labor, having been conceived as the labor of men outside the home boundaries, is a subject that demands a special effort to be perceived in special terms if it refers to women. Most of the legal and documentary sources for the colonial period relate to men and easily led to a lopsided picture of the historical reality.[38]

Since the earliest times, women's work has been recorded by visual arts or in the written word. Mochica pottery, for example, shows women spinning, and throughout the period prior to and after the discovery of America women continued in charge of that task. Most of the lovely examples of Peruvian textiles are the product of women's work. The illustrations of life among the Aztecs immediately after the conquest in Fray Bernardino de Sahagún's works offer a variety of women's occupations, from acting as midwives to gathering herbs for medical purposes.[39] The conceptual difficulty with much of women's work is that it has not been conceived as "productive" in a larger economic sense, despite its being essential to the community. As Elinor Burkett points out in her essay, the share of the Indian women in the economic processes prior to or after the conquest was vital, but has been easily relegated to oblivion due to its nature. Some other colonial sources also offer insights on women's work. The illustrations of Guamán Poma de Ayala and Bishop Martínez Compañón for late sixteenth and early eighteenth century Peru, respectively, are not only visually attractive, but historically accurate.[40] The late eighteenth-century series of oil paintings on *mestizaje* also depict popular types engaged in a number of daily activities.[41]

Almost all the essays in the present volume, to a greater or lesser degree, offer ample evidence of the multiplicity of women's occupations during the colonial period. Although these have only opened the path for future and deeper inquiries, they have hopefully helped to supersede the stage during which women's labor was not even registered as an economic factor. The diversity of sources offering data on women's labor, coupled with their often terse statements, have been an obstacle to research, but should not remain as such. Archival sections on litigations over land and water titles reveal a significant number of women landowners actively engaged in the administration of their land. The minutes of city councils (*ayuntamientos*) record women as miners, or as cattle owners bidding for the provisions of cities, or as bakers providing vital bread supply to some urban complexes. [42] Notarial records containing powers of attorney, sales and purchases of properties, loans, and testaments with inventories furnish a variety of vignettes of women as active members of the local economy. Church records add the extra dimension of religious institutions as property owners and banking institutions of no small importance. [43] The task for the future lies in determining the extent of such activities and the influence of women and feminine institutions on the various economic sectors compared to that of men. It would also be relevant to determine in what manner these activities merged with those of men or served as links between generations of male producers within the family. During the colonial period, widows had a substantial amount of economic power, but we do not know with certainty if they retained this role during the nineteenth or twentieth century. Thus, it is necessary to investigate changes throughout time, due not only to changes in political conditions, but also to cycles of production, scarcity, highs and lows in market demands, and other factors that affected the demand for women's labor or their activities as producers.

The sources cited above will probably yield information on women property owners and on those with their own businesses. Information on Indians, free and slave blacks, and *castas* will be more difficult to retrieve, especially if they belonged to the rural population. But the task is not totally impossible, and although the picture might be incomplete, it will be better than no picture at all. That a partial reconstruction is possible has been demonstrated by Burkett's work. Archival records on Indians, for example, should contain material on women that has not been tapped. The condition of slavery tended to obscure the labor of black women perhaps more than that of the Indian; but in both instances the varied activities of these women—as peddlers, main controllers of town markets, agricultural laborers on plantations or in truck gardening, workers in cottage industries, in the pottery-making trade, and even in the mines, tasks that have been bypassed by historians—may be partially reconstructed. [44]

The greater availability and use of sociological and statistical data for the nineteenth and twentieth centuries make easier the historian's consideration of women's economic activities. However, the bulk of the studies so far available are not historical and concentrate mostly on the twentieth century. Of these, many consider the general position of women in the labor market and deal mostly with the period from 1930 to the present. [45] There is a big lacuna for the earlier years of the twentieth century, and hardly anything exists on the nineteenth century. Interest in the present conditions of laboring women has taken precedent over the historical examination of the development of women's labor or of their continuous role as productive members of the economy. Thus, the need to learn more about the conditions that have shaped women's present circumstances is more urgent than ever. From the late eighteenth century, women began to be incorporated into certain industries, such as textile, garment, and cigar manufacturing. There are few monographic works on these subjects. [46] Significant changes took place in women's work patterns during the nineteenth century. It was then that as a result of industrialization the demand for women's labor in factories increased. Equally, urbanization spurred the migration of many women to the cities because they sought better economic opportunities or perhaps because an increase in the population, coupled with a diminishing availability of free land, offered fewer choices in the provinces. What motivated these women to migrate or to work in factories? From what social strata did they come? How have the economic cycles of different areas of Latin America affected these processes? [47] The urban middle-class women stepped out of the home to engage in activities, such as teaching in the nineteenth century or nursing, secretarial work, or government employment in the twentieth century. The economic and social implications and effects of such large-scale mobilization of women have not been analyzed. Did Latin women pass through the classic Marxist cycle of cottage industry to home piecework to industrial work? [48] Did political changes have a positive or negative effect on the working condition and working opportunities for women? The working conditions of women in the early industrial development of Latin America as well as those employed in traditional occupations remain to be even described, let alone analyzed.

The statistical data mentioned above could be used to start a methodical inquiry into the complex subject of the role of women in the economy. National censuses may not be perfect, but they can be tapped to try to determine the structure of employment in the cities, the number of women employed, their marital status, and other relevant data that will help to establish a firm basis for further research. [49] Parliamentary debates on labor legislation and labor conditions, governmental reports, newspapers, travelers' comments, and the writings of interested labor leaders are also good sources for this topic. [50] Available studies on the patterns of the incorporation of women into the labor market in Latin America seem to indicate that the special idiosyncrasies of each country determined differing modes and rhythms of assimilation. However, there is the intriguing possibility of investigating whether similar stages of development may have taken place in different countries at different chronological periods. [51] On the other hand, certain situations, such as the working conditions and motivation for work among the servant class, appear to be quite similar regardless of country or period.

The activities of women as professionals has been broached in some studies, but the emphasis has been on economic impact. The participation of women in the labor unions and their leaders is another possible line of research. The names of Carolina Muzzili, María Cano, or Luisa Capetillo may be completely unknown to the North American public, but they were leaders of significance in the labor movements of their countries in the early twentieth century. The study of women's activities in labor unions during the early stages of their development or during political crises will reveal surprising examples of leadership and activism. Political parties have supported specific feminine labor activities—as in Argentina, Cuba, and Mexico—but political histories do not often consider the significance of such mobilization, an omission that is much to everybody's loss,[52] since it leaves unanswered the ultimate and most important question about women in labor movements and as economic agents: the degree of power that they gained and the way in which they wielded it.

Although the percentage of women actively employed in Latin America—using the standard of wage earning, which might not be a fair form of assessment—may be favorably compared to some areas of the world, female participation in the labor force does not compare favorably with such other areas as Europe or Japan. This phenomenon is now being interpreted much less as a result of economic factors than of cultural attitudes emanating from the perception of sex roles in a given society.[53] Surveys carried out in Chile, in Colombia, and among Cuban exiles indicate a significant degree of resistance among middle-class men to their wives' working outside the home unless there is an urgent economic need for it.[54] Although these attitudes may be changing and becoming more flexible, their persistence will be more easily understood when the ideas and influence of educators, spiritual leaders, essayists, and others who shaped the process of female socialization are better known.

Many other topics related to the work and economic significance of women could be broached: the effect of women's increased economic independence on her family role; the relation between work and fertility; the relation between education and opportunities for employment; and the evolution of rural female work in countries undergoing an increasing rate of urbanization.[55] Space precludes the consideration of such topics, but they remain as challenges for future investigations.

In the past—and perhaps even today—feminism in Latin America has not always been a popular cause. Deprecated by some intellectuals—male and female—it has received a tepid or outright cold reception among the majority of the population. Feminism has been regarded as divesting women of certain qualities of femininity and "masculinizing" them as a result of the equalization of men and women that feminists advocate. As a result, feminists have spent a considerable part of their energies trying to destroy such concepts.[56] The tension resulting from the desire to gain rights while at the same time preserving femininity and respectability is a constant topic in the works of male and female writers, feminist and antifeminist, and one that offers fascinating implications for cultural history. Historically, the staunchest supporters of feminism have been a group of middle-class intellectuals who, since the last quarter of the nineteenth century, have lent their pens and energies to the cause. Any study of feminism in Latin America would have to distinguish between intellectual supporters and activist followers and their organizations, as well as consider the arguments of those who opposed it.[57]

Feminism and ideas on women's liberation in Latin America were inspired by European and North American sources, but eventually developed their own idiosyncrasies. Female and male advocates of feminism had several common goals, which appeared as basic themes in their writings and lent some commonality to their experience in Latin America. The most important goal was to provide women with equal standing before the law. This involved equal access to educational opportunities, the abrogation of nineteenth-century codes curtailing women's rights after marriage, and specific legislation for the protection of women and children. Suffrage was a goal, but almost as a derivative of the larger goal of legal equality. It never sparked the same kind of fire that it did in England or the United States. Important differences in the political systems, already pointed out, account for this. Moral reforms, on the other hand, had high priority among some feminists, such as Paulina Luisi.[58] This might be explained partially by the character of women's education and socialization, which for centuries had stressed women's selfless goodness and their role as educators and as moralizing and stabilizing agents in society.[59]

Another interesting characteristic of female feminists in Latin America is that they coaxed men's opinions; they acted persuasively, not aggressively. Radical feminism on a large scale did not appear in Latin America. Essentially, the middle-class Latin American feminist was a gentle reformer, but, as suggested in the Introduction, the many nuances of feminism in this area remain to be ascertained, studied in detail, and explained in terms of the class of its supporters and the general social, political, and economic situation of each nation. Was the advocacy of equal pay for women, coming mostly from non-working-class men and women, a purely intellectual attitude? Was it a response to growing economies that were fast integrating women into the labor pool? Was the moralizing campaign of some feminists a response to increasing socioeconomic deterioration of living standards among the urban working class? What was the relationship between feminists and working-class women? One expects some common historical conjunctions, but most countries followed different paths and different tempos in the adoption of legislation granting equal rights to women. Those variations need to be explained. What factors put Uruguay in the avant-garde in enacting protective legislation for women and adopting divorce? What moved Ecuadorean politicians to grant the right to vote to women as early as 1929, since it is obvious that, despite this, the socioeconomic status of women in that country has changed little and remains low?

Feminism has been linked to political parties or personalities who have espoused its cause. Such sponsorship could have been based on firmly held principles or adopted for political gain, perhaps both. In any study dealing with the political use of feminist slogans, there must be a distinction between feminism in general and the use of some of its goals—such as protective legislation or the right to vote. Most politicians have spoken of women's pursuits for the reform of certain social problems.[60] Anna Macías's essay in this volume illustrates that situation and serves as a guide to other investigations. The Socialist party in Argentina early in the twentieth century, Juan Domingo Perón, and Fidel Castro have had their own programs for women's liberation or women's rights, as they have seen it.[61] In the Dominican Republic both Rafael L. Trujillo and Joaquín Balaguer have been said to have manipulated the principles and implications of feminism for their own political ends.[62] The Aprista party of Peru alienated female supporters with its intrinsically conservative attitude toward women.[63] A full treatment of how women's activism has influenced political decisions concerning the female population or of how male politicians have either used or resisted demands for women's equality before the law remains to be done for almost all countries in Latin America.[64] The records of congressional discussion of such topics as legislation to establish divorce, the right to vote, or protective legislation for women are excellent sources for the study of these topics. Political speeches, the programs of political parties, and opinions vented in national newspapers should also be good indices of political attitudes toward women and feminism.

Investigation of the political aspects of feminism leads logically to the study of the gamut of personal opinions of the men and women who supported or opposed it. Many of the reforms or changes proposed by intellectual or active feminists stirred deeply rooted opinions on the interrelation of men and women, woman's role in society and the family, and the family itself. These writings also form a rewarding and fascinating body of sources for the study of social attitudes. A study of Latin masculine ideas on women in the past will have to rely to a large extent on such writings.[65] They are also a legitimate source for the study of women's self-expression. The general absence of records emanating from women themselves, characteristic of former periods, was finally superseded between the last quarter of the nineteenth century and the first decades of the twentieth. Once education made self-expression possible, women naturally turned to discussion of their own position in society and their own problems. Women's writings—whether liberal reformists, radical activists, or conservatives—constitute the richest source for examining self-perception and self-definition. A very important question raised by those writings is whether there has been a significant change in attitudes, advocacy of programs, and social or political concerns among Latin women throughout time.[66] Since not all issues of male-female equality, legal or social, have been solved in Latin America, and since new feminists continue to raise their voices and use their pens, a comparative study between "old" and "new" feminists may give a clue to the degree of consciousness regarding certain social problems among men and women, to the effectiveness of legislative measures affecting women, and, in general, to the kinds of problems that contemporary women expect to solve, compared to those that motivated women several decades ago. There are very few studies on Latin American feminism or feminists available in English or even in Spanish. These topics have enjoyed great popularity in American and European history, and it is time that they received greater attention in Latin American studies.

Feminism spurred the foundation of many women's organizations, which have expanded considerably during the twentieth century. However, these were not the first forms of feminine associations. They had historical predecessors although of a different character. In a broad sense, colonial nunneries, *beaterios*, and confraternities should be considered forms of female association: Christianity's answer to women's desire for a place of their own within the Church. Nunneries and *beaterios* required a high degree of personal commitment and were not merely aggregative associations, but true affinity groups, closely knit, hierarchically organized, and devoted to the pursuit of a clearly defined goal. They have no counterpart in the secular world, either in the colonial or in the contemporary period. The Incas had special feminine religious groups that were based on a similar concept of service to their gods and were as revered in their time as nuns were during the colonial period. Not much is known about the Inca concept of nunneries beyond what several colonial sources tell us, and it is unlikely that a great deal of new knowledge will be discovered. Other pre-Columbian civilizations had priestesses for their cults, but the idea of associations of women devoted to specific religious purposes seem to have been more European than indigenous. Throughout the colonial period some Indian towns had confraternities for women, and urban confraternities received women either as full members or as wives of the male members. In neither case do we know much about their activities or significance for women themselves, although they were obviously a very important form of female socialization. The purpose, organization, management, and socioeconomic meaning of the nunneries of Bahia and Mexico City have been studied by Soeiro and myself, but other colonial areas have yet to receive any attention. Since religious institutions mirrored the societies in which they developed, it must be assumed that the nunneries of Quito, Rio de Janeiro, or Guatemala have distinctive characteristics that merit other studies. Furthermore, the declining influence of convents as institutions throughout the nineteenth and twentieth centuries should not obscure the fact that many feminine orders are still active in Latin America. The appeal of a religious community for women in highly secularized times, the process of recruitment of nuns, their activities as teachers and nurses, the differences between the contemplative and the active character of past and present communities—are intriguing and unanswered questions that should generate future studies.[67]

Strictly secular women's associations developed after independence, mostly as voluntary associations for social welfare. These institutions furnished social services that the governments themselves could not provide. Charitable organizations proliferated toward the end of the nineteenth century, but, despite their significance, they have not received their historical due. Not only did they provide much needed services in bourgeoning cities, but, more importantly, they trained women of the middle and upper classes in institutional management. This was no mean accomplishment for women who had few such opportunities before. In the twentieth century the spectrum of activities of women's organizations has been significantly widened. Yet, there are few studies on organizations founded by women for a variety of purposes (such as gaining political or civil rights), professional organizations, cultural associations, women's sections in major political parties, labor-oriented groups, and many others that defy classification, all of which have catered to the greatly expanded activities of women outside the home. [68]

The creation of so many organizations is in itself an index to the extensive social changes undergone by Latin women in the last hundred years. However, this indicator may be deceptive unless properly evaluated. Participation in an association or organization may be undertaken with different degrees of commitment and might not indicate deep involvement. For some women membership in a given organization was—and is—a social act lacking a great influence on their private lives. Associations formed by a membership lasting for only a few years or requiring the limited attention of the members in their spare time are of aggregative character. Their appeal is temporary and may be determined by the interests of women in a particular stage of their life-cycle. This does not diminish their interest to historians, but it is necessary to note that their impact of women's lives is not very deep and that there are limitations imposed on their actions that are determined by the nature of their membership. A greater degree of commitment is demanded by associations affiliated with political parties or labor unions, and, significantly, there are far fewer women found in them.

Despite the need to observe such qualifications, studies of women's associations would be very useful, insofar as they would help to define the issues and interests that cause women to associate for the pursuit of common goals. Such studies would also help to gauge the degree of independence of some women from family affairs, the specific actions that women take within those associations, women's social or political consciousness, and even the breadth of their cultural horizons. In this respect, an appraisal of the variety, role, and goals of women's organizations in a country during a given period would be a commendable contribution to our knowledge of Latin women's actions in the public sphere. The beneficent societies and the national councils of women of several countries are obvious targets of studies. [69] These are upper- or middle-class associations, but a closer view of other social classes may be obtained from other professional or political organizations. The membership records of women's association should provide material for group profiles of the affiliated women. The minutes of the meetings of women's associations or women's conferences are the most logical sources to learn about their concerns, their strategies for action, and their effectiveness as pressure groups. [70] Perhaps the most important question posed by the study of women's organizations is that related to their power to influence other social groups, obtain favorable legal or governmental decisions, stir public opinion, and mobilize women themselves.

On retrospective consideration of the many topics of research in the history of women in Latin America, the materials available for that research, and the studies so far completed, it is evident that much remains to be done. Descriptive histories of institutions, biographical exercises, and general appraisals of women's contributions to society form the largest portion of the body of historical literature now available. Intra-Latin American comparative studies of the roles and action of women are scarce. Analytical works focusing on pre-twentieth-century female activities and circumstances are starting to appear, but as yet these are few. A significant number of the studies on twentieth-century women have been either inspired by the work of social scientists or actually carried out by them. Historians of Latin America will simply have to pick up the challenge and start providing answers for the new questions on women, the family, and society. Archival materials, printed documents, newspapers, women's writings, governmental records, and other sources are waiting to be utilized. Perhaps the most important tasks for the future are the proper evaluation and use of those sources and the development of an awareness of the significance of women in the process of history.

Notes

1. Ann Pescatello, "The Female in Ibero-America: An Essay on Research Bibliography and Research Directions," *Latin American Research Review* 7 (Summer 1972): 125-41; June E. Hahner, *Women in Latin American History: Their Lives and Views* (Los Angeles: UCLA Latin American Center Publications; 1976), pp. 175-81; Meri Knaster, "Women in Latin America: The State of Research, 1975," *Latin American Research Review* 11 (Spring 1976): 3-74; Meri Knaster, *Women in Spanish America: An Annotated Bibliography from Pre-Conquest to Contemporary Times* (Boston: G. K. Hall, 1977).

2. See, for example, the work of José María Ots Capdequí, mentioned in note 18 of Lavrin's essay (chap. 1) and the examples of normative literature quoted in Lavrin's (chap. 1) and Russell-Wood's (chap. 2) essays.

3. Hector P. Blomberg, *Mujeres en la historia americana* (Buenos Aires: Librerías Anaconda, 1933); Jorge Cornejo Bouroncle, *Sangre andina: Diez mujeres cuzqueñas* (Cuzco: H. G. Rozas Sucesores, 1949); Mirta Aguirre, *Influencia de la mujer en Ibero-america* (Havana: Imprenta P. Fernández, 1947). See others in the "History" section of Knaster's *Women in Spanish America*.

4. Louisa Hoberman, "Hispanic American Women: Types and Archetypes"; see note 11 in the Introduction. She discusses the continuity of models throughout several centuries by analyzing the historical literature and establishes the new types of the nineteenth century.

5. See, for example, Rafael Ceniceros y Villareal, *Páginas para mis hijas: Obra destinada a la educación católica de la mujer* (Zacatecas: Imprenta y Encuadernación

La Rosa, 1891); Joaquín Valentín Riera, *La mujer: Breves rasgos descriptivos de su naturaleza física y moral con relación a la sociedad* (New York: J. M. and Familton, 1856). The latter work starts with the premise that woman is the most disgraced being in nature, owing to her intrinsic debility. It seeks to help her overcome her handicaps through education and moral enlightenment. Meri Knaster, *Women in Spanish America*, mentions the following, which will also serve for this purpose: Mariano R. Ospina, *Carta a la señorita María Josefa Ospina, en la víspera de su matrimonio* (Bogotá: Imprenta de Silvestre, 1884); Adolfo Llanos y Alcaráz, *La mujer en el siglo diez y nueve: Hojas de un libro originales* (Lima: Librería Hispano-francesa, 1876).

6. See conservative writings of Pablo Luros, *La educación de las jóvenes* (San José: Imprenta Borrose Hermanos, 1938); María Velasco y Arias, *Juana Paula Manso: Vida y acción* (Buenos Aires: Talleres Gráficos Portes, 1937); Mirna M. Pérez-Venero, "The Education of Women on the Isthmus of Panama," *Journal of the West* 12 (April 1973): 325-34; Cecilia Grierson, *Educación técnica de la mujer* (Buenos Aires: Tipografía de la Penitenciaría Nacional, 1902); Alfredo M. Aguayo, *Tres grandes educadores cubanos: Varona, Echemendía, María Luisa Dolz* (Havana: Cultural, 1937); María Luisa Dolz y Arango, *La liberación de la mujer cubana por la educación* (Havana: Oficina del Historiador de la Ciudad, 1955). Also see the notes in Little's (Chap. 9) and Hahner's (chap. 10) works in this volume.

7. David Joaquín Guzmán, *El libro del hogar* (Managua: Tipografía Nacional, 1900); José V. Vázquez, *La mujer en el hogar* (Guatemala: Tipografía Nacional, 1929).

8. Angelina Lemmo, *La educación en Venezuela en 1879* (Caracas: Universidad Central de Venezuela, 1961), pp. 143, ff.

9. Gabriela Mistral, *Lecturas para mujeres* (Mexico: Editorial Porrúa, 1969). In the Introduction, Mistral states that "whether professional or worker, peasant or lady, [woman's] only reason for being in this world is maternity, material as well as spiritual" (p. xv). Further, "these Readings . . . are destined to strengthen the family spirit, which ennobles all life and has made great the best countries in the world: England, for example" (p. xvi).

10. Amanda Labarca H., *Historia de la enseñanza en Chile* (Santiago de Chile: Imprenta Universitaria, 1939); *Feminismo contemporáneo* (Santiago de Chile: Zig-Zag, 1947); *¿A dónde vá la mujer?* (Santiago de Chile: Ediciones Extra, 1934). C. M. Paul, "Amanda Labarca H.: Educator to the Women in Chile" (Ph.D. diss., New York University, 1967); published in Spanish by CIDHOC, Cuernavaca, Mexico. Labarca was a feminist in a sui generis manner. She defended divorce legislation, full civil rights for women, and their access to all the advantages of education. Yet, she could state without qualms that "the main task of women is, without doubt, the formation of a spiritual atmosphere in the home." In *¿A dónde vá la mujer?* (see pp. 55, 241-47) she drew up the balance achieved by feminism, citing as gains women's consciousness of their own value, their legal equality, and their greater economic freedom. On the opposite side she saw the loss of masculine respect (no further male homage to women) and the loss of chances to get married because educated women appealed less to men. She finished by advising women not to preach feminism, but to try to change male attitudes toward liberated woman. These remarks were written in 1934.

11. See the works of Mendelson (chap. 6), Little (chap. 9), and Hahner (chap. 10) in this volume for further bibliographical references. The best guide for available works is Knaster, *Women in Spanish America*, section on "Education." Of particular interest

are the works from mid-nineteenth-century and early twentieth-century educators, who had to argue all the fine points of the need for women's education over again, indicating that, despite all earlier discussions on the topic, it was still encountering opposition. In a similar vein are the works of Mexican educators graduating from the school for teachers in Puebla. For example, Trinidad Bonilla, *Algunas consideraciones acerca de la importancia de la educación de la mujer* (Puebla: Imprenta de la Escuela de Artes y Oficios, 1903), and Eva López Vallejo, *Ligeras consideraciones acerca de la influencia que la mujer ejerce en la educación* (Puebla: Imprenta Artística, 1902). The ideas discussed in the social gatherings of educator Juana María Gorriti in Lima represent the campaign for acceptance of women's education in a conservative country. See the works of Benicio Alamos González, "Enseñanza superior de la mujer"; Mercedes Elespuro y Lazo, "La instrucción de la mujer"; and Abel de la E. Delgado, "La educación social de la mujer," all in Juana M. Gorriti, *Veladas literarias de Lima, 1876-1877* (Buenos Aires: Imprenta Europa, 1892).

12. Lucy Cohen, "Women's Entry to the Professions in Colombia: Selected Characteristics," *Journal of Marriage and the Family* 35 (May 1973): 322-30 (hereafter cited as *JMF*); *Las colombianas ante la renovación universitaria* (Bogotá: Editores Tercer Mundo, 1971); Nora Kinzer, "Women Professionals in Buenos Aires," in Ann Pescatello, ed., *Female and Male in Ibero-America: Essays* (Pittsburgh: University of Pittsburgh Press, 1974), pp. 159-90. An interesting example of a text for domestic sciences is that of Peruvian Elvira García y García, *Ciencias Domesticas* (Lima: Editorial Librería Peruana, 1937). For a male-authored text on domestic science, see Néstor Morales Villazón, *Al pié de la cuna* (La Paz: González y Medina, 1919). He pontificates on child care.

13. For examples of educational programs, see *Reglamento de las academias de corte y confección por el Consejo Nacional de Educación* (Paraguay: Dirección General de Escuelas, 1920); Adela Schmidt de Alvarez, *Enseñanza artística de la mujer: Informe presentado al Ministerio de Instrucción Pública* . . . (Santiago: Encuadernación y Litografía Esmeralda, 1903); *Reglamento de la Asociación de Damas para la Instrucción de la Mujer* (San Juan, Puerto Rico: Tipografía de González, 1886).

14. The male marital right to lead the family is still accepted in full or modified forms in several countries of Latin America, such as Chile, Argentina, and Bolivia. Fidelity of the wife to the husband is still legislated in Venezuela. Lesser penalties for adulterous husbands are established in El Salvador, Honduras, and Uruguay. *Patria potestad*, or the father's legal authority over the children in preference to the mother's, is still upheld in Argentina, Chile, and Ecuador. For these and similar topics, consult María Gabriela Leret de Matheus, *La mujer*, cited in note 47, Chap. 1 of this volume.

15. See Knaster, *Women in Spanish America*, section on "Law." A brief perusal of the titles reveals a large number of works on the topic of women before the law, but few seem to go beyond the mere legal statement.

16. Recent works on women and crime in Latin America have taken a broader and more meaningful approach. See the works of Verena Martínez-Alier (note 4. Introduction) and Sylvia Arrom (note 6, Introduction). See also Patricia Aufderheide, "Hearing the Unsaid: Woman in Appeals Court, Brazil, 1780-1830," and Susan Socolow, "Women and Crime in Colonial Buenos Aires." (These two titles were papers read at the International Conference on Women's History, at the University of Maryland, College Park, 1977.)

17. Knaster, *Women in Spanish America*. The section on "Female Delinquency and

Penal Institutions" is a good index to the available literature. Of special interest to historians are titles that furnish information on attitudes or data on female deviance in the past. See, for example, Luis Lara y Pardo, *La prostitución en Mexico* (Mexico: Librería de la Viuda de Bouret, 1908); Pedro Dávalos y Lesson, *La prostitución en la ciudad de Lima* (Lima: Imprenta La Industria, 1909); Israel Castellanos, *La delincuencia femenina en Cuba* (Havana: Imprenta Ojeda, 1929). Also of interest is a woman'a view of female criminality, as represented by Felícitas Klimpel Alvarado, *La mujer, el delito y la sociedad* (Buenos Aires: Editorial El Ateneo, 1946).

18. Knaster, *Women in Spanish America*. See section on "Marriage and the Family." Of 204 titles in this section only 16 are truly historical.

19. See essays by Couturier (chap. 4) and Russell-Wood (chap. 2) in this volume.

20. See works by Linda Lewin (note 19) and Mary Felstiner (note 4) cited in the Introduction. See also Charles Wagley, "Luso-Brazilian Kinship Patterns: The Persistence of a Cultural Tradition," in Joseph Maier and Richard W. Weatherhead, eds., *Politics of Change in Latin America* (New York: Praeger, 1964), pp. 174-89.

21. See Juan Carlos Rebora, *La familia chilena y la familia argentina*, cited in chap. 7, note 23. Also Virginia Gutiérrez de Pineda, *Familia y cultura en Colombia* (Bogotá: Tercer Mundo, 1968); E. E. Arriaga, "Some Aspects of Family Composition in Venezuela," *Eugenics Quarterly* 15 (December 1968): 177-90; Emilio Willems, "The Structure of the Brazilian Family," cited by Russell-Wood, chap. 2, note 1; Donald Ramos, "Marriage and the Family," cited in Russell-Wood, chap. 2, note 1.

22. Herbert G. Gutman, *The Black Family in Slavery and Freedom, 1750-1925* (New York: Pantheon Books, 1976). Census taking was started regularly in most areas of Spanish America by mid-eighteenth century, although there are earlier samples. By the late nineteenth century many areas compiled censuses reliable enough to serve as useful research tools. For the early colonial periods the parochial census is the most available source. The urban scene is better covered by better preserved and easier to understand records of births, marriages and deaths, which were dutifully kept by the Church. Much of this data for Mexico and Central America is available in the U.S. in the microfilm archives of the Church of the Latter Day Saints (Mormons), which also have a fair sampling of nineteenth- and twentieth-century census data for all Spanish America. Josefina Plá, *Hermano negro: La esclavitud en el Paraguay* (Madrid: Editorial Paraninfo, 1972), contains information on the black family.

23. See Mendelson's essay, chap. 7. A fascinating source for pre-Columbian times and the early sixteenth century is Fray Bernardino de Sahagún; see his *Florentine Codex: General History of the Things of New Spain*, ed. Arthur J. O. Anderson and Charles E. Dibble, 12 vols. (Santa Fe; N.M.; School of American Research and University of Utah, 1950-69). There are several good editions in Spanish (*Historia general de las cosas de Nueva España*). For remarks on wet-nursing and other issues concerning women by a late nineteenth-century woman writer, see Josefina Pelliza de Sagasta, *Conferencias: El libro de las madres* (Buenos Aires, 1885), pp. 183-207. For wet-nursing treated as an historical subject see, George D. Sussman, "Parisian Infants and Norman Wet Nurses in the Early Nineteenth Century: A Statistical Study," *Journal of Interdisciplinary History* 7 (Spring 1977): 637-53. For sources on colonial medical concepts on women, consult Anastasio Chinchilla, *Anales históricos de la medicina* (cited in Mendelson's essay, chap. 7, note 42.) For models of writing on the topic of women and their medical problems, see Hilda Smith, "Gynecology and Ideology in Seventeenth Century England," in Berenice Carroll, ed., *Liberating Women's History: Theoretical*

and Critical Essays (Urbana: University of Illinois Press, 1976), pp. 97-114; Carroll Smith-Rosenberg and Charles Rosenberg, "The Female Animal: Medical and Biological Views of Women in Nineteenth Century America," *Journal of American History* 60 (September 1973): 332-56; Ann Douglas Wood, " 'The Fashionable Disease': Women's Complaints and Their Treatment in Nineteenth Century America," in Mary Hartman and Lois W. Banner, eds., *Clio's Consciousness Raised* (New York: Harper Torchbooks, 1974), pp. 1-22; Regina Morantz, "The Lady and Her Physician," in Hartman and Banner, *Clio's Consciousness*, pp. 38-53; Elvira García y García's *Ciencias Domésticas* is an example of the source book for the study of ideas on home management. See also Vázquez, *La mujer en el hogar*. Both were written in the 1920s.

24. See remarks on servants in García y García, *Ciencias Domésticas*, p. 106. On the general topic of servants, see Emily M. Nett, "The Servant Class in a Developing Country: Ecuador," *Journal of Interamerican Studies and World Affairs* 8 (July 1966): 437-52 (hereafter cited as *JISWA*). An excellent survey of the condition of contemporary female servants is found in Margo Lane Smith, "Institutionalized Servitude: The Female Domestic Servant in Lima, Peru" (Ph.D. diss., Indiana University, 1971). Elinor Burkett stresses the importance of class differences in the interrelation of women in Latin America since the sixteenth century. See her "Race, Class and Sex in Early Colonial Peru" (Paper delivered at the Ninety-first Annual Meeting of the American Historical Association, Washington, D.C., 1976); recently published in *Latin American Perspectives* 4 (Winter-Spring 1977): 18-26.

25. See Carroll Smith-Rosenberg, "Puberty to Menopause: The Cycle of Feminity in Nineteenth Century America," *Feminist Studies* 1 (Winter-Spring 1973): 58-72.

26. Terry J. Rosenberg, "Individual and Regional Influences on the Employment of Colombian Women," *JMF* 38 (May 1976): 339-53; Otilia Arosemena de Tejeira, *La mujer* (cited in note 18, Introduction), p. 74; Heleith I. B. Saffioti, *A mulher na sociedade da classe* (cited in note 11, Introduction), pp. 253, 258. See also her "Relationship of Sex and Social Class in Brazil," in Nash and Safa, eds., *Sex and Class, in Latin America* (see note 3, Introduction), p. 154; Elizabeth Jelin, "The Bahiana in the Labor Force of Salvador, Brazil," in Nash and Safa, *Sex and Class*, p. 135.

27. Kinzer, "Women Professionals in Buenos Aires," p. 168. Kinzer shows that marriage is still the goal of the single professionals in Buenos Aires. There is no reason to believe that the situation is much different anywhere in Latin America due to the similarity of socialization techniques.

28. See, for example, Steffen W. Schmidt, "Political Participation and Development: The Role of Women in Latin America," *Journal of International Affairs* 30 (Fall-Winter 1976-77): 243-60; Jane Jaquette, "Women in Revolutionary Movements in Latin America," *JMF* 35 (May 1973): 344-54; William Blough, "Political Attitudes of Mexican Women: Support for the Political System Among Newly Enfranchised Groups," *JISWA* 14 (February 1972): 201-24; Elsa M. Chaney, "Women in Latin American Politics: The Case of Peru and Chile," in Pescatello, *Female and Male*, pp. 103-39. See also works by JoAnn Aviel and Elsa Chaney on Costa Rican and Chilean women's political attitudes in Jane Jaquette, ed., *Women in Politics* (New York: John Wiley & Sons, 1974). The bulk of the literature on women and politics covers the following topics in descending order, according to the number of works in print: the winning of political rights and of the right to vote, women's role in politics and their attitudes, feminism, some women politicians, the activities of some women's groups and the

minutes and reports of women's congresses. Titles on women in the Cuban Revolution are also numerous. I have surveyed the titles in the sections on "History and Politics" and "Twentieth Century Revolutionary Movements" in Knaster, *Women in Spanish America*, for these generalizations.

29. See Irma Cairoli de Liberal, *Eulalia Ares: Revolucionaria y gobernadora, 1809-1884* (Buenos Aires: Editorial Goyanarte, 1963); Francisco A. Loayza, *Mártires y heroínas* (Lima: Talleres Tipográficos de Domingo Miranda, 1945); a study of Micaela Bastidas, wife of Tupac Amaru; Magda Portal, *El aprismo y la mujer* (Lima: Editorial Cooperative Aprista Atahualpa, 1933). The names of Marietta Veintemilla, "Pancha" Gamarra, Manuelita Saénz, Encarnación Ezcurra de Rosas, and Eva Perón come to mind as examples of women who were instrumental in their husbands' ascent to power or who took an active political role as their wives or relatives. For biographical data on Veintemilla and Gamarra, see Germán Arciniegas, *América Mágica*, 2 vols. (Buenos Aires: Editorial Sudamericana, 1961), 1: 77 ff. This includes biographical data on Manuela Beltrán, a *comunero* leader in eighteenth-century Colombia. For Gamarra, see Carlos Neuhaus Rizo Patrón, *Pancha Gamarra, la Mariscala* (Lima: Francisco Moncloa Eds., 1967). In the section "History Before 1900, Independence Era" of Knaster's *Women in Spanish America* there are thirty-five items on Manuelita Sáenz, Bolívar's mistress. One of the best biographies of Manuelita is that by Alfonso Rumazo González, *Manuela Sáenz, la libertadora del libertador* (Caracas: Edime, 1935). Eva Perón has elicited similar historical attention, although there are only fourteen titles recorded by Knaster in her work. Few of them are objective. Perhaps the best initiation to Eva Perón is her own adulatory ghostwritten biography, *My Mission in Life* (New York: Vantage Press, 1953). For further references, consult the sections on "History" and "Biography and Autobiography" in Knaster's bibliography.

30. See, for example, José Macedonio Urquidi, *Bolivianas ilustres*, 2 vols. (La Paz: Arno Hermanos Libreros Editores, 1919); María Luis Leal C., "Mujeres insurgentes," *Boletín del Archivo General de la Nación* 20 (October-December 1949): 543-604. This is a heavily suscribed field, like that of notable women, although not all titles are of equal quality. It is advisable to persue the sections in Knaster's work cited above to gauge the quantity and quality of the available titles.

31. Clara Villaseca, ed., *Cartas de Mariquita Sánchez* (Buenos Aires: Ediciones Peuser, 1952).

32. Morris Blachman, "Selective Omission and Theoretical Distortion in Studying the Political Activity of Women in Brazil," in Nash and Safa, *Sex and Class*, pp. 245-64.

33. The best example is that of Fidel Castro's speeches. See Linda Jeness, *Women and the Cuban Revolution: Speeches by Fidel Castro* (New York: Pathfinder Press, 1970).

34. Eva Duarte de Perón's speeches and her biography are representative. See the writings of activist Bolivian revolutionary Lydia Gueiler de Moller—for example, *La mujer y la revolución: Autobiografía política* (La Paz, 1959). For examples of official or semiofficial publications, see *La redención de la mujer mexicana por el ejido* (Mexico: Partido Nacional Revolucionario, Secretaría de Acción Agraria, 1934). José Fausto Riéffolo Bessone, *Los derechos sociales de la mujer: Sufragismo y feminismo* (Buenos Aires: Editorial El Ateneo, 1950), is a eulogy of Peronism and its work on behalf of women. Newspapers and magazines are some of the best sources for this topic. The most detailed bibliography on Cuban women so far published is Nelson P. Valdés, "A

Bibliography on Cuban Women in the Twentieth Century," *Cuban Newsletter* 4 (June 1974): 1-31. See also Louis A. Pérez, comp., "Women in the Cuban Revolutionary War, 1953-1958: A Bibliography," *Science and Society* 39 (Spring 1975): 104-8; Margaret Randall, *Cuban Women Now: Interviews with Cuban Women* (Toronto: Women's Press, 1974), which is available also in Spanish.

35. Michele Mattelart, "Chile: The Feminine Version of the Coup d'Etat," in Nash and Safa, *Sex and Class*, pp. 279-301. This work gives the views of the pro-Allende followers. For the opposite view, see María Correa Moraide, *La guerra de las mujeres* (Santiago: Editorial Universidad Técnica del Estado, 1974), and Teresa Donoso Loero, *La epopeya de las ollas vacías* (Santiago: Editorial Nacional Gabriela Mistral, 1974). For a brief description of the participation of Brazilian women in an anti-Goulart campaign, see John W. F. Dulles, *Unrest in Brazil: Political-Military Crises, 1955-1964* (Austin: University of Texas Press, 1970), pp. 274-78.

36. Steffen W. Schmidt, "Women in Colombia: Attitudes and Future Perspectives in the Political System," *JISWA* 17 (November 1975): 465-89.

37. Susan Kaufman Purcell, "Modernizing Women for a Modern Society: The Cuban Case," in Pescatello, *Female and Male*, pp. 257-71; Virginia Olesen, "Confluences in Social Change: Cuban Women and Health Care," *JISWA* 17 (November 1975): 398-410; Virginia Olesen, "Context and Posture: Notes on Socio-Cultural Aspects of Women's Roles and Family Policy in Contemporary Cuba," *JMF* 33 (August 1971): 548-60. In 1974 a new family code was issued in Cuba, which aimed at changing the traditional roles of men in the family. See Claude Regin, "Sex Equality in Cuba," in *The Washington Post*, 4 August 1974, sec. F 10. The code went into effect in March 1975, but there are no studies or reports on its effectiveness as a catalyst for social change.

38. See, for example, Silvio Zavala and María Castelo, comps., *Fuentes para la historia del trabajo en Nueva España*, 8 vols. (Mexico: Fondo de Cultura Económica, 1939-46).

39. J. Alden Mason, *The Ancient Civilizations of Peru* (Baltimore: Penguin Books, 1957), which is also available in Spanish. Mason devotes a chapter to the consideration of textiles in pre-Columbian South America. See also Fray Bernardino de Sahagún, *Historia general*, cited in note 23 above.

40. Guamán Poma de Ayala, *Nueva corónica y buen gobierno* (Paris: Institut d'Ethnologie, 1936); Bishop Baltasar Jaime Martínez Compañón, *Trujillo del Perú a fines del siglo XVIII* (Madrid: Talleres Gráficos de Bermejo, 1936). Using visual sources has become a valid method for gathering evidence, especially on social groups that were unlikely to leave more orthodox forms of historical records of their activities.

41. Isidoro Moreno Navarro, *Los cuadros del mestizaje americano: Estudio antropológico del mestizaje* (Madrid: Ediciones José Porrúa Turanzas, 1973). These paintings have often been used as illustrations for colonial histories. See Guillermo Fúrlong, *Historia social y cultural del Río de la Plata, 1536-1810*, 3 vols. (Buenos Aires: Tipográfica Editora Argentina, 1969), vol. 3, *El transplante social*.

42. *Libros del Cabildo de la ciudad de Quito, 1610-1616; 1650-1657* (Quito: Imprenta Municipal, 1955); Ramón López Lara, ed., *El obispado de Michoacán en el siglo XVII* (Morelia: Fimax Publicistas, 1973); Luis Capoche, *Relación general de la villa imperial de Potosí, 1585* (Madrid: Ediciones Atlas, 1959).

43. For example, the convent of Santa Clara of Querétaro (Mexico) monopolized the

overwhelming majority of registered liens on properties in that city from 1696 through 1720 and for much of the period thereafter was one of the main sources of liquid capital for the local entrepreneurs. See Joe Super, "Human Affairs in Colonial Querétaro, 1531-1810" (Manuscript), Appendix 2. I am grateful to Professor Super for this information. See also Lavrin, "El convento de Santa Clara de Querétaro," cited in note 56, chap. 1.

44. Mary Karasch of Oakland University has completed a manuscript containing information on the labor of slave women in nineteenth-century Brazil. There are more sources of information on these topics for the twentieth century. See, for example, "Employment of Women in the Bolivian Mining Industry," *International Labor Review* 49 (June 1944): 678. Anthropological interest in these subjects has produced such works as Kathleen Klumpp, "Black Traders of North Highland Ecuador," in N. E. Whitten, Jr., ed., *Afro-American Anthropology: Contemporary Perspectives* (New York: Free Press, 1970), pp. 245-62; and Rubén Reina, *Chinautla, a Guatemalan Indian Community* (New Orleans: Tulane University Middle American Research Institute, 1972). The latter work has a section on women in the marketplace.

45. See, for example, Gloria González Salazar, "Participation of Women in the Mexican labor Force," in Nash and Safa, *Sex and Class*, pp. 183-201; the author used data from the censuses of 1930 and 1960. Josefina Marpons, *La mujer en el trabajo* (Santiago de Chile: Editorial Ercilla, 1938). The best guide for the type of literature available is Knaster, *Women in Spanish America*, section on "Economic Life."

46. Ana María Hernández, *La mujer mexicana en la industria textil* (Mexico: Tipografía Moderna, 1940). For the opinion of an early nineteenth-century manufacturer on women's work in the textile industry, see Estevan de Antuñano, *Ventajas políticas, civiles, fabriles y domésticas que por dar ocupación también a las mujeres . . . deben recibirse* (Puebla: Oficina del Hospital de San Pedro, 1837); *La mujer y el movimiento obrero mexicano en el siglo XIX: Antología de la prensa obrera* (Mexico: Centro de Estudios Históricos del Movimiento Obrero Mexicano, 1975). Vol. 2 (June 1975) of *Historia Obrera*, a journal of the Centro de Estudios Históricos del Movimiento Obrero Mexicano, was totally devoted to the history of working women in Mexico.

47. The interesting work of Joan Scott and Louise Tilly on nineteenth-century working women in Europe illustrates the potential of the topic of women's work in that century and the current interpretive trends; see their "Women's Work and the Family in Nineteenth Century Europe," *Comparative Studies in Society and History* 17 (January 1975): 36-64. Studies on the immigration of women in Latin America have focused on contemporary conditions. See Lourdes Arizpe S., *Indígenas en la ciudad de Mexico: El caso de las "Marías"* (Mexico: SepSetentas, 1975); Margo L. Smith, "Domestic Service as a Channel of Upward Mobility for the Lower-Class Woman: The Lima Case," in Pescatello, *Female and Male*, pp. 191-207; Alejandra Moreno Toscano and Carlos Aguirre Anaya, "Migration to Mexico City in the Nineteenth Century: Research Approaches," *JISWA* 17 (February 1975): 27-42. For a study of the effect of migration and urbanization of the family, see Philip M. Hauser, ed., *Seminar on Urbanization Problems in Latin America* (New York: Columbia University Press, 1961). Among the few historical studies on women's work using census data is María C. Cacopardo, *Argentina: Aspectos demográficos de la población economicamente activa en el período 1869-1895* (Santiago de Chile: Centro Latinoamericano de Demografía, 1960). This center has produced several works on women's labor, mostly in the con-

temporary scene. See Aida Rodríguez and Susana Schkolnik, *Chile y Guatemala: Factores que afectan la participación femenina en la actividad económica* (Santiago de Chile: Centro latinoamericano de Demografía, 1974).

48. Although the assumption is that this was the case, there are few historical works furnishing evidence that this process indeed took place in Latin America. Both Isabel Picó Vidal for Puerto Rico and Elvira García for Peru provide information on women's needlework that suggests the existence of an intermediary stage known as piecework, mostly performed at home, but for industrial purposes. See Picó Vidal, "The History of Women's Struggle" (cited in note 17, Introduction), p. 206; Elvira García y García, *La mujer peruana a través de los siglos,* 2 vols. (Lima: Imprenta Americana, 1925), 2: 673. García y García mentions an organization called *Industria Femenil* that obtained a contract to provide uniforms for the army. It tried to eliminate the exploitation of women doing piecework, an abuse quite rampant in Lima at the beginning of the twentieth century.

49. Manuel Atanasio Fuentes, *Estadística general de Lima* (Lima: Imprenta Nacional de N. N. Corpancho, 1858). This is a good example of what similar sources may unearth. For example, there were 931 women vendors in the markets of Lima out of a total of 1,300. There were 3,147 washerwomen, 440 wetnurses, 1,248 cooks, 2,321 servants, and 2,040 seamstresses out of a total work force (male and female) of 41,338 individuals. Few women were employed in other forms of labor. Those mentioned had been "feminine" occupations since the sixteenth century. See also J. Capelo, *Sociología de Lima,* 4 vols. (Lima: Imprenta Masías, 1899). In addition to the works cited above, see some of the literature produced by the International Labor Office in Geneva, the U.S. Department of Labor, and the ministries of labor or institutions concerned with development in several Latin American countries. See, for example, *El trabajo de la mujer: Disposiciones legales* (Bogotá: Imprenta Nacional, 1953); *Informe sobre las labores de la mujer y de los menores trabajadores* (Mexico: Departamento del Trabajo, 1936); *Reglamento sobre el trabajo de la mujer* (Havana: Imprenta y Papelería Bouza y Ca., 1937); Mary M. Cannon, *Women Workers in Peru*, Bulletin 213, and *Women Workers in Paraguay*, Bulletin 210, (Washington, D.C.: U.S. Department of Labor, Women's Bureau, 1947). One problem with these sources is that they state an official governmental position or the country's legislation without reference to actual conditions or enforcement. A general evaluation of women's work in contemporary Peru, with bibliography and tables, is provided in Gabriela Villalobos de Urrutia, *Diagnóstico de la situación social y económica de la mujer peruana* (Lima: Centro de Estudiós de Publación y Desarrollo, 1975). This center has also produced other literature on women. Other bibliographical references will be found in Knaster, *Women in Spanish America*, under "Law-Employment Legislation" and "Economic Life."

50. Such sources have been used by June Hahner in her pioneering study on women's work in Brazil from 1850 through 1920. See note 82 in Hahner's essay (chap. 10) in this volume.

51. Compare remarks on the decline in the number of women employed in the textile industries and the labor force in general in Mexico and Argentina at the end of the nineteenth century. See Rodney D. Anderson, *Outcasts in Their Own Land: Mexican Industrial Workers, 1906-1911* (De Kalb: Northern Illinois University Press, 1976), and Cacopardo, *Argentina: Aspectos demográficos.*

52. María Ríos Cárdenas, *La mujer mexicana es ciudadana* (Mexico: A. del Bosque,

Impresor, 1942); Francisco A. Guido, *La mujer en la vida sindical* (Buenos Aires: Ministerio de Cultura y Educación, 1972); Picó Vidal, "The History of Women's Struggle"; Ignacio Torres Giraldo, *María Cano*, cited in note 17, Introduction; Lily Sosa de Newton, *Las argentinas*, p. 216.

53. Nadia H. Youseff, *Women and Work in Developing Societies* (Berkeley: Institute of International Studies, 1974); Jelin, "The Bahiana," p. 132; Schmidt, "Political Participation," pp. 249-50.

54. Geoffrey E. Fox, "Honor, Shame and Women's Liberation in Cuba: Views of Working-Class Emigré Men," in Pescatello, *Female and Male*, pp. 273-90; Terry Rosenberg, "Individual and Regional Influences;" Mattelart and Mattelart, *La mujer chilena* (cited in note 22, Introduction), p. 114.

55 See, Guadalupe Zetina Lozano, "El trabajo de la mujer y su vida familiar," in María del Carmen Elú de Leñero, ed., *Mujeres que hablan* (Mexico: Instituto Mexicano de Estudios Sociales, A.C., 1971); Juan C. Elizaga, "Participation of Women in the Labor Force of Latin America: Fertility and Other Factors," *International Labor Review* 109 (May-June 1974): 519-38; Peter Peek, "Female Employment and Fertility: Study Based on Chilean Data," *International Labor Review* 112 (August-September 1975): 207-16. Elizaga considers better female education and increased labor demand due to economic changes to be directly correlated to a lower fertility rate. Peter Peek adds an extra dimension by introducing the availability of social services, as well as child care, as a key element in female labor participation. For a recent study on the status of rural women in Chile, see Patricia M. Garret, "Some Structural Constraints in the Agricultural Activities of Women: The Chilean Hacienda," mimeographed (Madison: Land Tenure Center, 1976).

56. See, for example, Zoila Rendón de Mosquera, *La mujer en el hogar y en la sociedad*, 2d ed. (Quito: Imprenta Nacional, 1933), p. 29. She depicts "modern women," presumably feminists, as a third sex, half-men who lack the charm of old-fashioned women. A Quito newspaper that praised this book characterized women who left their homes to claim rights as *marimachos vocingleros* (vociferous tomboys). ibid., pp. xvi-xvii; María Abella de Ramírez, *Ensayos feministas* (1909), 2d ed. (Montevideo: Editorial El Siglo Ilustrado, 1965), pp. 69-74. In an impassioned defense of feminists Abella de Ramírez acknowledged a common prejudice against them, stemming from a vitiated picture of the feminist as an ugly, graceless, sexless women incapable of love. She was obliged to restate that "modern woman does not wish the absurdity of becoming a man. . . ." Women who claimed the right to vote in Colombia in the mid 1940s received caustic attacks in local newspapers. See Ofelia Uribe de Acosta, *Una voz insurgente* (Bogotá: Editorial Guadalupe, 1963), 205-06. She quotes from a newspaper: "To be ugly is the only thing that we cannot forgive in women, and to be a suffragette is the only thing that cannot be forgiven in ugly women." Victoria Ocampo. *La mujer y su expresión* (Buenos Aires: Editorial Sur, 1936), 57, 63. She states that what feminists want is not to take man's place, but to occupy their own fully, reasserting that the liberation of women aims at bringing men and women closer.

57. Feminism is a commitment to the cause of gaining legal and intellectual equality for women, It is the base for more specific efforts directed at the achievement of that equality. When those efforts are organized and pursued consistently by a group of men and women, one may talk of a feminist movement. Most often such movements aim at gaining specific rights, such as the right to vote. At all times, though, feminism remains

as a basic attitude or commitment. Thus, it is possible to find feminist writers who did not engage in any movement, either because they preceded such organized efforts or because they were not activists. The early supporters of women's education or those who wrote on behalf of women's legal equality may be considered feminists, although they did not participate in any campaign to stir public opinion. Many Latin American writers fall into this category.

58. Cynthia Little, "Moral Reform and Feminism," cited in note 13, Introduction; Abella de Ramírez, *Ensayos*, pp. 13-15. In a list of eighteen "minimum vindications" for women, most of the points refer to legal rights such as the preservation of women's property after marriage, the right to divorce, or the abrogation of *patria potestad*. Point 17, the next to last, referred to general political rights. Abella de Ramírez, however, departs from other feminists in advocating the toleration—but not the regulation—of prostitution. She based this demand on a very advanced idea for her times: women owned their bodies and, like men, were entitled to do what they wished with them. Lucila Rubio de Laverde, *Ideales feministas* (Bogotá: Editorial Nuevo Mundo, 1944), p. 138. As late as 1947, Rubio de Laverde, explaining some basic feminist postulates, placed political rights in fourth place after the rights for equal education, administration of their own property, and equal pay for equal work.

59. These ideas are repeated by feminists and nonfeminists as well. See Gregorio Sánchez Gómez, *Femina: Ensayo* (Cali, Colombia: Editores Sánchez Gómez Hermanos, 1950), p. 94. See also ibid., pp. 106-107, 123 ff., for other interesting concepts on women's feminity and their roles as single, engaged, and married women. Antonio Austregesilo, *Perfil da mulher brasileira*, 2d. ed. (Rio de Janeiro: Editôra Guanabara, 1938), pp. 122-23, 129-35; Ocampo, *La mujer y su expresión*, pp. 15-16, 25; Gutiérrez, *La mujer* (cited in note 14, Introduction), pp. 20-22; Israel Rojas R., *Dignificación femenina* (Manizales, Colombia: Casa Editora y Talleres Gráficos Arturo Zapata, 1941); Riéffolo Bessone, *Los derechos sociales*.

60. The word *feminism*, not having been very popular in Latin America, has not often been used by politicians. Peronists used it, but more frequently politicians have spoken of specific programs for the benefit of women or used terms such as *vindication* or *gaining rights*. Both feminism and women's liberation have been seen by radicals of the left and the right as alien to the Latin American character and situation, either as a bourgeois capitalist idea or as a foreign menace to the Iberian roots of the area. See, for example, the ideas of Vilma Espín, head of the Federation of Cuban Women, in Hahner, *Women in Latin American History*, pp. 164-71. Teresa Amadeo Gely, *Aspectos de la familia, el hogar y la mujer puertorriqueña* (Madrid: Imprenta Samarán, 1972), ascribes many of the "negative" changes in Puerto Rican family life to the substitution of Hispanic values by North American values. Margarita Loreto Hernández, *Personalidad (?) de la mujer mexicana* (Mexico: Impresora Galve, 1961), also sees a direct correlation between North American influence and feminism, and she disapproves of both. A thought-provoking examination of the prospects of women's liberation in Latin America, based on an interpretation of women's image, is that of Evelyn P. Stevens, "The Prospects for a Women's Liberation Movement in Latin America," cited in note 22, *Introduction*.

61. Nancy Caro Hollander, "Women: The Forgotten Half," cited in note 8, Introduction; Riéffolo Bessone, *Los derechos sociales*; Randal, *Cuban Women Now*. See also Cynthia Little's essay (chap. 9) in this volume. For an example of a study of the

connection between a political party and feminist activists, see Amy Hackett, "Feminism and Liberalism in Wilhelmine Germany, 1890-1918," in Carroll, *Liberating Women's History*, pp. 127-36.

62. Shoshana B. Tancer, "La Quisqueyana: The Dominican Woman, 1940-1970," in Pescatello, *Female and Male*, pp. 209-29; Vivian M. Mota, "Politics and Feminism in the Dominican Republic, 1931-45 and 1966-74," in Nash and Safa, *Sex and Class*, pp. 265-78.

63. Portal, *El aprismo y la mujer*; Rómulo Meneses, *Aprismo femenino peruano* (Lima: Editorial Cooperative Aprista Atahualpa, 1934).

64. The only book-length study in English of a Latin American suffrage movement is that by Ward M. Morton, *Woman Suffrage in Mexico* (Gainesville: University of Florida Press, 1962).

65. The lectures on feminism given by Uruguayan Carlos Vaz Ferreira in 1914 are an excellent example of a liberal feminist of that time. See Carlos Vaz Ferreira, *Sobre feminismo* (Buenos Aires: Sociedad Amigos del Libro Rioplatense, 1933). He claimed to be neither an antifeminist nor an outright feminist favoring total equality of men and women. Rather, he sought to balance some of the biological disadvantages of women with social compensations that would give ample opportunities for intellectual pursuit to those women who had such abilities. On suffrage, divorce, and male-female relationships he is a moderate liberal, never a radical. For the complete antithesis of Vaz Ferreira, and a good example of conservative thinking on women, see Clodomiro Cordero, *La sociedad argentina y la mujer*, cited in note 49, chap. 9. Other examples of conservative thinking may be found in Guillermo Sevilla Sacasa, *La mujer micaraguense ante el derecho de sufragar* (Managua: Talleres Gráficos Pérez, 1939); Eliseo Giberga, *El problema del divorcio* (Havana: Librería e Imprenta La Moderna Poesía, 1911). Supporting feminism or some of its aims are Arsenio López Decoud, *Sobre el feminismo* (Asunción: Imprenta de Luis Tasso, 1902); Marcial Zumaeta, *La cuestión femenina: El voto femenino* (Lima: Imprenta y Encuadernación de E. R. Villarán, 1917); *Iniciativa de algunos diputados de la Asamblea Nacional Legislativa sobre el divorcio* (Guatemala: Oficina Tipográfica El Progreso, 1883). For other titles, see M. Knaster, *Women in Spanish America*, section on "Perspectives on Women's Liberation."

66. Elsa M. Chaney, "Old and New Feminists," cited in note 21, Introduction; Blanca A. Cassagne Lerres, *¿Debe votar la mujer?* (Buenos Aires: Editorial Licurgo, 1945); Mirta Henault, Peggy Morton, and Isabel Larguía, *Las mujeres dicen basta* (Buenos Aires: Ediciones Nueva Mujer, 1972). This last book contains three different essays by the authors. María Lacerda de Moura, *A mulher e uma degenerada*, 3d ed. (Rio de Janeiro: Civilização Brasileira Editora, 1932); this ardent Brazilian feminist borrowed the title of her book from an antifeminist statement of psychiatrist Miguel Bombarda, who claimed that the only legitimate human type was the male. Rose Marie Muraro, *Libertação sexual da mulher* (Petrópolis: Editora Vozes, 1970); Carmen da Silva, *U homem e a mulher no mundo moderno* (Rio de Janeiro: Editora Civilização Brasileira, 1969). The works of Ofelia Uribe de Acosta, Lucila Rubio de Laverde, and Victoria Ocampo are representative of feminist writings in the 1960s, 1940s, and 1930s, respectively. For a radical leftist supporter of women's liberation, see the works of Vania Bambirra, as listed in Knaster, *Women in Spanish America*, pp. 582-83. The sections on "Perspectives on Women's Liberation" and "General-Miscellaneous" of Knaster's bibliography contain numerous references to women's writings.

67. The available historical literature focuses not on studies of religious communities, but on a handful of notable religious figures, such as Sor Juana Inés de la Cruz, Santa Rosa de Lima, and Mariana de Jesús of Quito. However, there are several studies based on archival records on the foundation and development of religious communities in the colonial period. See, for example, Josefina Muriel, *Conventos de monjas de Nueva España* (Mexico: Editorial Santiago, 1946), and *Los recogimientos de mujeres*, cited in note 36, chap. 1; Luis Francisco Prieto del Rio, *Crónica del monasterio de Capuchinas de Santiago* (Santiago: Imprenta de San José, 1911); D. Ventura Travada, *El suelo de Arequipa convertido en cielo en el . . . religioso monasterio de Santa Rosa de Santa María* (1752), in Manuel de Odrozola, ed., *Documentos literarios del Perú* (Lima: Imprenta del Estado, 1877), pp. 5-326. Colonial sources consist mostly of the rules of religious communities or the biographies of nuns. To reconstruct other aspects or activities of the convents, archival sources must be consulted. For other titles on religious associations, see Knaster, *Women in Spanish America*, section on "Magic, Religion and Ritual."

68. Helen N. Gillin, "The Other Half: Women in Colombian Life," in A. C. Wilgus, ed., *The Caribbean: Contemporary Colombia* (Gainesville: University of Florida Press, 1960); Angela Acuña de Chacón, *La mujer costaricense a través de cuatro siglos* (San José: Imprenta Nacional, 1969); Felicítas Klimpel Alvarado, *La mujer chilena* (Santiago: Editorial Andrés Bello, 1962); Villalobos de Urrutia, *Diagnóstico de la situación social y económica de la mujer peruana*, sec. 5. All these publications cite and describe women's organizations.

69. Evelyn G. Schipske, "An Analysis of the *Consejo Nacional de Mujeres del Perú*," *JISWA* 17 (November 1975): 426-39.

70. *Memorias del Primer Congreso Interamericano de Mujeres* (Guatemala: Tipografía Nacional, 1948); *Procedimientos e informes de las conferencias del día de Colón* (New York: Inter-American Press, 1926); *Orientación revolucionaria de mujeres de Bolivia: Primer Congreso Nacional* (La Paz: Imprenta y Librería Renovación, 1968). The many publications of the Inter-American Commission of Women include the minutes of inter-American women's conferences, the *Bulletin* of The Inter-American Women's Commission, and other official records of past and present activities. For a list of all women's organizations and congresses in Mexico from 1857 through 1958, see Kathleen H. O'Quinn, "A Cultural Portrait of Women in Mexico," mimeographed (1974).

Index

About the contributors

Asunción Lavrin has a Ph.D. in history from Harvard University and is currently an associate professor at Howard University. Her research has focused on ecclesiastical history and on women in religious and secular life in colonial Mexico. She is the author of several works on these topics, one of which was awarded the Robertson Memorial Prize in 1967. She is also a contributing editor for the *Handbook of Latin American Studies*.

A. J. R. Russell-Wood is professor of history at Johns Hopkins University. Educated at Oxford University, he was a research fellow of Saint Anthony's College. His research interests are the history of colonial Brazil, comparative colonialism in the Americas, and the Portuguese seaborne empire. He is the author of *Fidalgos and Philanthropists: The Santa Casa da Misericórdia of Bahia, 1550-1755* (Bolton Memorial Prize, 1969) and coauthor and editor of *From Colony to Nation: Essays on the Independence of Brazil*.

Elinor C. Burkett has a Ph.D. in history from the University of Pittsburgh and is assistant professor at Frostburgh State College, Maryland. She has published several works and reviews about women in Latin American history and is currently researching the relationship between the State and the social relations of the sexes.

Edith Couturier received her Ph.D. in history from Columbia University and is the author of *La Hacienda de Hueyapán: 1550-1936*. She has also written other works on the history of philanthropy, the family, and women in colonial Mexico. Currently she is finishing a book on the history of the family of the Counts of Regla. She has taught at SUNY, Albany, the University of Maryland, American University in Washington, D.C., and Northeastern Illinois University.

Ann Miriam Gallagher is president of College Misericordia, Dallas, Pennsylvania, where she was previously a member of the faculty. She obtained her Ph.D. in history from The Catholic University of America, Washington, D.C. Her research has dealt primarily with the role of women, especially that of nuns, in colonial Mexico society. She is a former assistant editor of *The Americas*.

Susan A. Soeiro obtained her Ph.D. in history from New York University and has taught at Stony Brook, SUNY, and York College, CUNY. Her main research interests involve the colonial Church and women and the family in Brazil. She is the author of several works and reviews on women's history in Brazil and Spanish America and is currently a member of the Institute for Research in History.

Johanna S. R. Mendelson received her Ph.D. in history from Washington University, Saint Louis. She has been interested in the preservation of women's history records and has worked as an archivist and freelance writer on that topic in Washington, D.C., and Atlanta, Georgia. She is currently a member of the staff of the Center for Defense Information, Washington, D.C.

Evelyn Cherpak is assistant curator of the Naval Historical Collection at the Naval War College, Newport, Rhode Island. She received her Ph.D. in history from the University of North Carolina and has presented several papers on women's history at professional meetings. She has taught at Central Connecticut State College and Salve Regina College, Rhode Island.

Cynthia Jeffress Little is a doctoral candidate in Latin American History at Temple University, Philadelphia. Her dissertation examines the development of health and social welfare institutions for women and children in nineteenth-century Buenos Aires. She has published several works and presented papers at professional meetings on Argentinian women of the nineteenth and twentieth centuries.

June E. Hahner received her Ph.D. in history from Cornell University and is associate professor at SUNY, Albany. She is the author of *Civilian-Military Relations in Brazil, 1889-1898* and editor of the documentary study *Women in Latin American History: Their Lives and Views* and *A Mulher no Brasil*. She has also contributed articles to scholarly journals in the United States and Latin America. She is a member of the editorial board of *The Americas*.

Anna Macías obtained her Ph.D. in history from Columbia University and is professor of history at Ohio Wesleyan University. She has also taught at Smith

College. She is the author of *Génesis del gobierno constitucional en Mexico: 1808-1820* and other works on the Mexican independence movement and women in Mexican history. She is currently completing a book on the feminist movement in Mexico from 1890 to 1940.